ASIAN COMMUNITY LIBRARY
1934 PARK BLVD.
OAKLAND, CA 94606
his book may be renewed by telephone, unless
reserve is filed.

LAKEVIEW

1976

East

Across

the

Pacific

D0721501

EAST ACROSS THE PACIFIC

A B C - CLIO INC. ®

AMERICAN BIBLIOGRAPHICAL CENTER
CLIO PRESS
Santa Barbara, California & Oxford, England

Historical & Sociological Studies of Japanese Immigration & Assimilation

edited by
HILARY CONROY
University of Pennsylvania
T. SCOTT MIYAKAWA
Boston University

© 1972 by ABC-CLIO, Inc.

All rights reserved.
This book or any part thereof may not be reproduced in any form
without the written permission of the publisher.

Library of Congress Catalog Card No. 72-77825
ISBN Paperbound Edition 0-87436-087-0
Clothbound Edition 0-87436-086-2

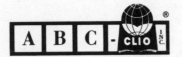

American Bibliographical Center - Clio Press
Riviera Campus, 2040 Alameda Padre Serra
Santa Barbara, California 93103

European Bibliographical Center - Clio Press
30 Cornmarket Street
Oxford OX1 3EY, England

To the Memory of

WILFRED TSUKIYAMA

JOE GRANT MASAOKA

Leaders in Encouraging the Study of

Japanese Contributions to America

Contents

Illustrations   ix
Foreword   xi

PART ONE
  HISTORICAL ESSAYS: HAWAII & THE PACIFIC ISLANDS
Introduction   3
"First Year" Immigrants to Hawaii & Eugene Van Reed   5
  MASAJI MARUMOTO, Supreme Court of Hawaii
R. W. Irwin & Systematic Immigration to Hawaii   40
  YUKIKO IRWIN & HILARY CONROY
Japanese Entrepreneurs in the Mariana, Marshall, & Caroline Islands   56
  DAVID C. PURCELL, JR., University of Hawaii, Hilo College

PART TWO
  HISTORICAL ESSAYS: MAINLAND NORTH AMERICA
Introduction   73
Japanese Immigrants on a Western Frontier: The Issei in California,
  1890–1940   76
  ROGER DANIELS, State University of New York, Fredonia
The Vancouver Riots of 1907: A Canadian Episode   92
  HOWARD H. SUGIMOTO, University of Pennsylvania
My Experience with the Wartime Relocation of Japanese   127
  ESTHER B. RHOADS, American Friends Service Committee
  with a bibliographical essay by HOWARD H. SUGIMOTO

PART THREE
  FROM HISTORY TO SOCIOLOGY
Introduction   153
Early New York Issei Founders of Japanese American Trade   156
  T. SCOTT MIYAKAWA, Boston University
Man of Two Worlds: An Inquiry into the Value System of Inazo Nitobe
  (1862–1933)   187
  SHARLIE C. USHIODA, University of California, Irvine

PART FOUR
  SOCIOLOGICAL ESSAYS
Introduction   213

An Immigrant Community in America   217
    S. FRANK MIYAMOTO, University of Washington
Acculturation & Childhood Accidents   244
    MINAKO KUROKAWA, University of Hawaii
Assimilation of Nisei in Los Angeles   268
    GEORGE KAGIWADA, University of California, Davis
Generation & Character: The Case of the Japanese Americans   279
    STANFORD M. LYMAN, New School for Social Research

Index   315

Illustrations

PLATES FOLLOWING PAGE xviii

1   Typical Japanese village of the sort from which many immigrants came in the Meiji period.
Photo from the collection of the late Anna Brinton.

2   A teahouse in Meiji Japan.
Photo from the collection of the late Anna Brinton.

3   The farming experience of Japanese immigrants was largely in rice planting.
Photo from the collection of the late Anna Brinton.

4   Robert W. Irwin and his wife in official attire to attend a celebration of the Meiji Constitution.

5   Robert W. Irwin Family: (front, left to right) Agnes Irwin, daughter; Iki Irwin, wife; R. W. Irwin; (back, left to right) Sophia Arabella Irwin, daughter; Robert Walker Irwin, Jr., son; Richard Irwin, son; two other daughters are missing.

6   Yukiko Irwin, co-author of essay and granddaughter of R. W. Irwin.

7   City Market of Los Angeles, 9th and San Pedro Streets, October 7, 1911. Japanese Diet member Shimada visits the Issei-organized and operated wholesale produce market.
Photo courtesy of Japanese American Research Project.

8   Issei picnic near the port of Los Angeles, May 26, 1907.
Photo by P. M. Suski from the personal files of Toyo Miyatake, courtesy Japanese American Research Project.

9   Hon. Rodolphe Lemieux, July 1911.
Photo courtesy of The Public Archives of Canada.

10   Damage from the anti-Japanese Riots, Vancouver, 1907.
Photo courtesy of The Public Archives of Canada.

11   Colorado River Relocation Center, Poston, Arizona, June 1942.
Photo courtesy of the Bancroft Library, University of California, Berkeley, California.

12   The War Relocation Authority caption reads: "Barrack Building typical of those at this (Poston, Arizona) War Relocation Center for evacuees of Japanese ancestry. Note the double roof construction for protection from the elements." June 1, 1942
Photo courtesy of the Bancroft Library, University of California, Berkeley, California.

13 *Landscaping by evacuees at Poston, Arizona, improved the Relocation Camp's appearance markedly. This was apparently done within the first year.*
Photo courtesy of the Bancroft Library, University of California, Berkeley, California.

14 *The Tule Lake—Newell, California Center was used for evacuees presumed to favor Japan. In this photo taken in February 1943, the muddy streets resulting from thawing ground are in evidence.*
Photo courtesy of the Bancroft Library, University of California, Berkeley, California.

15 *Although the evacuees were ingenious in developing agriculture in the inhospitable areas in which the centers were located, those at Tule Lake—Newell, California, had a special problem. The War Relocation Authority caption on this photo of some of the land they developed there reads: "View of wild geese on farm. These geese, which are protected by game laws, cause hundreds of dollars of damage to the crops."*
Photo courtesy of the Bancroft Library, University of California, Berkeley, California.

16 *An interior view of one section of the Mizunuma Silk Mills (reeling mill) from which came the first direct shipments of silk ever exported to the United States. Chotaro Hoshino, elder brother of Ryoichiro Arai, was the initiator and founder.*
Photo courtesy of Department of Sociology & Anthropology, Boston University, 232 Bay State Road, Boston, Massachusetts.

17 *Toyo Morimura (left) and Ichizaemon Morimura in 1889.*
Photo courtesy of Department of Sociology & Anthropology, Boston University, 232 Bay State Road, Boston, Massachusetts.

18 *Ryoichiro Arai in December 1910, at the age of fifty-five.*
Photo courtesy of Department of Sociology & Anthropology, Boston University, 232 Bay State Road, Boston, Massachusetts.

19 *Inazo and Mary Elkinton Nitobe with a young woman friend, 1931.*
Photo courtesy of Mr. Passmore Elkinton.

Foreword

This book attempts to bring together some results of recent research on Japanese immigration to and settlement in North America, Hawaii, and the Pacific islands with the hope of contributing to our present understanding of these developments and to an eventual synthesis of the historical and the sociological findings. The editors also hope it will help encourage students of European immigration to North America to include the Japanese and other supposedly "non-assimilative" Asians in their studies on immigration.

From the hindsight of the third quarter of the twentieth century, it is increasingly clear that in many ways the Asians were not more "alien" than others who have come to our shores. The rapid one-generation occupational mobility of the Japanese Americans into middle-class America in the face of exceptionally strong prejudices suggests, for example, that on the whole they had acculturated more rapidly to this country than several European ethnic groups, some of whose West Coast leaders were conspicuous in the pre-World War II anti-Oriental movements. The significant contributions of the Asian immigrants and their descendants to American economy and culture—far more substantial contributions, as have been observed, than their numbers might indicate—and their participation in a wide range of responsible roles show how mistaken were the contentions of the anti-Oriental organizations that Asians could not or would never "assimilate." Nevertheless, as educational research has found, many school textbooks and popular accounts, perhaps reflecting the inertia of the past, continue to ignore the Asian Americans or to depict them as "problems" and "unleavened alien lumps" in the body politic.

Now would seem to be a good time to gain some retrospective insights into the experiences of Japanese and other Asian immigrants and the subsequent generations in the United States rather than to perpetuate the old stereotypes which pictured their arrival as a bizarre and possibly dangerous deviation from the mainstream of immigration to this country. The United States, it would seem, is today better able to analyze even its racist heritage which, with its strong emotional overtones, justified in the minds of many Americans the indignities and inequalities deliberately imposed on Asian immigrants and Asian Americans. The emotion-laden activities of anti-Japanese organizations aggravated the tensions between the United States and Japan and influenced the course of events which ultimately culminated in the war in the Pacific. Unless understood and overcome, this racist tradition could help lead (some assert, it already has helped to lead) Americans to further conflicts with other Asian peoples.

Studies on the Japanese and other Asian immigrants and their American-born descendants are potentially important not only in themselves, but also as sources of comparative data to test the various explanatory generalizations regarding American ethnic and race relations and regarding the experiences of European immigrants. Most of these generalizations are derived from American research on European ethnics and Afro-Americans. A number of observers as diverse as Professor William Petersen and Daniel Patrick Moynihan, however, are beginning to question the adequacy or even the validity of some frequently applied explanations. To mention only one example, it is at times stated that the greater the differences between the American and the ancestral cultures of an immigrant group, the more difficult will be the family relations between the immigrant parents and their American-born children, and hence, the larger the delinquency and crime rates of the children. The Nisei probably had the lowest delinquency and crime rate of any substantial ethnic group in America, although many Nisei were acutely aware of the difficulty they had in understanding their parents and being understood by them.

Despite the many differences in the Japanese and Japanese American experiences from those of the European ethnic groups and Afro-Americans, we may first suggest that students of European immigration will recognize many of the specific attributes of Japanese immigration and Japanese American life, although Japanese history and culture obviously influenced the particular emphases and combinations of traits characteristic of their immigration. Our second observation is that the actual years of the Japanese immigration and the nature of the treatment accorded the Japanese after their arrival account for much of the difference in their American experiences. Finally, as noted below, some of the difficulties in understanding Japanese immigrants and their children arise from the inadequacy of the explanatory generalizations.

An obviously important historical and cultural factor was the absence in Meiji Japan of any tradition of mass migration such as some European countries already had. The Tokugawa regime prohibited Japanese travel abroad during the two and a half centuries when the nation was isolated. During those crucial years, Europeans were rapidly expanding throughout the world and even the Chinese had begun to go abroad. Indeed, during the Tokugawa era, the Japanese did not migrate extensively even within their own country. In addition, for some years after the "opening" of Japan, its government continued the ban against leaving the homeland. After emigration became possible, the number of Japanese who went to Hawaii and Mainland America was still small compared with the millions of Europeans who came to the United States.

As a result of this long period of seclusion, it was understandably the outsiders who took the initiative in promoting a group migration of Japanese, as distinct from the emigration of a few exceptional individuals. Hawaiian officials in Japan actively sought to recruit Japanese for Hawaiian plantations and certain influential Mainland Americans at the same time had interests which conflicted with those of Hawaii, even though Hawaii was still independent. Thus, although the initial impulse for the Japanese immigration was in response to the efforts of Hawaiian officials, it was from the first caught in a crossfire of conflicting interests. Van Reed and Irwin were Americans, but they represented Hawaii and did not fully realize that some American diplomats whom they regarded as friends were at times working behind the scenes to nullify their efforts. The activities of these two are almost equally a subject of diplomatic history or immigration studies but we shall stress their impact on Japanese immigration. They helped to make the Japanese immigration to Hawaii possible and to establish some basic patterns which later immigration at least partly followed. Irwin himself chose Hiroshima Prefecture as a source of immigrants and personally organized immigrant groups. Emigration thus became a familiar alternative to many Hiroshima residents so that decades later, even in Southern California, we find that more Issei had come from Hiroshima than from any other prefecture.

A partial exception to the above pattern of Japanese emigration involved a little-known group of early Meiji Japanese who opened contacts with a number of the Pacific islands, including some which came under Japanese mandate in the post-World War I years. These men promoted trade and also the immigration of Japanese to develop the resources of several islands. The number of immigrants, of course, was small compared with the total going to Hawaii, but these activities presaged the later growth of the Japanese overseas interests.

The Japanese immigration in numbers to the Mainland United States did not begin until almost the end of the nineteenth century. It followed far more varied patterns than did the earlier Hawaiian immigration. Many immigrants came individually, others at the invitation of friends and relatives who had preceded them, a number as recruits of immigration companies which arranged for their initial employment with large American corporations, and some originally as students. Still others first migrated to Hawaii and then moved on to the Mainland. Regardless of how they came, all those who settled in the Pacific Coast states almost immediately encountered an extensive discrimination and hostility against Asians, which anti-Chinese organizations had helped to create in the course of several decades of vigorous campaigns to exclude the Chinese. The experienced leaders of the earlier anti-Chinese movements soon had effective anti-Japanese organizations. By the end of 1907, the Japanese government had already begun to restrict immigration to the Mainland in conformity with the so-called Gentlemen's Agreement with President Theodore Roosevelt.

Despite the furor and tensions it created, the unrestricted Japanese migration to the Mainland lasted only about ten years. The census reported approximately 72,000 (six percent of them American-born citizens) Japanese in 1910 and 110,000 Japanese in 1920, and of the 1920 total, 27 percent were American-born citizens, not immigrants. For our understanding the census data are more meaningful than the immigration statistics which often summed up the Japanese entries into this country without subtracting the substantial Japanese departures. By 1910, the United States had nearly fourteen million foreign-born residents, mostly European immigrants. Yet, the opposition to the small Japanese minority was so intense that it created international tensions and later helped to eliminate the token quota of less than 200 proposed for Japan in the 1924 immigration law. Many leaders of the anti-Japanese movements openly referred to their racial views as the reason for their position, although some apologists tried to explain their long campaign of opposition in economic terms.

Europeans and Africans could become naturalized citizens, but Asians could not. As a result, the Japanese faced severe handicaps compared with non-Asians. Politicians found it advantageous to stir up anti-Japanese campaigns to gain votes. More directly, the denial of citizenship barred educated Japanese from nearly all civil service positions and many scientific and professional posts (some professional societies required citizenship). Many states used this ineligibility to citizenship as the basis of the sweeping anti-Oriental legislation which barred Asians from owning real property, including agricultural land, and from entering certain occupations. The leaders of the anti-Japanese movements did not confine their activities to the United States, but a number attempted to "export" their anti-Japanese programs to other countries, as illustrated by the essay on the Vancouver riots. During World War II, the American government persuaded the Peruvian government to expel Japanese and Peruvians of Japanese ancestry (expulsion resulted in the loss of their property) with no recourse to justice. The Brazilians were more successful in resisting American pressure. Some scholars concerned with Asian subjects and civil rights who are at least partly informed about the West Coast evacuation are barely aware of all the attempts to extend American racist practices in the past. It is equally important to take into account the continuous efforts of American organizations and individuals opposed to discrimination. In recent years, their views have won increasing numbers.

Publications on Japanese immigration to the United States have generally paid little attention to the role of Japanese immigrants and long-term residents in the development of the now giant trade between the United States and Japan. Each is the largest overseas market for the other, even without adding the great volume of exports to Japan sold by the overseas branches of American firms. In the early years of the Meiji era, however, the possibility of establishing normal trade relations between the two countries was unpromising and the economic value of the trade seemed limited. Japan's long seclusion left her without readily marketable products to sustain overseas trade and without the institutions, organizations, personnel, understanding, and experience needed to conduct and promote trade. The social and cultural differences between the United States and a Japan emerging from feudalism further complicated the situation. The essay on the East Coast Issei examines some of the reasons why the early Issei took the lead in fostering this trade, which was another significant contribution of the Japanese immigrants to the establishment of economic relations between the United States and Japan.

A number of other Japanese were active in the cultural and intellectual relations between the two countries. Their intellectual and artistic concerns required frequent changes of residence across the Pacific. Further research on this group is obviously needed. Since its members literally lived in the two "worlds," the cultural "bridges" they represented differed from those of the usual Issei or resident. It is difficult to decide in some cases whether a particular person was more a Japanese immigrant living primarily in America or a Japanese based in Japan who frequently lived in the United States. Nonetheless, their contributions as artists, musicians, writers, intellectuals, and scholars added significantly to Japanese American understanding.

The unusually rapid mobility of Japanese Americans into the mainstream of American occupational and cultural life has stimulated some scholars to ask how this was possible in the face of discrimination and the cultural gap between the Japanese and American. As already mentioned, several observers question the adequacy of generalizations based solely on European and Afro-American experiences.

It seems that Japanese "communities" in many Western cities helped their members to prepare for social mobility rather than permanently locking them in a "ghetto." As discrimination lessened, Japanese Americans moved into responsible positions and began to reside in essentially non-ethnic areas. The study of Seattle's representative Japanese community analyzes some of the complex and subtle interrelationships between the ethnic community and the larger society. It also suggests some bases for comparative studies on European immigrant and ethnic communities, which in some cases apparently handicapped their residents in their efforts to rise in the larger world.

European immigration to the United States continued over a longer period than did the free Japanese immigration to the Mainland, which was sharply restricted about ten years after its beginning. In many European ethnic communities in the United States, the American-born children of the earlier immigrants were older than most new immigrants. Age did not automatically categorize a person's cultural background or place of birth. Since a large percentage of the Japanese immigrants had come as young men during the brief period of open immigration, a significant proportion of the immigrants belonged to a single generation and their American-born children to another generation. The generation gap accentuated the cultural gap, and this sharpened separation no doubt influenced the Japanese and Japanese Americans to emphasize the intergenerational differences. Such generation theses as those of Hansen and Mannheim should be subjected to further tests. Studies on the Asians and Asian Americans in the United States can broaden and strengthen the research on other ethnic and racial groups.

We are greatly indebted to the Japanese American Research Project at the University of California, Los Angeles, which inspired this collection. Co-editor Miyakawa was one of the initiators and the director of that project. We are also indebted to the friends of Japanese American studies in Hawaii who encouraged co-editor Conroy to undertake the task. Our special thanks go to Dr. Mary I. Watanabe of Philadelphia, the Eastern District Chairman of the Japanese American Citizens League committee for Japanese American research, who first brought the editors together.

It is emphasized that the studies included here represent only a small part of the research currently under way or already completed. We believe, however, that they illustrate some of the problems and approaches scholars have been following. Professor Roger Daniels has mentioned many earlier publications on California's treatment of Japanese immigrants in his *The Politics of Prejudice: The Anti-Japanese Movements in California and the Struggle for Japanese Exclusion* (Berkeley and Los Angeles: University of California Press, 1962). *The Japanese in Hawaii, 1868–1967: A Bibliography of the First Hundred Years* (Honolulu: Social

Science Research Institute of the University of Hawaii, 1968) by Mitsugu Matsuda lists references on Hawaii. For Brazil, which unfortunately could not be included in the present volume, readers may consult *The Japanese and Their Descendants in Brazil: An Annotated Bibliography* (Sao Paulo: Centro de Estudos Nipo-Brasileiros, 1967) by Robert J. Smith, Hiroshi Sato, John B. Cornell, and Takashi Maeyama.

Recent publications include: John Modell, "The Japanese American Family: A Perspective for Future Study" and "Class or Ethnic Solidarity: The Japanese American Company Union," both in *The Pacific Historical Review,* XXXVII, 1 (February 1968) and XXXVIII, 2 (May 1969) respectively; Harry H. L. Kitano, *Japanese Americans: The Evolution of a Sub-Culture* (Englewood Cliffs, N.J.: Prentice-Hall, Inc., 1969); and Bill Hosokawa, *Nisei: The Quiet Americans* (New York: William Morrow and Company, 1969). Among the references to the war years are Daisuke Kitagawa, *Issei and Nisei: The Internment Years* (New York: Seabury Press, 1967); Allan R. Bosworth, *America's Concentration Camps* (New York: W. W. Norton, 1967); Audrey Girdner and Anne Loftis, *The Great Betrayal: The Evacuation of Japanese-Americans During World War II* (New York: The Macmillan Company, 1969); and Dillon Myer, *Uprooted Americans* (Tucson: University of Arizona Press, 1971). Howard H. Sugimoto prepared a special bibliographical essay on the war period and the relocation for this volume.

For editorial assistance we are grateful to Lloyd Garrison, Nancy Davidson, Barbara Monahan, and Charlotte Conroy, for typing assistance to Mary Baranski, and for spirited proofreading to Wayne Patterson, Toru Takemoto, Martin Bagish, and Melvin Ang.

HILARY CONROY & T. SCOTT MIYAKAWA
Editors

1 *Typical Japanese village of the sort from which many immigrants came in the Meiji period.*

2 *A teahouse in Meiji Japan.*

3   The farming experience of Japanese immigrants was largely in rice planting.

4 (left)   *Robert W. Irwin and his wife in official attire to attend a celebration of the Meiji Constitution.*

5 (below)   *Robert W. Irwin family: (front, left to right) Agnes Irwin, daughter; Iki Irwin, wife; R. W. Irwin; (back, left to right) Sophia Arabella Irwin, daughter; Robert Walker Irwin, Jr., son; Richard Irwin, son; two other daughters are missing.*

6 (right)   *Yukiko Irwin,*
co-author of essay
and granddaughter of R. W. Irwin.

7 (below)   *City Market of*
Los Angeles, 9th and San Pedro
Streets, October 7, 1911.
Japanese Diet member Shimada visits
the Issei-organized and operated
wholesale produce market.

8   Issei picnic near the port of Los Angeles, May 26, 1907.

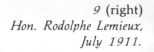

9 (right)
Hon. Rodolphe Lemieux,
July 1911.

10 (left)
Damage from the
anti-Japanese Riots,
Vancouver, 1907.

11   *Colorado River Relocation Center, Poston, Arizona, June 1942.*

12   *The War Relocation Authority caption reads: "Barrack Building typical of those at this (Poston, Arizona) War Relocation center for evacuees of Japanese ancestry. Note the double roof construction for protection from the elements." June 1, 1942.*

13 (right) Landscaping by evacuees at Poston, Arizona, improved the Relocation Camp's appearance markedly. This was apparently done within the first year.

14 (left) The Tule Lake—Newell, California Center was used for evacuees presumed to favor Japan. In this photo taken in February 1943, the muddy streets resulting from thawing ground are in evidence.

15   Although the evacuees were ingenious in developing agriculture in the inhospitable areas in which the centers were located, those at Tule Lake—Newell, California, had a special problem. The War Relocation Authority caption on this photo of some of the land they developed there reads: "View of wild geese on farm. These geese, which are protected by game laws, cause hundreds of dollars of damage to the crops."

16   An interior view of one section of the Mizunuma Silk Mills (reeling mill) from which came the first direct shipments of silk ever exported to the United States. Chotaro Hoshino, elder brother of Ryoichiro Arai, was the initiator and founder.

17 (right) *Toyo Morimura (left)*
and Ichizaemon Morimura in 1889.

18 (left) *Ryoichiro Arai*
in December 1910,
at the age of fifty-five.

19   Inazo and Mary Elkinton Nitobe with a young woman friend, 1931.

Part One

Historical Essays:
Hawaii & the Pacific Islands

Introduction

The Tokugawa Shogunate and the subsequent Meiji government both continued to prohibit the free emigration of Japanese, even after Japan was opened to the outside world and treaty relations were established with various Western powers in the 1850s and 1860s. The ban persisted partly as a cultural carry-over from the two and a half centuries of seclusion, but its retention also reflected some new factors. Not the least of the new influences was the reaction of Japanese officials, who in their early travels abroad became aware of the "inhuman" discrimination against Chinese immigrants in America and several other places. These officials felt that the forced acceptance of inferior status by the Chinese immigrants accentuated Western prejudices against the Chinese and lowered China's standing as a nation. They were opposed to having Japanese immigrants subjected to similar humiliations, both on human- itarian grounds and in consideration of Japanese national policy. The Meiji government, which was embarked on efforts to revise the unequal treaties imposed on Japan, sought equal status among world powers and tried to avoid situations which would adversely affect the standing of Japanese.

In view of Japan's long seclusion and its official reluctance to permit emigration, the first two essays show that it was the active initiative and organizational talents of the Hawaiian officials in Japan which were responsible for most of the earlier Japanese migration to Hawaii. Thus, the pattern of this earlier Japanese movement to Hawaii differed from that of many Europeans to North America, especially in the later years, in which there was a wide diversity in modes of immigration. The European colonial powers who occupied the New World did not seclude themselves as Japan did. They sent soldiers, officials, clergymen, traders, craftsmen, and other colonists, directly and through official companies, and they encouraged private immigration—individual, organizational, and commercial. There were other developments in Europe, religious wars and persecution, which also impelled many people to consider refuge in the New World.

The first two essays concentrate on two Americans, Eugene Van Reed and Robert Walker Irwin, who served as loyal and active official repre- sentatives of Hawaii in Japan and made possible the early Japanese migration to the Islands. The authors also mention several conflicts of interest between Hawaii and certain influential elements in the United States. Some of those Mainland Americans were opposed to Hawaiian efforts to expand trade relations with East Asia and thus strengthen its economy. A stronger Hawaii would be less susceptible to their influence. Masaji Marumoto's essay suggests that they were able to block Van Reed on several crucial occasions, and that he was unaware of their activities. In the light of the strong anti-Oriental racism in the United States, it is intriguing to note that the Hawaiian government originally wanted Japanese immigrants not merely for economic reasons, but also to help replenish the native Hawaiian population. Hawaiian officials sought population objectives which post-annexation American authorities in Hawaii would find distasteful or directly objectionable because of their Mainland racism and vested interests.

A number of individual Japanese of the early Meiji era considered migrating to other islands in the Pacific, especially the Marianas, Carolines, and Marshalls, to establish personal business or trade. Nevertheless, there was a relatively large-scale early Japanese emigration to Hawaii (small in total numbers when compared to the millions of Europeans who immigrated to America) which depended on the systematic program developed by Robert W. Irwin. In the second essay, Yukiko Irwin and Hilary Conroy describe that program. The third essay by David C. Purcell shows that the Japanese resident traders were able to compete successfully in many of the Pacific islands which were still under German and Spanish rule. That token immigration into Micronesia perhaps presaged the greater interest many Japanese developed in immigration in later years. The growing trade relations developed in the Pacific may be symbolic of an eventual world-wide trade with areas remote from historic Japanese horizons.

These first historical essays reveal quite clearly the importance of seemingly minor "historical accidents" (e.g., a lost letter, chance meetings, and individual arrangements) at the start of a migration process. These essays describe the beginnings from which a vast network of later relationships between Japanese and North Americans developed.

"First Year" Immigrants to Hawaii & Eugene Van Reed[1]

MASAJI MARUMOTO

The first group of Japanese laborers recruited to work in Hawaii arrived in Honolulu on June 19, 1868, on the British ship *Scioto,* a three-masted sailing ship of 855 tons registered in Gibraltar.[2] The ship left Yokohama with 150 persons, but one died on the way. When it docked in Honolulu, there were 149 souls aboard: the group leader or headman, 141 male workers, six women, and one infant.[3]

Among the Japanese in Hawaii, the members of this group are known as "Gan-nen-mono," or "First Year Men," because they came in the first year of the reign of Emperor Meiji (1868–1912).

Eugene Van Reed, an American citizen commissioned by King Kamehameha IV as the Hawaiian consul general at Kanagawa, directed the recruitment of the group. He was also responsible for shipping the members out of Japan under circumstances which made him *persona non grata* to Japanese officials.

The idea of getting Japanese laborers to Hawaii was broached by the Hawaiian foreign minister, Robert C. Wyllie, in a letter dated March 10, 1865, to Van Reed. Besides being a government official, Wyllie was a businessman with a substantial stake in the Hawaiian sugar industry. He was an owner of the Princeville Plantation on Kauai.

At the time Wyllie wrote to Van Reed, Hawaiian officials were looking for solutions to two problems which had confronted the kingdom for many years. One was the necessity of finding new sources of labor supply as a consequence of the rapid growth of the sugar industry, which became a factor in the Hawaiian economy after the founding of Koloa Plantation in 1835. The second problem was the need for repopulation, which arose from a steep decline in native population during the period that the sugar industry was enjoying its growth. The latter problem was complicated because of the belief held in official circles that the kingdom should be repopulated with people of cognate racial origin, who would readily amalgamate with native Hawaiians.

The Royal Hawaiian Agricultural Society tried to obtain laborers from a new source in August 1851 by entering into an agreement with

Captain Cass, of the British bark *Thetis,* to import Chinese labor. Captain Cass brought 180 laborers from Amoy in January 1852, and 100 more later in the same year.

The Chinese were engaged for five years at three dollars per month, plus transportation, food, clothing, and housing. They were generally satisfactory to sugar planters, and the president of the society congratulated the kingdom for having obtained such "quiet, able and willing men."[4] However, the presence of the Chinese soon resulted in criticism from other elements of the population. In 1855 Kamehameha IV stated to the legislature:[5]

> It is to be regretted that the Chinese coolie emigrants, to whom has been given a trial of sufficient length for testing their fitness to supply our want of labor and population, have not realized the hopes of those who incurred the expense of their introduction. They are not so kind and tractable as it was anticipated they would be; and they seem to have no affinities, attraction or tendencies to blend with this, or any other race. In view of this failure it becomes a question of some moment whether a class of persons more nearly assimilated with the Hawaiian race could not be induced to settle on our shores.

Despite such criticism, sugar planters continued to import Chinese because they could find no other satisfactory source of labor supply. In October 1864, Kamehameha V told the legislature:[6]

> Our agricultural enterprises have been urged forward with such energy on every island of the group as to render importation of laborers necessary. . . . The wants of our agriculture, the dictates of humanity and the preservation of our race demand that the Government should control this operation.

In compliance with this message, the legislature passed "An Act to Provide for the Importation of Laborers and for the Encouragement of Immigration," which became law on December 30, 1864. This act created a bureau of immigration, more generally called the Board of Immigration, and was the basis for the government's exclusive control of immigration.

Soon after it came into existence, the Board of Immigration had the king appoint Dr. William Hillebrand as commissioner "to procure, contract and import into this Kingdom Labourers, from such countries in Asia, as can best supply them." Under this appointment Dr. Hillebrand proceeded to Hong Kong, and subsequently shipped 522 Chinese to Honolulu. He went to India on the same trip, but not to Japan, although he carried letters of introduction from Wyllie to Van Reed and to Joseph Heco, a naturalized American citizen, whose Japanese name was Hikozo Hamada.[7]

While these events were taking place, Japan was in the throes of a great political upheaval which ended in the spring of 1868 in the restoration of imperial rule, after more than six centuries of rule by shoguns. Japan also emerged from more than two centuries of isolation by entering into a treaty with the United States which opened the ports of Shimoda and Hakodate to American ships. That agreement was followed by a more comprehensive treaty which opened the port of Kanagawa, in place of Shimoda, and four other ports, including Hakodate, to trade with the United States. Commodore Perry negotiated and on March 31, 1854 signed the earlier agreement for the United States. Consul General Townsend Harris negotiated the later treaty which he signed on June 19, 1858. Both treaties were negotiated and signed by shogunate officials for Japan, but without imperial consent. The treaties were extremely unpopular in Japan, and they were factors in accelerating the downfall of the shogunate government.

Kanagawa is now a part of Yokohama, but at the time of its designation as a treaty port, it was the principal seaport town in the area, and Yokohama was a small fishing village. The United States opened its consular office in Kanagawa in July 1859, with Consul General Dorr in charge, and Heco and Van Reed as secretaries.[8]

Heco first came to the United States as a shipwrecked Japanese sailor, who had been rescued by an American ship. He subsequently was educated and naturalized in the United States. Being bilingual in English and Japanese, he was able to give invaluable services to the United States and Japan in the early years of their intercourse. But this is not the place to dwell on his career. Suffice it to say, he became acquainted with Van Reed about 1853, taught him some Japanese, and undoubtedly nurtured Van Reed's interest in Japan. He visited Van Reed in Reading, Pennsylvania, in June 1858, just before he left the United States to return to Japan.

Van Reed was born in Reading, in 1835. His father took him to San Francisco when he was 16 years old. There he first met Heco. Van Reed arrived in Kanagawa in June 1859. After a brief stint at the American consulate, he went into private business. Early in 1864, he was associated with Augustine Heard & Co. in Yokohama.[9] While in Yokohama he met a friend of Wyllie, U. W. Cryder of Hong Kong, who was on a visit to Japan, and their conversation turned to the subject of the relationship between Hawaii and Japan.

On March 15, 1864, upon his return to Hong Kong, Cryder wrote to Wyllie suggesting that Hawaii initiate treaty negotiations with Japan:

> The matter has been particularly brought to my notice by Mr. Eugene M. Van Reed, an American gentleman resident of Yokohama, & connected in

business with the well known house of Messrs. Augustine Heard & Co. of China. Should you think it advisable to act on my suggestion, I do not know of a more suitable person to manage the negotiations, & act as consul for your Government.

Wyllie did not act on this letter for almost a year, although in the meantime Van Reed had sent him an application for appointment as the Hawaiian representative in Japan. Van Reed's father had also sent him a request for favorable consideration of his son's application.[10]

Then, on March 10, 1865, Wyllie wrote to Van Reed the previously mentioned letter. In that letter, he stated:

I have before me your letter of 1 May from Kanagawa, and one from my friend Mr. U. W. Cryder of 15th March from Hong Kong, strongly recommending you for the office of the King's Consul General in Japan.

It is my purpose to nominate you for that office to the King, whose prerogative it is to make such appointment, and I shall take care to inform you each of the result, which I expect will be favorable.

I enclose the Hawaiian Gazette of 18th February, containing 3 ordinances, relating to the importation of Chinese and other Foreign Labourers. We are in much want of them. I myself could take 500 for my own estates. Could any good agricultural laborers be obtained from Japan or its dependencies, to serve like the Chinese, under a contract for 6 or 8 years? If so, send me all the information you can and state at what cost per head they could be landed here; and if their wives and children could be induced to come with them. They would be treated well, enjoy all the rights of freemen, and in our fine [islands], under our beautiful and salubrious climate, they would be better off, as permanent settlers than in their own country.

Thus, it was Hawaii's need for labor, rather than its quest for a treaty relationship with Japan, which provided Wyllie with an impetus to act. Van Reed was appointed Hawaiian consul general at Kanagawa on April 7, 1865. Wyllie died six months later, on October 19. Upon Wyllie's death, Charles de Varigny became foreign minister.

On January 27, 1866, Van Reed arrived in Honolulu for a stopover of three weeks on his way back to Japan from a trip to the United States. During his stay, he conferred with Varigny and made a study of local conditions. He also had an audience with the king.[11]

Although there is no record of the subjects Varigny and Van Reed discussed, it is evident from their later correspondence that they decided to give priority to treaty negotiation, and to subordinate the obtaining of laborers to the accomplishment of that primary object. Van Reed thought that once the treaty was signed permission for Japanese laborers to come to Hawaii would be granted as a matter of course.[12]

Van Reed left Honolulu on February 18 on the Bremen bark *Libelle,* bound for Hong Kong. On March 4, the ship was wrecked on a reef off Wake Island, which at that time was a desolate, uninhabited coral atoll without water. After spending three weeks there, the ship's crew and passengers headed for the Marianas in two open boats, with a short supply of provisions and water. One boat with nine persons aboard was lost. The other boat with 22 persons aboard, including Van Reed, reached Guam after negotiating the distance of 1,400 miles from Wake in 13 days. From Guam, Van Reed proceeded to Hong Kong and finally got back to Kanagawa on June 30.[13]

On July 3, Van Reed wrote to Varigny informing him about the shipwreck, and stating: "In a few days, as soon as I have recuperated a little, I shall meet the Japanese Officials and explain the wishes of His Majesty." Varigny received this letter on September 10. Two weeks later, he wrote to Van Reed encouraging him to proceed with negotiations with the Japanese government.

On August 18, General Robert B. Van Valkenburgh arrived in Yedo, the administrative capital of Japan, to assume the post of American minister to Japan. Four days later, Van Reed called on the minister to seek his aid and friendly cooperation in arranging the preliminaries of a treaty of friendship and commerce between Hawaii and Japan.[14]

Van Valkenburgh obliged, and had the American legation approach the Japanese foreign office. The legation reported the result to Van Reed on October 8, as follows:

> A despatch from the Governors of Foreign Affairs by order of the Gorojin for Ministers of Foreign Affairs concerning the conclusion of a Treaty with the Hawaiian Kingdom, that at present they cannot enter into negotiation to that effect owing to the death of the Tycoon and the ceremonies of interment. A period of mourning then follows, but as soon as that period shall have expired Plenipotentiaries to negotiate with you will be appointed.

The period of mourning ended in November,[15] and on January 26, 1867, the Japanese government reported to Van Valkenburgh the appointment of its commissioners to negotiate and conclude a treaty with the Hawaiian kingdom.[16]

However, at this auspicious moment, Van Reed did not have a letter of credence from the king. In the absence of such a letter, the Japanese commissioners refused to enter into any discussion. So, the negotiation was stalemated at the very outset.[17] When Van Reed was in Honolulu, he apprised Varigny of the necessity of a letter of credence in any treaty negotiation. Again, on September 10, he wrote to Varigny, shortly after his call on the American minister, and stressed the importance of a letter of credence. Varigny received this letter on November 14, but at that time, the king was on the island of Hawaii, and did not return to Honolulu until sometime after January 7.[18] Varigny did not make any special effort to get the king's signature to a letter of credence while the king was away from Honolulu because, as he wrote later to Van Reed, he did not know that the document was absolutely necessary to the success of Van Reed's negotiation.[19]

A letter of credence was finally signed by the king and mailed to Van Reed on January 21, 1867. Instead of being carried directly to Kanagawa, however, it went first to San Francisco, then to China, and finally to Kanagawa. It was not delivered to Van Reed until May 24.[20] While awaiting the letter of credence, Van Reed wrote to Varigny on April 30:

> To this date, neither myself or the Japanese Government have received any information from His Majesty relative to forwarding me sufficient Powers to sign the Treaty. . ., and my position in such absence is becoming one of a peculiarly sensitive character.

This letter was delivered to Varigny on June 26. Soon after that, Varigny decided to have D. C. Waterman hand-carry a duplicate of the letter of credence which was mailed on January 21 to Van Reed. Waterman left Honolulu on August 3 and arrived in Kanagawa on September 26. At the time of Waterman's departure, Varigny did not know that Van Reed had received the original letter of credence. In the meantime, immediately upon receipt of the letter of credence, Van Reed gave notice of its arrival to the Japanese government. In response to this notice, the Japanese foreign office wrote to Van Reed:

> Having received your letter of the 24 May, we had the honor of knowing that you are charged now by Hawaiian Government with the full power of concluding the Treaty of friendship and commerce between Hawaiian Kingdom and Japan. Consequently, we having not neglect [*sic*] to appoint our Authorities, have elected as our Commissioners: Edzure Kagano Kami, Ishino Tsikdzenno Kami, Governors for Foreign affairs, and Shimmi Sagamino Kami, Ometsuke (inspector); hoping that you will negotiate with them about every point relating to the Treaty.

On June 16, the Japanese commissioners presented themselves to Van Reed, and, after an exchange of credentials, tentatively agreed to enter into a treaty similar to the Italian treaty, to be ready for signature in the presence of the American minister upon his return from his contemplated trip to the west coast of Japan.[21]

Van Valkenburgh returned from his trip in mid-August, and Van Reed wrote to Varigny on August 23 that he hoped to have the pleasure of sending the treaty for ratification by the king within two weeks. On September 4, Van Reed wrote to the Japanese commissioners:[22]

I beg to return herewith the Italian Treaty and to inform Your Excellencies that I am having a copy made similar, commencing from Article III, merely inserting the Hawaiian, instead of the Italian Name.

The Heading of the Hawaiian Treaty as far as Article III, I also enclose. I shall write out the Treaty as thus agreed upon in Japanese, and am ready to meet Your Excellencies to sign it, at the American Legation, at any date you may designate.

When Waterman arrived in Kanagawa on September 26, he had with him the duplicate copy of the letter of credence and also an undated ratification of the treaty signed by the king. On the same day, Van Reed again wrote to the Japanese commissioners informing them of Waterman's arrival with documents investing full powers in him to sign the treaty already agreed upon, and requesting that the treaty be signed at their earliest convenience at the American legation.

To Van Reed's dismay, the Japanese commissioners wrote to him on October 20 that they could not recognize him as the Hawaiian plenipotentiary to sign the treaty because he was a merchant and not a person of high rank. The communication read:

We have the honor to state to you that His Majesty the Tycoon having consented to conclude a treaty of amity and commerce with the Hawaiian Government at the request of the Minister of the United States of America we were appointed Commissioners to negotiate with the American Minister, but entered into negotiation with you when we learned that you were authorized by that Government to treat with us.

During these negotiations your appointment as Minister Plenipotentiary from the Hawaiian Government was announced to the Government of Japan.

We regret that your appointment to this office of high dignity cannot be recognized by our Government since, during your long residence in Japan you have engaged in trade as a merchant here.

Besides the negotiation of a treaty between two countries is very important since it established a warm and lasting friendship, therefore, proper respect should be shown by the appointment, only, of persons of high rank for that purpose. Such has been the case with America, England, France and Holland and all the other powers with whom treaties have been made. The Japanese Government is willing to conclude this treaty; they only object, to its being negotiated by you for the reason above mentioned, and at any time when the Hawaiian Government shall appoint a person not engaged in trade in this country to represent it, the Government of Japan will make the treaty in the same manner as has been done with other foreign powers.

The Minister for Foreign Affairs, by whose direction we address you, has written further on this subject to the Minister of the United States.

At the time of this communication, Japan was still a feudal state with a highly stratified social structure of four classes, of which warrior-

OAKLAND PUBLIC LIBRARY
OAKLAND, CALIFORNIA

administrators were at the top, then farmers, artisans, and lowest in the scale, merchants. Consequently, the reason given by the Japanese commissioners for rejecting Van Reed was plausible enough. But was that the real reason?

When the Japanese commissioners met Van Reed on June 16 to exchange credentials, they did not raise any question regarding Van Reed's qualification predicated on his social status. As a matter of fact, on that occasion, it was they who presented themselves to Van Reed, instead of the other way around. After the exchange of credentials, they negotiated with Van Reed to the point where there was nothing left to do except sign the treaty. Thus, some reason for rejection other than the one given in the communication must have risen.

What was that other reason? On July 22, 1866, about the time Van Valkenburgh went to Japan as the American minister to that country, General Edward M. McCook arrived in Honolulu as the American minister resident in Hawaii.[23] Like Van Valkenburgh, he was one of several generals and colonels who exchanged military commands for diplomatic posts after the close of the civil war. On the same ship which took Waterman to Japan, McCook dispatched a letter to Van Valkenburgh in which he wrote:[24]

> An envoy of the Hawaiian government sails for Japan today for the purpose of endeavoring to negotiate a treaty with Japan which will admit the sugars and other products of that kingdom on an equality with the products of the U.S., England, etc. I should think it will be your policy to oppose the consummation of such a treaty by every means in your power. The Pacific States of the U.S. are almost entirely dependent on the Hawaiian Islands for their supply of sugar and the planters here depend on the Pacific States just as entirely for a market. This circumstance has been instrumental in maintaining American influence here, although all the sympathies of the government are probably English; and as soon as they can find another market which will render them independent of the U.S. our political and commercial influence on the islands will be lost.
>
> I hope that you will concur with me in the view I have taken and throw every obstacle you can in the way of the success of Capt. Waterman.

In the light of this letter, and because the American legation in Yedo was intimately involved in the treaty negotiation, it is reasonable to conclude that Van Valkenburgh was behind the Japanese commissioner's rejection of Van Reed. This conclusion becomes even more credible in view of the Japanese government's failure to question the qualifications of Townsend Harris to sign a treaty on behalf of the United States eight years earlier in 1858. Harris also was a merchant before he was appointed American consul general at Shimoda.

Van Reed reported briefly on his rejection to Varigny on October 24. In this report after referring to other documents which had nothing to do with the treaty, he merely stated:

I . . . beg also to enclose the last Despatch received in which His Majesty the Tycoon reiterates his readiness to make the Treaty with the Hawaiian Government, after certain preliminaries have been arranged, particulars of which Waterman, Esq., will inform Your Excellency.

The report was hand-carried by Waterman, who returned to Honolulu on December 5. Waterman delivered the report to Varigny, and, at the same time, informed him that the matter relating to the treaty was arranged so that further negotiation was unnecessary, that the designation of Van Valkenburgh as plenipotentiary would be agreeable to Van Reed and the Japanese Government, and acceptable to Van Valkenburgh.[25] Neither Van Reed nor Waterman knew about McCook's letter to Van Valkenburgh.

On December 7, Varigny forwarded to Van Reed a special commission authorizing Van Valkenburgh to sign the treaty negotiated by Van Reed, and wrote:

We sincerely hope that after so many proofs of friendship towards this Government, General Van Valkenburgh will accept the honor conferred upon and the trust reposed in him, and will consent to add one more obligation to those under which he has already placed us.

Van Reed received the special commission sometime before March 7, 1868. At the time of its receipt, Van Valkenburgh was absent from Yedo so Van Reed delivered it to the American *chargé d'affaires*.[26] Van Valkenburgh did not acknowledge its receipt until April 12, when he wrote to Varigny that because of the unsettled political situation in Japan, "no negotiation with the object of entering into Treaty relation with the Country could be commenced with any prospect of success." Van Valkenburgh never signed the treaty, and Hawaiian Foreign Minister Stephen H. Phillips, who succeeded Varigny, recalled the commission on October 24, 1868.

During the period of two years following his stopover in Honolulu, Van Reed had devoted his major efforts to the conclusion of the treaty between Hawaii and Japan, although he did not altogether ignore the problem of getting Japanese laborers to work in Hawaii. From time to time, he reported to Varigny on this problem. The first of those reports was made on March 27, 1867, when he wrote to Varigny:

Any proposition by the Government for Japanese Emigrants or Coolies, I think would be favorably received. Wages $30-50 per annum, for a term of two or three years service, with an obligation to return them at such expiration, might prove satisfactory, and be a benefit to the Japanese.

Then on March 30, he reported:

> The American Bark *Swallow* will, I believe, succeed in procuring from the Japanese Government passports for 50 men from the ages of 20 to 30 to become laborers on the Island of Guam, for the period of two years at a monthly stipend of $4, and the men to be returned free of expense should they so elect.
>
> I need not inform Your Excellency that a precedent having been once established that it will be an easy matter to procure the agreement of the Government to a larger number who may wish to emigrate, and that the people would readily agree to serve on the Islands in a climate healthy and agreeable to the Japanese.
>
> No better class of people for Laborers could be found than the Japanese race, so accustomed to raising Sugar, Rice, and Cotton, nor one so easily governed, they being peaceable, quiet, and of a pleasant disposition.

Five days later he made a further report to Varigny, stating:

> I have but a moment to inform Your Excellency that although Mr. Burdick of the *Swallow* had procured passports for Fifty Japanese to enable them to emigrate to Guam as Farmers, I have influenced the Japanese Government not to allow of their leaving, the good name of the Governor of Guam being as I have reason to believe, jeopardized, Burdick having no written authority for using the Governor's name.
>
> I have closely watched this Emigrant scheme, knowing that should irresponsible characters succeed in removing Japanese under great promises which are not to be fulfilled, and that in such case it will mitigate against whatever bona fide transactions other parties might have in view.

Varigny acknowledged receipt of these reports in his letter of June 6 to Van Reed, and stated that he would communicate the information to the Board of Immigration.

The Board of Immigration met for the first time in almost a year on March 19, 1868. At that meeting, after some discussion about importing Portuguese laborers from Azores and Cape Verde Islands, Varigny and the president of the board made a strong argument for the importation of laborers from Japan. According to the minutes:

> ...They stated in their opinion Japanese were more like the natives of these Islands, than any other we could get to immigrate here. The Japanese considered themselves of the same origin with these natives; they certainly resembled our native race very much, and there was not the slightest doubt that they would most readily amalgamate.

After listening to this argument, the board unanimously voted to remit the unexpended balance of the biennial appropriation made to it in June 1866, amounting to $1,925, to Van Reed "with instruction to expend that amount in sending immigrants, males and females from Japan to this country under Contracts."

Varigny sent the money to Van Reed on the ram *Stonewall,* on March 24, with a covering letter in which he stated:

> The question of Japanese immigration to this Kingdom is one that is attracting every day more attention. . . . We are desirous of giving such assistance as we can toward promoting an immigration of laborers, servants &c not only for the services they may render but in the hope that they may locate here, and amalgamate with our people with whom they have a remarkable affinity.

Van Reed received Varigny's letter and the remittance on April 25. For at least two weeks before that time he had been active in procuring Japanese laborers to go to Hawaii. On April 10, he wrote to Varigny:

> All my ingenuity has been taxed to procure from the Japanese Government the privilege of sending Laborers to improve the Sugar Plantations of Hawaii, and I have cause to know it will result in success. It is my intention to send a vessel the moment I can procure a hundred or two Laborers for Honolulu, and shall be compelled to draw on Your Excellency for the expenses: all of which I hope may prove in order. I proposed to the Japanese to give them in the name of the Government $4 each per month and found, contract three years: To advance $10. To give the parties who supplied the men one or two Dollars each. To pay their passages and feed them. Should their wives accompany them, well, but no wages to be assigned them except finding them. There are many petty official squeezes which the Laborers are to pay out of the advance money of $10. Preference given to men ages 20 to 35.
>
> I hope if all moved well to have the Japanese on the way within a month. These people are accustomed to labor, are extremely versed in the culture of Silk, Sugar, Cotton, Rice, and their fields are the admiration of Foreigners from the tidy and thorough manner of cultivating.

Van Reed's activity resulted from his discovery, noted in another letter to Varigny, that this was "a moment in the affairs of [Japan] precious in establishing a precedent for employing Japanese in large numbers."[27] Van Reed did not say what the precious moment was, but he probably was referring to the permission granted by the Japanese government to a Prussian firm, upon the request of the governor of Guam, to take 42 of its subjects to work as agricultural laborers on that island. The Japanese laborers departed for Guam on May 2 without incident.[28]

By April 24, the day before Van Reed received Varigny's letter with the remittance, three Japanese innkeepers named Hanbei, Kumehachi, and Yonekichi, had recruited approximately 400 Japanese who were interested in going to Hawaii under the terms stated in Van Reed's letter of April 10 to Varigny, and Van Reed had obtained passports for 350 of them, including 20 women.[29] The shogunate officials issued 300 on April 22 and 50 on April 24.[30] At the time the passports were issued, imperial officials had taken over most of the governmental offices and functions in Japan but shogunate officials were still in charge of the port of Kanagawa and the function of issuing passports.

Van Reed was disappointed with the small amount of remittance. On April 27, he wrote to Varigny:

> Without sufficient funds in hand, I shall search for a smaller vessel and having repicked the men, retain but about 180 for trial, and shall send them by first opportunity, drawing on Your Excellency to pay their way.

Van Reed had two reasons for retaining only 180 of the 350 persons for whom he had passports. First, the remittance barely covered the advance to be paid to that number of persons. Second, the bark *Recife*, the smaller vessel which he found, had a capacity for carrying only 180 passengers.[31] After selecting the 180 persons to be placed aboard that vessel, he returned 170 passports to the shogunate officials who issued them.

Sometime between April 27 and May 5 Van Reed changed his mind. He chartered the *Scioto* on May 5 to carry not more than 350 Japanese passengers in steerage to Honolulu; with one foreigner in charge of them, and his servant, and two Japanese, in the cabin. Their charter cost $8,900; $3,000 Mexican was to be paid on the day of departure, and $5,900 in American gold coin was to be paid five days "after sight" upon a draft drawn by Van Reed on Varigny. The *Scioto's* master provided wood and water and the charterer supplied provisions for the voyage.

There is no record to exactly explain Van Reed's change of mind. But his statement in a letter dated May (blank) 1868, sent to Varigny on the *Scioto*, suggests some of his reasons:

> Prior to the arrival of the Ram *Stonewall* 25th April . . ., I had procured some four hundred men for the Government, hoping to charter a vessel at reasonable rates to take them to Honolulu, arrival of the Ram placing but a small sum of money at my disposal, but confirming my anticipations that you desired LABOR for the Islands, and looking to Japan for such, *reassured* me in my action, and especially so when the Japanese clamorous to leave demanded to be sent to Hawaii, the country beyond their vision for which they appeared to have an infatuation, which was not to be dispelled. I therefore, in order to save the good name of Hawaii which all classes of the people here already entertain for her, determined to charter the *Scioto* and send the

Japanese to you. The best was done that could be done, the largest and most commodious Ship to be obtained was chartered, at a rate which would make the rate of passage considerably under $30 each, . . .

The charter party provided that the loading of passengers should commence 24 hours after the master gave written notice to the charterer that the ship was ready for loading.

Van Reed, however, placed 180 Japanese aboard on May 6, before the *Scioto* was ready. They were the same persons he had picked to go on the *Recife.* All were examined and passed by Dr. David J. Lee, an American physician hired by Van Reed to check on their physical fitness.[32]

The *Scioto* was still not ready on May 9, and its master notified Van Reed to take the passengers off until the ship was ready, or else he would hold him responsible for any damages that their presence aboard might cause. Van Reed did not remove the passengers. Instead, he directed Dr. Lee to examine additional persons to be placed on board. He evidently anticipated no difficulty in obtaining passports for the additional men, for his relationship with the shogunate officials charged with their issuance had always been cordial.

Van Reed's objective and hopes were thus expressed to Varigny:[33]

It has been my especial aim in all matters to make my position here one of credit to the Hawaiian Government and benefit to both countries, and in case of sending you Laborers I sincerely hope that both sides may be benefited through the intercourse thus happily inaugurated, and should the Japanese report favorably of their treatment by Hawaii you will receive by every installment a superior order of men to the last, until every acre of your luxurious Islands is crowded with a happy, thrifty and contented race far superior to any of the East.

Van Reed's hopes were dashed by the Meiji Restoration on May 9, when imperial forces entered the Kanagawa area, and officials of the new regime took over the administration of that area from shogunate officials. The new administration was headed by General Michitomi Higashikuze, governor, and Naohiro Nabeshima and Tozo Terashima, vice governors. It also had an official whose title was *kumigashira,* probably a senior administrative officer. These officials administered an office called *saibansho* which means "court house." But the office as operated by these officials was not a judicial tribunal, rather it was an administrative arm of the new regime.

Van Reed and Terashima were old acquaintances. While Van Reed was secretary of the American consulate at Kanagawa in 1859, Terashima was an interpreter at the custom house. Terashima had a special reason to remember Van Reed. In 1863, he was a prisoner on a British man of war, following an incident in southern Japan, and Van Reed was instrumental in obtaining his release after the vessel arrived at Kanagawa.[34]

The new administration required Van Reed to return the 180 passports he had retained on the very day of their takeover. Van Reed complied and explained his reason for doing so in the following note to Varigny.

> Took receipt from the Officer for the 180 passports returned him in order to be exchanged under the new Mikado Government with additional 170 men. He promised reply by 12 tomorrow.

Van Reed did not receive the reply as promised by noon on the following day. He dispatched a letter addressed to the governor and vice governors requesting that "the Passports which were to be exchanged today may be granted at the earliest possible moment as the *Scioto* is now under a heavy charter and sailing orders." Later that afternoon, a subordinate official informed him that his request was denied because "Hawaii was unknown to the Mikado and no Treaty had been signed with Sandwich."

Van Reed wrote to Higashikuze on May 11 in reply to the denial of his request noting that shogunate officials had previously agreed upon a treaty, that the civil war which raged in Japan at that time presented obstacles to its signing, and that in the meantime they had recognized his official acts. As a matter of fact, he received his consular exequatur from the shogunate officials on March 31.[35]

Van Reed conferred with Terashima on May 13, and at his suggestion wrote another letter to Higashikuze requesting that 350 passports be issued in confirmation of the acts of the former government. Alternatively, he requested payment of expenses he had incurred as agent of the Hawaiian government and damages for cancellation of the charter party. The total he estimated at about $9,000 to $10,000. He also stated that if the Japanese government desired a bond for the return of the laborers at the expiration of the contract period, he would be willing to give such bond but preferred that a Japanese consul be sent to Hawaii to look after the Japanese interest.

The Japanese officials rejected Van Reed's proposal for the dispatch of a consul to Hawaii because they felt it was too expensive. They countered with a request that he obtain a guarantee from one of the resident ministers of the treaty powers. Van Reed initially gave some consideration to this counterproposal. On May 15 he wrote to the *kumigashira* that the British minister had informed him of his plan to call a ministers' meeting to discuss the matter. Presumably, the British minister did not call such a meeting. Van Reed finally ignored the counterproposal as an insult to Hawaii, and did not answer the request of the *kumigashira* for a report of the outcome of the ministers' meeting.

The *Scioto* was cleared for sailing on May 16 by the custom house, and the master received his papers from the British consul. Van Reed then wrote to Terashima:

> The *Scioto* has waited ten days for the courtesy and confirmation of the acts of the former Government and owing to the expenses cannot wait longer. She has cleared at the Custom House and H. B. M. Consul has delivered the Captain his Papers today and will positively sail in the morning over all of which I have no control.
>
> If the new Government positively refuses to confirm the acts of the old the amount of the money expended by me for the Hawaiian Government must be refunded or the Japanese passengers will depart by the *Scioto* in conformity with the release granted by the Tycoon. . . .
>
> In conclusion I would say it certainly is very inconsistent for the Japanese Government to ask one Foreign Nation to guarantee the acts of another when in the letter making this request they refuse to guarantee the acts of their own and therefore I must refuse to ask of the Foreign Ministers the unprecedented request of a guarantee in your favor, but will abide by the privileges granted by the Tycoon.

Van Reed also wrote a letter to the *kumigashira* in similar tenor, which he closed by stating:

> I now propose in order to come to a friendly and honorable settlement of the question to return the Japanese back to Government upon payment of the money actually expended on my part of about (under) $4,000, and shall leave the case of the charter and great delay of the ship *Scioto* to be equitably decided by the English consul.

With regard to this proposal, it is noted that Van Reed made a similar proposal in his letter of May 13 to Higashikuze. In that letter, he mentioned a settlement figure of $9,000 to $10,000, which included his estimate of damages for cancellation of the charter party. In the proposal to the *kumigashira,* the figure of $4,000 covered Van Reed's out of pocket expenditures only, and, "the case of the charter and great delay of the ship" was left to the equitable determination of the British consul. There was no inconsistency in the two proposals.

Van Reed waited for an answer from either Terashima or the *kumigashira* until nine o'clock of the morning of May 17. Receiving none, he decided to order the *Scioto* to depart with the passengers who were then aboard. Upon making this decision, he went to the ship, reported the circumstances to the assembled passengers, and stated that those who desired to get off were at liberty to do so because the ship would positively sail.[36] He also paid the master $3,000 (Mexican) required at the time of the ship's departure.

The *Scioto* left Yokohama at two o'clock in the afternoon. Aboard were 141 Japanese passengers remaining from the 180 who originally went on board eleven days before, and nine persons had been smuggled aboard later as stowaways, among them a young couple and their infant child.[37]

Van Reed described these Japanese in a letter he sent on the *Scioto* to Varigny, as follows:

> You will find the men far more tractable than any other race, have a great notion of honor in a "yakunin," or official, and abide rigidly to their decisions, take a great pride in the result of their labor, and desire to excel, and I will venture to assert that after a year's intercourse with Hawaiians (a race beyond a doubt from the same original source) you will find these men settled down as happy contented beings whose greatest anxiety will be that the day of their compulsory return with its servile labor and rigid laws draws near to sever associations deeply formed.

In another letter he sent to Varigny at the same time, he stated:

> By the course of the new Government in not upholding the acts of the old, the most careful arrangements have been frustrated, and instead of 350 men clamorous to leave for Hawaii, but about 120 can depart, they having been on board some 11 days. It is even better that this number be sent than that the honor of Hawaii be doubted, or impediment be placed in the way of free intercourse between the two Nations. I have been advised by my friends to abide by the concessions made by the Tycoon's Government and were I to release the Japanese on board the *Scioto* without recompense for the outlay made while reposing on the good faith of the new Government, I would place Hawaii beyond countenance in future intercourse with Japan.

Van Reed placed D. A. Baum, an American businessman, in charge of the passengers. Tomisaburo Makino, who will hereafter be referred to as Saburo because he came to be known by that name in Hawaii, was the *yakunin* mentioned in Van Reed's letter to Varigny. He was of samurai stock and an armor maker by occupation.[38] Also accompanying the group was Dr. Lee, whose presence on the ship was required by Sir Harry Parkes, British minister to Japan. Parkes had instructed the British consul at Kanagawa not to permit the ship to depart without a medical attendant.[39]

The departure of the *Scioto* threw the Japanese officials into consternation. On the day after the departure, the *kumigashira* asked Van Reed for an explanation. Van Reed merely elaborated on what he had written to Terashima.[40] On May 25, Higashikuze complained to Van Valkenburgh. Van Valkenburgh responded by publishing the following notice on May 26:[41]

> In pursuance of the 4th Section of the Act of Congress giving certain Judicial powers etc. approved June 22nd, 1860, I, ROBERT B. VAN VALKEN-BURGH—Minister Resident of the United States in Japan do hereby decree the following regulation, which shall have the force of law in the Courts of the United States in Japan.
>
> The Act of Congress to prohibit the Coolie trade etc. approved February 19th, 1862—and which was framed with regard to China, is hereby made applicable to Japan.

At the same time, however, he informed the Japanese officials that, although he regretted the incident, he could do nothing about it because the *Scioto* was a British ship. Upon further prodding, he wrote the same officials:[42]

> I am not acquainted with the circumstances of this case, neither have I been able to comprehend why. . .Your *saibansho* did not prevent their emigration, as nothing would have been easier for them to do so.

The Japanese officials were unable to obtain aid or comfort from the British minister. On June 12 Parkes received the following report in reply to an inquiry made to the British consul at Kanagawa:[43]

> I have had no positive information as to the exact relation between the shipper Mr. E. Van Reed, who is an American citizen, and the Emigrants. I have no reason to suppose, however, that their departure was not purely voluntary and that they comprehended whither they were going and the nature of the contract they made. . . . No objection was at any time made at this Consulate by the Japanese Authorities in the circumstances of a British ship conveying these passengers, and the master got his clearance at the Custom House, apparently without difficulty, which he presented at this Consulate before he got the papers of his ship.

The *Scioto* took 34 days to cross the Pacific to Hawaii, and arrived in Honolulu on June 19. One of the stowaway passengers, Yonekichi Sakuma, kept a brief diary of the voyage. His diary reveals that the Japanese passengers did not know in which direction Hawaii lay. Day after day, Sakuma noted that the ship headed east and then south. As late as the 17th day at sea, he wrote: "The ship still is pointed south." He recorded several highlights of the trip in the diary which revealed that the ship was loaded with 500 bags of unpolished rice, 20 bags of polished rice, and a sufficient supply of soy sauce, soy bean paste, and firewood. The passengers, however, apparently suffered from a shortage of fish, fowl, and other supplementary food items. The first three days in the open sea were stormy, and not a soul had a meal. The days after the storm were long and monotonous, and the more energetic passengers engaged themselves in pounding and dehusking unhulled rice. On one occasion, a Chinese cook had an altercation with some passengers and flashed a knife, but serious trouble was averted by Saburo's timely appearance on the scene. On a couple of occasions, violators of the ship's strict no-smoking rule were handcuffed. A person named Wakichi died from an unknown cause on the 21st day at sea. He was wrapped in sailcloth and tossed into the ocean. When the *Scioto* arrived in Honolulu the king welcomed the passengers by sending them a barrel of salted fish.[44]

On June 20, Dr. Lee submitted a report to the Board of Immigration, in which he stated:

> The Japanese now arrived were with some exceptions, together with one hundred others, selected by myself, from about four hundred presented as laborers desirous of emigrating to Hawaii.
>
> It is a well known fact that at least two-thirds of this class of Japanese are afflicted with diseases of the skin, of scrofulous and venereal character. It was then an extremely difficult matter to select such as were entirely free from such diseases; but their present condition will show that none have been taken with any virulent form of skin disease and most of them free from disease in any form.
>
> I would here remark that several of this list of passengers were rejected on account of their condition in this respect, and several others because of age and other reasons, but so anxious were the Japanese to leave, that these rejected applicants were by their friends smuggled on board without papers. As I had no authority or part in their shipment I could but make the best of the matter after they were found on board.

The Board of Immigration held a special meeting on June 22 to consider the questions presented by the arrival of the Japanese immigrants. The Board spoke of them as immigrants even though they originally came with the understanding that they would be returned to Japan at the end of three years. The board considered several questions, among them: how to distribute the immigrants and how to recover the costs of bringing them to Hawaii.

In considering the first question, the Board had information from a poorly translated Japanese document which contained the agreement under which the immigrants were recruited. The terms of the agreement were essentially the same as those set forth in Van Reed's letter of April 10 to Varigny, except that the monthly wage was to be paid two dollars in cash and the balance at the end of each year. The minutes of the meeting indicate that the Board had entered, or was in the process of entering, into a contract on those terms with each of the 147 immigrants, except for the infant and Saburo, the headman, who was in a separate category. The Board voted to assign those contracts to various employers. Some of the employers were sugar planters who wanted the immigrants as plantation workers, and others were individuals who wanted them as domestic servants.

Information concerning the costs of importing the immigrants came from three drafts, totaling $10,150, drawn by Van Reed upon Varigny, one in favor of the master of the *Scioto* for $5,900, one in favor of Baum for $2,750, and one in favor of Bishop & Co. for $1,500. The Board also had a request from Van Reed addressed to Varigny to pay $150 to Dr. Lee for his services as medical attendant on the *Scioto.*[45] The Board voted to charge seventy dollars for the assignment of each contract in order to meet these payments. The total of those charges was $10,290.

When the Board decided on the contract assignment price of seventy dollars per person, it did not have a complete report from Van Reed of his expenditures. Van Reed's complete report was submitted to Varigny on June 1. The final accounting, after this report came in, revealed that the costs of importing the immigrants was actually $12,770, as follows: charterage, $8,900; advance payment to immigrants and other costs incurred by Van Reed, $3,174; Dr. Lee's services as ship's physician, $150; exchange, $546. Deducting $10,290 in contract fees and an additional $48 collected by Van Reed for Chinese passengers and freight from $12,770 left the Board with a net unreimbursed expenditure for the immigration of $2,432.

In May Van Reed wrote to Varigny that he had conducted everything "in an honorable and open way . . . without an iota of profit to myself in any possible way." Van Reed's accounting to Varigny supports this statement. He expended $3,174 including a $10 advance to each immigrant, payment for Dr. Lee's services in Japan, and costs of provisions.

The Hawaiian Gazette of June 24 reported on the impression created by these immigrants:

> They are very good natured and lusty looking set of fellows, and seem to enjoy the sights about town, so new and novel to these untravelled subjects of the Mikado's Empire. They are very polite withal, having picked up our salutation of 'aloha' and are not without a small degree of shame-facedness in regard to their appearance in coarse and sea-soiled clothing.
>
> They are favorably received by our population, both Hawaiian and foreign, and the impression is prevalent that they will make peaceable and efficient laborers, and give satisfaction.

On June 27, one week after arrival, Saburo wrote to Van Reed:[46]

Availing myself of good opportunity, I submit this report to you. We left Yokohama at dusk on May 17, and after 35 days at sea, we arrived safely in Honolulu. . . . On the ship and upon arrival, we received exceptionally courteous treatment and we are overjoyed that this capital city is much better than we were told in Japan. . . .

On the ship, quite a number of persons were seasick, but nothing serious happened, except to a person named Wakichi. He was a very good man. He became seriously ill and died on the 21st day out at sea. It is most regrettable. . . .

There is not a drunkard or a ruffian on the street during daytime or at night, and the people have a gentle disposition. So, we are very fortunate. . . .

Dr. Lee, the American physician, has been very kind not only to the sick but in other matters. When you have a chance, please convey our appreciation to him.

The mutual feeling of good will, evidenced in the Hawaiian Gazette article and Saburo's letter quoted above, did not last long. Soon after the immigrants were taken over by the assigned masters, the Board of Immigration began receiving complaints from the employers as well as from the immigrants.

Two employers, M. McInerny and Theo. H. Davies, asked the Board to refund payments made for immigrants who were ill and therefore of no use to them.

McInerny had taken an immigrant named Nakasuke to use as a household servant. Nakasuke was ill from the day he arrived in the McInerny home and required hospitalization and medical care. Apparently he had tuberculosis. McInerny wrote to the Board:[47]

Under these unfortunate circumstances and in view of the fact that the man was unquestionably sick when I took him (although I did not notice it when I saw him on the vessel) I trust your Honorable Board will take this case into your favorable consideration and relieve me of the man, reimbursing the amount advanced by me for his services as well as $7.50 I have paid to the Queen's Hospital.

Davies was agent of Kaalaea Plantation, to which 25 contracts were assigned. One of the men died before he did any work. In requesting the Board that the plantation be relieved of the expense incurred in obtaining this man's contract, Davies stated:[48]

On inquiry I find that this man never raised his hand for a single half hour's work, but was on the contrary the occasion of much delay as he had to be tended by the men who were greatly needed at their own work thus causing considerable loss apart from that occasioned by his own unfitness.

The immigrants soon complained about the withholding of one-half of their monthly four-dollar wage until the end of each year. The resulting monthly stipend of two dollars was not sufficient to buy even the necessities. Kaalaea Plantation considered that the complaint was justified and agreed to pay the entire wage in cash at the end of each month.[49] But S. G. Wilder, owner of a neighboring plantation, resisted, and wrote to the Board:[50]

I am willing to accede to any change of contract - in reason - that may be asked of all the *planters,* but I am not willing to accede to a demand of these people directly against the contract simply because they demand it. ...

I am sorry to trouble you, but I do not wish to take any step, that will not be for the best for all concerned.

The Board considered the immigrants' complaint at its meeting on August 6, and unanimously resolved that the following circular be sent to each employer:

The Board wishes it to be well understood that they disavow any claim to a right on their part to change the contracts made between employers and their Japanese laborers; at the same time they feel satisfied from representations, which have been made to them, that the men never would have agreed to receive one-half their wages in paper at the end of each month, had they known the prices of clothing, tobacco, and other articles which they look upon as necessaries. It seems clear that the sum of two dollars per month will not purchase the clothing, etc. necessary to their wants, and under these circumstances, it was unanimously agreed by the Board that they do recommend, "That all those persons who have contracted with the Board of Immigration for Japanese Immigrants, be advised to pay their men the full amount of their wages due them at the end of each month, if the laborers themselves should so desire."

The Board adjusted many other complaints with Saburo's assistance, despite the difficulty imposed by his woefully weak command of English. In an attempt to remedy this situation the Board voted to send Saburo to school at Punahou but apparently he did not go because the student roster for the academic year 1868–1869 does not show his name.

The chief grievance of the immigrants concerned long hours of work under the tropical sun. Many of the immigrants were unable to withstand the field work to which they were subjected. Contrary to Van Reed's representation to Varigny most of the immigrants were not laborers accustomed to such work, but were men unadapted by education or habits for the service at which they were being employed. Their skills were more aptly characterized by the Japanese ambassador who later came to Hawaii in response to the appeals of the immigrants to the home government for assistance.

ASIAN COMMUNITY LIBRARY
1934 PARK BLVD.
OAKLAND, CA 94606

The first report received by the Japanese government that the immigrants were having difficulties in Hawaii came from Seiichi Shiroyama, a retainer of the Lord of Uwajima, of whom Van Reed wrote to Phillips on October 27:

I have the honor to inform Your Excellency that notwithstanding the ill reports spread against the action relative to Immigrating to Hawaii by the Foreign Ministers to the Japanese Government I have succeeded in procuring a reaction, and so far as to have the Government to send Shiroyama Seichi [sic] to Hawaii. It is conceded by his friends that the rank of Consul will be forwarded him by next steamer, his Prince Oowajima being the Minister of Foreign Affairs of the Mikado, and as the above party is an especial favorite there is not doubt that my application will have its weight with Govt. Although young he is quite an intelligent youth who is impressed with the intention of opening up intercourse between the two countries.

It may be inferred from this letter that it was written after Shiroyama had departed from Japan and that he did not have a consular commission.

Shiroyama arrived in San Francisco early in December, accompanied by Katsukichi Sasebe and Shinsuke Takado.[51] Upon arrival there, he saw a newspaper article which reported that the Japanese immigrants in Hawaii were good as servants but were not good as farm workers; that they were finding it difficult to adjust themselves to the climate and to live on their meager monthly wage of four dollars, from which they had to purchase their clothing and other sundry necessities. The article further mentioned that the immigrants were frequently ill from unaccustomed climatic conditions and hard labor and that there were deductions from their wages when they did not appear for work, even when their absence was caused by illness. The newspapers added that because of such difficulties one or two of them had committed suicide and that Shiroyama was on his way to Honolulu as the Japanese consul to look after the interests of the immigrants.

Although Shiroyama had originally intended to go to Hawaii, he changed his mind and decided to return to Japan immediately, when he read the newspaper article and heard other similar reports about the immigrants.[52] His two companions proceeded to Honolulu.

Sasebe and Takado arrived in Honolulu on December 20 and stayed until December 26.[53] When they left Honolulu, they carried with them an appeal for assistance, dated December 25, addressed to the saibansho, signed by Saburo and a person named Sentaro, and also a letter from Saburo and Sentaro to Shiroyama requesting his assistance in getting the immigrants back to Japan.[54]

In their appeal to the saibansho, Saburo and Sentaro charged the

Hawaiian employers with ill treatment of the immigrants and violation of their contracts with them, and stated that the hardships of employment had caused three deaths among them, one in Ulupalakua by suicide, and two in Kaalaea by burning tropical heat.

Shiroyama returned to Japan, ahead of his companions, early in January 1869. On January 6, he sent a translation of the San Francisco newspaper article regarding the immigrants to Sozo Tsuzuki, an official in the Japanese foreign office, with a covering letter in which he stated that he went to San Francisco as an agent of a Yedo merchant named Hisajiro Ogiya and had intended to go to Honolulu on business, but decided to forego the trip, lest he embarrass the Japanese government, in light of the false rumors spread by Van Reed that he would be the Japanese consul there.[55]

That Shiroyama had some basis for his apprehension is indicated in Van Reed's letter of January 25 to Phillips, which he wrote after learning about Shiroyama's report to Tsuzuki, stating that:

> . . . I advanced money to enable Shiroyama to reach Hawaii, being confident that as he was a protege of the present Minister of Foreign affairs who was secretly aware of Shiroyama's intended departure that he would be induced to send the necessary documents as Japanese Consul, whereby he would not be placed in a false position and the Mikado not disgraced before the world.

It appears that Sasebe and Takado returned to Japan sometime in March, with the appeal of Saburo and Sentaro to the *saibansho*.[56] The appeal undoubtedly contained distortions and exaggerations. For instance, the Davies letter shows that one death in Kaalaea occurred even before the immigrant "raised his hand for a single half hour's work."

When Van Reed learned about the appeal, he wrote to Phillips on March 25 suggesting that Japanese evincing a desire to return prior to the expiration of their contract should be permitted to do so, regardless of the circumstances. He added the following reason for his suggestion:

> My desire is to have an amicable feeling between the two people, which can only be brought about by mutual concession, the present advantages should be in my mind not securely grasped in order that the *future* may be clear for a field to procure Laborers in.

Phillips replied to this suggestion on April 22, stating that it was a subject of deep regret that mistaken impressions should have reached Japan in regard to the treatment of the immigrants. He noted that some misunderstandings had been traced to the inability of the immigrants to communicate with their employers in a language both understood, and, that it was quite likely that cases had been magnified in the imagination of the immigrants because they were unable to obtain sympathy and advice in a familiar language. He added:

> It will probably occur to you upon more mature reflection, that it may be difficult to extricate laborers now under special obligation of voluntary agreement; but you can assure all with whom it may become your duty to communicate, that the rights of individual Japanese, in His Majesty's dominions, will be carefully protected, and that any Complaints of individual wrong will be kindly received, and promptly and thoroughly investigated.

When the Japanese officials received Shiroyama's report and the appeal of Saburo and Sentaro, they were still trying to obtain redress for Van Reed's action through the American minister. But, by April 1869, it became evident that they could not depend for any solution of the problem through that channel. On April 26, Van Valkenburgh wrote to the Japanese officials:[57]

> As I have informed Your Excellencies in previous communications, I regret that the emigrants were permitted to sail by the *saibansho,* but under the statement of facts as I have received them from Mr. Van Reed . . ., I cannot see he has been guilty of the breach of any of the laws of the United States.

So, the Japanese foreign office processed a recommendation made on April 16, by an official whose title was *Gaikokukan Hanji* to *Gyoseikan Benji,* a superior official, that a meeting be called to discuss the question of sending a mission to Hawaii. On July 23, it appointed an embassy headed by Torataro Hanabusa, as ambassador, assisted by Hoichi Miwa, as associate. The departure of the embassy was delayed. On September 22, Hanabusa was replaced by an official of the *saibansho,* Keisuke Ueno, who was given the title of *Kantoku no Kami.*[58]

Ueno and Miwa left for Hawaii, via San Francisco, on October 31, with letters of introduction from Van Valkenburgh to Henry A. Peirce, the American minister, and from Parkes to James H. Wodehouse, the British commissioner, in Honolulu.[59] Ueno carried with him a commission which read:[60]

> The Japanese Government hereby appoints Weyno Kantoku no Kami Special Ambassador to the Government of the Hawaiian Islands; giving him full power and authority to settle all matters relating to certain Japanese Subjects now on said Islands, and bring them back to Japan.

Before the departure of the embassy, Van Reed visited with Miwa, and wrote to Phillips:

> It affords me extreme pleasure to inform Your Excellency . . . that Miwa Hoichi, one of the Embassy was the translator of the original agreement by which Hawaii was assured her Treaty, and being of the old Government, was

steadily my friend; at parting with him on board the Steamer at 5 p.m. (Weno Keski being closeted with H. B. M. Minister) he assured me that the smoke now enveloping the Hawaiian horizon and my own credit would be swept away by his investigation, and result in peace and satisfaction to us all.

Ueno and Miwa arrived in Honolulu on December 27, after a briefing in San Francisco by Charles W. Brooks, an American who was acting as the Japanese consul in that city, and by H. W. Severance, the Hawaiian consul there. Upon their arrival in Honolulu, they were cordially greeted by Charles C. Harris, who had succeeded Phillips as foreign minister, and were quartered in the same house which the Duke of Edinburgh, son of Queen Victoria of England, had used during his visit to Honolulu. They were also warmly received by Peirce and Wodehouse, who vied with each other in rendering friendly services to them. Colonel Isaac H. Hooper, secretary of the American legation, took a leave of absence from his office in order to serve as secretary to the embassy.[61]

On December 31, Ueno addressed an official communication to Harris, in which he presented two alternative propositions, the first of which was worded as follows:

All the Japanese subjects brought here in the *Scioto* who are now living shall be collected together at Honolulu, and delivered to the Embassy, or to its agent duly appointed to receive them, for the purpose of being returned to Yokohama, and at the expense of the Japanese government for transportation only from Honolulu.

The second proposition read as follows:[62]

The Embassy will receive now a part only of said subjects, and return them to Japan, the expense of their passage to be paid by the Embassy.

In the class as above named, the whole number may amount to forty persons, more or less, and consists namely of, Mechanics, who may elect to return home. Men, unadapted by education or habits for the service at which they are now employed.

Also, all the sick, deformed, and disabled.

Those Japanese subjects not embraced as above mentioned, shall remain at service until the expiration of their present contract of labor, at the end of which time or previous thereto, they shall be returned to Yokohama at the entire expense of the Hawaiian government.

Should any of the above named class of persons be too ill, or from other unforeseen causes be unable to embark for Yokohama, they shall be properly cared for, and ultimately returned by the Hawaiian government at its own expense, due notice to be given to the Japanese government as to the cause or causes which may prevent such persons from being sent at the proper time with the others.

Ueno further wrote that Van Reed's act in shipping the immigrants to Hawaii on the *Scioto* violated the laws of Japan. He indicated that he had been instructed to take all of the immigrants back to Japan, but was presenting the second proposition as an alternative, being aware of "the hardship and pecuniary loss that such a course might work to innocent parties here, and having full powers to compromise and arrange with the Hawaiian Government the whole matter in question." He also added:[63]

It is the desire and purpose of the government of Japan to live in terms of friendship and good neighborhood with the Hawaiian nation, and to that end will be pleased to entertain treaty relations between the two nations, but it is thought necessary by the Japanese ambassadors to first settle satisfactorily the matters which are the subject of this communication.

Harris was a Harvard-educated lawyer, who was attorney general before he became foreign minister. He answered Ueno's communication on January 5, 1870, stating:

I do not think it necessary at present for me to enter into any account of the facts and circumstances attending the leaving Yokohama by the laborers alluded to, which undoubtedly are fresh in Your Excellency's mind, but would you be kind enough if you have the information upon which to do it, to give me a list of those persons who would be included in your proposition and the places where they are now employed. Saboro who came with them ought to be able to supply you with the information which you may desire for this purpose.

Harris followed this with an unofficial and informal dispatch on January 8 to Ueno, stating that "His Majesty's Government will give you all aid in their power towards the carrying out of your second proposition," and by a formal communication of January 11, informing Ueno that, after due consideration by the king in cabinet council, the Hawaiian government would accept his second proposition, subject to the stipulation that the immigrants who desired to remain in Hawaii after the expiration of their contracts be permitted to do so. Ueno and Miwa objected to the inclusion of such stipulation in a formal document, but, at the suggestion of Peirce and Wodehouse, agreed to sign a separate declaration that "should any desire to remain the Hawaiian government has no authority to compel them to go."[64]

With their principal mission thus concluded, the ambassadors went on a four-day trip around Oahu as guests of the Hawaiian government, visiting the plantations at which the immigrants were employed. Of this trip, Ueno wrote to Harris on January 19:

I desire . . . to express to Your Excellency that the visit we have lately made to the various plantations on the Island of Oahu, by Your Excellency's kind invitation has given us great pleasure.

We have everywhere found our countrymen well cared for, and kindly treated by their Employers.

Before the departure of the embassy for Japan, Ueno took care of a few housekeeping details, and also conferred with Harris on the terms of a treaty between Hawaii and Japan. On January 18, he informed Harris that he had appointed Hooper to act as his agent in receiving and forwarding the immigrants who were to be returned immediately to Japan, and also appointed Saburo as special agent to look after the interests of those who remained to serve out their contracts. He also told Harris that he would be gratified to be assured "that the said Laborers shall have the same treatment, in regard to time of Labor, holidays, rules and regulations, and rights and privileges, which are granted, by the Hawaiian Government, and the Planters in general, to the native and Chinese Laborers."

On January 19, Harris wrote to Ueno, taking notice of the two appointments, stating that he hoped Saburo would be more diligent in the future than in the past, and assuring equal treatment of the Japanese immigrants and Chinese laborers as follows:

The proprietors of Plantations generally leave off work at 3 o'clock, and always at 4 o'clock on Saturdays. It is the intention that all persons shall be treated alike in this respect. The Chinese Laborers, by *their contracts,* stipulated to have 3 days on Chinese New Year, but the Japanese did not. Since we know from Your Excellency that the Japanese have the same custom as regard the New Year, as the Chinese, especial pains will be taken to procure for the Japanese the same privileges. . . .

The undersigned further wishes to convey the idea, that it has been the desire of H. M.'s Government to guard and protect all the rights of the Japanese, and they have been diligent in doing so heretofore. The undersigned himself and the Minister of Interior have, at all times, lent their personal attention to the complaints of the humblest Japanese, and will continue always so to do, for we have looked upon their coming to this country, as an ultimate means to establish the closest relations with the Japanese Government.

With respect to the treaty, Ueno and Harris agreed upon a draft of six articles, which were embodied in a memorandum signed by them on January 19. Harris promised Ueno that a treaty containing the articles as so drafted would be confirmed by the king immediately upon its acceptance by the emperor of Japan, and Ueno promised Harris that he would recommend the acceptance of such treaty to the Japanese government.[65]

Before departing from Hawaii, Ueno obtained from Peirce and Wodehouse, as United States and British representatives respectively, a statement that in the settlement "all that it was possible to concede, consistent with the general law of Nations and the laws of Hawaiia [sic], was yielded by the latter power."[66]

The ambassadors left for San Francisco on January 20. Nine days after their departure, forty immigrants were selected and sent directly to Yokohama on the bark *R. W. Wood.* Two others from Kauai, who did not make the *R. W. Wood,* were returned to Japan by way of San Francisco.[67] Some employers complained to the Hawaiian government about the selection of their men for return to Japan. So, on February 1, the Board of Immigration adopted the following resolution:

> Resolved - That the Board allow to those persons, from whom Japanese were taken to return to their own country, a proportioned part of the money first advanced for passages, according to the time served.

The repatriating immigrants on the *R. W. Wood* arrived in Yokohama on March 7. Three weeks later, on March 25, they created a minor irritation by sending to the editor of the *Japan Herald,* a letter, sealed with their blood, reiterating the charges of contract violation and ill treatment by the Hawaiian employers, and promising to render free service to their "merciful government" as a gesture of thanks for extricating them from their sad plight.[68] However, on June 21, Van Reed wrote to Harris that five of them had requested him, on their knees, to be sent back to Hawaii; that he had obliged them by sending two on the *Wm. Rotch* and three on the *Champion,* and that "were communication more frequent, quite a number would leave on their own responsibility."

The immigrants who remained in Hawaii served out their contracts in an atmosphere of growing understanding with their employers. On September 24, Saburo wrote to Miwa, as an illustration of improved treatment of the immigrants:[69]

> The employer at Haiku Plantation is a warm and patient person. He not only observes the contracts, but also gives spending money to the sick and provides English instruction to those who have time in the evenings. In Honolulu, also, the employers are gradually showing sympathetic understanding. For all of this I wish to express to you our appreciation.

As the time for the expiration of their contracts approached, the immigrants who desired to remain in Hawaii or go to the United States, after serving out their contracts, inquired of the Japanese government, through Saburo, whether they might do so. In response to the inquiry, the Japanese foreign office informed Saburo on February 16, 1871, that it would grant such permission in compliance with the demand of the Hawaiian government and also because the matter had a bearing on the progress of the pending negotiations for a treaty between Hawaii and Japan.[70]

When their contracts expired in June, eleven of the immigrants chose to return to Japan, and were shipped back on the *Vesta* at the expense of the Hawaiian government.[71] This left ninety of the *Scioto* immigrants either to remain in Hawaii or to go to the United States, that number being accounted for as follows:

Number departing on the *Scioto*		150
Died at sea and in Hawaii	7	
Returned to Japan, per Ueno-Harris agreement	42	
Returned to Japan on contract expiration	11	60
Number remaining		90

Saburo was one of those who chose to go to the United States. He left Honolulu on October 24.[72] Harris provided his passage to San Francisco, and also agreed to instruct Severance to pay his passage from San Francisco to Yokohama, should he decide to return to Japan. In addition, he was given a gratuity of $150.[73] There is no evidence that he ever returned to Japan. Sometime before his departure from Hawaii, he wrote to the Hawaiian foreign office:[74]

Often we had been to complain to you by some trifling matters. But I have all known always you was so troublesome indeed. We have very sorry to you. Please pardon to us for them.

Reading this letter, written three years after Saburo's arrival in Hawaii, and considering that Saburo provided the only line of communication between the immigrants and their employers, the wonder is not that there were so many misunderstandings between them but that the misunderstandings were not greater.

The treaty between Hawaii and Japan, discussed by Harris and Ueno, was finally concluded on August 19, 1871, with Charles E. De Long, who had succeeded Van Valkenburgh as the American minister to Japan, acting as the Hawaiian plenipotentiary. But before that, on February 21, 1871, Van Reed resigned as the Hawaiian consular representative in Japan. The Japanese officials adamantly refused to negotiate so long as he had any official connection with the Hawaiian government. Harris accepted Van Reed's resignation on April 25 with regret that it should be necessary. Yet, Van Reed had been prepared to resign at any time. As early as October 31, 1869, he wrote to Phillips, "if it be found necessary to sacrifice anyone, in order to make the treaty with and for His Majesty rather than lose it, let me be the one to prove my sincerity for the welfare of the country."

On December 1, after the treaty had been in effect for three months, De Long inquired of Terashima, who was then vice foreign minister, whether he would accept Van Reed as the Hawaiian consul general. Terashima stated that he would, if Van Reed's powers should be strictly limited to the discharge of consular duties and not extend to diplomatic matters. De Long then gave Van Reed a temporary appointment as consul general.[75] Van Reed commented on Terashima's action in his letter of December 22 to Harris, as follows:

> I have to thank you for your continued good wishes and attention to my welfare. Surely you can appreciate my happiness in feeling that that Treaty was actually an accomplished fact! To think that such ill luck should have followed the defeat of the Tycoon, and that a Japanese (Terashima) who should have been my best friend should have risen to the rank of Minister for Foreign Affairs only to be the very man of all others to be my persistent enemy and be the cause of severing the good feelings which should exist between two nations, is indeed hard to believe; - but such ill will was duly taken advantage of by learning that it was my person alone which stood in the way of making two nations friends, and on my resignation and request of the American Minister to conclude the Treaty the ill will of Terashima culminated in concluding a Treaty within one week, where other ministers have taken as many months to accomplish; and now the consistency of Terashima is shown by his recognition of my appointment as acting Consul General awaiting your further pleasure. It merely goes to prove that the ill will and spleen of an enemy once a friend is of the most intense kind, and withal the most foolish.

The Hawaiian government regularized De Long's temporary appointment of Van Reed as acting consul general by issuing a commission as consul general to him on September 10, 1872. By then, Van Reed had contracted pulmonary tuberculosis. He died on February 3, 1873 while on his way back to San Francisco at the still young age of 38 years.[76]

The death of Van Reed may be the proper place to bring this account to an end. But, the story is not complete without an evaluation of Van Reed's role in the affair, and a consideration of the meaning of the *Gan-nen-mono* in the subsequent history of Hawaii. Though officials of Japan's new Meiji government regarded Van Reed as a villain of sorts, in his behalf one might ask a few rhetorical questions. Who else would have risked more than $4,000 of his own money in a venture from which he stood to make not a cent of profit for himself, without a definite commitment for reimbursement? Who else would have defied the government of a nation many times larger than Hawaii just to send 150 untried laborers to a land where their acceptance was still in question? Would there have been the *Gan-nen-mono,* except for Van Reed? And, without the *Gan-nen-mono,* would the subsequent history of Hawaii have been the same?

As for the *Gan-nen-mono* themselves, after the malcontents were repatriated to Japan, many of the remaining male members married Hawaiian women, and melted and merged into the stream of native life, as Van Reed and Varigny confidently predicted. Because of the problems raised by the venture, immigration from Japan was not resumed until 1885, but once resumed, it brought more than 65,000 Japanese to Hawaii by the end of 1899. The floodgate was not opened by Japan, but by the persistent prodding of Hawaiian officials, who, through their experience with the *Scioto* immigrants, held firmly to the view that the Japanese were desirable not only as laborers but as a repopulating element. This view was most clearly expressed by John M. Kapena, whom King Kalakaua appointed on September 23, 1882 as envoy extraordinary and minister plenipotentiary to Japan in Hawaii's continuing quest for immigrants from Japan. At a dinner he gave in Tokyo, soon after his arrival in Japan, honoring three imperial princes and the nation's department heads, Kapena stated:

> His Majesty [Kalakaua] believes that the Japanese and Hawaiians spring from one cognate race and this enhances his love for you. He hopes that our people will more and more be brought closer together in common brotherhood. Hawaii holds out her loving hand and heart to Japan and desires that Your People may come and cast in their lots with ours and repeople our Island Home.

Kapena's statement also expressed the view of Walter Murray Gibson, then the premier and foreign minister of Hawaii, who had taken the contracts of four of the *Scioto* immigrants to work on his sugar plantation on Lanai. In a letter of instruction to Kapena, Gibson wrote:

> You will urge upon the consideration of the Imperial Government, the recognition of His Majesty as one of the family of Asiatic Princes, and that to strengthen his hands is to elevate the sovereign of a cognate and friendly race. This can be most effectually done by the migration of Japanese people to the Hawaii Islands.

The Aloha Week celebration held on October 20-26, 1968 in Honolulu provided a dramatic sequel to the merging of *Gan-nen-mono* into the Hawaiian society. The festival king was James Kaanapu, a swarthy, handsome young man, as Hawaiian-looking as any person can be, a natural to play the monarch in a Hawaiian festival. Neither the media nor the celebrants noticed that he was the great-grandson of Sakuma, the immigrant who kept the diary of the *Scioto* voyage.

A final word about the only *Gan-nen-mono* woman who remained in Hawaii. Her name was Tomi, wife of Kintaro Ozawa. She gave birth to three children, Yotaro, Itoko, and Arthur Kenzaburo. Yotaro spent his adult years as a member of the Hilo police force, undoubtedly the first policeman of Japanese ancestry in Hawaii. Itoko is reputed to have spoken English as well as any Caucasian. At the age of twelve, she acted as interpreter at a hearing held by Robert W. Irwin,[77] Hawaiian minister to Japan, in connection with the proposed immigration convention between Hawaii and Japan. Irwin was so impressed by Itoko that he took her to Japan and gave her a good Japanese education. Itoko married Kenji Imanishi, manager of the Honolulu branch of The Yokohama Specie Bank. Imanishi later became the manager of the New York branch (and a prominent leader of the local Japanese community). In that position he gave such yeoman service in selling Japanese bonds during the Russo-Japanese war that he was decorated by Emperor Mutsuhito. A large measure of his success has been attributed to the English-speaking ability and social grace of his wife. Arthur graduated from Michigan Law School and was admitted to the Michigan bar and the Hawaiian bar in 1910. He died on June 21, 1917, at the age of forty years. By that time he had established such a solid position and gained such respect in the community that his funeral was attended by Governor Lucius Pinkham, General Frederick Strong, commanding general of the United States army in Hawaii, Japanese Consul General Rokuro Moroi, Chinese Consul General Wu Fan, Food Commissioner James Dole and other notables. The Bar Association of Hawaii in its memorial spoke of "his loyalty to his professional obligations, his patriotic American citizenship derived through his birth in Hawaii, and his high standards of integrity in his professional and everyday life," which endeared him to all who knew him.

NOTES

1. This article is based principally on letters and other documents preserved in the Archives of Hawaii. Additional materials necessary to fill the gaps and for achieving continuity of the narrative have been obtained from duly cited sources. Archives materials are not noted, except where they are mentioned without dates.

2. Y. Baron Goto, *Children of Gan-nen-mono: The First Year Men* (1968); Kenpu Kawazoe, *Imin Hyakunen no Nenrin* (1968), p. 3.

3. Soen Yamashita, *Gan-nen-mono no Omokage* (1968), p. 73; list of Japanese on *Scioto* and disposition of same, made out by Tomisaburo in 1871. This list contains 151 names, including Wakichi, who died at sea, and Harukichi, who was born in Hawaii. The Yamashita publication will hereafter be referred to as "Yamashita 1968."

4. Katherine Coman, *The History of Contract Labor in the Hawaiian Islands* (1903), p. 12; Ralph S. Kuykendall, *The Hawaiian Kingdom 1778–1854* (Honolulu: University of Hawaii Press, 1938), p. 329.

5. Speeches of His Majesty Kamehameha IV, p. 15, quoted in Kuykendall, *The Hawaiian Kingdom 1854–1874* (Honolulu: University of Hawaii Press, 1953), p. 76. This Kuykendall volume will hereafter be referred to as "Kuykendall 1854–1874."

6. Coman, p. 17.

7. Kuykendall 1854–1874, p. 180; Wyllie to Heco, March 15, 1865; Wyllie to Van Reed, March 20, 1865.

8. Hideo Matsunaga, "Van Reed's Life," part 1, *Hawaii Times,* June 11, 1968.

9. Hideo Matsunaga, part 2, *Hawaii Times,* June 12, 1968.

10. J. Van Reed to Wyllie, January 26, 1865.

11. Kuykendall, *The Earliest Japanese Labor Immigration to Hawaii* (1935), p. 4. This publication will hereafter be referred to as "Kuykendall, Japanese Immigration."

12. Van Reed to Varigny, April 4, 1867.

13. Van Reed to Varigny, July 3, 1866.

14. Van Reed to Varigny, September 10, 1866.

15. Van Reed to Varigny, November 13, 1866.

16. Van Reed to Varigny, January 27, 1867.

17. Van Reed to Varigny, February 26, 1867.

18. Varigny to Van Reed, January 7, 1867.

19. Varigny to Van Reed, April 5, 1867.

20. Van Reed to Varigny, May 25, 1867.

21. Van Reed to Van Valkenburgh, June 17, 1867.

22. Varigny to Van Reed, July 29, 1867.

23. Kuykendall 1854–1874, p. 209.

24. McCook to Van Valkenburgh, August 3, 1867, quoted in Hilary Conroy, *The Japanese Frontier in Hawaii 1868–1898* (Berkeley: University of California Press, 1953), p. 18.

25. Varigny to Van Reed, December 7, 1867.

26. Van Reed to Varigny, March 7, 1868.

27. Van Reed to Varigny, May (blank) 1868.

28. Soen Yamashita, *Gan-nen-mono Imin Hawaii Toko 88 Shunen* (1956), p. 15. This volume will hereafter be referred to as "Yamashita 1956."

29. Van Reed to Varigny, April 27, 1868.

30. Yamashita 1968, p. 19.

31. Van Reed to Varigny, June 1, 1868.

32. Lee to Board of Immigration, June 19, 1868; Van Reed to Van Valkenburgh, April 20, 1869.

33. Van Reed to Varigny, May (blank) 1868.
34. Kawazoe, p. 75; Matsunaga, part 3, *Hawaii Times,* June 22, 1968.
35. Van Reed to Varigny, April 10, 1868.
36. Van Reed to Van Valkenburgh, April 20, 1869.
37. Yamashita 1968, p. 29.
38. Yamashita 1968, p. 64.
39. Lee to Board of Immigration, June 19, 1868.
40. Yamashita 1956, p. 74.
41. Van Reed to Varigny, June 1, 1868.
42. Van Valkenburgh to "Their Excellencies," April 26, 1869, quoted in Conroy, p. 33.
43. Fletcher to Parkes, June 12, 1868, quoted in Kuykendall, Japanese Immigration, p. 12.
44. Yamashita 1968, p. 34.
45. Van Reed to Varigny, May 17, 1868.
46. Yamashita 1968, p. 37.
47. McInerny to Hutchison, August 3, 1868.
48. Davies to Hutchison, August 4, 1868.
49. Minutes of Board of Immigration, August 6, 1868.
50. Wilder to Hutchison, August 6, 1868.
51. Kuykendall, Japanese Immigration, p. 18.
52. Yamashita 1956, p. 82.
53. Phillips to Van Reed, December 26, 1868.
54. Yamashita 1968, p. 44. There is some question regarding the identity of Sentaro, who signed this appeal. There was a Sentaro among the *Scioto* immigrants and another Sentaro who came to Hawaii two years earlier on a whaling ship. Neither of them appears to be the Sentaro in question. It is probable that the signer of the appeal was the Sentaro who was shipwrecked in 1851 with Heco, later joined Commodore Perry's fleet, where he was befriended by a sailor named Goble, taken by Goble to Hamilton, New York, where he received an English education, known in New York as Samuel Sinthan and in Hawaii as Samuel Sentharo, and greeted the *Scioto* immigrants when they arrived in Honolulu.
55. Yamashita 1956, p. 82.
56. Van Reed to Phillips, March 13, 1869.
57. Van Valkenburgh to "Their Excellencies," April 26, 1869, quoted in Conroy, p. 33.
58. Yamashita 1968, p. 45, 61.
59. Kuykendall, Japanese Immigration, p. 20.
60. Conroy, p. 35.
61. Kuykendall, Japanese Immigration, p. 21.
62. Kuykendall, Japanese Immigration, p. 21.
63. Harris to Ueno, January 5, 1870.
64. Kuykendall, Japanese Immigration, p. 23.
65. Kuykendall, Japanese Immigration, p. 23.
66. Conroy, p. 40.

67. Yamashita 1968, p. 50.

68. Conroy, p. 41; P. C. *Advertiser,* July 9, 1870.

69. Yamashita 1968, p. 52.

70. Yamashita 1968, p. 52.

71. Twelve went on the *Vesta,* but one was Harukichi, a child born in Hawaii.

72. Yamashita 1968, p. 67.

73. Harris to Peirce, October 21, 1871.

74. Saburo to Hawaiian Foreign Office, May 23, 1871.

75. Kuykendall, Japanese Immigration, p. 26; Conroy, p. 46.

76. Matsunaga, part 6, *Hawaii Times,* June 27, 1968.

77. See the following essay on Irwin.

Robert Walker Irwin &
Systematic Immigration to Hawaii

YUKIKO IRWIN

HILARY CONROY

The tale so well told by Oscar Handlin of the "uprooted,"[1] the thousands of European immigrants who reached the eastern shore of the United States in the late nineteenth century, is singularly different from that of the Japanese immigration to Hawaii in one aspect at least. There was no "tsar" of the European migration, no overseer with a master plan in his head, indeed hardly any organization at all. It was broad, diffuse, and largely spontaneous, as individuals and families driven by destitution in Europe and responding to rumors of opportunity in America made their way to continental European and English ports and somehow negotiated passage for America. Once there they were welcome in a general sense but often without organized assistance of any sort.

It was not so in Hawaii. Though the system broke down later, the first decade of the Japanese immigration to Hawaii, during which 28,691 Japanese men, women and children were transported to "paradise," was organized, regulated, and inspected to a remarkable degree. And it had a man in charge, Robert Walker Irwin, Hawaiian consul general and special agent for immigration in Japan from 1885 to 1894. He was such a key figure that the system of immigration which operated in those years might appropriately be called the "Irwin System." It is quite clear from the voluminous immigration records housed in the Archives of Hawaii that Irwin was in charge of the immigration system, not only overseeing the actual shipment of the immigrants, but also conducting high-level and delicate negotiations with both Hawaiian and Japanese government officials to make sure everything went smoothly at both ends of the immigration line.

This was no easy task, given the difficult human elements in the immigration equation. These included planters in Hawaii, whose preoccupation was cheap, dependable, machine-like labor; touchy Hawaiian government officials who wanted a diseaseless, apolitical, well-behaving, hard-working population increment; even touchier Japanese officials, concerned above all with national dignity, willing to have an outlet for Japan's economically depressed agricultural population but only if it would not sully the national image; and the immigrants themselves, who though willing to work and seeking a better life, were by no means so machine-like that they did not have difficult problems of adjustment.

In today's world such a project would engage the talents of highly trained sociologists and professional diplomats, but the nineteenth century was an era of amateurs. Robert Irwin was an amateur, yet he managed to blend his talents and opportunities to produce what must rank as one of the best organized mass migrations in history.

Who was Robert Irwin, what were his talents and opportunities, and what was his "magic formula" for Japanese immigration?

Robert Walker Irwin was born in Copenhagen, Denmark in 1844, the son of William Wallace Irwin, former mayor of Pittsburgh, Pennsylvania and member of the United States House of Representatives, who on the expiration of his term there was appointed *chargé d'affaires* at Copenhagen by President Tyler. His mother, Sophia Arabella Bache of Philadelphia, was a fourth direct descendant of Benjamin Franklin.

Other children of this marriage were Richard Biddle Irwin (later colonel), elder brother of Robert, and three daughters, Agnes, Sophy, and Mary. Agnes and Sophy, neither of whom married, were the founders of the Agnes Irwin School for Girls in Philadelphia, which Sophy directed after Agnes left Philadelphia to become the first dean of Radcliffe College in 1894. Mary, the third daughter, married Dennis McCarthy of New York, later to be lieutenant governor of New York and "a devout Roman Catholic." The father's marriage to Sophia Arabella Bache was his second. The first, to Frances E. Smith, had also produced a son, John Irwin (later admiral), whose assignment to Hawaiian waters in 1893 was to provide a latter-day link with his half-brother, Robert.

His family had a strong influence on Irwin. His father was a prominent lawyer and Democratic politician, and, according to his obituary, an "accomplished scholar." He died in 1856 when Robert was twelve years old. His mother, who was a member of Holy Trinity Protestant Episcopal Church of Philadelphia, wore her Franklin heritage proudly and was actively interested in many charitable organizations. She died in 1904.[2]

His educator sisters, though neither was a college graduate, were cultured and stylish women considered somewhat liberal by Philadelphians because of their devotion to women's education and their actively intellectual social life. At their school Agnes was known as Miss Irwin and Sophy as Miss Sophy, revealing their difference in manner. Agnes was considered critical, ironic and somewhat coldly intellectual, while Sophy was warm, effusive, and inclined to be emotional, though both were said to be full of wit and humor at their frequent teas and social hours. As dean at Radcliffe, Agnes was too aristocratic and demanding to be popular with the majority of the students, but conservative enough to please a "reluctant Harvard extending a chill hospitality to Radcliffe."[3]

Robert kept in touch with his mother and sisters even when he was far away in Japan or Hawaii. He sent them various oriental treasures, which sometimes mystified them. Once, for example, he sent them a special kind of tea, very rare and delicious "which the Japanese Emperor favored for his own use," and the ladies arranged a tea party to celebrate its arrival. Miss Sophy brewed it with great care, but it turned out to be extremely unsavory. After watching the guests' polite but unsuccessful efforts to drink it, Agnes Irwin put down her cup and announced, "The company is excused from drinking its tea." Later the maid discovered that a small ornate box, inside the larger one, contained the "emperor's tea." Miss Sophy had inadvertently brewed the packing material.[4]

Elder brother Richard provided Robert Irwin with his first opportunity to go to Japan. After the Civil War, from which he emerged as a colonel in the Union Army, Richard accepted a position with the Pacific Mail Steamship Company, with which he remained as its San Francisco agent until 1872. After that he conducted his own business in San Francisco until 1878. Meanwhile Robert had been sent to Japan in November 1866, as the Pacific Mail steamship agent in Yokohama. His first duties were apparently in connection with preparations for receiving and handling the regular trans-Pacific steamer service of the company, inaugurated with the steamer *Colorado* in 1867.[5]

The other activities Robert undertook in Japan during the next few years are not clear, but by 1872 he was active in the Yokohama firm of Walsh, Hall and Company, called *Ameichi* in Japanese. There he became acquainted with Masuda Takashi (later baron), who had been working for the firm as an interpreter and had left to become an official of the Ministry of Finance. Another Japanese acquaintance was Okada Heizo. Either Masuda or Okada or both of these men introduced Irwin to Finance Minister Inoue Kaoru, who became Irwin's highly placed friend in the Meiji government over the succeeding years. Inoue at the time was concerned over the new government's precarious financial condition, particularly its need for foreign exchange.

With Irwin's advice and assistance Inoue, Masuda and Okada decided to organize a company to promote exports, especially the export of rice to London. As a result in 1873 they established Senshu Kaisha, a trading company, with Inoue as president, Masuda vice-president and Masuda and Okada in charge of its Tokyo and Osaka offices respectively. Irwin arranged for Walsh, Hall and Company to develop its connections abroad on very favorable terms. In 1874 Irwin and Walsh had a falling out and Irwin left Walsh, Hall and Company to enter a partnership with Edward Fisher, taking the Senshu Kaisha business with him. In December 1874, Inoue was appointed special envoy to Korea and resigned as president of Senshu Kaisha.

The firm was then reorganized twice, to emerge in July 1876 as Mitsui Bussan Kaisha (Mitsui Trading Company). Masuda became its president on Inoue's recommendation. Irwin remained the key figure in its overseas trading activities, with rice, silk, and tea as the principal exports of the company and ammunition, wool, fertilizer, and used copper the principal imports. The business activities of this company helped resolve the problem of foreign exchange in Japan, and as purchasing agent for the army, it secured 100,000 Snyder guns which the government forces used to put down the Satsuma rebellion of 1877.

In 1876, Inoue Kaoru (now marquis) traveled to America and Europe to study financial markets, tax and currency systems, and trade. He left Yokohama for San Francisco on June 25, 1876, accompanied by his wife, his daughter Sueko, and some 20 Japanese assistants and students aboard the Pacific Mail Steamship *Alaska* under the tour leadership of Robert Irwin. Irwin stayed with the Inoues at the Palace Hotel in San Francisco, led them to Nevada to meet Charles DeLong, former U.S. Minister at Tokyo, and on to Chicago, Niagara Falls, and Philadelphia, where a World's Fair was in progress. On September 2, after two weeks in Philadelphia and a week in Washington, Inoue and his immediate party sailed from New York for London, and Irwin again accompanied them. In London they established residence in the house of an acquaintance of Irwin's and planned to remain there for two years. At that point Irwin seems to have left them and returned to Japan, although it is possible that before leaving he accompanied the marquis on a tour of the continent.[6]

In any event he soon returned to London. According to a memorandum he wrote, "I left Yokohama on April 23, 1877 and arrived in London in June the same year," to open a London branch of Mitsui Bussan Kaisha. This, his memorandum states, "is a successor of Senshu Kaisha." He added that he opened the agency "under my own name, for the reason that the name of Mitsui was virtually unknown there."[7]

Business developed so briskly that his elder brother Richard was invited to London, and "in August 1878, after closing his business in San Francisco, Colonel (Richard) Irwin went to London to manage the business of his brother, Robert W. Irwin, in rice, etc. on account of the Japanese government, from Japan to Europe."[8]

Meanwhile, Inoue was called back to Japan to become minister of industry on July 29, 1878. Irwin waited in London until a Japanese representative of Mitsui Bussan Company, Sasase Motoaki, who was selected on his recommendation, arrived to assist his brother in the management of the London office. Then he too returned to Japan, where upon his arrival in November 1879, he regained his old title as "counselor" (of the Mitsui Company) with privileges and power equal to those of the president, Takashi Masuda.[9]

Most importantly, Robert Irwin had become a firm and trusted friend of Inoue Kaoru.

About 1880 Inoue decided that his good friend should have a Japanese wife, and he initiated a search for a proper young lady, which culminated in Irwin's marriage to Takechi Iki, whose ancestry included both samurai and merchants. This was the first American-Japanese marriage to be based on thorough legal arrangements between the United States and Japan, and it took more than a year before the final papers were signed, on March 15, 1882. The first child of Robert and Iki Irwin, born on November 24, 1882, was a daughter, named Sophia Arabella Irwin for her American grandmother. The Irwins had six children; all were educated in the United States as well as Japan. Two of the four girls did not marry; one, a Bryn Mawr graduate, married a Harvard professor; and one, a Vassar graduate, married a Japanese businessman. The sons attended Princeton and married Japanese girls.

In addition to their own children, Robert and Iki raised two others, a niece, Iki, and a boy named Hayashi Tadamichi, who was legally adopted by the Takechi family on the understanding that he would marry the niece and become the family head, since there was no male heir. The adoption was made in 1882, when Iki, who had acted as family head after her stepfather's death, officially "left" the family by marrying Irwin. The boy, aged 12 at the time, was the son of a wealthy overseer for Echigoya (Mitsui) business interest and proved to be a very able young man. He was schooled at Keio and Punahou (Honolulu) and eventually became Robert Irwin's secretary, general assistant and manager in various Irwin enterprises, including the Hawaiian immigration. At the age of twenty, he was chief immigration officer at the Hawaiian legation in Tokyo. When he married the Takechi niece in 1893 the official go-between was the stepson of Inoue Kaoru.[10]

These then were Irwin's Japanese connections.

His first opportunity to enter into Hawaiian affairs came in 1880, when the Hawaiian consul general to Japan, Harlan P. Lillibridge, took a leave of absence to return to the United States. He recommended that Robert Irwin be appointed to fill in for him in his absence, and noted in his letter of recommendation that his nominee had close business and social connections with Inoue Kaoru, now Japan's foreign minister.[11] Thus Irwin became acting consul general for Hawaii in Japan. The following year King Kalakaua of Hawaii and an entourage of high officials from Honolulu visited Japan. They were favorably impressed by Irwin, and upon learning that Lillibridge would not return to his post, they appointed Irwin consul general and gave him diplomatic functions as *chargé d'affaires* as well.[12] The idea of making a major effort for Japanese immigration was formulating in their minds.

As mentioned in the previous essay, American planters in Hawaii needed a stable and dependable source of laborers for their enlarging sugar plantations. At the same time, the king and his political friend and advisor, Walter Murray Gibson, also saw the Japanese as a potential source of support for the Hawaiian throne against increasing American inroads.[13] These diverse elements were thus agreed, temporarily at least, that Japanese immigrants were both needed and desirable. The one dark cloud on the project was the circumstances surrounding the previous immigration attempt in 1868, the "First Year" discussed in the previous essay. The Hawaiian government wanted to avoid a repetition of the incidents which had occurred at that time.

The Hawaiian officials, however, perceived that the chief problem in the previous immigration attempt was their agent Van Reed. Judge Marumoto's essay shows that Van Reed may not have deserved the condemnation heaped upon him. Certainly he was loyal to the Hawaiian interests he represented, and he was in many ways the victim of peculiarly unfortunate circumstances. But the Japanese government regarded his pragmatic behavior in those circumstances as extremely devious and unprincipled, and his connections and credentials in Japan were not sufficient to overcome their mistrust.[14]

Robert Irwin was different. Unlike Van Reed he was far from "devious," he was meticulous, and his connections and credentials were the best to be found among foreigners in Japan. He was the man Hawaii needed and her leaders knew it.

As negotiations for a new Japanese immigration to Hawaii developed, Irwin played a large role. He assisted Colonel Curtis P. Iaukea, a Hawaiian envoy who came directly from Honolulu, in preliminary conversations with Japanese Foreign Minister Inoue, in which it developed that the Japanese government was not willing to make a formal immigration convention as yet, but was "not inclined to impose any obstacle" to a properly arranged resumption of immigration. Irwin accompanied Iaukea back to Hawaii, where he explained Japanese needs, problems and feelings on the matter to Hawaiian officials and then returned to Tokyo armed with additional appointments as commissioner of immigration and special agent of the (Hawaiian) Board of Immigration to organize the first shipment of immigrants. Foreign Minister Inoue assured Hawaii that "the nomination of a man of such ability and so well acquainted with the affairs of Japan as Mr. Irwin cannot but be satisfactory to His Imperial Majesty's Government."[15]

The Hawaiian legislature voted $50,000 for Japanese immigration and the project began.[16]

Since one of the co-authors has written elsewhere about the development of the immigration program and its social, political and international consequences in Hawaii,[17] this essay will emphasize Irwin's role.

The selection of emigrants in Japan is not explained in earlier studies, or by documents on the immigration in the Archives of Hawaii. It is clear from Hawaiian records that most of the immigrants came from Yamaguchi and Hiroshima prefectures, but there is no explanation why this was so, except for Irwin's rather stereotyped assurances to the planters that the immigrants were "from the agricultural districts" of Japan. However, from the Mitsui Bussan Company newspaper we learn that Inoue Kaoru, a native of that prefecture, selected Yamaguchi as a preferred place for obtaining immigrants. The governor there, Hara Yasutaro, approached the Mitsui Bussan Company, which was helping Irwin recruit, with an offer to supply immigrants. Of the first shipment 420 persons, nearly half the total number, were from Yamaguchi, especially from its Oshima district, which in addition to a drought of 1883 and a storm and flood in 1884 was suffering from over-population.

Regarding Hiroshima, Irwin received the following advice from Masuda Takashi, the Mitsui company president:

You can judge the character of people of various prefectures by analysing the philosophy of the outstanding scholar of that prefecture. The outstanding scholar of Hiroshima prefecture was a sensible man and his philosophy was sound and pacifistic, with nothing radical or revolutionary in it. Therefore I think that people of Hiroshima prefecture must be sound and law abiding.[18]

Masuda also approved of Yamaguchi prefecture as a source of immigrants because its people "are not timid or afraid to go to far away places . . . even to foreign countries." And he adds the following:

Irwin followed my advice and it proved successful. However, during my absence from Japan on my tour of Europe, Onaka, manager of the immigration office, recommended that he send immigrants from Higo [Miyazaki-Kumamoto area]. I heard of this from Irwin after my return. I told Irwin that people from Higo Kumamoto work very hard, but they are quick tempered and unless they are handled with care, they may make some trouble. My prediction unfortunately proved correct later. Immigrants from Higo set fire to a sugar plantation and this became a big issue between the Japanese and Hawaiian governments.[19]

It is clear that the Mitsui Bussan Company was intimately involved with the recruiting of immigrants. According to the company history,

Irwin asked our company to help him with the task of handling the immigration business. Because of his involvement with our company we agreed wholeheartedly and decided to give our fullest cooperation. We dispatched our employees to Yamaguchi, Hiroshima, Fukushima and Kumamoto prefectures and handled their recruitment, transportation, etc. Later we handled the shipment of rice, medicine and other daily necessities to the immigrants in Hawaii. However, such business could hardly be called profitable. Later we were asked to handle transfer of the immigrants' money from Hawaii to Japan. Some of them wanted to deposit their savings with us, so we made an arrangement with the Ministry of Foreign Affairs. This arrangement continued until the Sino-Japanese War.[20]

The Mitsui Bussan Company also provided Irwin with a publicity medium for the Hawaiian immigration, the newspaper *Chugai Bukka Shimpo,* a creation of the Shimpokata (or Shimpoho), the overseas news section of the company, organized in 1876. In 1882 the Shimpokata became an independent company, moved its office out of the Mitsui Bussan headquarters at No. 5 Kabutocho into No. 3 Kabutocho and changed its name to Shokyosha. This agency carried immigration recruitment advertising in its newspaper, and during 1884 "carried on all necessary business concerning the immigration" organized at that time.[21]

Irwin's careful supervision of the start of the immigration is evidenced by the fact that, with his wife and first daughter Bella (Sophia Arabella), he personally accompanied the first shipload of immigrants, which reached Honolulu on February 8, 1885 aboard the Pacific Mail steamer *City of Tokyo.* There was an unanticipated charge of fifty cents per immigrant for "passport handling" and he paid the entire bill himself (over $450). Irwin was determined to maintain a Japanese inspection staff of doctors and interpreters in Hawaii to help the immigrants and prevent friction with plantation managers. The responsibility for paying the inspection staff was at first a moot point, but Irwin brought Nakayama Joji (George Nacayama) along on the *City of Tokyo* as "inspector of immigrants" and got the Hawaiian government to take him on its payroll at $100 per month.

There was no such "inspector" in the abortive 1868 immigration unless we regard Tomisaburo as such. It will be recalled that Tomisaburo was the "headman" of the immigrants. Because of his limited prestige and command of English he was less helpful in settling disputes than he might have been.

Irwin not only brought Nakayama, he served notice that others were needed. The Hawaiian authorities were apparently noncommittal, for the matter was unsettled until the third shipment when Irwin brought along nine or ten more inspectors and seven doctors to add to Nakayama's staff. He employed them in the name of the Hawaiian Bureau of Immigration and advanced $5,000 out of his own pocket for their passage and salaries. The Hawaiian government then reprimanded Irwin for exceeding his instructions.[22]

The inspectors and doctors remained in Hawaii, and the question of who would pay their salaries was unanswered. Irwin paid them himself for the next few months, all the while insisting that it was the responsibility of the Hawaiian government or the planters to do so.

Meanwhile his good friend Foreign Minister Inoue came to the rescue. The foreign minister at first demurred at the idea of a formal convention. After sending his adopted son Katsunosuke with the second shipment of immigrants and receiving a report from him as well as from Irwin, he decided that disputes and misunderstandings were more likely to be avoided if the basic immigration arrangements were formalized in an Immigration Convention between Japan and Hawaii. He instructed the newly appointed Japanese consul in Hawaii, Nakamura Jiro, to ask Hawaiian Foreign Minister Gibson to give Irwin power to negotiate such a convention with the Japanese government.[23]

Despite misgivings about the inspection staff, the Hawaiian government and the planters were so pleased with the Japanese labor force they were acquiring that the necessary powers were forwarded to Irwin, who proceeded to negotiate a convention of eleven articles, which he and Foreign Minister Inoue signed at Tokyo on January 28, 1886, for their respective governments. Articles 6 and 7 specifically made the Hawaiian government responsible for employing "a sufficient number" of inspectors and doctors to serve the immigrants.[24]

Despite this the government of Hawaii made no move to pay the salaries, and Irwin was still paying them in April 1886. He then wrote to the Hawaiian Board of Immigration urging that an appropriation be sought from the Hawaiian legislature to take care of the problem.[25] The legislation was not passed and later in the year Irwin was told that the cost of importing Japanese immigrants was too high. Reluctantly, he agreed to try to obtain modifications in the arrangements so as to shift some of the cost to the immigrants themselves.[26]

The negotiations which followed were lengthy and difficult. Irwin's problems were complicated when his friend Inoue resigned as foreign minister in September 1887 to become a counselor of the imperial household, and Gibson was replaced as Hawaiian foreign minister by Godfrey Brown, who was less friendly than Gibson had been.

Irwin obtained preliminary agreements from Inoue to revise article 6 of the Convention so as to limit Hawaii's responsibility to the payment of *one* inspector and interpreter and to eliminate article 7 (responsibility for paying doctors).[27] When Premier Ito assumed the foreign minister's portfolio after Inoue's departure, Irwin urged him to accept the new arrangement on the grounds that the price of sugar had dropped, causing financial difficulties in Hawaii. Meanwhile, certain other financial rearrangements made Ito willing to accept the modifications proposed. These involved the transfer from the Hawaiian to the Japanese government of custody of a 25 percent reserve fund withheld from the immigrants' wages for payment upon completion of their contracts and/or return to Japan, and the reconstitution of a so-called Nippu Shokai (Japan-Hawaii Trading Company) which had been handling the immigrants' remissions of money to their families in Japan.[28]

According to a brief history of these matters compiled by the Japanese foreign office in 1900, the Nippu Shokai trading company should have been suspect *(ayashimubeki)* from the beginning. Through it Irwin controlled the immigrants' deposits, which he used as collateral for loans from the Mitsui company, according to the report. As a result of the rearrangements made in 1887 the sum of $120,458.59, representing the savings of 2,200 workers, was turned over to the Japanese government in 1888.

The details of these financial transactions are far from clear, but it seems possible that Irwin used this money (or loans secured by the Mitsui Bussan) to pay the costs of the inspection bureau during its first three years, which the government of Hawaii refused to pay. Certainly the latter-day Foreign Office report took a jaundiced view of Irwin's financial juggling.[29] However, it should be added that Shoji Seya, who recorded the matter in 1893, said, "Rich as Irwin was he could not forever pay the expenses of more than 10 people every month, so from the fourth shipment they started collecting $70 or $80 for the payment of their salaries under an item called 'protection of immigrants' . . . The whole thing was a result of breach of contract by the Hawaiian government, and Irwin was the only one who honorably followed the contract."[30]

At any rate, in late September 1887 Ito authorized the Japanese consul in Honolulu to inform the Hawaiian government that subsequent expenses for the inspection staff were to be deducted from the wages of the new immigrants and that a "voluntary contribution" was to be taken from previous immigrants to that end.[31] At the same time he informed the Hawaiian premier and minister of finance, William Green, that the Japanese government would henceforth receive the deposits of the immigrants, a course "actuated not by any unfriendly feeling toward the Hawaiian government, or by any feeling of uneasiness as to the security of the funds, but solely by a strong solicitude to enable the parties interested to realize a greater amount of profit than they do at present availing of the present opportunity."[32]

The inspector-doctor issue was scarcely settled when Irwin had to contend with a political controversy which threatened to upset the immigration. Gibson's ouster from the Hawaiian government in July 1887 presaged a general reorganization in which the propertied Caucasian elements of the population limited the power of the Hawaiian monarchy and enhanced their own. King Kalakaua was forced to accept a new constitution giving Caucasian *residents* of the Islands voting rights which gave them effective control of the legislature; prior to the new constitution only those who had chosen to become *subjects* of the Hawaiian king had voting rights. Orientals, unmentioned in the new constitution, were therefore excluded from the franchise. Consul General Ando Taro speedily pointed out the unequal treatment of Japanese inherent in this arrangement.[33] A long dispute developed as to whether this was being done intentionally or unintentionally and whether the discrimination would remain.

By July of 1888 Ando was irritated and disgusted enough to recommend a halt in the immigration until Hawaii had changed the offensive clauses. Irwin, however, counseled patience, and the Japanese foreign minister, now Okuma Shigenobu, decided that stopping the immigration was not the best diplomatic course.[34] Despite the tensions engendered by the dispute the immigration continued and accelerated, with Irwin watching the details assiduously.

He maintained an elaborate system of health precautions to prevent diseased or even scrawny looking individuals being sent from Japan, and he anticipated the sort of complaints and outside interference which might disrupt his system. Such interference seemed in the offing in 1890 when the convention came up for renewal and the Hawaiian government sent Paul Neumann as its special agent to Tokyo to negotiate better terms. By the time Neumann arrived Irwin had arranged a compromise which left Neumann with no recourse but to express admiration for the skill with which Irwin operated.[35]

Between 1891 and 1893 Irwin was caught several times in a crossfire between Hawaiian planters and the Japanese government. The planters insisted on reducing labor costs because of the dire effects of the McKinley tariff on Hawaiian sugar. The Japanese government insisted that the terms of the Convention as amended be honored. Irwin shaved the immigrants' wages a bit at one end and his own remuneration at the other and so managed to keep the immigrants coming, the inspection-medical staff operating, and the system generally intact. He even managed to increase the percentage of women emigres.[36]

It took the Hawaiian revolution of 1893 to undo Irwin and his immigration system, although he made a valiant, if rather pathetic effort to survive even that. He was not unaware that the American annexationists who dethroned Queen Liliuokalani and established the provisional government might look critically at the Japanese immigration and even mistrust him, but he thought he could win them over. He even hoped he could get them to adopt an enlightened racial policy toward propertied Japanese, allowing them the franchise on equal terms with Caucasians and Hawaiians.

To these ends he came to Hawaii in December 1893, with several factors working in his favor: his long association with many high-placed Americans in Hawaii (for example, the former Hawaiian foreign minister, Godfrey Brown, who had visited him in Tokyo two years earlier); the fact that his half-brother, Admiral John Irwin, was in command of the U.S.S. *Philadelphia* in Hawaiian waters; and his own diplomatic agility. He revealed his inner thoughts on these matters to his adopted nephew and secretary, Tadamichi.

> I arrived here on the 4th at noon, went immediately aboard the flagship *Philadelphia* where I remained for two weeks, sleeping on board at night, going to bed at 10 o'clock, rising at 6:30 a.m., breakfast on board with my brother, then at 9 went ashore every day . . . On the 23rd took a small cottage on Makiki St. ($25 gold per month) . . . borrowed bedstead, etc. from Nacayama [Nakayama, Chief Inspector]. . . . I have talked with President Dole and the Cabinet, Thurston and others about the Electoral franchise. . . . Tell Mama that my old friend Armstrong is here. He came with the King to Japan in 1881 and dined with the King and Judd at our House. He lives with Thurston on Judd St. up Nuanu Valley.
>
> I have spent one morning and one evening with them. I think Thurston will advocate the electoral franchise for Japanese but as yet cannot say positively. I am not forcing the matter, but arguing patiently.
>
> I say "No franchise—No emigration. No assurance, no immediate emigration." With assurance emigration will continue, but the Japanese must be given the same privileges as other foreigners.
>
> I have often met and talked with Consul General Fujii. He is prudent and able and has been nice to me. I have advised him to keep quiet about the

franchise at present and let me put in my work so that he can act when a settled Government is made. I cannot say positively but I am working hard to succeed. I believe I am popular here. I have declared positively that I have no ambition here and I have none.

My career is in Japan. Nothing will ever change this. So as this is true people trust me. Then! I am a fairly good politician anyhow with discretion and diplomatic experience.

On the other hand there are a lot of low fellows who have drifted from San F. [,] Yokohama and Kobe—the scum and refuse of the earth—idle, dissolute, worthless—Now, these fellows, egged on by clergyman Okabe and others to become political agitators in Hawaii. . . . These kind [*sic*] of people give a bad name to Japan. Thieves like Dr. Mitamura and Seya who both stole money of Japanese. . . .

On the other hand the high character of Captain Togo and his officers of the *Naniwa Kan* as well as the good conduct of the sailors of the *Naniwa* and their manly, clean, orderly appearance have greatly raised the estimation of Japan in the minds of all classes here. If the young Japanese Naval Officers could only dance they would be very popular. As it is, I think they are all much liked and respected. . . .

Newman [Paul Neumann] has been and is very sick. So, I have employed and sent a lawyer, Creighton, to Hilo to attend court (Circuit Judge Austin presiding) to prosecute the Kukuihaele Luna (overseer) who shot a laborer Ito last June. You will inform H. E. Mr. Mutsu [Foreign Minister] that every effort will be made to have this Luna thoroughly prosecuted and convicted, if guilty. The deputy Attorney General will also prosecute.

Of course, we only know one side now, namely the poor Japanese who was shot. We do not know what the Luna's defence will be. Anyhow Justice will be rendered and we have spared no expense. . . .

Of course, no resistance was ever really intended against the United States forces. A demand of surrender to the military power of the United States could not and would not be resisted. On the other hand the Provisional Government will never surrender to the Queen and if the United States places the Queen on the throne, she can only be kept there by the Military force of the United States and that force will not be used for any such purpose I am sure. A Republic will at once result.

I am well but homesick. . . .[37]

This long letter, the main points of which are reproduced above, tells a great deal about Irwin's attitudes and his diplomacy, both in the positive and the negative sense. He had a rather paternalistic regard for orderliness (e.g., his evaluation of Togo and the *Naniwa*) and a penchant for gentlemanly politics. His sense of justice and fair play was strong. His understanding of the urgency of equal treatment of Orientals for the healthy political future of Hawaii was a half century ahead of its time. It may be playfully wondered if disciplinarian Togo had ordered his sailors to spend their off-duty hours learning to dance, would the dominant Caucasians in Honolulu have been more inclined to listen to Japanese arguments for the franchise?

Irwin, however, was wrong on two points. The provisional government authorities trusted him less than he thought. Further, they were more prejudiced and fearful than he had anticipated. They refused his advice, and insulted him in a shameful way. His application for "a certificate of Special Rights of Citizenship" in the Republic of Hawaii, which he filed in 1894, was denied by the Board of Examiners on the grounds that "Mr. Irwin has failed to establish that he took the active part or 'rendered substantial service' required by the Constitution."

Irwin's application cited his eight years as a Hawaiian resident (at the Hawaiian legation in Tokyo), his frequent stays in Hawaii, and noted that from December 4, 1893 "actively, hourly, and daily, I stood shoulder to shoulder with President Dole and his Cabinet, placing myself under the orders of President Dole."[38]

He wrote Dole effusively: "I am delighted with the proclamation of our Republic and Constitution on July 4, a day of glorious memory to all of us." And he underlined the following: "I am always proud that my ancestor Benjamin Franklin took active part in the American Declaration; and I am proud that I in a humbler way have taken part in our declaration of a Republic."[39]

Alas, in trying to save the immigration system its architect humbled himself too much. It would have been better to base his application on the grounds that he had offered the leaders of the provisional government and the Republic of Hawaii sound and sage advice on fair play for Japanese immigrants. They would have rejected him, no doubt, for his horizons were wider than theirs, but his record would have escaped having a blot of sycophancy on the last page.

NOTES

1. Oscar Handlin, *The Uprooted* (Boston: Little, Brown and Co., 1951), pp. 7-62.

2. *Pittsburgh Post,* September 16, 1856, obituary of William Wallace Irwin; *The Public Ledger,* Philadelphia, March 25, 1904, obituary of Sophia Arabella Bache Irwin.

3. Agnes Ripplier, *Agnes Irwin: A Biography* (New York: Doubleday, Doran and Co., 1934), see especially p. 68; Gertrude B. Biddle and Sarah D. Lowrie, *Notable Women of Pennsylvania* (Philadelphia: University of Pennsylvania Press, 1942), see especially p. 202; LeBaron R. Briggs, "Not Always to the Swift," *Radcliffe Quarterly* (Cambridge, Mass.: Radcliffe Alumnae Assoc., 1927); Yukiko Irwin, personal interviews with Miss Edith Bache and Miss Emily Bache of

Philadelphia, Pa., cousins of Robert W. Irwin, and Miss Bertha Laws, former headmistress of the Agnes Irwin School for girls, Philadelphia.

4. Ripplier, *op. cit.*, p. 48.

5. *New York Tribune*, April 27, 1892, obituary of Col. Richard B. Irwin; letter from W. G. MacDonald, American President Lines, to Yukiko Irwin, October 20, 1965.

6. Inoue Kaoru Denki Hensankai (Inoue Kaoru Biographical Compilation Society), comp., *Segai Inoue Kō Den* [Life of Marquis Inoue] (Tokyo: Nagai Shoseki Kabushiki Kaisha, 1933–34), II, pp. 43, 523, 538, 713-739; *Jijo Masuda Takashi Den* [Autobiography of Masuda Takashi] (Tokyo, 1939), pp. 165-168.

7. Memorandum by R. W. Irwin in *Mitsui Bussan Enkakushi* [History of the Mitsui Company], Vol. IV, book 1, p. 121; quoted in Matsunaga Hideo, "Hawaii Imin to Mitsui Bussan" [Hawaiian Immigration and the Mitsui Company], *Sanyū Shimbun* (Mitsui Co. newspaper), December 10, 1964.

8. *New York Tribune*, April 27, 1892, obituary of Col. Richard B. Irwin.

9. Matsunaga, *Sanyū Shimbun*, December 10, 1964.

10. Genealogy of Iki Takechi Irwin, compiled from interviews and family papers by Yukiko Irwin.

11. Lillibridge to Kapena, August 1, 1880, Archives of Hawaii, Foreign Office and Executive file, Consul General, Japan.

12. Green to Irwin, May 7, 1881, Archives of Hawaii, F.O. and Ex. file, Treaty Documents, Hawaii and Japan, 1881–1885.

13. Hilary Conroy, "'Asiatic Federation' and the Japanese Immigration to Hawaii," *Report of the Hawaiian Historical Society for the Year 1949* (Honolulu, 1950), pp. 31-42.

14. See Masaji Marumoto, "'First Year' Immigrants to Hawaii and Eugene Van Reed," above; see also Hilary Conroy, *The Japanese Frontier in Hawaii, 1868–1898* (Berkeley: University of California Press, 1953), pp. 15-43.

15. Inoue to Iaukea, April 26, 1884, Archives of Hawaii, F.O. and Ex. file, Immigration.

16. Hawaii *Session Laws*, 1884, chap. vi., p. 6.

17. Conroy, *The Japanese Frontier in Hawaii;* see also Segawa Yoshinobu, "Nippu Imin Mondai" [The Japan-Hawaii Immigration Problem], *Kokusaihō Gaikō Zasshi* LXVI, nos. 1, 3 (June, October, 1967), pp. 67-96, 264-292.

18. Matsunaga, *Sanyū Shimbun,* February 11, 1965, quoting the Autobiography of Masuda Takashi.

19. *Ibid.,* February 4, 1965.

20. *Ibid.,* December 10, 1964.

21. *Ibid.,* February 11, 1965. The *Chūgai Bukka Shimpō* became the *Chūgai Shōgyō Shimpō* in 1889, and later the *Nihon Sangyō Keizai Shimpō.* Today it is the *Nihon Sangyō Shimbun,* one of Japan's leading financial newspapers.

22. Gibson (Hawaiian Foreign Minister) to Irwin, February 22, 1886, Archives of Hawaii, F.O. and Ex. file, Japanese Minister, Tokyo; see also Seya Shoji (Inspector of Immigrants), *Hawaiikoku Imin Shimatsusho* [A Detailed History of Japanese Immigration to Hawaii] (1893), quoted in *Hawaii Nihonjin Imin Shi* [A

History of Japanese Immigrants in Hawaii] (Honolulu: United Japanese Society of Hawaii, 1964), pp. 109-111.

23. Nakamura to Gibson, November 7, 1885, Archives of Hawaii, F.O. and Ex. file, Japanese Commissioner and Consul, 1885. This folio also contains various letters and reports on the discussions with Inoue Katsunosuke.

24. The Convention is printed in English in Conroy, *The Japanese Frontier in Hawaii,* appendix C, pp. 148-150, and in Japanese in Gaimushō (Japanese Foreign Office), *Nihon Gaikō Bunsho* (hereafter *NGB*) (Japanese Foreign Affairs Documents), XIX, pp. 463-465.

25. Irwin to Gulick (President, Board of Immigration), April 8, 1886, Archives of Hawaii, Interior Dept. file, Immigration, Box 55.

26. Irwin to Gibson, December 1, 1886, Archives of Hawaii, F.O. and Ex. file, Japan, Minister Tokyo.

27. *NGB,* XX, pp. 422-423.

28. Ando (Japanese Consul General, Honolulu) to Foreign Minister Inoue, September 6, 1887 and enclosures, *NGB,* XX, pp. 420-424; Irwin to Ito, September 27, 1887, *ibid.,* pp. 429-433.

29. "History of the Hawaiian Immigrant Fund," document dated 1900 and printed next to letter from Ando to Inoue, January 14, 1887 in *NGB,* XX, pp. 356-361.

30. Seya Shoji, *op. cit.,* p. 110. The recent study by Segawa Yoshinobu says only that "it was rumored that Irwin retained the immigrants' money for over a year and used it to manipulate Mitsui Company debts." Segawa, *op. cit.,* p. 85.

31. Ito to Ando, two letters, both dated September 28, 1887, *NGB,* XX, pp. 434-435.

32. Ito to Green, September 29, 1887, *NGB,* XX, pp. 437-439.

33. Ando (Honolulu) to Inoue, July 29, 1887, *NGB,* XX, pp. 399-402.

34. Ando to Okuma, July 28, 1888, *NGB,* XXI, p. 424; Okuma to Irwin, September 29, 1888, *ibid.,* pp. 445-446; Okuma to Ando, September 27, 1888, *ibid.,* pp. 443-444.

35. Neumann to Spencer (Report), March 18, 1891, Archives of Hawaii, Interior Dept. file, Immigration, Box 55.

36. Conroy, *The Japanese Frontier in Hawaii,* pp. 108-110.

37. "Strictly private" letter from R. W. Irwin to Takechi Tadamichi, Honolulu, December 28, 1893, Japanese Foreign Office Archives, Tokyo, Hawaiian Immigration, 1887–1894, folio 6. A photocopy of this letter is in the authors' possession.

38. Irwin (Tokyo) to James A. King, Minister of Interior, August 8, 1894 (two letters); Board of Examiners to King, no day, September 1894, Archives of Hawaii, Minister of Interior file. Photocopies in authors' possession.

39. Irwin to President Dole, August 8, 1894, Tokyo, Archives of Hawaii, Minister Tokyo, January–August, 1894. Photocopies in authors' possession. President Dole had previously approved citizenship "except the right to vote" for Irwin on July 28.

OAKLAND PUBLIC LIBRARY
OAKLAND. CALIFORNIA

Japanese Entrepreneurs in the Mariana, Marshall, & Caroline Islands

DAVID C. PURCELL, JR.

During the last decade of the nineteenth century and the early years of the twentieth, Japanese entrepreneurs made several attempts to establish commercial and agricultural enterprises throughout the Mariana, Marshall and Caroline Islands.

The international status of these Micronesian islands was defined by the Treaty of Tordesillas in 1494, which placed the entire Pacific Ocean under the nominal jurisdiction of Spain. Despite this carte blanche for territorial aggrandisement, the Spanish were content to focus their attention on Guam, a port of call along the galleon route from the Philippines to Mexico, and the islands of the Northern Marianas. Spain was slow to exercise control over the Carolines, and never did establish ascendancy over the Marshalls, which remained a no man's land until the 1880s. In 1885 Germany declared a protectorate over the Marshall Islands, and in 1899 purchased the Marianas and the Carolines from Spain for $4.5 million. These islands remained under German control until the end of World War I, when they were assigned to Japan as a Class C mandate under the League of Nations, and were administered as such until 1945.

The beginnings of Japanese commercial relations with Micronesia are traditionally associated with Mizutani Shinroku. Mizutani, who resided in the Bonin Islands and raised cattle for a living, heard about the wonders of the *Nanyō*[1] area from a native of the Bonins. In 1887 Mizutani set sail in a forty-five-ton vessel, the *Sōyō Maru,* and made his first stop on Mutok harbor on Ponape. He was immediately apprehended by Spanish officials there, who informed him that it was illegal to trade at Mutok, and ordered him to proceed to Santiago harbor, where the *Sōyō Maru* was inspected. Since Mizutani behaved circumspectly during this episode, and his ship was small, the Spanish officials simply fined him for trying to trade illegally with the natives, and ordered him to leave immediately. From there Mizutani sailed to Pingelap and throughout the Mokil Islands, where he clandestinely traded with the natives in such items as lamps, kerosene, hardware, and food. He returned to the Bonin Islands in October 1887.[2]

Mizutani related his adventures to Yorioka Shōzō, who lived on one of the small islands in the Bonins and also raised livestock for a living.[3] While on a trip to Tokyo, Yorioka told a friend, Ueda Kimon, about Mizutani's activities, and suggested the establishment of a Japanese-controlled commercial network throughout the islands of Micronesia. Yorioka and Ueda then discussed this matter with Ugawa Momirō, an economist, and shortly thereafter Taguchi Ukichi, a strong advocate of economic individualism, was made privy to these conversations.[4]

Takazaki Goroku, the mayor of Tokyo, learned of these discussions, and in December 1889 proposed that Taguchi, Ugawa and Seki Naohiko, a promising young politician, take the lead in establishing a marine products enterprise in the Bonin Islands.[5] At first Taguchi hesitated, claiming that the prospects for such an enterprise were not good, but when asked to reconsider two months later he agreed to undertake the project, which was to be financed with a grant from the ex-samurai employment fund *(shizoku jusankin)*.

Taguchi purchased a ninety-ton vessel, the *Tenyū Maru,* established a company called the Nantō Shōkai, and assembled a sixteen-man crew to make the voyage to the Bonin Islands. However, he immediately encountered opposition from a group of samurai who complained bitterly that the mayor of Tokyo had exceeded his authority in providing a subsidy for Taguchi. In response to these complaints, the head of the prefectural assembly, Kusumoto Masataka, attempted to impound the vessel, but Taguchi, aware of these developments, hastily sailed from Yokohama on May 15, 1890, a festival day when government officials were occupied elsewhere.[6]

The voyage of the *Tenyū Maru,* which lasted six and a half months, was fraught with difficulties from beginning to end, and demonstrated that Taguchi had no intention of establishing a marine products enterprise in the Bonin Islands.[7] He made only a brief stop there while a man named Matsunaga Ichitarō and a companion joined the crew, and also visited the island of Rota, before proceeding to Guam on June 10. The crew members were not permitted to go ashore because they did not have health certificates from the Spanish consul in Yokohama, but after waiting for four days they were rescued by Oda Shinzaburō, a resident of Guam who was employed by an Australian trading company. Through Oda's efforts the crew was eventually permitted to land, and Taguchi was informed that he would be fined fifty yen for violating harbor regulations. However, the fine was waived when Taguchi explained that he hadn't been aware of the health certificate requirement.

The next stop was Yap on June 26, where Taguchi received permission from Spanish officials to engage in commercial activities. The *Tenyū Maru* then proceeded to Palau, where Taguchi encountered some resis-

ASIAN COMMUNITY LIBRARY
1934 PARK BLVD.
OAKLAND, CA 94606

tance. D. D. O'Keefe, an independent trader who was trying to compete with the Jaluit Company, which had a monopoly on German commercial and agricultural enterprises in the Caroline and Marshall Islands, regarded Taguchi as an interloper. O'Keefe had established a foothold in the Caroline Islands in 1872, when he began quarrying huge quantities of stone on Palau and brought it to Yap, where it was used as currency by the natives. This activity enabled him to gain extensive commercial privileges from the chieftains of Palau and Yap. He informed the Japanese that Ponape was a center of commercial activity and had an excellent climate, and suggested that Taguchi look into the possibility of establishing a commercial outlet there.[8]

Taguchi, sensing that he faced insurmountable competition, sailed immediately for Ponape, where he encountered further difficulties. After arriving there on September 7, he spent the next two weeks battling bad weather, heavy seas, and recalcitrant Spanish officials before he was permitted to land. After prolonged negotiations, he was granted permission to establish a store at Santiago harbor, which was placed under the management of Sekine Sentarō, Matsunaga Ichitarō and Seto Toyokichi.

After establishing this store on Ponape, Taguchi returned directly to Tokyo. Upon his arrival there on December 2, 1890, he learned that the original opposition to his activities had not abated. He was accused of misappropriating the money from the ex-samurai employment fund because he had made no attempt to establish a marine products enterprise in the Bonins. When Mutsu Munemitsu, the minister of agriculture and commerce, joined the chorus of criticism, Taguchi paid back the money and surrendered control of the Nantō Shōkai to the government on February 4, 1891. Shortly thereafter, when the government put the company up for bids, it was purchased and renamed the Ichiya Shōkai by Komida Kigi, a retainer of the Matsudaira Chūi family from Nagasaki prefecture.[9] Komida sailed to Ponape during June 1891 on the *Tenyū Maru* to supply his newly acquired business there. Sekine Sentarō and Matsunaga Ichitarō changed hats and continued as managers of the Ichiya Shōkai venture on Ponape. Subsequently, the *Tenyū Maru* was sent on two more voyages, one to Ponape and the other to Truk, where a store was established, but the Ichiya Shōkai soon languished from neglect.[10]

Other Japanese continued commercial activity in Micronesia. For example, in 1891 Mizutani Shinroku made another attempt by establishing the Kaitsusha and opening a store on Truk. Unfortunately, his ship, the *Kaitsu Maru*, ran aground off Hokkaido while on a voyage to

Japan and was destroyed. He purchased another ship and announced plans to transport freight between Japan and the Caroline Islands, but nothing more was heard of this enterprise.[11]

It was also in 1891 that Enomoto Takeaki (Buyō) and some friends established the Kōshinsha, a company which concentrated its activities on Palau. The Kōshinsha remained in business until December 1917, when its assets and property were purchased by the Nanyō Bōeki Kaisha.[12]

Two years later, in 1893, Samoto Tsunekichi initiated another venture in Micronesia. Samoto, who had been a crew member of the *Tenyū Maru* when Komida Kigi sailed it to Ponape in 1891, went to his native village of Hioki in Wakayama prefecture to seek capital to establish a trading company. With the assistance of a close friend, a wealthy landlord named Mitsumoto Rokuyūeimon was persuaded to invest 8,000 yen, which was used to purchase a 134-ton vessel from the government of Siam and establish the Nanyō Bōeki Hioki Gōshi Kaisha. A year later Mitsumoto invested another 4,000 yen in the company, and after five years of careful management and vigorous expansion Samoto claimed assets of 100,000 yen, which included four sailing vessels and a network of commercial outlets and numerous agricultural enterprises on Truk, Yap, Guam, Saipan, Rota, Ulio, and Elato.

However, the Nanyō Bōeki Hioki Gōshi Kaisha, which handled both general merchandise and copra, experienced financial difficulties after 1900. The amount of copra which the company produced on Saipan was always so meager that the profits on its operations there never exceeded ten percent, and thus Samoto was obliged to develop the bulk of his copra trade with the rest of the Marianas. When a severe storm curtailed the production of copra in these islands, the company weathered the ensuing financial crisis only because the price of copra remained high in Japan. Truk also presented a problem, although of a different nature. The company was constantly involved in disputes with German colonial officials there, as well as with British and American merchants who resented competition from the Japanese. Eventually the store on Truk was closed because the Japanese sold weapons to the natives in violation of German law.[13]

Another entrepreneur, Murayama Sukichi, a resident of Yokohama, established the Nanyō Bōeki Murayama Gōmei Kaisha in 1901. Sekine Sentarō, formerly in the employ of the Nantō Shōkai and the Ichiya Shōkai, was hired to manage the Murayama store on Ponape, but immediately encountered difficulties. Because of the sale of arms to the natives by Samoto's representatives, German officials were suspicious of any Japanese activity in Micronesia, and in January 1901 expelled four-teen Japanese residents from Ponape. Sekine signed an agreement with a Spanish merchant to act as a forwarding agent for the Murayama company's cargo on Ponape, and was able to establish stores on Guam and Saipan. Murayama was subsequently granted permission by Ger-man authorities to establish commercial outlets on Palau and Yap, as well as throughout the Faraulep, Lamotrek and Ifalik atolls. In 1906 the Germans tightened trading regulations for the East Caroline Islands, but Murayama persuaded the Japanese Foreign Office to intercede in his behalf. After prolonged negotiations with the German government, Murayama was permitted to establish trading stations on Truk and Ponape, with the latter under the management of Sekine Sentarō.[14]

On June 27, 1908 Murayama merged his enterprise with Samoto's Nanyō Bōeki Hioki Gōshi Kaisha to form a new organization, the Nanyō Bōeki Kaisha. Mitsumoto Rokuyūeimon, Samoto's backer, became president of the new company, which had five ships and a growing commercial network throughout Micronesia. The company intensified its efforts and continued transporting freight, maintaining a chain of retail outlets which sold articles of everyday living to Japanese and natives throughout the islands, carrying mail and passengers, and producing copra. After the merger in 1908, the Nanyō Bōeki Kaisha was capitalized at 150,000 yen. Five years later it listed assets of more than 300,000 yen.[15]

As World War I spread to East Asia, Japan sought to expand the boundaries of the empire. She also sought revenge for Germany's role in the Triple Intervention of 1895. She thus embarked on an offensive in the Marianas, Marshalls and Carolines.[16] Between September 29 and October 14, 1914 the Japanese Navy took possession of Jaluit, Kusaie, Ponape, Truk, Palau, Angaur, and Saipan in that order. A state of martial law was declared and all activity throughout Micronesia was placed under the Japanese minister of the navy or his officially desig-nated representative.[17]

In 1914 the Nanyō Bōeki Kaisha was placed under the protective wing of the Navy Ministry, and by October 1915 the company's ships began scheduled sailings between Japan and the islands to transport provisions and military personnel, for which the government paid it 42,000 yen per month. By this time the company had a fleet of four steam-powered vessels and five sailing ships, which in 1915 made thir-teen trips to the islands and ten return voyages to Japan. The total volume of exports handled in 1915 amounted to 295,000 yen and the total imports to Japan were valued at 796,000 yen. This represented the largest volume of trade which the company had handled in any one year since it was established, and resulted in an annual profit of 48,750 yen. By 1916 the Nanyō Bōeki Kaisha listed assets of 1,000,000 yen, which increased to 3,000,000 yen in 1917 with the purchase of the Kōshinsha. For the next three years the Nanyō Bōeki Kaisha expanded its interests in Micronesia because it received preferential treatment from the Japanese government. By 1920 it had a monopoly on all trading operations there.[18]

Tokyo was preoccupied with events in China and Korea, as well as with Russian activity in northeast Asia, during the initial period of Japanese entrepreneurship in Micronesia from 1890 until 1914 at which time the Japanese Navy seized the Marianas, Marshalls and Carolines. The volume of trade with these islands comprised a very small fraction of Japan's total foreign commerce, and the islands were of no strategic consequence. For these reasons the Japanese government did not officially sponsor Japanese immigration to Micronesia as an adjunct to Japanese commercial activities there.[19]

By the middle of July 1913 there were fifty-six Japanese living on Palau and in the West Carolines, and about fifty-one living in the Marianas. However, their influence was greater than their numbers suggest.

> From the time of their commercial establishment in the Marianas in the late 1890s the Japanese practically monopolized the foreign trade of the region. ... The Japanese control of the Marianas trade declined somewhat in later years; nevertheless, it was so nearly complete that the Pagan Gesellschaft, under German government sponsorship, had no choice but to ship its copra to Yokohama.[20]

What was true for the Marianas in general was the case with Guam in particular. In his annual report submitted June 30, 1905, the American Governor General noted that there were forty Japanese living on the island, and went on to say that

> The absence of a line of freight-carrying craft between San Francisco, Guam and Manila throws all the trade with this island into the hands of the Japanese. They have established stores, regular lines of schooners, and practically monopolize trade and fix prices. Under these conditions living expenses for the natives are cruelly high.[21]

Again in 1908 the Governor General wrote in his annual report that

> ... practically all the trade of Guam is in the hands of the Japanese, who are gradually acquiring commercial mastery and buying up all the choice lands of the island. They introduce, on their small schooners, at risks few mer-

chants would care to take, large quantities of cheap and inferior goods of antiquated patterns which are sold at irregular and exorbitant prices.[22]

In 1909 the Japanese population of Guam was ninety-five, but the volume of Japanese trade with the island continued to increase. The value of imports entered at the customs house for the fiscal year ending June 30, 1909 was $82,250.83. Of this, goods from the United States represented 17.9 percent; from Manila, 11.1 percent; from Honolulu, 0.2 percent; and from Saipan, 2.4 percent. Japan accounted for 68 percent of the imports.[23] Two years later the Governor General noted that

> There are five Japanese schooners trading between Guam and Yokohama. The Japanese export all the copra produced in the island and control the prices thereof. Also, the Japanese are the principal merchants of the island, controlling more or less the price of imports.[24]

In June 1914, however, this situation changed completely, as a result of stringent shipping regulations established by the United States. All trade under foreign flags was confined to Japanese vessels which, by special exemption, were authorized to trade between Guam and Yokohama. Only Japanese merchants who lived on Guam and who owned schooners wholly or in part by themselves were able to qualify for this exemption. Consequently, only two Japanese schooners were given permission to trade with Guam. Furthermore, the right to trade exclusively between Saipan, at that time a German port, and Guam was denied to all Japanese vessels. Finally, only two Japanese vessels of less than five tons each were permitted to pass from Apra harbor to the other harbors on Guam in order to supply the Japanese residents in these places.[25] The Americans succeeded in drastically reducing Japan's role in the Guam trade. In 1915 imports from Japan dropped to $34,912.28,[26] and in 1916 to $29,557.98, while at the same time annual copra exports to Japan dropped to 958 pounds.[27]

The other islands in Micronesia nevertheless felt the increased presence of Japanese, as Tokyo encouraged immigration to reinforce Japan's military and commercial presence there. At the end of 1920, there were 3,671 Japanese living in Micronesia (1,758, 1,715, and 198 in the Marianas, Carolines, and Marshalls respectively). Of these, 3,403 were from Japan proper, while 268 were classified as Koreans.[28] Among the 3,671 Japanese, about 470 were military personnel attached to the South Seas Temporary Defense Garrison.[29] After 1920 the Japanese population of the islands increased steadily, reaching 77,257 by 1939.[30]

Shortly after the beginning of World War I, Nishimura Sōshirō became the leading Japanese entrepreneur in Micronesia. He was the owner of a large fishing company based in Shimonoseki, and was reasonably familiar with the Marianas, Marshalls and Carolines because of the activities of his fleet. In the latter part of 1914, Nishimura sent his adopted son, Ichimatsu, to reconnoiter the Micronesian islands for the purpose of locating new fishing grounds. Ichimatsu, while enroute, was told that the islands had considerable potential for the development of the sugar industry. He visited Saipan and drew up a written plan for the establishment and operation of such an enterprise, and then went to Truk, where the headquarters of the Japanese occupation forces was located. He consulted with Japanese officials there and was given permission to lease land for the purpose of cultivating sugar. After he returned to Shimonoseki and consulted with his father, Nishimura decided to invest in this venture.[31]

For a number of years Japanese entrepreneurs, often with strong government support, had attempted to cultivate and refine sugar for consumption in Japan, but investment in such enterprises was limited until after 1905.

> Until Formosa was acquired as a colony in 1895, little sugar was produced within the Empire. Prior to 1902 only 2.7 million yen was invested in eight refineries and the nation was compelled to rely heavily on imported sugar. Plans progressed rapidly, however, for the expansion of sugar cane farms in the colony of Formosa and sugar refining investments rose from 9.2 million yen in 1908 to 15 million yen in 1912.[32]

Entrepreneurs such as Nishimura falsely assumed that the topographical, climatic and other conditions under which the Japanese were successfully producing sugar on Taiwan were identical to those in Micronesia, and that there was, therefore, a reasonable chance for success in the Marianas, Marshalls and Carolines. The prewar boom in the sugar industry and its burgeoning market in Japan provided a compelling motive for experimenting with sugar in new areas.

Under these circumstances, the large-scale cultivation of other crops on a commercial basis was never given serious consideration. The market potential for vegetables, fruits and rice was limited in both Micronesia and Japan. The inhabitants of the islands produced enough food to satisfy their needs. Japan became increasingly dependent on overseas sources for foodstuffs after 1890, but the situation was not critical enough in 1912 to warrant the cultivation of such items for commercial purposes in Micronesia. Copra had commercial possibilities, but its export was under the control of the Nanyō Bōeki Kaisha, and Nishimura seems not to have considered producing or trading it.

Workers from the Nishimura enterprises in Yamaguchi and Nagasaki prefectures were sent to Saipan in February 1916, under Ichimatsu's

general supervision. He unfortunately knew nothing about the cultivation of sugar, let alone the refining process. Progress was slow from the
very beginning; the men brought as laborers were actually fishermen
and did not like the idea of clearing land. The arrival of 400 Korean
laborers created other problems. They quarreled among themselves and
with the Japanese. Nevertheless, by the spring of 1919, 300 acres of land
were cleared and a refinery, warehouse, trunk line, and dormitory for
the workers were constructed.[33] When the first sugar crop was har-
vested and delivered for processing, no one knew what to do with the
juice after it had been extracted from the cane. The juice was boiled but
no sugar was produced, and it was subsequently stored in a tank in the
hope that it would ferment and produce a low-grade alcohol. This too
was unsuccessful and the juice was finally poured into the ocean.

In the meantime, Nishimura reorganized his Micronesian enterprise
as the Nishimura Shokusan Kaisha, capitalized at 5,000,000 yen with
himself as president and Ichimatsu as vice-president. Despite this
change the fortunes of the company did not improve. The second sugar
crop suffered the same fate as the first, and by this time many of the
workers had died from tropical diseases and fire destroyed some of the
company buildings.

However, the high price of sugar on the international market enabled
Nishimura to obtain a loan of 900,000 yen to finance one further attempt to produce sugar in Saipan. That attempt also failed and the
operation was abandoned, along with the laborers who were left on the
island to survive by their own ingenuity.

Another organization, the Nanyō Shokusan Kaisha, attempted to
establish a sugar refining enterprise in Micronesia in 1917, bringing
eighty tenant families from the Bonin Islands and 300 Japanese laborers
to Saipan. A refinery was constructed on the north side of the island,
the side opposite the Nishimura operation. Once again poor planning,
lack of experience, and mismanagement caused the enterprise to fail. For
example, the company's main office and the laborers' living quarters
were three miles over a mountain from the refining facilities.[34]

Despite the fact that the Nanyō Shokusan Kaisha was able to produce 300 barrels of sugar while the Nishimura refinery was being constructed, the company immediately had trouble with field supervisors
who embezzled funds and spent large sums of money on lavish dinner
parties and entertainment. When the home office dispatched a man to
investigate conditions on Saipan, he found that the company treasury
was empty. After this, the company lost a great deal of money in the
Philippines due to the failure of a jute crop in which it had invested.
Then came the world financial panic of 1920, and this was more than

the company could endure. The owners abandoned the operation and left the laborers and tenant families on Saipan to fend for themselves.

In addition to the failure of the Nishimura and Nanyō Shokusan ventures, Tōyō Seitō Kaisha (Orient Sugar Company) lost heavily in Micronesia. In 1916, with the aid of the Suzuki Brothers Trading Company, Orient Sugar conducted a large-scale investigation into the sugar-producing potential of the islands. Operations were established on Ponape, but too much rain and extensive insect damage made it necessary to abandon the venture in 1920 at a loss of 300,000 to 400,000 yen.

Due to these initial failures, it was not quite as easy as it had been to persuade Japanese businessmen to invest in such enterprises after 1920. The large Japanese sugar companies on Formosa did conduct investigations between 1915–20 into the prospect of sugar production in the Marianas. All considered, however, that the islands were too small to make the operation profitable. The natives could not be relied upon to work with any regularity, and it would be very expensive (if not impossible, because of the natural features of the islands) to bring in the heavy machinery necessary for refining the sugar.

Despite this bleak forecast, a few individuals were convinced that the islands which the Japanese occupied during the war could produce sugar profitably. One such person was Matsue Haruji, who had worked for several different sugar companies prior to 1920. In 1921, while in Tokyo, he met Takatsuhisa Ueimon, board chairman of the Osaka sugar exchange, who asked Matsue to investigate the prospects for sugar production in the Marianas for him. Accordingly, Matsue left for Saipan in February 1921.[35]

During his tour of the island Matsue lived with a minor chief of the Chamorro tribe and made careful surveys of the land. He also traveled on Tinian, where he discovered fields which he felt were ideal for the cultivation of sugar. At the same time he discussed the pitiful plight of the Japanese laborers abandoned by Nishimura, Nanyō Shokusan and the Orient Sugar Company with the chief of the civil affairs section attached to the Japanese military forces in the Marianas, who requested that the government assist these people. The Japanese government, while insisting that these laborers would be removed from the islands at its expense only as a last resort, attempted to persuade Ishitsuka Eizō, the president of Tōyō Takushoku Kaisha, to begin some type of industry in Micronesia which would employ these men. Ishitsuka made it clear that he was not interested in taking any financial risks, but did mention that in the fall of 1920 he had sent two men to Saipan to investigate the situation there.

In the meantime, Matsue tried to persuade an old friend, Kaneko

Naokichi, to provide some capital for a sugar refining operation in the Marianas, which could use the abandoned Japanese laborers. Kaneko argued that this would be a very risky venture and that the government should be persuaded to guarantee a subsidy for such an undertaking. However, Matsue soon discovered that a government subsidy was out of the question.

Clearly the situation had reached an impasse. It was at this point that Ishitsuka's emissaries returned from Saipan and recommended that he invest in cotton production there. He sent Matsue, whose business acumen and ambition had impressed him, to Saipan for one final appraisal of the situation, while Ishitsuka managed the financial negotiations in Tokyo. He took out a loan of 600,000 yen from a bank and borrowed another 300,000 yen from Kaigai Kōgyō Kaisha, an organization with interests in Brazil and Peru, which had been established in December 1917. Ishitsuka then purchased the assets of the Nishimura Shokusan Kaisha, which at this time amounted to the cultivation rights for various areas of land on Saipan, Rota and Tinian, for 500,000 yen. At the same time he issued new stock which the former stockholders of the Nishimura Shokusan Kaisha purchased for three million yen, and shortly thereafter purchased the land and machinery of the Nanyō Shokusan Kaisha on Saipan for 500,000 yen. This financial maneuvering culminated on November 20, 1921 with the creation of the Nanyō Kōhatsu (Development) company.[36]

Matsue returned from Saipan to Tokyo, arriving on October 6, 1921. He persuaded Ishitsuka to forget about the cultivation of cotton and concentrate on sugar, was named director of the Nanyō Kōhatsu company, and on December 6, 1921 left for Saipan to begin the cultivation and refining of sugar. For the next twenty-five years this company, with ample government assistance and protection, became the leading Japanese business organization in Micronesia.

Thirty years elapsed between 1891, when Taguchi Ukichi established the Nantō Shōkai, and the creation of the Nanyō Kōhatsu company, which was the most important economic force in the Mariana, Marshall and Caroline Islands until 1945. During that period Japanese entrepreneurial activities in those islands experienced varying degrees of success. Both the agricultural and commercial enterprises failed primarily because of a lack of capital, but in each instance other factors contributed to their failure.

The commercial operations suffered from a lack of markets, due to the sparseness of the Japanese population in the islands and because of restrictive measures against Japanese traders by Spanish, German and American colonial officials. The influence of the Japanese traders was greater than their numbers or capital investment would indicate, however, because they controlled a large portion of the trade in the Marianas, Marshalls and Carolines. This can be explained in part by the absence of powerful competition from either European or American companies. But the eventual success of the Japanese was due mainly to their remarkable tenacity and commercial skill under conditions which few merchants would have tolerated. Taguchi's Nantō Shōkai, which after its initial failure was salvaged to become the Ichiya Shōkai and later the Nanyō Bōeki Hioki firm (which evolved into the Nanyō Bōeki company) attests to the remarkable persistence and ingenuity of the Japanese commercial adventurers.

A similar lack of capital affected the agricultural enterprises, especially those involving the cultivation and production of sugar. They failed due to a lack of technical skill, poor planning and inept management. The labor problems which they experienced were not critical in determining the success or failure of the ventures.

The factors essential to the success of Japanese commercial, agricultural and industrial enterprises in Micronesia—capital, absence of restrictive trade measures, technical skill, and government support—were not present until after World War I. The alliance which Ishitsuka Eizō forged among Nanyō Kōhatsu, Tōyō Takushoku, and Kaigai Kōgyō in 1921 was extended in 1933 to include Nanyō Bōeki. The alliance remained intact until 1945 to assure an adequate source of capital.[37] The remaining prerequisites for success were provided when these islands were assigned to Japan as a Class C mandate by the League of Nations on December 17, 1920.

NOTES

1. Nanyō, literally "south seas," is the term used by the Japanese to refer to Southeast Asia, and the islands of both the North and South Pacific.
2. Gō Takashi, *Nanyō Bōeki Go Jū Nen Shi* [Fifty Years of Commerce in the South Seas] (Tokyo: Nanyō Bōeki Kabushiki Kaisha, 1942), pp. 3-4.
3. Oka Seishi, *Yorioka Shōzō Den* [The Life of Yorioka Shōzō] (Kobe: Nissa Shōkai, Ltd., 1936), pp. 11-23. In 1910 Yorioka went to Sarawak, where he became a pioneer in developing Japanese mining, commercial and agricultural interests. Takumushō, Takumukyoku, *Kaigai Takushoku Jigyō Chōsa Shiryō Dai San Jū Shichi Shū: Sarawakku Ōkoku Jijō* [Materials on the Investigation of Enterprises Overseas-Number 37: The Kingdom of Sarawak] (Tokyo: Takumushō, 1938), pp. 195-196.
4. Sumiya Tetsuji, *Nihon Keizai Gakushi,* rev. ed. [Studies on Japan's Economy] (Tokyo: Mineruva Shobo, 1967), pp. 129-150.
5. Seki Naohiko was a successful candidate in nine elections for the Diet

from 1890-1924. Peter Duus, *Party Rivalry and Political Change in Taishō Japan* (Cambridge: Harvard University Press, 1968), p. 20.

6. Sekine Sentarō, "Nanyō Guntō Mukashibanashi," [Legends of the South Sea Islands] in Nanyō Keizai Kenkyūjō, *Nanyō Shiryō,* No. 473 (Tokyo: Nanyō Keizai Kenkyūjō, 1944), pp. 1-3.

7. For an account of the voyage see Irie Toraji, *Meiji Nanshin Shiko* [A Short History of Southward Expansion in the Meiji Era] (Tokyo: Iwanami Shoten, 1943), pp. 102-110.

8. Office of the Chief of Naval Operations, comp., *Civil Affairs Handbook: West Caroline Islands* (Washington: Navy Department, 1944), p. 28. Hereafter cited as *West Caroline Islands.*

9. Sekine, pp. 3-4.

10. Gō, pp. 12-13.

11. Gō, p. 13.

12. *West Caroline Islands,* p. 29 says that as early as the Spanish period Japanese business interests had become strongly entrenched in Palau. When the Germans arrived they found the Japanese in control of nearly all the trade of this island group. In 1912, 73 of the 122 foreigners living in the Marianas and the West Carolines were Japanese, and approximately one-third of the foreign trade of this area was with Japan.

13. Watanabe Masasuke, "Yon Ju Nen Mai no Nanyō Bōeki," [Commerce in the South Seas Forty Years Ago] in Nanyō Keizai Kenkyūjō, *Nanyō Shiryō,* No. 473 (Tokyo: Nanyō Keizai Kenkyūjō, 1944), pp. 23-24.

14. Gō, pp. 44-46. Sekine, p. 15.

15. Gō, pp. 78-80.

16. For the negotiations which led to Japan's entering the war see Madeleine Chi, *China Diplomacy, 1914-1918* (Cambridge: Harvard University Press, 1970), pp. 5-21.

17. MT 5,2,6,22-2; Reel 515, pp. 01-9. For a description of these and other pertinent Japanese Foreign Office documents see Cecil H. Uyehara, ed., *Checklist of Archives in the Japanese Ministry of Foreign Affairs, Tokyo, Japan, 1868-1945, microfilmed for the Library of Congress, 1949-1951* (Washington: Library of Congress, 1954).

18. Gō, pp. 81-87.

19. From 1899, the earliest year for which statistics are available, to 1920, 27,583 Japanese traveled to various islands of the Pacific, other than the Ryukyus, Taiwan and Hawaii. Eighty-five percent of these were contract laborers who went to the Philippines, Guam, Ocean Island, New Caledonia or Tahiti. Nearly all of them returned to Japan after completing their terms of service. Therefore, it was not until after 1920 that Japanese communities of significant size appeared throughout the Pacific islands. Takumu Daijin, Kanbō Bunshoka, *Takumushō Tōkei Gaiyō* [A Statistical Summary of the Department of Overseas Affairs] (Tokyo: Takumushō, 1931), p. 28.

20. Office of the Chief of Naval Operations, comp., *Civil Affairs Handbook: Mandated Marianas* (Washington: Navy Department, 1944), p. 29.

21. U.S., Department of the Navy, comp., *Annual Report of the Naval Station,*

Island of Guam, 1905, pp. 43, 47. General Records of the Department of the Navy, National Archives, Record Group 80. Hereafter records in the National Archives are indicated by the symbol NA, followed by the record group (RG) number.

22. U.S., Department of the Navy, comp., *Annual Report of the Naval Station, Island of Guam, 1908,* p. 23. NA, RG 80.

23. U.S., Department of the Navy, comp., *Annual Report of the Naval Station, Island of Guam, 1909,* pp. 7, 20. NA, RG 80.

24. U.S., Department of the Navy, comp., *Annual Report of the Naval Station, Island of Guam, 1911,* p. 2. NA, RG 80.

25. U.S., Department of the Navy, comp., *Annual Report of the Naval Station, Island of Guam, 1914,* p. 18. NA, RG 80.

26. U.S., Department of the Navy, comp., *Annual Report of the Naval Station, Island of Guam, 1915,* p. 18. NA, RG 80.

27. U.S., Department of the Navy, comp., *Annual Report of the Naval Station, Island of Guam, 1916,* p. 22. NA, RG 80. Imports from Japan for 1917, 1918 and 1919 were $44,780.88, $73,695.09 and $41,259.45 respectively, probably due to American supply problems resulting from the war. However, imports dropped to a record low of $17,279.13 in 1920, indicating that the United States was determined to limit Japanese trade with Guam.

28. Nanyōchō, *Nanyōchō Shisei Jū Nen Shi* [The South Seas Bureau: A Ten-Year History of Its Administration] (Tokyo: Nanyōchō, 1932), p. 12. MT 5, 2,6,32; Reel 522, pp. 3093-3096.

29. Nanyōchō, *op. cit.,* pp. 39-44. Nanyōchō, *Nanyōchō Tōkei Nenkan: Dai Ikkai* [Statistical Yearbook of the South Seas Bureau: Number One] (Tokyo: Nanyōchō, 1933), pp. 36-37.

30. Nanyōchō, *Nanyōchō Tōkei Nenkan: Dai Kyūkai* [Statistical Yearbook of the South Seas Bureau: Number Nine] (Tokyo: Nanyōchō, 1939), p. 2.

31. There are two sources of information about the Nishimura enterprise and related activities: Irie Toraji, *Hōjin Kaigai Hatten Shi* [A History of the Expansion of the Japanese Overseas] (Tokyo: Ida Shoten, 1942), Vol. II, pp. 239-256 and Matsue Haruji, *Nanyō Kaitaku Jū Nen Shi* [Ten Years of Developing the South Seas] (Tokyo: Nanyō Kōhatsu Kabushiki Kaisha, 1932), pp. 20-44.

32. Hugh Borton, *Japan's Modern Century* (New York: Ronald Press Company, 1955), p. 273.

33. Matsue, p. 30.

34. For an account of this company see Matsue, pp. 38-44.

35. Matsue, pp. 45-52.

36. Yanaihara Tadao, *Nanyō Guntō no Kenkyū* [A Study of the South Seas Archipelago] (Tokyo: Iwanami Shoten, 1935), pp. 90-91. Matsue, pp. 65-70.

37. For the relationship of these four companies in the late 1930s see Nanyō Keizai Kenkyūjō, *Nanyō Kankei Kaisha Yōran* [A General Survey of Companies Connected with the South Seas] (Tokyo: Nanyō Keizai Kenkyūjō, 1939), pp. 32, 102, 123, and 144.

BIBLIOGRAPHY

Borton, Hugh. *Japan's Modern Century*. New York: Ronald Press, 1970, rev. ed.
Chi, Madeleine. *China Diplomacy, 1914–1918*. Cambridge: Harvard University Press, 1970.
Duus, Peter. *Party Rivalry and Political Change in Taishō Japan*. Cambridge: Harvard University Press, 1968.
Gō Takashi. *Nanyō Bōeki Go Jū Nen Shi* [Fifty Years of Commerce in the South Seas]. Tokyo: Nanyō Bōeki Kabushiki Kaisha, 1942.
Irie Toraji. *Hōjin Kaigai Hatten Shi* [A History of the Expansion of the Japanese Overseas]. Tokyo: Ida Shoten, 1942. Vol. II.
———. *Meiji Nanshin Shikō* [A Short History of Southward Expansion in the Meiji Era]. Tokyo: Iwanami Shoten, 1943.
Matsue Harutsugu. *Nanyō Kaitaku Jū Nen Shi* [Ten Years of Developing the South Seas]. Tokyo: Nanyō Kōhatsu Kabushiki Kaisha, 1932.
Nanyōchō. *Nanyōchō Tōkei Nenkan: Dai Ikkai* [Statistical Yearbook of the South Seas Bureau: Number One]. Tokyo: Nanyōchō, 1933.
———. *Nanyōchō Tōkei Nenkan: Dai Kyūkai* [Statistical Yearbook of the South Seas Bureau: Number Nine]. Tokyo: Nanyōchō, 1939.
———. *Nanyōchō Shisei Jū Nen Shi* [The South Seas Bureau: A Ten-Year History of Its Administration]. Tokyo: Nanyōchō, 1932.
Nanyō Keizai Kenkyūjō. *Nanyō Shiryō* [Historical Materials on the South Seas]. Tokyo: Nanyō Keizai Kenkyūjō, 1944. No. 473.
———. *Nanyō Kankei Kaisha Yōran* [A General Survey of Companies Connected with the South Seas]. Tokyo: Nanyō Keizai Kenkyūjō, 1939.
Office of the Chief of Naval Operations, comp., *Civil Affairs Handbook: Mandated Marianas*. Washington: Navy Department, 1944.
Office of the Chief of Naval Operations, comp., *Civil Affairs Handbook: West Caroline Islands*. Washington: Navy Department, 1944.
Oka Seishi. *Yorioka Shōzō Den* [The Life of Yorioka Shōzō]. Kobe: Nissa Shokai, Ltd., 1936.
Sumiya Tetsuji. *Nihon Keizai Gakushi* [Studies on Japan's Economy]. Tokyo: Mineruva Shobo, 1967, rev. ed.
Takumu Daijin, Kanbō Bunshoka. *Takumushō Tōkei Gaiyō* [A Statistical Summary of the Department of Overseas Affairs]. Tokyo: Takumushō, 1931.
Takumusho, Takumukyoku. *Kaigai Takushoku Jigyō Chōsa Shiryō Dai San Jū Siti Shū: Sarawakku Ōkoku Jijō* [Materials on the Investigation of Enterprises Overseas-Number 37: The Kingdom of Sarawak]. Tokyo: Takumusho, 1938.
U.S., Department of the Navy, comp. *Annual Report of the Naval Station, Island of Guam*. General Records of the Department of the Navy, National Archives, Record Group 80.
Uyehara, Cecil H., ed. *Checklist of Archives in the Japanese Ministry of Foreign Affairs, Tokyo, Japan, 1868–1945, microfilmed for the Library of Congress, 1949–1951*. Washington: Library of Congress, 1954.
Yanaihara Tadao. *Nanyō Guntō no Kenkyū* [A Study of the South Seas Archipelago]. Tokyo: Iwanami Shoten, 1935.

Part Two

Historical Essays:
Mainland North America

Introduction

The Japanese immigration to mainland America and Canada developed more widely varied forms than did the early migration to Hawaii. Many Japanese immigrants came to the United States singly or as individuals with relatives and friends already in America. A few came as students, but exhausted their financial resources. Some were recruited by immigration companies at the specific request of American and Canadian industrialists and later moved into independent activities. Others first went to Hawaii and subsequently decided to reemigrate to the continent. Still others arrived as crew members of ships and were permitted to remain ashore between voyages. Some of those became permanent residents. Indeed, a number of the Issei came as crew members of American warships and stayed in this country when their enlistment term expired.

Regardless of how they came, Japanese immigrants in the Western states encountered varying degrees of discrimination and overt hostility instigated by anti-Oriental organizations. These states had a tradition of discriminating against the Chinese. In that racist climate, it was easy for the anti-Oriental groups to try to treat the Japanese in the same manner as the Chinese. The Issei had to make their way in the face of relentless and pervasive hostility, which Roger Daniels describes in the following essay. It is a striking commentary on the irrationality of racism that the anti-Japanese movements readily persuaded the majority of the West Coast voters to oppose the Japanese immigrants, despite the significant contributions they made to the economic well-being of the Western states.

In examining the anti-Japanese movements, the actual number of immigrants should be kept in mind. The Japanese have always been a small minority. In 1910, the total in all the continental United States was only 72,000, including 41,000 in California. At that time, approximately 13,360,000 foreign-born persons, mostly European immigrants, were living in the United States. In 1920, there were 110,000 "Japanese," including 72,000 in California. Of that total, 27 percent were American-born citizens. In comparison, there were over 14 million foreign-born people, mostly European immigrants, residing in this country. In 1940, there were 127,000 ethnic Japanese (including 94,000 in California) in mainland America, of whom 63 percent were American-born citizens. The foreign-born population (mostly of European origin) then was almost 11.7 million.

The more thoughtful post-World War II publications have helped interested readers better understand the contributions which Japanese immigrants and their American and Canadian descendants have made to the United States and Canada. They have also begun to explain some of the causes and consequences of the anti-Japanese movements and the broader domestic and international implications of American and Canadian racist traditions. More research is obviously needed on the interrelations between the racial attitudes and practices of the United States, especially of the Western states, and those of other American hemisphere countries. For example, the role of the American government in the 1942 evacuation of Canadians and Latin Americans of Japanese ancestry should be studied. One obvious research topic is a follow-up to Professor Edward N. Barnhart's 1962 paper on the expulsion and internment of Japanese Peruvians as a part of the American domestic evacuation of Japanese Americans.

In the second essay in this section, Howard Sugimoto reviews the Vancouver riots of 1907 and the ensuing national and international repercussions. The immediate stimulus for the riots was the simultaneous arrival of a number of groups of Japanese, including Japanese en route to the United States, returning Japanese Canadian residents who had gone to Japan on a visit, Hawaiian Issei who decided to reemigrate to Canada, and laborers recruited by an immigration company under a contract with a large Canadian firm. Only the last two groups added to the small number of Japanese in Canada. The situation in British Columbia affected Canada, Great Britain, the Commonwealth, and the United States. The leaders of American anti-Oriental and labor organizations actively intervened to encourage and accentuate the racist concerns of the Canadian movements. Some Canadian politicians benefited from the anti-Japanese campaigns, as did many American political leaders, among them a number of alleged advocates of American democratic traditions.

Post-World War II studies on the domestic aspects of the 1942-1945 evacuation and relocation of the Issei and Japanese Americans clarify why this action is now regarded as one of America's "worst blunders" in World War II. The studies concentrate on the background and consequences of the evacuation, its administrative processes, and the evacuees themselves. Aside from occasional personal reminiscences, less information is available on the individuals and organizations sympathetic to the Japanese Americans and their civil rights. In the face of misunderstanding and hostility, these friends defended the loyalty of the Japanese Americans, sought to report accurately on the events, gave vital personal assistance to the evacuees, and worked valiantly for their return to the larger society. These unsung friends of democracy were of widely varied backgrounds and they contributed in diverse ways. Each was unique, but many shared the common spirit richly exemplified by Esther B. Rhoads, a former teacher in the Friends School of Tokyo and later a member of the American Friends Service Committee. In the third essay in this section, she discusses the crucial events from the perspective of an involved and dedicated person who did outstanding work behind the scenes to help mitigate the moral damage of the evacuation and keep alive the faith of the evacuees and indeed of this country in its professed ideals.

Japanese Immigrants on a Western Frontier: The Issei in California, 1890-1940

ROGER DANIELS

The immigration of Japanese[1] to the United States falls conveniently into three periods:
1. 1890–1924—the initial immigration
2. 1924–1952—the period of exclusion
3. 1952–present—the period of renewed immigration.

This essay deliberately ignores that periodization since it is concerned with the social history of the first generation of Japanese within the United States rather than with the ebb and flow of trans-Pacific migration.

The hostility that the Issei pioneers of the first generation encountered is well known and need only be summarized here. They inherited the West Coast prejudice against the Chinese and almost coincident with their initial arrival were assailed with verbal and physical indignities by the populace and subjected to legislative and judicial discrimination by local, state and federal governments. Anti-Japanese hooliganism in the early years of this century was a prelude to the infamous San Francisco School Board Affair involving the attempt to segregate ninety-three Japanese pupils. President Theodore Roosevelt quashed that attempt through the extra-legal use of presidential power and then caused the ill-fated Gentlemen's Agreement to be negotiated with Japan during 1907–08. Under this agreement the Japanese government agreed to limit the immigration of its laborers to the United States. Concurrently, each biennial session of the California legislature considered and discussed anti-Japanese bills in an inflammatory manner. Few were passed. The most significant of these were the Alien Land Acts of 1913 and 1920, which were designed so that they affected only Asians. These laws sought, without success, to drive Issei farmers off their lands. In 1922 the U.S. Supreme Court confirmed the special status of Japanese (and other Asians) as "aliens ineligible to citizenship." In 1924 the U.S. Congress brought the first period of Japanese immigration to an end by striking from the immigration act of that year a provision which would have allocated a token quota of 100 immigrants a year to Japan, and instead, barred Japanese completely. (All other Asians, save Filipinos who were "American nationals," had been barred by previous acts.)[2]

These measures were accompanied by (and in part made possible by) massive and persistent doses of anti-Japanese propaganda. Much of this propaganda was of the "Yellow Peril" variety, which, in its characteristic American form, envisaged Japanese troops landing in California and marching east.[3] In addition to "fright" literature, there were a number of war scares, real and imagined. By the 1920s Japan was well established in the public and military mind as America's most probable enemy.[4]

This anti-Japanese heritage was so strong and pervasive that, when war did come in December, 1941, most Americans were convinced, despite a lack of any real evidence, that Japanese resident in the United States were all potential spies and saboteurs. No distinction was made between the alien Issei and their native-born (and therefore United States citizen) children, the Nisei. Some, in fact, argued that the citizen generation posed an even greater threat than the alien. As Lieutenant General John L. De Witt, the officer in charge of the West Coast defenses put it, "a Jap is a Jap." In more polite language the eminent columnist Walter Lippmann denied the existence of constitutional rights for Japanese of either generation resident on the Pacific Coast, because, in his words, it was a "battlefield," and constitutional rights could not survive on a battlefield. Both the general and the pundit advocated the same course: the establishment of concentration camps for the West Coast Japanese. Ten such camps were established in the interior of the United States in 1942. About two-thirds of those incarcerated in what the government euphemistically called "relocation centers" were Nisei and thus native-born citizens of the United States.

The establishment of these camps and the detention in them of more than 110,000 human beings was hailed during the war by a broad consensus ranging from the Communist Party on the left to the most racist elements in American life on the right. Even more important, similar views were held by the overwhelming majority of what is usually called the "establishment" in the center.

That view prevails no longer. The establishment of these camps is now regarded as "our worst wartime mistake."[5] The Japanese Americans, once despised even more than Negroes, are now hailed by some as "our model minority."[6] The general public, according to the respected Gallup Poll, once perceived Japanese as innately "treacherous," "sly," "cruel" and "warlike." Fifteen years after the war it found them "hard-working," "artistic," "intelligent" and "progressive."[7]

This new, positive American image of the Japanese is, of course, due to many factors: the changing world situation, the favorable American experiences in and with post-war Japan, and the recent trend toward ethnic egalitarianism all have to be taken into account. Some of the change, however, must be due to the interaction between Japanese immigrants, their descendants, and the rest of the population. The Issei —when they are not simply ignored—are often treated as ciphers on whom history acted, as victims of rather than participants in events. Victims, certainly, most mainland Issei became, but they were also pioneers, and it is that pioneering aspect of the Issei experience which will be treated here.

*   *   *

The entry of Japanese into the United States was relatively small. In the year of heaviest immigration, 1907, some 30,000 came; total immigration into the United States that year was 1.25 million. Up to 1940, a quarter of a million Japanese were recorded as entering the continental United States. But when students, emigrants, and multiple entries by individuals are taken into account, it becomes apparent that fewer than 200,000 persons were involved. During the same period, 1890–1940, immigration from all sources to the United States was on the order of 25 million. Considering the relative size of the Japanese immigration the amount of controversy it generated is almost ludicrous.

Despite a thriving but not exceptional birth rate, the total Japanese population was always tiny. The highest incidence of Japanese in the population, including both immigrant and native born, was two and one tenth percent (.021) of the population of California and one tenth of one percent (.001) of the population of the continental United States.[8] If they had been spread evenly throughout the United States—as United States Secretary of State William Jennings Bryan and President Franklin Delano Roosevelt each proposed—there would have been fewer than fifty Japanese in each American county.[9]

While it is useful for perspective to get the figures right, questions of racial antagonism, since they are largely arational if not irrational, cannot be made a mere matter of numbers. Apart from the phenomenon that sociologists call "high social visibility"—people who appear different stand out and thus seem to be more numerous than they really are —the Japanese in the United States were concentrated in a relatively few geographical areas and in an even narrower range of occupations.

The overwhelming majority of the Issei and their children settled in California; the censuses of 1910, 1920, 1930 and 1940 showed that 57 percent, 65 percent, 70 percent and almost 75 percent of all mainland

Japanese lived in the Golden State. Within the state they were also concentrated. In 1920 more than half were in just six counties, while forty-two other counties had only 10 percent of the total. And, of course, even within the areas of highest Japanese population the immigrants and their families tended to cluster into enclaves in both town and country: a "Little Tokyo" or "Little Osaka" in the larger cities, a less desirable street or two in the smaller towns, and little "colonies" of Japanese farms or ranches in the countryside. Had they not so clustered by choice, de facto segregation and restrictive covenants would have forced them to do so.

This clustering into enclaves and turning areas of American cities into linguistic and cultural extensions of the mother country is typical of patterns of immigration to America from most non-English-speaking lands. The Issei pioneers, in many ways, paralleled the contemporary experience of their European counterparts elsewhere in the nation. The Italians of New York and San Francisco, the Poles of Buffalo and Hamtrammack, the Czechs of Chicago, to name just a few, all tended to cluster into highly visible and often notorious sections. They, too, met resistance, disparagement, and discrimination. The Japanese experience must not be thought of as an experience somehow discrete from the basic patterns of immigration. The Issei, were, first of all, immigrants and most of the generalizations that apply to other immigrants of the same era apply to them and other Asians.[10]

But, if the Issei conform to certain general characteristics common to most immigrants and thus are less "special" than most historians of immigration have tended to assume, there are, nevertheless, three things, apart from race and the complications stemming from race, which set them somewhat apart: their relation to their government at home, the area in which they settled, and the economic activities which they pursued.

While relations between governments and their subjects and citizens who emigrated to America have been quite varied depending upon the countries, the emigrants and the particular situation, it is almost axiomatic that the original governments have tended to have little interest in their departed people. Exceptions have to be made for particularly atrocious behavior, such as the lynchings of Italians in New Orleans and the massacre of Chinese in Rock Springs, Wyoming, which stirred the Italian and Chinese governments to file protests and claim indemnities, and for times of war when governments have tried to get their nationals and ex-nationals to return to fight for the fatherland. Rather than concerning themselves with the welfare of their expatriates, some governments actually subsidized emigration.

The Japanese government demonstrated an early and persistent concern for her emigrants, but for reasons not necessarily connected with their welfare. Hilary Conroy has described the Japanese government's insistence on certain minimum standards of living and working conditions for Japanese laborers who went, under contract, to work on sugar plantations in the Kingdom of Hawaii. He concludes that "her ever jealous watch against discriminatory treatment abroad" was chiefly motivated by the desire to protect "her own prestige as a nation."[11] The same attitudes, not surprisingly, caused the Japanese government to take what seems like an inordinate interest in the lives of the Issei in America.

As early as 1891, when there were perhaps 3,000 Issei in the whole country, Consul Sutemi Chinda, reporting to the Foreign Ministry about some Japanese prostitutes in San Francisco, bewailed the "deplorable situation that their being the object of public scandals must cause unnecessary hardships in our endeavour to maintain the reputation of the Japanese as a whole." Such scandals, he felt, would "indeed impair Japan's national honor." Apart from that, which was dire enough in itself, it appeared to Chinda that "the ignominious conduct of Japanese prostitutes [and pimps] will, if not inhibited, be used, sooner or later, as a pretext for attacking the Japanese residents by those who openly advocate the exclusion of the Oriental race from the country."[12]

In a later dispatch the far-sighted Chinda assured his superiors in Tokyo that "an unrestricted mass-migration of lower class Japanese . . . will, without doubt, arouse and aggravate" trade union opposition to the Japanese and provide opportunities for unscrupulous politicians looking for an issue to exploit. The Japanese consul felt that San Francisco, the city to which he was posted, provided a key contact point between Orient and Occident and that there the Japanese should try "to uphold our national glory and prestige." The Chinese, he pointed out, "are now detested and discriminated against wherever they migrate simply because they failed to grasp the seriousness of the situation at the outset. Their failure must be a lesson to us Japanese." He urged his government "to adopt appropriate measures so as to prevent the departure of these undesirable Japanese to this country in the future."[13]

Later in 1891, Chinda sent an investigator, Yoshiro Fujita, up to the Pacific Northwest to investigate conditions prevailing among Japanese there. He discovered widely varying circumstances. In Seattle, Washington, for example, he found all but ten of the 250 Japanese residents deeply involved in illegal, but tolerated, prostitution and gambling. In neighboring Tacoma, however, he reported happily that all the Japanese residents were "enterprising young men" in legitimate occupations.[14] If

Chinda and Fujita are representative of the official Japanese view—and I think that they are—it is clear that they were applying a very rigid yardstick to Japanese abroad, expecting them to conform to standards considerably higher than those prevalent in either Japan or the western United States, still a relatively "wide open" frontier area in which prostitution, gambling and loose living were endemic.

Japanese consular personnel thus acted quite differently than the officials of other nations. While many European countries consciously "exported" their less desirable population and tried to keep the better sort at home, Japanese policy, for reasons of prestige, was to be just the opposite. Its government was urged, first by its own officials and then by the United States government, to limit emigrants to the better sort. The Japanese government, in general, adopted such a policy, and, in addition, took a great deal of trouble to see that its emigrants in America behaved "properly."

That even the better sort of Japanese—and it was largely they who came—created so much animosity between the two nations and drew so much antagonism to their own persons must have been particularly galling to Japanese officialdom. Despite the constant counseling regarding proper behavior provided the immigrants by both Japanese officials and the semi-official Japanese Association of America (which the government encouraged and subsidized), the enmity of most of California's population against the Issei steadily increased. In fact, the more the immigrant population prospered the more it was despised. In the nineteenth century attacks against the Chinese had been justified partly on the grounds that they brought no women and children with them and had no families. In the twentieth century Japanese were attacked for bringing women with them and having families. As the hostility and the attacks increased, the government of Japan, directly and indirectly, did more and more for its nationals.[15] Certainly in the entire history of immigration to the United States no other nation evinced so much and so lasting a concern for its departed countrymen.

This concern was particularly appropriate, since the Issei, along with other Asians, were aliens ineligible for citizenship. In addition, American government, particularly at the state and local level, was openly and implacably hostile to them. They were denied, by statute and constitutional law the right to public employment, the right to practice certain professions and to enter certain occupations. Extralegally they were often denied effective police protection and their complaints against Caucasians were often ignored by local officials.

The Japanese government provided both behavioral and legal advice. The Issei were exhorted to dress in the western fashion, not to carouse in public, and, in general, to make as low a social profile as possible. Most of the legal advice came through competent local attorneys whose services were, when necessary, subsidized through intermediaries. These lawyers became specialists in federal immigration law and the various laws and ordinances aimed at Asians, especially the alien land laws. In a manual which two of these attorneys prepared, the Issei were advised:

> to obey carefully all the laws of the land of their adoption and particularly those state statutes which deny to them the right of ownership of real property, especially such property as is used for real estate.[16]

In practice, however, the function of these attorneys was to help the Issei circumvent the spirit if not the letter of these laws.

In addition to fostering attitudes and institutions which tended to Americanize the Issei and their children, the government of Japan also encouraged and abetted the perpetuation of their native culture through Japanese language schools, newspapers and other institutions typical of most first-generation immigrants. This continued identification with their homeland—while far from unique—was often used as part of the nativist argument against the Japanese. United States Senator James D. Phelan, a Roman Catholic, a Democrat and a leading Japanophobe, liked to argue that the real aim of the language schools was to "delay, if not thwart" the process of Americanization. He also insisted that:

> It is well known that the schools which the Japanese maintain in America teach also Japanese imperialism, the divinity of the Mikado and the allegiance due him by all Nipponese at home and abroad. So really, the Japanese position today is to hold all its subjects in foreign lands to allegiance; to fight, if necessary, for the Mikado, and spurn the hand that feeds them; to economically drain a generous land and leave it open to its enemy. More than that, if its enemy be Japan, to not only "give aid and comfort to the enemy"—a treasonable offense everywhere—but to take up arms in his behalf.[17]

Apart from the imaginary dangers cited by Phelan and others, there was the real and growing threat of Japanese expansion into East Asia. The Japanese thus became international villains and much of the hostility generated by Japan's imperialistic foreign policy was transferred to her nationals and their descendants in the United States. At the same time continued mistreatment of Japanese in the United States did much to discredit democracy in Japan. As George F. Kennan has pointed out, the "long and unhappy story" of U.S.-Japanese relations in the first four decades of this century was continually exacerbated "by our immigration policies and the treatment of people of Japanese lineage in this country."[18]

Just as the land of their origin continued to exercise one set of influences upon their lives, the Issei were also significantly affected by the special characteristics of the American West, where almost all of them settled. Most significantly, perhaps, the West was, within the frame of reference of the American economy, an underdeveloped region. As an early Japanese minister to the United States, Munemitsu Mutsu, reported to Tokyo in 1888:

> These states on the Pacific Coast of the United States, are, generally speaking, very vast in their territorial extent and sparsely populated. But they have developed very rapidly in recent years. Hence, even in domestic and menial labor fields, a demand for workers far exceeds the supply, and these menial jobs pay very well.[19]

This is an almost classic description of the basic attraction to America —what historians of immigration call the "pull" of the host country, as opposed to the "push" or expelling forces existing within the homeland. This economic pull has been, over the years, the major attractive force on immigrants to the United States, regardless of nationality. Apart from the fact that economic opportunity was greater in the West than in the country at large, there were other significant regional characteristics which had grave consequences for the Issei and their children.

Unlike other frontier regions in the United States, which were, at one time or another, in Frederick Jackson Turner's phrase, "the hither edge of civilization," the Pacific Coast was (or considered itself) a frontier against outside intrusion, a racial frontier against what one popular writer of the 1920s styled "the rising tide of color against White world-supremacy."[20] The West Coast had its own variant of that racism which has been a central theme of American history since the seventeenth century.[21] Before significant numbers of Japanese arrived, Yankee Californians had demonstrated virulent hostility toward three different ethnic groups: the aboriginal Indians, the native Mexicans (or Californios) and other Latins, and Chinese. The anti-Chinese precedent, as Consul Chinda noted, was the single most important factor in the development of organized prejudice against the Issei. It should be remembered, however, that this kind of hostility flourished within a generally racist climate of opinion whose basic assumption was that the United States was a white man's country.

Despite their chronological and geographical propinquity, the two major streams of immigration from Asia were quite different. The Chinese and Japanese did come from the same part of the world, had (to most Occidental eyes at least) a common physical appearance, and each entered the labor force at the very bottom. But the political, economic and demographic aspects of Chinese and Japanese immigration were dissimilar.

Politically, Japan was a rising and respected major power while China was weak and relatively helpless, a victim rather than a predator among nations. The international political "clout" of Japan forestalled discriminatory federal legislation for some time, and even when it did pass it was couched in somewhat diplomatic terms. Opponents of Japanese immigration long envisaged and agitated for a Japanese Exclusion Act modeled on the Chinese Exclusion Act of 1882. When exclusion was enacted in 1924, as part of the immigration act of that year, the Japanese were not mentioned but were excluded by the "aliens ineligible to citizenship" formula. Had Japan not been a major power, a Japanese Exclusion Act probably would have passed Congress before the election of 1908.

The basic demographic difference was the much greater sexual imbalance among the Chinese. California census figures show that just prior to the end of Chinese immigration (1880), males outnumbered females by almost twenty to one. The comparable census figures for Japanese (1920), show men outnumbering women by fewer than two to one. The Chinese population, therefore, declined steadily for almost half a century after immigration ceased, while Japanese numbers continued to grow.

The Chinese, after their early employment in mines, railroad construction and various forms of manufacturing, were soon driven from these fields by trade union opposition.[22] Chinese then tended to find either menial employment—the Chinese ranch cook is almost ubiquitous in "western" fiction—or become proprietors of small enterprises, particularly restaurants and laundries. The Japanese, conversely, started in domestic service and as stoop laborers, becoming in the latter capacity members of the agricultural proletariat that in much of the West outnumbered the industrial. When Issei were able to advance economically, they tended to become agricultural or horticultural proprietors or went into immigrant community-oriented businesses.

After the 1870s, the Chinese were more widely dispersed with every census. The Japanese tended, until they were forcibly uprooted in 1942, to cluster. San Francisco was—and remains—the major continental center of Chinese population. The Japanese were at first also most numerous in the Bay City, but early in the twentieth century Los Angeles became, and remains, the major cluster area.

But, despite their differences, the Chinese immigrants of the mid-nineteenth century and the Japanese immigrants of the early twentieth were attacked by exactly the same forces—the labor movement and the politicians who depended upon labor for their support. Labor's opposition to the Chinese, however deplorable it may have been, was at least based upon tangible economic grievances. The presence of relatively large numbers of Chinese male laborers in California lowered wage rates and if their immigration had continued unabated, wage rates probably would have been lowered even further. At the height of the anti-Chinese agitation non-union Chinese were employed in significant numbers in some industries that had a relatively high degree of unionization throughout the nation, notably cigar making and shoe manufacturing.

The Japanese almost never entered into competition with organized labor[23] and were never numerous enough vis-a-vis the labor force to affect wage rates significantly. Yet organized labor and its political allies launched the anti-Japanese movement and even after the Gentlemen's Agreement of 1907-08 effectively inhibited the migration of laborers, labor continued to oppose the Japanese with almost the fervor it had shown against the Chinese. This seeming anomaly is readily explainable. West Coast laboring men had an inherited prejudice against immigrants from Asia that continued long after the original economic grievances against them had disappeared.

In addition to their other woes, Asian immigrants in the United States opposed one another, covertly and overtly. Although Chinese and Japanese are often lumped together as Orientals, their communities in the United States have been discrete. Neither group has married much outside itself, but members of both groups are more likely to marry non-Asians than to inter-marry. At the turn of the century, in what may have been the first political demonstration by Japanese in America, delegates to an anti-Chinese convention in San Francisco were advised by leaflet and oratory that while it was quite proper to exclude Chinese, Japanese were different and should not be shut out. In the 1920s, a Japanese newspaper editor in Hawaii could attack incoming Filipinos as "cheap Oriental labor."[24] And, to cite a final example of inter-group hostility, just after Pearl Harbor Chinese often sported buttons which proclaimed, "I'M NO JAP," or "I'M CHINESE—I HATE JAPS TOO."

But the accomplishments of the Issei are much more important than what was done to them. The Issei were pioneers, pioneers in a pioneering region, pioneers whose eventual achievement is archetypically American, paradoxical as that may seem in view of their reputed "alienness" from the mainstream of the American tradition.[25] When one examines the Issei accomplishment, it turns out to be a minor variant of the American dream, if that rather nebulous entity is defined as hard work, modest aspirations, upward social mobility, a desire for education, good citizenship, and patriotism.

Most of the Issei, if not actually penniless, came to America in straitened circumstances. George Shima, the "potato king" of California who became the first Issei "millionaire," had about $1,000 when he came, but he was an exception. By the eve of World War II most Issei were mildly prosperous members of the lower middle class. By that time Issei families owned farms and businesses to a much greater degree than did the general population. Their industry was proverbial: to their admirers, their detractors, and their overworked and underpaid offspring.

The most easily measurable index of the Issei achievement is in agriculture. Rather than displacing existing farmers, as anti-Japanese propaganda alleged, Issei farmers more often opened up new lands with their labor-intensive, high-yield style of agriculture, as opposed to the resource-intensive agriculture characteristic of American farming. In addition, they introduced new commercial crops.

The growth in immigrant entrepreneurship can be seen in the data on land ownership and leasing in California. In 1900 Japanese farmers controlled some 4,500 acres; by 1919 they controlled more than 450,000 acres. Although this latter figure represents only about one percent of the land under cultivation in the state, the market value of the crops produced on that land was just over ten percent of the dollar volume of California agriculture. The disparity between the last two percentages is due to the type of crops the Issei raised—strawberries, asparagus, and flowers, to name a few.

Considered as a sector of California agriculture, the Japanese farmers supplemented rather than competed with other California producers. It is clear that the Japanese did not "spurn the hand that feeds them" as exclusionists like Phelan claimed, but rather, to mix the metaphor, were feeding the hand that slapped them. It was, in part, Japanese food production that made California's dramatic population growth possible: the state grew from 1.5 million in 1900 to 3.4 million in 1920 and 6.9 million in 1940.

But perhaps the most meaningful index to the Issei achievement is the record of their offspring, most of whom have yet to reach the zenith of their careers. By 1960, fewer than one Japanese in three was still involved in agriculture and a larger number—more than 38 percent—were in professional, technical and white-collar fields. The 1970 census figures will undoubtedly reveal an even more impressive shift in occupation as more and more of the surviving Issei and older Nisei leave the labor force and the younger and better-educated Nisei and Sansei enter it. By 1960 the educational achievements of California's Japanese sur-

passed that of the general population despite an influx of poorly educated war brides and newly-admissible elder relatives of the Issei.
About four-fifths of the Japanese population over fourteen years of age
completed high school (80.5 percent of males, 75.6 percent of females).
The figures show a "median school years completed" of 12.4 for Japanese males and 12.3 for Japanese females, while the comparable figures
for the total population were 11.7 and 12.0 respectively.[26]

But quantitative data, however useful, tell us nothing of the quality
of the lives that the Issei lived. Even before the trauma of World War
II and the attendant concentration camps—which fall beyond the scope
of this essay—the life of the immigrants from Japan must have been,
in most ways, even more schizoid and ambivalent than that of most
other contemporary immigrants.[27] One might expect, therefore, to find
marked examples of social pathology within the Japanese American
community: high crime rate, frequent juvenile delinquency, and an
inordinate amount of mental illness. But such is not the case. Japanese
American crime, delinquency and mental illness rates have remained a
minor fraction of those for comparable population groups, whether in
America or Japan.[28] Put more positively, the Issei and their descendants
have been hard-working, law-abiding citizens. All the factors responsible for this rather startling behavior pattern are not readily apparent but
there must be some relationship between the values that the Issei incul-
cated into their children and the resultant behavior.

The Issei are now rapidly passing from the scene, but their heritage
will persist. It is important to appreciate and understand that heritage,
but it is almost equally important not to overstate it or to use it as an
analogy for other minority groups.[29] The Issei were a small, self-confi-
dent group entering a fertile region with a rapidly expanding population. They came with almost all the skills and technological know-how
necessary to reach the bottom rungs of the ladder of success. They
brought with them the ethnic pride of a successfully emerging nation
about to assume the leadership of a continent. They came at a unique
moment in the history of their two countries: their experience cannot
be repeated.

NOTES

Source Materials and Suggestions for Future Research

The most valuable kinds of materials for the study of Japanese Americans of
the Issei generation are community newspapers, letters, diaries and business

papers. Unfortunately, in the period between Pearl Harbor and the evacuation of the West Coast Japanese, many of these materials were deliberately destroyed, especially those written in what was then an enemy language. In some cases the files of Japanese American newspapers were "donated" to scrap paper drives by Caucasian patriots. The greatest single collection of surviving materials of this type is in the Japanese American Research Project at the University of California, Los Angeles, which is also systematically interviewing survivors on an unprecedented scale. The project has an ambitious publication program. When its major publications appear and its materials are fully available to scholars not associated with the project it will be possible, in a statistical sense at least, to be much more precise about the Issei generation.

Because they were an acknowledged "problem" the West Coast Japanese received special attention from contemporary scholars and government experts and we know much more about them than about coeval ethnic groups like the Mexican Americans. The published materials of the United States Immigration Commission, as well as its files in the National Archives, contain a wealth of statistical data, as do the files of certain California agencies and commissions, particularly the State Board of Control and the Commission on Immigration and Housing.

There are also illuminating materials in the papers of anti-Japanese politicians, including some correspondence with Japanese American community leaders. The papers of Hiram W. Johnson III, James D. Phelan and Chester H. Rowell, all in the Bancroft Library, and the papers of Franklin Hichborn, at the University of California, Los Angeles, are most significant.

More sympathetic materials may be found in the papers of leading educators; outstanding in this regard are the President's Files of the University of California, in the University Archives at the Bancroft Library, and the papers of David Starr Jordan at Stanford. Also in the former are a few copies of Japanese American student publications dating from the mid-1930s. In the past few years the University of Washington and the University of Arizona have been collecting Japanese American materials, some of which cover the pre-war period.

Various aspects of the Japanese "problem" have received academic scrutiny in almost every West Coast educational institution. Literally scores of unpublished theses and dissertations shed light on the Issei experience: most significant are those at Berkeley, the University of Southern California, and the University of Washington. For a full but not complete listing see William Wong Lum, compiler, *Asians in America: A Bibliography of Master's Theses and Doctoral Dissertations,* published by the Asian American Research Project of the University of California, Davis (Davis, California, March, 1970). The published literature is extensive and no attempt to list it will be made here. The fullest bibliographies appear in Roger Daniels, *The Politics of Prejudice: The Anti-Japanese Movement in California and the Struggle for Japanese Exclusion* (Berkeley and Los Angeles, 1962), in William Petersen, *Japanese Americans: Oppression and Success* (New York, 1971), and in John Modell, "The Japanese in Los Angeles: A Study in Growth and Accommodation, 1900–1946," unpublished Ph.D. dissertation, Columbia University, 1969.

Although the wartime evacuation falls outside the chronological scope of this essay, materials assembled during and after the war shed light on the pre-war period. The most significant collections are those of the Japanese American Evacuation and Resettlement Project in the Bancroft Library, and the War Relocation Authority papers in the National Archives (some of these materials are in the Bancroft Library, the University of California, Los Angeles library and at the University of Arizona). Some materials are in the papers of the Secretary of War, the Provost Marshal General and the Western Defense Command, Record Groups 107, 389 and 394 in the National Archives. There are also a few items in the Conrad-Duveneck Collection, Hoover Institution Archives, and the John Anson Ford papers, Huntington Library.

From these and other materials, for example, city and county records, it should be possible in the near future to advance our knowledge of the development and growth of the Japanese American community significantly. We need sophisticated studies, like John Modell's on Los Angeles, for San Francisco, Seattle and other urban centers of Japanese American population. An equally important area of study is the development of rural Japanese American communities.

Other worthwhile and virtually untouched topics need to be explored. There is the whole question of relations between subordinate minority groups—between Japanese and Chinese, Filipinos, Mexican Americans, and blacks. Some sociologists, following Gunnar Myrdal who has talked about an essentially ethnic American "under class," have assumed the existence of a kind of united front of the dispossessed. In fact, the relations between disadvantaged ethnic groups have been characterized by conflict.

Studies of the Japanese Americans deal almost exclusively with a majority within the minority: for the Issei generation this meant the various Japanese Associations; for the Nisei generation, the Japanese American Citizens League. In actuality the Japanese American community was never as united as the literature indicates. Both generations had a significant if miniscule left wing, which has been almost completely ignored. Also the various "pro-Japanese" activities of members of both generations, particularly after the "China incident" began, have been noted but never investigated by anyone more scholarly than the investigators employed by the House Committee on Un-American Activities.

There is also significant work to be done in Japan. Practically nothing has been written about Issei and Nisei who returned to Japan and what happened to them there. A sophisticated treatment of this topic, on the order of Theodore Saloutos, *They Remember America* (Berkeley and Los Angeles, 1956), which deals with Greek Americans, would be a contribution of real value to students of both countries. Perhaps equally useful would be comparative studies of Japanese in the American West with their Canadian counterparts and with the distinctly different development in Hawaii.

Japanese American studies are still in their infancy. In the last few years courses in the Asian American experience have been inaugurated in West Coast colleges and universities. Some now just enrolling in these courses may not only accomplish the modest agenda outlined above but raise even more significant questions of their own.

Footnotes

1. The terminology in an essay of this nature can be problematical. My usage will vary. All persons of Japanese ancestry will be called Japanese, regardless of citizenship. Similarly, all Japanese domiciled in the United States will be called Japanese Americans. The special terms, Issei, for the immigrant generation, and Nisei, for their children, will also be used.

2. Documentation for this and other historical material otherwise undocumented here will be found in Roger Daniels, *The Politics of Prejudice: The Anti-Japanese Movement in California and the Struggle for Japanese Exclusion* (Berkeley and Los Angeles: University of California Press, 1962). (An Atheneum paperback is in print.)

3. *Ibid.*, pp. 65-78; for an evaluation of the yellow peril as a worldwide phenomenon, see Heinz Gollwitzer, *Die Gelbe Gefahr* (Gottingen, 1962).

4. For a convenient summary of these relations see William L. Neumann, *America Encounters Japan* (Baltimore: Johns Hopkins, 1963); an interesting contemporary article in view of later events is Franklin D. Roosevelt, "Shall We Trust Japan?", *Asia*, July, 1923.

5. The phrase is Eugene V. Rostow's; for an analysis of the wartime evacuation, see Roger Daniels, *Concentration Camps, USA: Japanese Americans and World War II* (New York: Holt, Rinehart & Winston, 1972).

6. William Petersen, "Success Story, Japanese-American Style," *New York Times Magazine*, January 9, 1966.

7. Gallup Polls reported in Los Angeles *Times*, May 1, 1961.

8. Daniels, *The Politics of Prejudice*, pp. 1-2, 111.

9. For fuller details see Daniels, "William Jennings Bryan and the Japanese," *Southern California Quarterly*, September, 1966, and Daniels, *Concentration Camps, USA*, p. 154.

10. I have made this point at some length in "Westerners from the East: Oriental Immigrants Reappraised," *Pacific Historical Review*, November, 1966. This essay views the matter from a different angle.

11. Hilary Conroy, *The Japanese Frontier in Hawaii, 1868–1898* (Berkeley and Los Angeles: University of California Press, 1953), p. 140.

12. The Japanese diplomatic dispatches cited here were translated by Mr. Yasuo Sakata for Professor Robert Wilson of UCLA. I am indebted to both of them for permission to use their research. This one is Chinda to Aoki, March 10, 1891.

13. Chinda to Aoki, April 25, 1891.

14. Yoshiro Fujita to Chinda, enclosed in Chinda to Hayashi, July 20, 1891.

15. Some of these relationships can be seen in Monica Sone, *Nisei Daughter* (Boston: Little, Brown & Company, 1953), which is perhaps the most useful memoir in English by a Japanese American.

16. Albert H. Elliot and Guy C. Calden, *The Law Affecting Japanese Residing in the State of California* (San Francisco: 1929), p. v. In an interview in 1959 Calden told me that he suspected, but could not prove, that some of his fees were in fact paid by the Government of Japan, although he was never so paid directly.

17. James D. Phelan, *Travel and Comment* (San Francisco: 1923), p. 39.

18. George F. Kennan, *American Diplomacy, 1900–1950* (Chicago: University of Chicago Press, 1951), p. 49.

19. Mutsu to Okuma, ca. May, 1888.

20. Theodore Lothrop Stoddard, *The Rising Tide of Color Against White World-Supremacy* (1920; reprint ed., Westport, Conn.: Negro Universities Press).

21. For a summary of California race relations see Roger Daniels and Harry H. L. Kitano, *American Racism: Exploration of the Nature of Prejudice* (Englewood Cliffs, N.J.: Prentice-Hall, 1970).

22. Ping Chiu, *Chinese Labor in California, 1850–1880: An Economic Study* (Madison, Wisconsin: The State Historical Society of Wisconsin for the Department of History, University of Wisconsin, 1963), contains useful data, but has quite different conclusions about the effect of Chinese labor.

23. John Modell, "Class or Ethnic Solidarity: The Japanese American Company Union," *Pacific Historical Review*, May, 1969.

24. Sister Mary Dorita Clifford, "The Hawaiian Sugar Planter Association and Filipino Exclusion," in Josefa M. Saniel, ed., *The Filipino Exclusion Movement, 1927–1935*, Occasional Papers No. 1, Institute of Asian Studies, University of the Philippines, Quezon City, p. 23.

25. For examples of this view, see Edith Abbot, *Immigration: Select Documents* (1924; reprint ed., New York: Arno), p. ix, and Carl Wittke, *We Who Built America* (1940; reprint ed., Cleveland: Press of Case Western Reserve University), p. 458.

26. A most useful source for statistics is *Californians of Japanese, Chinese, Filipino Ancestry* published by the State of California Fair Employment Practices Commission, 455 Golden Gate Avenue, San Francisco, June, 1965.

27. The classic, if perhaps overstated, account of this trauma is Oscar Handlin, *The Uprooted* (Boston: Little, Brown & Company, 1951).

28. A forthcoming study by Harry H. L. Kitano on Japanese American mental illness will establish some of these matters quantitatively.

29. To cite merely one example of misuse of the Issei analogy, see a story in the Los Angeles *Times*, July 6, 1963, headlined "Nisei Tells Negroes to Better Themselves."

The Vancouver Riots of 1907:
A Canadian Episode

HOWARD H. SUGIMOTO

Immigrants to Canada often risked an unfriendly reception from many of those who had already made their homes there. As late-comers to the new land, Japanese settlers experienced extreme difficulties during periods of violent opposition to their arrival and settlement, but they endured them with philosophical restraint. The Vancouver Anti-Japanese Riots represent only one of the manifestations of the general hostility against immigrants and are therefore in themselves of little moment, except that they afford us an opportunity to study in detail the forces surrounding such violent acts.

The difficulties of the Japanese arose mainly from cultural and racial differences between the immigrants and the residents. The Japanese were not the only new people to face hostility, however, for all those who missed the early phase of immigration—South and East Europeans and Asians—were confronted in varying degrees with problems of adaptation to a society in rapid evolution.

The Asian immigrants, because of the wide gap in their racial and cultural background, as well as the language barrier, found adjustment and communication especially difficult. They were regarded as being unable to make the transition rapidly enough to the new social and political order that was coming into being. The alleged slowness of their adaptation to the accepted living patterns left them vulnerable to attacks as "outsiders" and prevented their effective participation in community and political affairs.

Moreover, in addition to antagonisms inherent in racial and cultural differences, the Asians unconsciously added to their unpopularity by retaining many of their customs and habits, based largely on Confucian or other similar concepts, which stressed cooperation and submission to authority. Often, a deep sense of duty, loyalty, and obligation to employers governed much of their everyday conduct and sometimes led them inadvertently into such acts as strikebreaking and the undermining of wage structures. This tended to alienate many of the established Caucasian workmen, who soon strongly opposed the entry of these immigrants.

Before long, the Japanese found themselves in the midst of a hostile community which sought by every social and political means to thwart their attempt to settle permanently in the Pacific coastal regions. At its worst, the opposition in British Columbia agitated for the complete exclusion of Asians from the province. But the exigencies of international politics did not always permit the Dominion government to carry out regional wishes which might interfere with British Empire commitments.

Because the federal authorities were reluctant to restrict openly Japanese immigration, the exclusionists tried to draw the attention of federal government officials to the mounting opposition to an increasing tempo of "yellow penetration." As a preliminary step toward this end, the Asiatic Exclusion League was formed in Vancouver in the summer of 1907 with the aid and direction of American "exclusionists" of the West Coast states, where anti-Asian organizations had been founded or reestablished during 1905–1906.

Having obtained substantial public support, the League organized a parade and a mass meeting to press for the total exclusion of Asians, particularly the Japanese. Unfortunately, during the evening, some of the more unrestrained elements in the crowd went on an orgy of destruction, first in the Chinese quarter and later in the Japanese section of the city. The Japanese fought the mobs vigorously and finally dispersed them, with some bloodshed. For this reason and also because the demonstration was aimed principally at the Japanese, the disturbance has been generally known as the Vancouver Anti-Japanese Riots.

The day of the riots, Saturday, September 7, 1907 dawned on Vancouver without any suggestion that it was to be a bad one for the city, except that the stifling humidity contributed to a general sense of discomfort and oppressiveness.[1]

A parade and mass meeting were planned by the Vancouver Asiatic Exclusion League as a protest against the continuing flow of Japanese immigration to the western ports of Canada.[2] The league's activities were designed to draw the attention of the federal government to the seriousness of the local sentiment against further Asiatic immigration. The afternoon issue of the Vancouver *Daily World* announced great expectations for the evening. The paper anticipated that "the demonstration will be the biggest ever held in the city" and looked forward to the energetic participation of trade unions, fraternal organizations, veterans' groups, sympathetic citizens, and delegates from nearby New Westminster.

The parade formation left the pre-arranged assembly center at the Cambie Street grounds shortly after seven o'clock in the evening. The parade marshal led the formation of demonstrators, accompanied by three brass bands,[3] west on Georgia Street to Granville, followed this street north to Hastings, and then proceeded east for a mile or more to Westminster Avenue.[4] The destination was City Hall, located on the west side of Westminster, literally a stone's throw to the south of the intersection. The mass meeting was scheduled for nine o'clock.

The carriages carrying officials of the Asiatic Exclusion League, speakers for the evening, and lady sympathizers were at the head of the parade.[5] An estimated 5,000 men followed on foot. Banners appeared at intervals among the marchers warning onlookers that an Asiatic influx endangered the white man's security.[6] An effigy of Lieutenant Governor Dunsmuir was prominently displayed, accompanied by a banner announcing that it would be burned at the City Hall that evening. The demonstrators planned the burning as a protest against the lieutenant governor's failure to support fully provincial laws seeking to exclude Japanese immigrants destined for British Columbia.[7]

On arrival of the crowds, the City Hall was filled to capacity, and thousands milled around the street outside where the effigy was suspended. Following a number of emotional speeches, the figure was set ablaze "amidst the waving of a thousand small white banners labeled 'For a White Canada.' "[8] The crowd shouted itself hoarse with delight.[9] While the effigy was still burning, some speakers came from the meeting inside the hall and harangued the overflow crowd on Westminster Avenue. Among the speakers was Arthur E. Fowler, an ardent anti-Japanese agitator and secretary of the Seattle Japanese and Korean Exclusion League.[10] He delivered an inflammatory speech which further excited the crowd and "his speech seemed to set things going. . . ."[11]

The atmosphere, already tense with emotion, now became riotous as a reckless feeling of abandon engulfed the spectators. The burning and Fowler's speech "had a bad effect on the hoodlum element that is to be found in every mob. Before the flames had died away, a group had commandeered some of the banners and started down nearby Dupont Street. . . ."[12]

The Chinese and Japanese sections of the city were not far from the City Hall. The Chinese center was only half a block south, on Dupont Street. The first exuberant groups started their raucous tour there, but apparently did little damage at this time. Two young boys broke two small windows. The pleased crowd then "yelled and cheered in a very indiscriminate manner."[13] The Japanese section was a few blocks north and east of the City Hall, in the opposite direction from the Chinese part of town. The choice of the meeting place between the two areas was unfortunate.

Inside, the City Hall "was packed to the doors and a mass of people was banked around the walls."[14] The number of people in the vicinity was variously estimated. One source stated that the number originally at the scene was 8,000 and that subsequent arrivals increased the total to 30,000, half of whom took part in the action that followed.[15] Once gathered the crowd shared a sense of anticipation, and the natural curiosity of the people held them in the district. Wild rumors of bloodshed soon increased the crowd's excitement to "fever heat."

The meeting in the hall, with the president of the Asiatic Exclusion League of Vancouver as chairman, was orderly except for an excess of vocal enthusiasm whenever the speakers denounced Asiatics.[16] In general, the speakers counselled moderation and the use of constitutional methods to achieve their goals.[17] The Reverend Dr. H. W. Fraser, one of four ministers scheduled to speak, delivered a representative speech when he declared that:

> He was body and spirit with the movement, as he almost felt that unless some steps were taken to stop the influx his own pulpit would soon be in the hands of a Jap or a Chinaman. There is no such thing as this cheap or common labor that was talked about. It was pure Anglo-Saxon blood that had made the Empire and it would never be made with a mixture of Asiatic blood.[18]

"Howls of applause greeted this declaration."[19]

The Reverend G. H. Wilson sympathized with the movement and expressed the hope that a solution would be reached without the violence which had occurred so recently in the United States. He aimed to "solve the problem in a Christian sense."[20] Fowler advocated the absolute and perpetual exclusion of Asiatic people. W. A. Young, an organizer of the American Federation of Labor from Seattle, deplored the "yellow blight" but supported the use of constitutional procedures. Harry Cowan blamed the immigration laws solely on the dominion government and demanded a continuation of the agitation to make the federal authorities realize that if they did not do something, the citizens would find it necessary to initiate direct action.[21] J. E. Wilson, a visiting New Zealand laborite, described the methods employed by the other colonies of the empire to exclude the Chinese from their shores.[22]

The meeting passed a resolution requesting the dominion government to exclude Japanese immigrants from British Columbia by allowing the British Columbia Immigration Act of 1907 to become law. The resolution further requested a dominion enactment to ban Asiatics from the entire country. Immigration was a delicate subject of considerable importance in the maintenance of good will between the British empire and Japan, which Great Britain was at great pains to preserve. In the light of these circumstances, the senior governments were scarcely expected to approve the British Columbia Immigration Act. Furthermore, the British North American Act and the interpretation of dominion-provincial rights involved a legal problem. There were other strong reasons for disallowing the act. Canada, on its own initiative, had adhered to the provisions of the Anglo-Japanese Treaty of Commerce and Navigation only the year previously, and also to the Anglo-Japanese Treaty of Alliance of 1902 and 1905.

The meeting threatened to become a political controversy when some participants denounced Richard McBride, the provincial premier, for collaboration with the lieutenant governor of the province to prevent the exclusion of Asiatics.[23] The president of the Conservative Association, however, defended McBride and it was finally decided to invite the premier to the League's next meeting to defend himself.[24]

Outside the hall, the initial excitement abated soon after the burning of the effigy, and groups of people on the streets began to drift about, looking for something to do. Crowds appeared on Carrall Street, two blocks directly west of the City Hall between Hastings and Dupont Streets. A youth tossed a stone which shattered the plate glass window of a Chinese tailor shop.[25] This act ignited the crowd's tense emotions and it then gave way to a wild orgy of destruction. As if by signal, people began gathering stones and throwing them at the windows of Chinese shops and dwellings. Shrieks of delight followed each crash of shattering glass. People moved helter-skelter up and down the streets seeking unbroken storefronts. The violence lasted but a short time, and the fury of the attack ended before the crowd fully comprehended what had happened.

The Chinese, caught unaware by the first crash of breaking glass, fled to nearby points of security and locked the doors and barricaded their premises. They did not come out in fear of the consequences. Glass from smashed windows and storefronts littered the sidewalks. The crowds left and not a soul disturbed the eerie silence.

The mob, after dissipating some of its energy against the Chinese, soon realized that the major target was the Japanese. People left the Chinese area and began to recongregate on Westminster Avenue, between Cordova and Powell streets, only two to three blocks north of City Hall. There, the attackers directed their fury toward Japanese property. The full force of the mob was brought to bear on a store on the southeast corner of Westminster and Powell streets. Missiles were thrown through the broken windows, damaging the men's furnishings, drygoods, toys, candy, and tobacco which were the store's stock in trade.[26] At this point, the mob was estimated to be more than 1,000 but hundreds of non-participating onlookers were drawn to the scene out of curiosity and excitement.[27]

The police department dispatched men to the trouble spots—especially to the corner of Westminster and Powell. Patrolmen from other parts of the city were called in and by ten o'clock virtually all of the men on duty were engaged in bringing order to the Oriental sections of the city.[28] The police used clubs to restore order and "calls were sent in for the fire brigade because of the fear that the mob might eventually decide to add to the list of its other crimes."[29] Seven men were arrested in one place and charged with rioting.[30] The seven were representative of the population at large, being of various races and occupations.

The law enforcement officers performed under an obvious handicap in the midst of the crowd. The identification, capture, and arrest of lawbreakers taxed their ingenuity and physical resources, and the crowd's attempts to rescue prisoners caused them considerable distress.[31] One newspaper account described an incident in which "five officers stood shoulder to shoulder and succeeded in taking their man to a hack."[32] Consequently, the police hoped only to discourage looting and arson and to prevent even greater violence by forcing the crowds back against the curb, keeping individual mobility to a minimum. One of the city's dailies described the plight of the officers as follows:

> The police on the scene were utterly unable to cope with the mass of struggling, cursing, shouting humanity which surged back and forth under the glare of the street arc lights. While in front the police were pushing and crowding the mob back, bricks and stones came from the rear over the heads of those in the van.[33]

The public and the press later admired and praised the conduct of the police. The following is typical of their comments:

> The police deserve great credit for the manner in which they handled the disgraceful outbreak. They were firm and they acted promptly and in a manner which said plainly that they would stand no nonsense.[34]

The rioters met resolute opposition from the Japanese shortly after they turned onto Powell Street. The defenders gathered weapons and put them to effective use.[35] The Japanese stayed indoors until objects hurtled through the windows of their shops and homes. Then, patience taxed to the limit, they charged into the street with long piercing shouts and hurled themselves into the midst of the approaching mass. The fighting then became a pitched hand-to-hand battle, much to the dismay of the demonstrators. Blood flowed and men ran about shouting and cursing in disarray. After each thrust the defenders quickly regrouped and charged again. They quickly withdrew their casualties into nearby buildings for treatment and protection. They brought "ammunition" to the roof-tops of their buildings, and from this vantage point, hurled them at the attackers below. Bottles, bricks, stones, and chunks of wood all came whistling down on the milling mob on the street. This unexpected and demoralizing response forced many of the invaders into hasty retreat, some deserted altogether, while others continued the offensive.

The police rushed in with drawn revolvers to take control.[36] Slowly and relentlessly the vanguard of the rioters was forced ahead by momentum from the rear. This close-formation fighting continued for three blocks until the offensive forces were badly decimated, and their remnants dispersed in the region of Oppenheimer Park.[37] This one-block-square playground between Powell Street on the north and Cordova Street on the south afforded a fine route for a quick and silent retreat.

The recently dedicated Japanese Methodist church, on the corner of the next block at Powell and Jackson, went unscathed.[38] Sections of the press credited the rioters for sparing the church—more likely, the attacking forces lost their vitality before they reached it. Two houses on this block, on the opposite side on Powell Street, were damaged in the turmoil,[39] and they marked the extreme point penetrated by the rioters.

Detached groups drifted slowly back to the area of the original disturbance at the corner of Hastings and Carrall Streets as the evening wore on. By eleven o'clock, a large crowd gathered there again, and many people tried to regain entry to the Chinese settlement. The police prevented a recurrence of the earlier violence by ordering barricades to block off Carrall Street and by placing guards there and at other strategic points. Chief of Police Chamberlin successfully confined the crowd to an area in which it was relatively harmless.[40] The Fire Department, realizing the seriousness of the situation, dispatched one of its units to the troubled area during the evening. Rumors persisted that some men were preparing to set fire to buildings with kerosene.[41]

By this time several leaders of the anti-Asiatic movement, including Fowler, came to the scene from the City Hall meeting. Some of them spoke to the people, urged them to disperse, refrain from violence, and return to their homes. The speeches had an effect on those nearest the speakers, but people on the periphery of the crowd continued to throw rocks at the Chinese premises and there was general approval from the rioters each time they made a direct hit.[42] Finally, most of the crowd left the area, leaving a few people to wander in the streets until daybreak.

During the violence virtually every building occupied by Chinese was damaged. In the Japanese sector fifty-nine properties were wrecked and the Japanese language school set afire, though this was saved by Japanese firefighters.[43] Miraculously, there were no fatalities, although several among both defenders[44] and rioters[45] were badly cut by stones or glass, and there were at least two stabbings.[46] After the rioters dispersed, the Japanese formed a security patrol for their area. On Sunday morning a delegation from their community requested the Chief of Police to keep his men out of the Japanese section and assured him that they were capable of maintaining order.[47] Earlier in the morning, Powell Street was barricaded at Westminster Avenue, and a policeman stood guard. One newspaper reported that the guard was not needed to protect the residents against violence from the outside, rather he was needed to keep outsiders from a "hornet's nest."[48] There was little fighting on the streets on Sunday, and incidents were confined to fights which occurred when suspicious-looking outsiders entered the "guarded-zone." The Japanese "patrolmen" were so efficient that two men on their way to work needed a police escort to get past them. That evening the Japanese posted extra pickets and patrols ready to repel any attack.

It is interesting to note that there was no looting or stealing despite the many broken windows and storefronts. Also, there was no violence directed against individual Japanese—the safest place for them was among the crowd. "They [the Japanese] mingled freely with the crowd. At its most exciting moments Hindoos, Japanese, and Chinese made their way to and fro through the mob without attracting any attention."[49] Therefore, there was some justification in the report that "the crowd was big, but it was swelled by the most good-natured lot of people that ever got classed as a destructive mob."[50] All of this confirmed the claim that the rioters had no malicious intent and were merely overwhelmed by an excess of exuberance and high spirits.[51]

The mayor, police chief, Japanese consul Morikawa Hideshiro, and the special commissioner from Japan, Ishii Kikujiro, met Sunday morning.[52] Except for the serious subject under discussion, the meeting had some of the humorous undertones of a comic opera. "The consul demanded that the Japanese be protected from the whites, the mayor demanded the whites be protected from the Japanese, and Ishii, in the name of the Japanese government, demanded full compensation for all the Japanese nationals."[53]

The preparedness of the police and their ample warning, the determined stand taken by the Japanese and Chinese, and the good common sense of the people of Vancouver prevailed so that few acts of violence were committed by the rioters on the second night of the disturbances. There was no doubt that the Orientals meant business:

Both [Chinese and Japanese] were practically standing under arms and both stated openly that there would be bloodshed if any further attempt were made on them by the mob. The Chinese mostly kept indoors, with all lights out in the front of the buildings, but the Japanese paraded in front of their houses on Powell Street and had pickets posted at the approaches to the Japanese quarter. These men were all armed with clubs or guns or knives or all three. Revolvers stuck out of hip pockets, sheath knives hung from belts and the least sign of disturbance caused doors to open and more men, armed even with axes, to appear.[54]

Toward evening people began to gather again near the junction of Hastings and Carrall and at Hastings and Columbia. The police were alert to the potential danger and cordoned off the area from outsiders. Similar measures were taken by the police near the Japanese section. "The mob was not obstreperous and were swept like sheep back to the corner of Hastings Street and Westminster Avenue. The police had complete control of the crowds so that nothing of a serious nature occurred."[55]

One of the more ironic sidelights of the Saturday night riots was an apocryphal account published by the Seattle *Post-Intelligencer* and other newspapers on the West Coast. The story referred to the docking of the steamship *Charmer* which arrived in the evening of September 7 at about the time the anti-Japanese parade was getting under way. With dramatic emphasis the report related how "scores of rioters scented the arrival of the brown men and started for Canadian Pacific wharf, where the new arrivals were debarking. Unceremoniously seven of the Japanese were thrown into the tide. Others dropped their baggage and fled. The men were rescued from the inlet."[56] According to reliable eyewitness accounts by people who were at the dock to meet the *Charmer,* no such incident occurred. The *Charmer* arrived between half past seven and eight o'clock on Saturday evening, with fewer than 75 Japanese aboard, not 500 as reported in the press. The passengers disembarked without being molested and went quietly uptown to their destinations. In the words of an observer: "There was no crowd of any kind on the docks to meet the boat, nor was there the slightest disturbance. ... There was no one thrown into the water, nor was there any scuffle or dispute of any kind. Absolutely nothing happened. I was there the whole time and saw everything that took place."[57]

On the Sunday following the outbreak the bright, warm weather was an invitation for many Vancouverites to take a leisurely afternoon stroll. The area in which the riots of the previous night occurred was a favorite destination. The Japanese section was out of bounds and grim-looking guards patrolled the streets, so Chinatown was a mecca:

Curious sightseers, whites, Hindoos and Japanese, men, women and children, gazed on the unusual spectacle of a mob's work in Vancouver. Not for twenty years, when the workmen who had helped to build the C.P.R. and clear Vancouver townsite started to drive the Chinamen out of the infant city, has anything of the kind occurred. Then they kept the Chinamen from returning by building bonfires in the streets and patrolling all night. The Victoria militia and a warship from Esquimalt made a fast trip here to put an end to that.[58]

The warm autumn sun brought dwellers and storekeepers in the ravaged area outside to board up gaping holes in their wrecked homes and storefronts. Broken glass lay inches thick on the sidewalks.

The citizens of Vancouver were shocked that the riot had taken place. The press and responsible citizens promptly deplored the thoughtless acts of violence and destruction. The *Daily News-Advertiser* on September 8 headed its editorial "Vancouver Disgraced." The editors predicted that the riots would evoke regret and shame among sensible and law-abiding people and that the incident would prejudice the success of the anti-Oriental movement. They demanded punishment for the guilty and called for citizens to respect law and order. The paper reminded its readers that the Chinese and Japanese were entitled to the same legal protection as other citizens of the city. In reference to the probable demand by the Japanese for compensation for damaged property, the editorial continued: "But the pecuniary loss that the taxpayers will suffer . . . is insignificant compared to the injury which the City's reputation will suffer from such disorderly proceedings." It concluded the editorial by stating: "It must be made quite plain that every person who is orderly and peaceable can be assured of protection as long as he is within British jurisdiction, whatever his race or nationality may be. No departure from that can or will be tolerated."

The paper absolved the organizers of the parade and meeting of responsibility for the riots and attributed the cause of the disturbances to a "gang of hoodlums" who took advantage of the anti-Japanese meeting. It gave the general impression that the people, including the agitators, were not opposed to Orientals as individuals so much as they were against the admission of Asiatic hordes.

Not everyone agreed with the *News-Advertiser* regarding responsibility for the outbreak. The Japanese, with some justification, considered taking legal action against the parade master and other leaders of the demonstration. Significantly, both the local Japanese and Chinese language newspapers issued special editions which counseled moderation and listed only the names of people who suffered damage and of those who had been arrested. According to the *World*, "The Japanese claim that the demonstration caused the trouble and comment bitterly on the fact that Christian pastors were among the speakers." Had they known, they might also have deplored the fact that Mayor Bethune himself was a devoted member of the Vancouver Asiatic Exclusion League.

The *World* indicated that official circles believed Canada would have to apologize to Japan for the damage caused in the riots. It quoted the Dominion Secretary of State's position that the Japanese had every right, by treaty between Canada and Japan, to enter and reside in any part of the dominion and its territories in the knowledge that their liberty and the full protection of law were guaranteed. It also mentioned the history of the relationships established by the treaty, which had been in force for ten years between Great Britain and Japan before Canada seriously considered becoming a party to it. The paper noted that British Columbia had not protested Canada's adoption of the resolution to the British government which requested Canada's inclusion in the treaty. The *World* (September 9-12, 1907) deplored the "undesirable notoriety" brought to the city by the "disgraceful folly of a few young men and boys."

On September 15, the *Daily News-Advertiser* expressed the hope that Japan, despite the treaty rights, "with the clearness of vision and its quick perception which characterize Japanese statecraft, would consent to a modification of the terms of the Treaty as will limit the immigration into Canada in the future." It implored its readers not to overlook the fact "that Canada and not Japan is the party to the contract which has brought about the present situation, and that it is Ottawa and not Tokyo which has to ask for its modification," and expressed the hope that the friendly relations between the British and the Japanese governments would prove an important factor in bringing about a settlement satisfactory to Canadian popular sentiment.

The *Province* on September 9 quoted an unidentified but prominent member of the Vancouver Asiatic Exclusion League who expressed regret over "the mob that broke loose." The source was quoted as feeling that a few thousand dollars worth of broken glass was not too great a price to draw "the attention of the provincial, federal and imperial authorities . . . to recognize the fact that British Columbia people will not permit this country to be made a dumping ground of yellow cheap labor." The exclusionist who was quoted held that the people of Vancouver were not to blame, since the federal government had failed to heed the urgent appeals of the province for the exclusion of the Japanese. He contended that, "unless some such trouble had occurred protests would have continued to pass unheeded. Now I expect that Ottawa and the imperial authorities will realize that the people here are not fooling and will take steps to prevent a recurrence of the trouble."

Elsewhere in Canada it was believed that the involvement of American labor and exclusion leaders in the Canadian anti-Asiatic movement was responsible for the riots. A Vancouver man reported in the London *Chronicle* that "unquestionably the whole of the violence came from the labour element alone, and was engineered from the United States." To support his view, he named A. E. Fowler and W. A. Young as two of the chief speakers at the mass meeting on Saturday evening. The Hamilton *Herald* speculated that an international intrigue, in which American agitators were the tools of higher sources, sought to embroil Canada and Great Britain in a quarrel between the United States and Japan. An American historian of a later period made an interesting comment on this point: "The British derived what comfort they could from the thought, which appears to have contained a considerable amount of truth, that the people of Vancouver had been inflamed by American labor agitators."[59]

The action of the British ambassador in Washington confirmed the general British suspicion of the role which American participants played in Canadian anti-Japanese activities. The ambassador requested the Canadian government to provide any information concerning the intimate interrelation of the anti-Asiatic movement in British Columbia and the Pacific states. He attached special importance to the activities of American agitators in Vancouver, and asked British consular officials on the American West Coast to transmit information on them to the Canadians.

The press in the United States was generally excited over the prospect of an Anglo-Japanese settlement that would moderate Japanese demands for losses incurred in several incidents in San Francisco the previous May. The procedures used in the settlement of the Vancouver incident were also expected to serve as a pattern for negotiations between Britain and the United States on damage claims in connection with the raid on the Hindus at Bellingham, Washington on September 5.[60] The Vancouver riots put the British in an embarrassing position, both as allies of Japan and because they had vehemently denounced American behavior in the San Francisco riots only four months previously. The Everett *Daily Herald* was quick to comment on this on Monday, Sept. 9:

This is the most important development that occurred since the Japanese question came to the front. If America's position has been embarrassing, what will Great Britain's be, considering the fact that she is Japan's sworn ally? Judging from reports the San Francisco disturbances must have been tame affairs compared with the Vancouver outbreak.

On September 10, the Seattle *Post-Intelligencer* editorialized that Japan would be entirely warranted in taking the same attitude toward the Vancouver outbreak as it did toward the anti-Japanese outrages in San Francisco in May. It also reflected that, in view of the cordial relations between Great Britain and Japan, a small provincial affair, the result of an irresponsible mob, was hardly likely to mar their friendly relationships.

On the Atlantic coast, the New York *Times* on Monday, September 9, briefly reported the Vancouver affair and delivered an optimistic appraisal of the situation. It attributed the influx of immigrants to Canada to immigration from Hawaii and indicated that it was the source of anxiety in Vancouver. The paper explained that, when the immigration to the continental United States was closed to Japanese residents of Hawaii in the spring of 1907, hotelkeepers and a number of lawyers in Honolulu devised a scheme to send people to Canada.

The *Times* exonerated the Japanese government of the responsibility for the large and rapid increase in the number of immigrants entering the west coast ports of Canada. In defense of its stand, the *Times* noted the efforts of the Japanese consuls in both Vancouver and Honolulu to discourage the migration.

> It is not difficult to realize that the Japanese government does not desire to do anything likely to cause irritation to Canada, a part of the British Empire, Japan's most important ally. The belief generally held by the best informed people in Vancouver that the Japanese government has honestly kept its promise to discourage its subjects from emigrating to Canada, induces a feeling that some means will be found at Tokio to stop any large movement in that direction.

The front page of Tuesday's edition, September 10, carried the headline: "Washington Is Curious, Wonders If Japan Will Be As Angry With Britain As With U.S." This story implied that American officials and diplomats were eagerly awaiting the Japanese reaction to mob violence inflicted on the subjects of Japan by Britons. The paper expected the same attitude to be taken by Japan on an official level but entertained a "doubt whether anything like the feeling displayed against the Americans will be manifested in the Japanese Parliament and among the Japanese people against Britain."

On September 11 the New York *Times* suggested that a settlement of the Bellingham Hindu affair depended largely on the demands submitted by the Japanese government to settle the Vancouver incident. The story suggested that the close ties between Britain and Japan would induce the Japanese to act in moderation. In turn Britain would adopt a similar approach toward the United States. Thus, it was thought that the settlement of both the San Francisco and the Bellingham riots would follow the difficult precedent that Japan would initiate in the settlement of the Vancouver riots.

Across the Atlantic the *Pall Mall Gazette* of London, which was known to be hostile towards Oriental settlers in British Columbia, indicated on September 9 that the news of the attacks on the Japanese and the Chinese in Vancouver was no surprise to Colonial and Foreign Office officials in London who had long feared an outbreak against the Asiatics in western Canada. The paper recognized the seriousness of demonstrations aimed directly at "the subjects of Great Britain's eastern ally." It referred to the embarrassing position of the English newspapers which had severely criticized the San Francisco riots but now were maintaining silence about the Vancouver affair.

The New York correspondent of the London *Times* reported confirmation of the belief that American agitators had instigated the anti-Japanese riots in Vancouver and named the leaders—Frank Cotterill, president of the Washington Federation of Labor; A. E. Fowler, secretary of the Japanese and Korean Exclusion League of Seattle; and A. P. Listman, prominent Seattle labor leader. He continued:

> American newspapers are inclined to be sarcastic over the outbreak in British territory, coming as it does after some severe comments made by the English newspapers on anti-Japanese troubles in California, but they will probably change their tone when they realize that it is citizens of the United States that are responsible for the rioting in Canada.

In a later issue, the *Times* maintained that the Japanese had treaty rights to immigrate to Canada and that the maintenance of these rights of the Japanese residents was a matter of imperial duty. It looked forward to an amicable arrangement and commented:

> The Mayor, Mr. Bethune, who has hitherto apparently been supine, has at last been moved to call the city council together for the purpose of interdicting a meeting of the Anti-Asiatic League on Thursday. The city police force is greatly undermanned, as many of the best men resigned recently owing to poor pay.

It ridiculed the idea that a few thousand Japanese were likely to convert British Columbia into a yellow province.

Reports in Japanese newspapers during the two weeks following the riots displayed relative calm, attributing the incident to irresponsible conduct on the part of a small number of people. According to the Tokyo *Asahi,* the press and government officials expressed little anxiety regarding the question of immigration, and in general the authorities expressed faith that the incident would be satisfactorily settled. Editorial comment was withheld, pending receipt of details and subsequent developments, so only a meager account was published. The *Asahi* (September 14) warned its readers against retaliation.

The calm and hopeful attitude of the Japanese was clearly expressed by the *Nichi Nichi* of Tokyo (September 13):

> It is reassuring to know that the Canadian and English press are unanimously condemning the Vancouver outbreak and it is hoped and trusted that full justice will be meted out. Should the Canadian government in this instance find a solution of the problem which would serve as a model and example in dealing with the same problem in the Pacific Coast states of the United States, it would be a case of fortune snatched out of miseries. Let us hope that this expectation will be realized and that permanent tranquility will be assured along the coasts of the ocean bearing the name of peace.

Jiji Shimpo (September 12) expressed faith in British law and justice, held that the dominion government had more power over the provinces than did Washington over the states and praised the police in Canada as being more efficient and more reliable during crises than the police in San Francisco.

In Vancouver, most Japanese returned to their usual duties after the weekend riots. On Monday afternoon they left to attend a mass meeting of Japanese at the Powell Street grounds. Monday's *World* asserted that, "They state that they are in no fear; that they are quite prepared to take care of themselves and dozens admit that they are armed." In contrast, the same paper remarked of the Chinese: "Practically without a single exception not a Chinaman in Vancouver is working today. They have, for the most part, retired to their warrens in Chinatown and announce that until the present unrest is completed, they will not stir out."

The Japanese consul in Vancouver and the commissioner from the Japanese Foreign Office brought about a feeling of moderation among their people, and should receive credit for preventing the Japanese from taking more severe retaliation. Commissioner Ishii spoke on Sunday to a local Japanese audience at the schoolhouse on Alexander Street and counseled a moderate attitude toward the incident and toward the people of Vancouver. He felt that the riots would not affect the friendship between Great Britain and Japan. He persuaded his people to remain patient and expressed confidence that a just settlement would be made for damages incurred in the riots. He exhorted his listeners to behave as good citizens and, as people of a great nation, to keep the name of their country unsullied. In an interview with a *World* reporter, the consul assured him that the Japanese would work as usual.

Consul Morikawa forwarded reports of damage to Consul General Nosse in Ottawa and Nosse promptly contacted the Prime Minister of

Canada to request security for the Japanese in Vancouver. The Prime Minister gave full assurance that every effort would be made to prevent a renewal of violence and sent the following message to the mayor of Vancouver:

> His Excellency the Governor General has learned with the deepest regret of the indignities and cruelties to which certain subjects of the Emperor of Japan, a friend and ally of His Majesty the King, have been victims and he hopes that peace will be promptly restored and all the offenders punished.[61]

The mayor of Vancouver sought to minimize the involvement of the city beyond that of preventing further disturbances, an attitude which was supported by the citizens of the community. The mayor also issued a statement regretting the riots and urged the people of the city to behave with moderation. At the City Council meeting on September 10, Bethune made it clear that he would not take sides in the controversy. He indicated that it was his duty as mayor to extend protection to all residents. The council ordered the Vancouver Asiatic Exclusion League to cancel its meeting scheduled for Thursday. The aldermen supported the mayor's stand unanimously. The community also condemned the acts of violence—even leading labor men deprecated the outrages and declared that the riots would only harm their cause.

As indicated by its Consul General, the Japanese government intended to leave matters to the Canadian government, which "could be trusted to make good the loss without the formality of a demand by Japan." Clearly, the Japanese government did not wish to make of the incident a matter of great international concern. The *Daily Colonist* of Victoria, in confirming this view, reported a London press release of September 9, stating:

> The action of the Japanese embassy here, it is understood, will be governed largely by the attitude the Canadian government assumes and whether the latter takes steps to protect the Japanese at Vancouver from a repetition of the incidents and recompense them for their losses.

Meanwhile, the question of responsibility for settlement was in the minds of federal and civic officials. The mayor of Vancouver, of course, disclaimed civic responsibility for restitution of damages, thus leaving the task of assessment and payment of losses to the dominion government. In any event, international considerations made that the most expedient course that could be taken.

On October 12 Canadian Premier Sir Wilfred Laurier cabled a message to the British ambassador at Tokyo, for transmission to the Emperor of Japan, expressing the Governor General's profound regrets over the riots and his assurance that the Canadian authorities would do their utmost to prevent a recurrence. The courteous reply to this communication was ample evidence of the friendly relations existing between Japan and the British Empire. The Foreign Minister, Count Tadasu Hayashi, stated that the Japanese government had every confidence in the action of the Canadian officials in the satisfactory disposition of the incident and expressed "the hope that in view of the cordial and friendly relations existing between Japan and Canada, the case may be settled at Ottawa independently of the British government and without going through the usual diplomatic channels."[62]

Under these favorable circumstances, the Canadian Privy Council auspiciously appointed W. L. Mackenzie King as a one-man commission to conduct an inquiry into the losses and to assess the damages sustained by the Japanese victims of the riots.

Commissioner King arrived in Vancouver from Ottawa on October 22 and accumulated evidence for eleven days. He then recommended awards totaling $9,036; $1,523.60 for actual damages and $7,512.40 for resultant losses. The federal government approved the amounts and forwarded the required sum to Vancouver on November 13 for disbursement by the commissioner. In addition, $139 was paid to the claimants for legal expenses they had incurred in connection with the preparation of their declarations. The commissioner, mindful of the degree to which the Japanese Consulate had facilitated the work of investigation by its engagement of legal counsel and by aiding in the careful preparation of claims, recommended that the consulate be reimbursed $1,600. The government at Ottawa concurred, but the Japanese consul in Vancouver very graciously declined the offer in behalf of his government in a letter of appreciation to the commissioner:

> While appreciating the high and honourable motives which have prompted you and your government to send me the cheque for $1,600, I regret that it is impossible for my government to accept a reward for protecting the interests and property of the subjects of Japan. This, and this only, is my reason for returning to you the cheque for $1,600.
>
> You may assure your government of my grateful acknowledgement of their generous course, a policy which, I am sure will make for an increase of good feeling between our people.[63]

The commissioner examined eighty witnesses, including the claimants, Chief of Police Chamberlin, civic officials, the appraiser engaged in assessing damages, and the individuals who prepared the claims. A total of 107 claims were reviewed, 54 for actual damages and 53 for resultant losses.

The report itself was only twenty-two pages long, and, significantly enough, it did not discuss the riots as such. It made every effort to appraise damages to property and losses arising out of the destruction justly and fairly. From the evidence, the commissioner concluded that "the claimants had in mind an 'amend honorable' rather than full compensation."[64] The Chinese claims for damages were not considered until the middle of the following year. King received high commendation for his investigation and the adjudication of awards. The commendation especially noted his courteous and judicious handling of a difficult assignment. The thoroughness and fairness with which he dispatched his duties brought these words of appreciation from the Japanese consul at Vancouver:

> I cannot too strongly express the satisfaction and approval of my government in your award and adjustment of the losses and damages sustained by the Japanese residents here, a feeling, I am sure, shared by every claimant. If I may be permitted to say anything of a personal character, I would assure you that the great skill, unvarying patience and urbanity which marked your conduct of the Commission has done much to restore the feeling of my countrymen here that the Canadian government and the people of Canada are opposed to every element whose purpose is to defy the ordinary rules of decency in life, and the wider laws which bind nations in friendly accord.[65]

While the investigation of Japanese claims was still in progress, the commissioner convinced the federal authorities of the usefulness of a commission of inquiry to investigate the reasons for the sudden rise in immigration of the Japanese and other Asiatics to Canada in 1907. The government approved King's proposal on November 5 and King began his new task on November 11. The second commission completed its work on November 30. The report on the Japanese immigration was presented to Parliament on January 20, 1908, and a companion study on the Chinese and Hindu laborers followed on July 13. Japanese immigration received the keenest scrutiny.

This emphasis was to be expected since the riots stemmed directly from agitation over the sudden and unanticipated rise in the number of Japanese immigrants in 1907. Unfortunately, the peak migration from Hawaii coincided with the period of heaviest immigration from Japan itself. The influx of Japanese reaching the ports of Victoria and Vancouver during the spring and summer of 1907 doubtless appeared like an invasion to some observers.[66] The anxious citizens of British Columbia did not know that only about half of those who disembarked at these points would settle in Canada. The majority of those who entered the country were either en route to the United States or were residents returning to Canada after a short visit to Japan. Many of the "returnees" were Canadian citizens.

The most obvious public concern was the influx from Hawaii. During

ASIAN COMMUNITY LIBRARY
1934 PARK BLVD.
OAKLAND, CA 94606

the first three months of the year 115 Japanese arrived from there.[67] After March, however, the numbers began to increase, and the April total was 326, in May 285. The July figure was an alarming 1,444. One ship alone—the *Kumeric*—carried 1,189, and its arrival set off the first strong popular agitation for drastic action to curb the influx. There was difficulty in accommodating such a large number on short notice, and the situation received undue attention when the Japanese consul found it necessary to call on the Vancouver civic authorities for special transportation facilities to move people to wherever accommodation could be procured, including outlying areas.

Among the Asiatic witnesses called to testify before the commission were thirty-five Chinese, twenty-seven Japanese, and fifteen Hindus. The ultimate objective of the investigation was to determine the actual number of Orientals who entered and remained in Canada, the reasons for their coming, and the means by which they were induced to leave their homeland for Canada. According to official statistics 11,440 Orientals reached the West Coast in the first ten months of 1907; 8,125 Japanese, 2,049 Hindus, and 1,266 Chinese.[68]

The investigation disclosed that the Japanese government maintained rigid control over the emigration of its people by restricting the issuance of passports for individuals leaving the country. Any change in general public policy was immediately made effective by instructions to prefectural governors, who controlled the number of emigrants from their respective areas in accordance with regulations determined from time to time by the Japanese Foreign Office.

Two methods of procuring passports were open to prospective immigrants. They could either apply on an individual basis through the municipal and prefectural governments, or through emigration companies which dealt directly with the Foreign Office and made all arrangements for a nominal legal fee of 20 to 25 yen. The Foreign Office thus maintained a record of all emigrants. The commission was to determine how, under these circumstances, such great numbers of Japanese immigrants arrived during the first ten months of 1907.

The investigation revealed that the Canadian Nippon Supply Company, Limited, was involved in a scheme to promote immigration and arrange contracts for labor, and to engage in domestic and international trade. The company was incorporated by British Columbia charter on December 17, 1906, and organized by Saori Gotoh, a labor contractor from Vancouver with previous experience in the United States, and Frederick Yoshy, a former employee of the Japanese consular service in Vancouver and Honolulu. Two prominent Vancouver businessmen, Charles Gardiner Johnson and William Washington Boultbee, were the president and treasurer respectively. The four men constituted the directorate and, to fulfill statutory requirements, Gotoh's secretary became the fifth shareholder. William John Bowser was the firm's solicitor. He provided legal advice to the officers of the company, especially on immigration problems, and prepared labor contracts between the company and large employers such as the Canadian Pacific Railway Company.

The Canadian Nippon Supply Company was loosely organized, so it was not surprising that the commissioner commented on the unorthodox manner in which its plans were made and executed. The company and its clerical staff of seven, however, received considerable praise. Only Gotoh and Yoshy had full knowledge of company business. Johnson, for example, was completely unaware of business developments and the commissioner was quick to note that this was unusual. Yoshy's testimony damaged the company's reputation with dishonest and evasive replies to queries put to him by the commissioner, who reported:

> More unfortunate in the suspicion it arouses . . . was the positive denial by Mr. Yoshy, of any kind of connection between the company of which he was an organizer and chief director, and the emigration companies of Japan. Not only did he disclaim all relationship between the Canadian Nippon Supply Company, but he was certain that no employment agency was connected in any way with the emigration companies of Japan. His testimony on this point is unhappily only too plain.[69]

The role played by Bowser was more serious since he was the provincial attorney-general and a member of the legislature. He exploited his position to serve his own political purposes on the basis of private and confidential information accessible to him as the company lawyer. [See p. 117 for further details of his inflammatory activities.] Without this politician's legal advice, Gotoh and Yoshy could hardly have succeeded in bringing over so many Japanese workers—the same ones whose presence angered Bowser's constituents. In this connection it was pointed out in the House of Commons that ". . . if the Gotoh contracts had not been put into force we would never have had any Japanese difficulty in the province of British Columbia."[70]

The Canadian Nippon Supply Company Limited was formed in anticipation of a possible relaxation in the policy of rigid restrictions on emigration which the Japanese government had imposed since the turn of the century. Recent conditions seemed to assure a good demand for labor by the larger firms in the province at a time when the local supply of labor was insufficient to meet the needs. Gotoh went to Japan in January 1907, and Yoshy followed in April to induce Japanese authorities to liberalize their emigration policies. The happy combination of Gotoh's experience in labor promotion and Yoshy's familiarity with official government procedures, fortified by the "Bowser Contracts" and the backing of emigration companies in Japan, induced the Japanese Foreign Office to issue passports to prospective immigrants with the certification of the consul in Vancouver that they would be employed on valid contracts from reputable firms requesting workers.

Under these conditions, the Nippon Supply Company succeeded in monopolizing both ends of the immigration traffic. In Canada it gained exclusive rights to supply Japanese laborers to such large firms as the Canadian Pacific Railway and the Wellington Collieries, and in Japan, it made exclusive arrangements with the Tokio Emigration Company for the recruitment of emigrants for Canada. The Canadian company established a branch office in Yokohama to maintain more efficient communication between the two countries.

Twenty-six immigrants arrived in May as the first group under the auspices of the Tokio Emigration Company and the Canadian Nippon Supply Company. Subsequently, 245 arrived during the month of June, 344 in July, 151 in August, 76 in September, and 14 in October. After the investigation began an estimated forty-four immigrants arrived, making the total from this source 900.[71]

By the latter part of October, 871 of the men sent by the Tokio Emigration Company were among a total of 1,468 men working under the direction of the Canadian Nippon Supply Company.[72] The remaining 597 were made up of 139 from Hawaii, six from the United States, and 156 listed as former residents of Canada. This left 296 whose former place of residence was not definitely known, but which was presumed to have been Canada. They consisted mostly of Gotoh's former employees taken over by the company at the time of its incorporation.

There was little doubt that the Canadian Nippon Supply Company was a responsible firm which carried out its business efficiently. For this it received praise from the commissioner:

> The business of the Canadian Nippon Supply Company appears to have been conducted from start to finish with an attention to details on which it would have been difficult to improve. With the labourers in its employ the company seems to have been fair and just and the charges made for its services, all things considered, appear to have been entirely reasonable. As an arrangement between corporations and large bodies of inexperienced foreign labourers, it is doubtful whether a more perfect system could be worked out to the advantage of all parties concerned.[73]

In addition to authorizing two King commission investigations, the federal government decided to negotiate with the Japanese authorities for an amicable arrangement to prevent a repetition of the large influx of Japanese immigrants to Canada. But the preservation of friendly relations between Japan and Canada and the rest of the British Empire was still of primary importance. The government's choice of Rodolphe Lemieux, the postmaster general and minister of labor, as the emissary to Tokyo was a fortuitous selection. Lemieux, determined on a conciliatory policy, left the Canadian capital on October 23 with his assistant, Joseph Pope, and arrived at Yokohama on November 13 and at Tokyo the following day.

The Japanese, for understandable reasons, based their position on the terms of the Anglo-Japanese Treaty of Commerce and Navigation of 1894, which established the legal basis for freedom of entry, movement, and residence of the nationals of each respective country in the domains of the other, save for areas specifically excepted. This mutual recognition of rights was further reinforced by the inclusion of Canada, at its own request, in the protocol some ten years after the privilege of adherence was first offered to the British colonies. The particular section under examination during the conference was the first paragraph of Article I which stated:

> The subjects of each of the two high contracting parties shall have full liberty to enter, travel, or reside in any part of the dominion and possessions of the other contracting party, and shall enjoy full and perfect protection for their persons and property.[74]

The Japanese insisted, as they had every right to do, that Lemieux recognize the basic rights set forth therein prior to any discussion and they emphatically declined:

> To enter into a formal written compact, as this would be to cancel without compensation a part of the rights to which she is entitled by treaty and which to forego would, in her eyes, be to submit to a national indignity.[75]

Canada rested its case on the declarations made by the Japanese consul general in Canada in correspondence with the Canadian prime minister and other government officials. Canada accepted these declarations as a "tacit understanding" for limiting Japanese immigration to not more than a few hundred a year. The final assurance made by the same Japanese representative, on January 18, 1907, stated, "that the Japanese government would issue no passport under any pretext whatever," and reinforced the Canadian belief in the existence of a definite limitation. Unfortunately, the consul general had exceeded his authority and the implications connected with his actions led to his recall. The Japanese officials repudiated his agreements.

ASIAN COMMUNITY LIBRARY.
1934 PARK BLVD.
OAKLAND, CA 94606

Under these circumstances, Lemieux was convinced that agreement was possible only if the Japanese government and its own legal machinery were allowed to control Japanese emigration to Canada. He recognized the futility of seeking an absolute numerical limitation which would be tantamount to a treaty revision. Japan was in no mood to permit remission of its treaty rights and was keenly sensitive to the suggestion that an absolute limit would be imposed on the basis of race —especially since immigration from Europe remained without restrictions of any kind. Lemieux reported to Ottawa and emphasized that the Japanese attitude was extremely sensitive to treatment different from that accorded other nationalities. So long as treatment was based on equality, he observed, there was considerable freedom of action in the negotiations. For example, he maintained that Japan was quite agreeable to the control of Japanese migration from Hawaii by means of the Alien Labour Law of Canada, which was equally applicable to all contract labor from the United States.

Lemieux was sympathetic toward the Japanese position and his greatest task was not winning Japanese acquiescence but convincing his own superiors to accept the Japanese offer of voluntary restriction, especially after the Japanese repudiation of their consul general's "tacit understanding." The Japanese claimed this agreement had been weakened by a speech in the Canadian House of Commons on June 22, 1905 by Sydney Fisher, the Minister of Agriculture, as well as by Fisher's letter to the Japanese Foreign Minister which, in effect, relinquished Canada's claim to numerical restriction of Japanese immigration.[76]

The final arrangement by "Gentleman's Agreement" restricted Japanese immigration to Canada to those already domiciled in Canada and members of their families; workers required on farms and in homes of Japanese who were unable to obtain suitable local labor, bona fide students, merchants, tourists, and travelers in transit; and laborers when specifically requested by the Canadian government.[77] The Gentlemen's Agreement together with the Canadian Order-in-Council of January 8, 1908, (by which Canada required all prospective immigrants to come to Canada on continuous voyage from the land of their birth or citizenship on a through-passage paid for in the country of origin) effectively regulated all immigration to Canada, including that of Japanese from both Hawaii and Japan.

Japan proved the seriousness of its intentions by increasing the deposit required of the emigration companies to 50,000 yen. This new requirement reduced the number of these companies from seventeen or more to only three. Furthermore, the minister of foreign affairs told a group of the companies' shareholders that when interests between diplomacy and emigration conflicted, diplomatic considerations took precedence as a matter of national policy.

Canada had two alternatives in its response to the Japanese position: either accept the agreement or abrogate the treaty. Abrogation meant the loss of commercial advantages and trade involving a market supported by 50 million people, whereas acceptance meant the realization of the aims of the Canadian government in maintaining and extending the existing cordial relations and enhancing the prospects for increased trade. Outright exclusion was not considered as an alternative, for any such measure constituted a serious breach in the close ties established by the Anglo-Japanese Treaty of Alliance.

On January 21, 1908, eleven days after his return to Ottawa, Lemieux presented a resolution in the House of Commons for the adoption of his report and recommended acceptance of the Gentlemen's Agreement as a solution to the problems posed by the threat of heavy Japanese immigration. The Parliament passed the resolution by an overwhelming majority of over two to one. The preponderance of support from the press, the people, and the members of Parliament signified the beginning of a new approach to Japanese-Canadian relations in which the Gentlemen's Agreement, after an initial period of anxiety in Canada, successfully withstood the practical test of time.

Since the Gentlemen's Agreement did not specifically state any numerical limitation, Foreign Minister Hayashi, upon representation from Lemieux, furnished a supplementary understanding in a confidential letter to the British ambassador in Tokyo. His statement expressed the Japanese government's expectation that the maximum number of new emigrants per year would remain under four hundred.[78] The figure soon became public knowledge in Canada, and the Japanese foreign office protested this breach of secrecy. Some confusion also arose over the inclusiveness or exclusiveness of those Japanese resident in Canada and members of their families, but after the initial year under the agreement, these sources of friction were eliminated. Revisions to lower the maximum figure were made in 1923 and in 1928, and the agreement came to an end in 1941.

Of the 8,125 Japanese who came to Canada in 1907, 8,048 landed; the remaining seventy-seven were rejected and subsequently returned to their port of origin. Of the 8,048, 3,619 had passports for the United States, where they proceeded shortly after landing.[79] Only 4,429 remained in Canada, and only 1,641 of those came directly from Japan. Those from Japan included the 900 for whom the Canadian Nippon Supply Company was responsible. The remaining 741 included an estimated 300 already domiciled in Canada. Moreover, among these 741 were 151 whose original destination was the United States but who, upon rejection at the border, returned to become immigrants to Canada. Therefore, the actual number of immigrants coming through the normal channels was only 290, of whom approximately 100 were merchants, officers, students, and travelers who normally remained in the country for only a limited period of time. This left only 190 who were immigrants in the ordinary sense of the word, and they were relatives and friends of Japanese already established in Canada and who had received their passports through certification of the Japanese Consul in Vancouver. A third source—Mexico—was responsible for nine Japanese immigrants.

The abnormally large number of arrivals, therefore, was attributable to the great exodus from Hawaii and to the groups who came under the auspices of the Canadian Nippon Supply Company. Approximately 80 percent of those who landed in Canada were accounted for by the 3,619 immigrants whose destination was the United States and the 2,779 who came from Hawaii. Of those destined for Canada, the Hawaiian and the Canadian Nippon Supply Company groups together made up approximately 65 percent of all arrivals and 83 percent of those who landed and remained in Canada.

On the foregoing basis, the investigating commission concluded that the Japanese government in 1907 did observe the "tacit understanding" in so far as the ordinary immigrants were concerned.[80] Misunderstanding arose over the 900 who came under the scheme of the immigration company and the influx of 2,779 from Hawaii, the latter beyond the control of the Japanese government. With the 900, however, the Japanese government could not be completely absolved of responsibility, for the Foreign Office issued the passports, and these were examined by Commissioner King at the Vancouver office of the Canadian Nippon Supply Company. The considerable pressure exerted by the emigration companies at the instigation of Gotoh and Yoshy, backed by certified copies of valid contracts for labor with reputable Canadian firms, was the immediate cause for the Japanese government's relaxing its restrictions.

The greatest single cause for the 1907 demonstration and the riots was the seemingly unending influx of Japanese immigrants to the coast during that summer. Lack of detailed statistics distorted the public perception of reality. The Japanese were the main target, despite official statements to the contrary by such people as the mayor of Vancouver, Commissioner King, and Prime Minister Laurier. Concern about the Japanese is found in the official Canadian and British government correspondence which refers to the riots. The Parliamentary debates in Canada also dwelt on the Japanese almost to the exclusion of the Chinese and the Hindus. Special Agent McInnes reported to the federal government that "The uneasiness against the Asiatics is caused by the Japanese. The Chinese and Hindus alone do not cause anxiety. The Japanese competition is feared because they do not take an inferior position and give competition."[81] The same report continued that there was no Chinese question because:

> They never assert a position of equality with the whites. They are limited to subordinate occupations, they do not compete seriously with the masses of the white population. The Chinese attitude is "peace at any price."

A statement by the Governor General noted that the people of British Columbia now genuinely feared the Japanese, while they almost favored the Chinese and showed pity for the Hindus.[82]

While the Japanese were the object of such hostility, the number of Chinese and Hindu immigrants was also increasing and creating a larger total number of Asian immigrants. The commissioner concluded in his report: "If anything more were needed to occasion unrest, it was to be found in the simultaneous arrival from the Orient of Hindus by the hundreds and Chinese in larger number than those of immediately preceding years. It was an alarm at numbers, and a cry of a white Canada was raised."[83]

The Chinese, after virtual cessation of immigration following an increase in capitation tax to $500 at the beginning of 1904, began to enter the country again in increasing numbers in response to the demand for Chinese labor. In 1904–05 only eight Chinese came to Canada; in 1905–06, twenty-two; and in 1906–07, ninety-one. Then in 1907–08, Chinese immigration suddenly rose to 1,482.[84] Similarly, Hindus began to immigrate to Canada for the first time during this same crucial period, and by 1907 their numbers had reached substantial proportions. From 45 in the fiscal year 1904–05 and 387 in 1905–06, the Hindu immigration rose to 2,124 for 1906–07 (9 months) and 2,623 for the year 1907.[85]

As already noted the situation was not nearly as threatening as generally believed at the time. The increasing anxiety of the citizens was understandable, however, in light of the paucity of reliable reports showing the actual circumstances.

The part played by politicians in arousing the public by directing undue and often misguided emphasis on the subject of Japanese immigration cannot escape our attention altogether, as illustrated by Attorney-General Bowser's actions. In a campaign speech in Victoria on the eve of the 1907 election, at a time when the opposition had no opportunity for refutation, Bowser spoke at some length on a supposed contract arrangement for labor in the construction of the Grand Trunk Pacific Railway.[86] Knowing the facts to be otherwise, Bowser nevertheless alleged that the Canadian Nippon Supply Company had already entered into an agreement to supply 50,000 Japanese laborers for the construction of the railway to the Pacific Coast and that officials of the firm were at that very moment recruiting workers.[87] He attributed the successful consummation of the alleged contract to the close relations between the Liberal Party and the Grand Trunk Pacific Railway.

The whole thing, of course, was a sensational fabrication, but it served its purpose by convincing the public that a genuine commitment existed. No doubt, the whole story was based on a quite innocuous hand-written letter which E. G. Russell, an agent of the Grand Trunk Pacific, had sent to Gotoh in reply to the latter's enquiry regarding workers for the Grand Trunk project.[88] The figure of 50,000 was a figment of Bowser's imagination, for his intent was to frighten the electorate into voting the Conservatives back into office. In this he was eminently successful.

Once re-elected, however, Bowser was faced with two allegiances. In his private capacity as solicitor for the Canadian Nippon Supply Company, he found it necessary to prevent the effectiveness of any legislation aimed at stopping Japanese immigration, and, as the province's attorney-general, he was duty-bound to legislate against the entry of Japanese into the province. The attorney-general, however, was no ordinary person. He took a course which pleased both sides, making certain to protect his client and his legal fees. He worded the Immigration Act of 1907 so that persons not able to read English or another European language could nevertheless be admitted to the province as immigrants. The people of British Columbia, unaware of the stratagem, naturally thought the act effectively kept Japanese out of the province.[89] This ruse protected his company and also the Canadian Pacific Railway Company, which required the workmen then being recruited in Japan.

Thus, at one stroke Bowser satisfied his clients, the Canadian Pacific (his party's supporters), and the people of British Columbia who were duped into believing that their province was saved from yellow penetration. If the act passed, Gotoh's company and the CPR were legally safeguarded; if it was disallowed, the lieutenant governor, the dominion government, the Liberal Party, and the Grand Trunk Pacific Railway interests could be made the scapegoats.

Bowser's campaign allegations, based on knowledge gained as the solicitor for the Canadian Nippon Supply Company, gave all the appearances of being confirmed, if for no other reason than that his clients followed the attorney-general's legal advice. Ensuing developments en-

couraged the stand taken by the West Coast politicians, the "exclusionists," and the agitators. The immigrants arrived in large and increasing
numbers during the summer, the legislature passed the Immigration Bill
to which royal assent was withheld, and the dominion government, for
obvious reasons, had no alternative but to employ moral and legal
restraint in order to abide by treaty arrangements in dealing with the
Japanese government.

The year 1907 was a divisional point in the history of Japanese-
Canadian relations. For many years prior to this, issues between Japan
and Canada were few and of little consequence, so that problems were
solved as they arose and disposed of as expeditiously as circumstances
warranted. No clear-cut policy existed to serve as a guide for the increasingly complex questions that came up with greater frequency by
the turn of the century. By this time the crucial racial issue and immigration produced difficult problems, and the task was to seek an arrangement to satisfy Canadian sentiment and yet to preserve the goodwill of
the Japanese toward Canada and the Empire.

The immigration crisis and the riots of 1907 finally prompted the
federal government to seek clarification of the basic issues involved. As
a result, Canadian policies based primarily on the information and recommendations supplied by Mackenzie King and Rodolphe Lemieux
ushered in a new diplomatic era and constituted the watershed for a
fresh new approach to Japanese-Canadian affairs. This new direction in
international relationships tended to influence all subsequent dealings
with the Japanese and was, for example, largely responsible for the
many regulatory provisions enacted prior to and during the Pacific War.
Mackenzie King was the master architect during this period, for no
other person in Canadian government was so well acquainted with the
problems. Again it was Mackenzie King who in 1944 attempted to set
the pattern for the general policy of total exclusion of Japanese in the
period following World War II.[90]

Within the last few years, however, a new concept in immigration
policy in Canada has ended determinants based exclusively on race.
Such a move was not unexpected in the light of the world-wide trends
in the second half of this century. Yet, new policies alone cannot alter
the tacit recognition by the majority of Canadians of the tenet, so well
established by 1907, that "Canada is white man's country and must
remain a white man's country." Already faint echoes of its old anti-
Asiatic sentiments have sounded over the horizon of British Columbia.

As for the investigation and the subsequent settlement of damages
caused by the 1907 riots, the Canadian government acquitted itself well
by acting promptly and fairly, without making international involve-

ment necessary. This step helped to maintain the existing cordial ties between Japan and Canada and the rest of the British Empire. Most noteworthy of all were the close and friendly relations which existed throughout the period of the investigations in Vancouver and during the negotiations of the Canadian envoys in Tokyo on their difficult and sensitive mission. Indeed, in the latter instance, so intimate were the sentiments between the two countries that the Canadian representatives did not meet with the American Ambassador at Tokyo, although he evinced a strong desire to deal jointly with Canada on the problem of Japanese immigration. In reciprocating, the Japanese delayed concluding the Gentlemen's Agreement with the United States until the negotiations with Canada were completed and its emissaries were safely back in Canada.

The unfortunate incident was brought to a satisfactory conclusion, and, in the process, an enduring understanding was also consummated on the basis of international diplomacy. For Canada, this was also its initial experience in international negotiations, exclusive of trade agreements, and Canada thus entered a new stage of responsibility among the nations of the world.

NOTES

1. The Vancouver *Daily Province,* September 6, 7, and 8, 1907.
2. The Asiatic Exclusion League, organized in Vancouver on August 12, 1907, was one of several leagues on the West Coast devoted to the exclusion of Asiatics in general, and the Japanese in particular, from Canada and the United States. The first such organization was formed in San Francisco on May 7, 1905 and immediately gained wide support, especially among the labor groups. Most of the coastal cities, including Seattle and Bellingham, had their "Leagues." For further details, see J. Castell Hopkins, *The Canadian Annual Review of Public Affairs, 1907* (Toronto: The Annual Publishing Company, Limited, 1908), p. 384 (hereafter cited as CAR) and also George Kennan, "The Japanese in the San Francisco Schools" in *The Outlook* LXXXVI (June 1907) 246-52.
3. This is the site on which the bus terminal is presently located.
4. *Daily News-Advertiser,* September 8, 1907. Westminster Avenue has since been renamed Main Street.
5. Vancouver *Daily World,* September 9, 1907.
6. *Ibid.*
7. *Daily News-Advertiser,* September 8, 1907. The Lieutenant Governor, James Dunsmuir, and his family were interested, as owners, in a number of coal mines on Vancouver Island, and they were at this time employers of Asiatic laborers. In the eyes of labor groups, they were capitalists profiting from Asiatic immigration. It must be noted, however, that, as Premier of British Columbia,

Dunsmuir wrote to the Prime Minister of Canada in October 1900 and recommended restrictive measures on Asiatic immigration. See letter, Dunsmuir to Laurier, Canada, Parliament, House of Commons, *Sessional Papers,* XLII (1907–8, v. 18), 74b (1907), p. 55, P.C. 2457. (Hereafter cited as *Sessional Papers.*)

The idea for the British Columbia law had its origin in the *Natal Act* passed by the Colony of Natal in 1897 in an effort to curb immigration from India by imposing a literacy test which demanded knowledge of a European language. The British Columbia legislature passed a *Natal Act* at almost every session, starting in the year 1900, which was as often disallowed by the dominion government.

8. *Daily News-Advertiser,* September 8, 1907.

9. The Vancouver *Daily Province,* September 9, 1907.

10. Arthur E. Fowler was a resident of Seattle who devoted much of his time to leading anti-Japanese activities in the north coastal regions, including Vancouver. "He was known as a cook, but preferred to think of himself as an artist." He had a record as an inmate of the Washington State Asylum at Steilacoom for a time and was one of the leaders in the attack on the Hindus of Bellingham two days before the Vancouver Anti-Japanese Riots. (See Seattle *Post-Intelligencer,* September 14, 1907.)

11. *Daily Colonist,* September 10, 1907. From an eyewitness account by one who saw the proceedings in front of the City Hall on Westminster Avenue.

12. Vancouver *Daily World,* September 9, 1907.

13. *Ibid.*

14. *Daily News-Advertiser,* September 8, 1907. The attendance at the hall was estimated at 2,000.

15. Alan Morley, *Vancouver: From Milltown to Metropolis* (Vancouver: Mitchell Press, 1961), p. 122. See also the Vancouver *Daily Province,* September 9, 1907. Since the total population of the city was only 75,000 (the figure given at the City Council meeting as reported in the *Daily News-Advertiser* on September 11), either the estimate was high or the turnout exceedingly good. It was well known, however, that entire sections of the city, such as the West End, were not aware of the riots in the East End at the time. (Interview with Major J. S. Matthews, December 4, 1961, Vancouver City Archivist, who saw the riots.) Eyewitnesses, nevertheless, stated that the streets in the area of the riots were so seriously congested that street cars were brought to a standstill. See *Daily News-Advertiser,* September 11, 1907.

16. A. W. Von Rhein, an American citizen, was the president of the Vancouver Asiatic Exclusion League and, according to a "Special Agent's" report, was known as "a walking delegate of the Bartenders' Union" at Vancouver. See Public Archives of Canada, *Mackenzie King Papers,* M.G. 26, J 4, vol. 13, File 75, C8684. (Hereafter cited as the *King Papers.*)

The Special Agent was T. R. E. McInnes, a former lawyer of Vancouver, who used the cover name of W. E. McInnes in his reports to the Honourable Frank Oliver, the Minister of the Interior, to whom he was directly responsible. A son of a former Lieutenant Governor of British Columbia, he offered his services to the Prime Minister immediately after the riots to make a secret assessment of the undercurrent developments in the anti-Japanese movement at the West Coast and was accepted.

17. *Daily News-Advertiser,* September 8, 1907 and the Vancouver *Daily Province,* September 9, 1907.

18. *Daily News-Advertiser,* September 8, 1907. The Reverend Dr. H. W. Fraser, the minister at the First Presbyterian Church at the corner of Hastings Street and Gore Avenue, was an American citizen of Canadian birth who declared in one of his sermons, "his opposition to the landing of one Oriental or a million," and complained that, "we are vassals of Britain and England runs things in the Dominion of Canada pretty much as she pleases." He maintained that, "as a body, the missionaries were exclusionists who did not aid Chinese and Japanese to come to the United States or to Canada by helping them to learn English." See CAR, p. 388 and also The Vancouver *Daily Province,* October 7 and 8, 1907.

19. *Daily News-Advertiser,* September 8, 1907.

20. Vancouver *Daily World,* September 9, 1907. The Reverend G. H. Wilson was the Rector of St. Michael's Church, Westminster Road, Mt. Pleasant.

21. Harry Cowan was "an influential Liberal labour man." He appeared before the Commission investigations of the riots as the League's appointed representative and attended all the sittings, assisting counsel but not taking part in the cross-examination of witnesses.

22. *Daily News-Advertiser,* September 8, 1907. See also CAR, p. 386, for references to the *Oregonian* (n.d.) which listed F. W. Cotterill, president of the Washington State Federation of Labor, and G. P. Listman, another Seattle labor leader, as present at the meeting.

23. For details, see speech in the House of Commons by Duncan Ross (Liberal, Yale-Cariboo) referring to McBride's statement to the Secretary of State on April 16, 1907, implying that the B. C. Immigration Act of 1907 would not receive royal assent. This information was offered two days before the Act was to have received its second reading in the legislature and seven days before the Lieutenant Governor was to have made his decision. A *quid pro quo* arrangement between the two men was suspected. See Canada, Parliament, House of Commons, *Debates,* LXXXII (1907-8, v. 1), pp. 1756 and 1757. (Hereafter cited as *Debates.*)

24. *Daily News-Advertiser,* September 8, 1907.

25. The Vancouver *Daily Province,* September 9, 1907.

26. *Ibid.* The firm, operated by U. Kawasaki and Brother, was awarded damages amounting to $2,400.10, by far the highest of all individual payments. See also *Sessional Papers,* 74g, p. 21.

27. The Vancouver *Daily Province,* September 9, 1907.

28. *Ibid.*

29. *Ibid.*

30. *Daily News-Advertiser,* September 9, 1907.

31. Interview with retired Police Sergeant William Kuner of 1836 Venables Street, Vancouver, B. C., December 10, 1961. Sergeant Kuner was on the Vancouver City Police force in 1907 at the time of the riots. According to his

recollection, the force at the time was not large, and, as far as he could remember, not many more than six or seven men were on the beat at any one time. He recollected that his badge number was 42 and that among the numbers posted some no longer had names listed opposite them.

32. *Daily News-Advertiser,* September 8, 1907.

33. The Vancouver *Daily Province,* September 9, 1907.

34. *Daily News-Advertiser,* September 8, 1907.

35. Knives, stones, clubs, bricks, blocks of wood, iron bars, and bottles, as well as the more conventional types of weapons, were used. (*Sake* and whiskey bottles were always plentiful in Japanese communities.) On the day following the initial riots, countless rooftops of Japanese shops and homes were virtual arsenals lined with bottles and other weapons. See the Vancouver *Daily Province,* September 9, 1907. Also confirmed by Major J. S. Matthews during interview on December 4, 1961. Bottles broken at the neck were effectively used as daggers in the "*banzai* charges."

36. *Daily News-Advertiser,* September 8, 1907.

37. Today's Powell Street Grounds.

38. Vancouver *Daily World,* September 9, 1907. The church was dedicated in 1906.

39. *Sessional Papers,* 74g, Appendix.

40. The Vancouver *Daily Province,* September 9, 1907.

41. *Daily News-Advertiser,* September 8, 1907 and the Vancouver *Daily Province,* September 9, 1907.

42. *Ibid.*

43. Telegraphic message, Morikawa (Japanese Consul, Vancouver) to Nosse (Japanese Consul General at Ottawa), September 10, 1907. Public Archives of Canada, *Laurier Papers.* M.G. 26, G l(a), vol. 477, p. 128812. (Hereafter cited as *Laurier Papers.*)

44. *Daily News-Advertiser,* September 8, 1907.

45. *Ibid.*

46. *Ibid.*

47. Interview with Sergeant Kuner, *op. cit.,* December 10, 1961.

48. *Ibid.* Sergeant Kuner himself had his turn at the barricade on Sunday morning. He related with some amusement an incident which concerned a brash young man, who, disregarding the Sergeant's good advice, was about to enter the guarded zone, whereupon the policeman pointed out to him the "men on sentry duty" on the other side. The man beat a hasty retreat!

49. Vancouver *Daily World,* September 9, 1907.

50. *Ibid.*

51. The Vancouver *Daily Province,* September 8, 1907.

52. Kikujiro Ishii of the Commerce Department of the Japanese Foreign Office, who, as Special Commissioner, was making a tour of inspection of Japanese communities in the major cities of the West Coast because of the prevailing anti-Japanese feeling, arrived in Vancouver in the midst of the riots and thus was able to transmit first-hand accounts of the demonstration to the Foreign Office of Japan. See telegraphic message, Ishii to Consulate General of

Japan at Ottawa, September 8, 1907, *Laurier Papers,* M.G. 26, G l(a), vol. 477, 128808 and also 128799-128801 (Special Agent's Report).

53. Morley, *op. cit.,* p. 122.

54. Vancouver *Daily World,* September 9, 1907.

55. *Daily News-Advertiser,* September 10, 1907.

56. *Daily Colonist,* September 10, 1907, quoting the report by the Victoria *Times* and the Seattle *Post-Intelligencer;* see also the Vancouver *Daily News-Advertiser* of September 8, 1907 for a similar account, differing only in details.

57. Statement by F. W. Bayliss, quoted in the *Daily Colonist,* September 10, 1907. Bayliss, a member of the James Bay (Victoria) Athletic Club team which had competed in Vancouver, was on the docks when the *Charmer* arrived on the evening of September 7. See also The Vancouver *Daily Province,* September 9, 1907 which also made reference to the erroneous report then current and concluded with the statement: "No encounter of any nature occurred on the wharf."

58. Vancouver *Daily World,* September 9, 1907.

59. Thomas A. Bailey, *Theodore Roosevelt and the Japanese-American Crises: An Account of International Complications Arising from the Race Problem on the Pacific Coast* (Stanford: Stanford University Press, 1934), p. 253.

60. Two nights before the Vancouver riots, the anti-Asiatic group in Bellingham was instrumental in carrying out a violent attack upon the "Hindus" (actually most of them were Sikhs from the Punjab), who were British subjects. Many Hindus were pulled out of bed in the dead of night and seriously injured, while some others were forced into the waters of the bay. The mob action proved successful in driving out the Hindus from Bellingham, never to return. Made homeless when their living quarters and household possessions were destroyed, most of the victims went to Vancouver. The British government officials were outraged and demanded an investigation into the losses caused by the incident and appropriate compensation by the United States government.

61. *Daily News-Advertiser,* September 10, 1907.

62. *Sessional Papers,* 74b, p. 165, P.C. 2170. "Extract from a Report of the Committee of the Privy Council, approved by the Governor General on the 12th October, 1907," noted a memorandum to this effect, received by the Secretary of State for Canada on September 28, 1907.

63. *Ibid.,* p. 15.

64. *Sessional Papers,* 74g, p. 12.

65. Morikawa to King, November 19, 1907. See *Sessional Papers,* 74g ("Report by W. L. Mackenzie King, C.M.G., Commissioner, Appointed to Investigate into the Losses Sustained by the Japanese Population of Vancouver, B. C. on the Occasion of the Riots in That City in September, 1907."), p. 14.

66. Rumors that the Japanese government connived with emigration companies to increase the number of immigrants had fanned suspicions. The source of these is discussed subsequently in this paper.

67. W. L. Mackenzie King, *Report of the Royal Commission Appointed to Inquire into the Methods by Which Oriental Labourers Have Been Induced to Come to Canada* (Ottawa: Government Printing Office, 1908), p. 55. (Hereafter cited as *Royal Commission on Oriental Labourers.*)

68. *Ibid.,* pp. 14-15. The figures represent totals for all those who crossed the Pacific, regardless of whether or not they landed or proceeded to the United States. An arithmetical error appears in the report; the correct figure for the Hindus is 2,047.

69. *Ibid.,* p. 27.

70. *Debates,* LXXXII (1907-8, v. 1), p. 1748.

71. *Royal Commission on Oriental Labourers,* p. 42.

72. *Ibid.,* p. 44.

73. *Ibid.,* p. 45. This type of arrangement was the source of much criticism by labor and political leaders, but the conclusion reached in this study is that it hardly deserved adverse comment. It was peculiarly suited to the Japanese whose social and economic organization was based on a system of obligations and thus served a necessary and useful purpose.

74. *Sessional Papers,* 74b, p. 124.

75. Cablegram, Lemieux to Laurier, December 10, 1907. *Laurier Papers,* M.G. 26, G l(a), vol. 489, 132183.

76. Cablegram, Lemieux to Laurier, December 10, 1907. *Ibid.,* 132146.

77. Hayashi to MacDonald, December 23, 1907. Public Archives of Canada, *Lemieux Papers,* M.G. 27, II, D10, vol. 7, 823. A supplementary section of the *Agreement* consisted of a confidential letter from the Japanese Foreign Minister to the British Ambassador, stating that, in the opinion of the Japanese government, the total number of Japanese emigrants leaving for Canada was not expected to exceed 400. The confidence was not entirely observed in Canada, and the press made free use of this information, and this action was protested by the Japanese. See MacDonald to Lord Grey, July 9, 1908, *ibid.,* 952.

78. Hayashi to MacDonald, December 23, 1907. *Ibid.,* 823.

79. *Royal Commission on Oriental Labourers,* pp. 22-24, 41-48, and 54-63.

80. *Ibid.,* p. 67.

81. Report of the Special Agent to the Minister of the Interior, October 2, 1907. *King Papers,* M.G. 26, J 4, vol. 13, File 75.

82. Grey to Elgin, November 14, 1907. Public Archives of Canada, *Grey of Howick Papers,* M.G. 27, II, B2, vol. 14, 003843.

83. *Royal Commission on Oriental Labourers,* p. 21.

84. *Ibid.,* p. 70.

85. *Ibid.,* p. 75.

86. Report of the Special Agent to the Minister of the Interior, October 2, 1907. *King Papers,* M.G. 26, J 4, vol. 13, File 75. The speech was delivered at the Victoria Theatre in Victoria on the evening of February 1, 1907 and was reported in the press the following day—election day.

87. For details of the alleged contract for 50,000 men, see the Vancouver *Daily Province* of February 1, 1907. The information for the newspaper's articles apparently came from a garbled version of the communications between E. G. Russell, the local agent for the Grand Trunk Pacific Railway, and Gotoh of the labor agency, as furnished by the latter's solicitor. Gotoh and Yoshy were actually at the time recruiting workers in Japan for the C. P. R., the great friend and supporter of Bowser and the Conservatives.

88. E. G. Russell to S. Gotoh, December 10, 1906. For the letter in longhand, see *King Papers,* M.G. 26, J 4, vol. 106, 207. See also the Special Agent's Report, *ibid.,* vol. 13, File 75. Russell was the Pacific Coast agent for the Grand Trunk Pacific Railway Company and also manager of the United Supply and Contracting Company, Limited, a firm which was to engage in furnishing supplies to the railway company. Investigation of Japanese immigration to Canada failed to reveal the existence of any contract for labor between the railway company and any other firm or individual. The terms in the fictitious contract alluded to were apparently taken from the C. P. R. contract which Bowser himself had drawn up.

89. *Debates,* LXXXII (1907-8, v. 1), p. 1754. The Act, commonly known as the Bowser Bill, stated:

The immigration into British Columbia of any person who, when asked to do so by the officer appointed under this Act, shall fail himself to write out and sign, in the English language, or any language of Europe, an application to the provincial secretary of the province of British Columbia to the effect in the form set out in Schedule B to this Act annexed, as well as read in English or any language of Europe, any test submitted to him by the officer appointed under this Act, shall be *lawful* (italics added).

90. The Vancouver *Daily Province,* August 5, 1944. King, as Prime Minister, declared in the House of Commons on August 4: "No immigration of Japanese will be permitted after the war." The paper on the following day editorialized in part as follows:

When the dust and passion of the conflict in which all our emotions are surcharged shall give way to calmer judgments of peace, it is very unlikely that Mr. King's present announcement of policy about our Japanese will stand up to the realities of practical politics.

My Experience with the
Wartime Relocation of Japanese

ESTHER B. RHOADS*

with a bibliographical essay by HOWARD H. SUGIMOTO

On December 7, 1941 the Japanese in America were as shocked as everyone else in the United States when they learned of the attack on Pearl Harbor. The truck farmers were at work in the fields, the nursery men and the store owners were at their usual jobs or relaxing at home, and children were helping their parents, studying or returning from Sunday school when they heard the news.

In addition to the thousands of Japanese in Hawaii, there were more than 127,000 persons of Japanese ancestry in the continental United States. About 63 percent of these were born in this country, but because of their youth only about 15 percent were of voting age. The immigrants came from a great variety of backgrounds and from many parts of Japan, but the great majority were from western Japan, second or third sons of farmers or fishermen from crowded areas where the inheritance was too small to be divided. They had come seeking a better life for themselves and their children.

In the still rather feudal system of Japan, the one chance of improving one's social status was through education. America offered unlimited educational and economic opportunities if one worked hard. Despite discrimination and the inability of the first-generation parents to become citizens, many Japanese settled on the West Coast.

Some were businessmen, priests, and teachers influential in their

*Esther B. Rhoads lived in Japan for 20 years before 1941. A teacher at the Friends (Quaker) School in Tokyo, she was one of few Americans who could speak Japanese. Home on furlough at the beginning of the Pacific war, she began work in February 1942 with the Quaker-sponsored American Friends Service Committee program to help persons of Japanese ancestry and continued in this until June 1946. Then she returned to Occupied Japan to work with the AFSC relief program and teach at the Friends School until 1960. In this essay the term "Japanese" is sometimes used in the old-fashioned way of ethnic identification. It should be remembered that even during the Pacific war period more than half the "Japanese" in North America were actually Japanese Americans or Japanese Canadians.

communities; some were successful farmers, nurserymen and fishermen; and many were laborers working on truck farms or ranches all along the West Coast and in Arizona. Most of the Issei (first generation) emigrated between 1900 and 1915. Their wives were often younger, having come after their husbands were well established; hence there were a large number of minor children. Many of the men never married, as immigration laws after 1924 prevented the admission of more Oriental immigrants.

During the depression some families returned to Japan, where the children were often unhappy. They longed for the better life in the United States and did not want to take Japanese citizenship and be subject to military conscription there. As they approached the age of 18 some returned to the United States and were known as "Kibei." There were some in this group who were extremely critical of the United States, having been exposed to anti-American attitudes in Japanese schools. Many were without relatives to guide and steady them.

The Issei women had much less opportunity than their husbands to learn English and American ways. Many could express themselves adequately only in Japanese, while their American-educated children spoke only enough Japanese to ask for material things at home. Communication about abstract ideas was almost impossible, making the gap between generations great indeed.

After Pearl Harbor, the FBI interned some of the Japanese leaders in Hawaii, though most were left to continue life as usual, but Californians were frightened. If the United States defenses at Pearl Harbor were so easily incapacitated, what might happen to California? The FBI immediately began picking up prominent leaders and the fishermen who were familiar with the coast near important naval bases. The Japanese Navy pushed south, taking the Philippines, Hong Kong and Singapore. With each victory more Japanese men were arrested in the United States. During these first three months, most men kept a small over-night bag ready in case they were taken. Curfew regulations were enforced. Chinese, fearing that they would be confused with Japanese, wore buttons saying "I am Chinese." Suspicion and false alarms were rife.

In February 1942 after air raid warnings had blocked out the coast, orders were issued to all persons of Japanese ancestry living on Terminal Island near Los Angeles, and Bainbridge in Puget Sound, to leave within 48 hours. As most of the fishermen were interned, their wives felt ill-prepared to care for their families, but inland Japanese opened their homes to acquaintances and church groups opened hostels where the larger families found shelter. I was connected with one of these hostels, where over 100 homeless persons came, bringing some furniture and other possessions. There was very real solidarity in this group. Food supplies were pooled. Japanese truck farmers brought vegetables and for a remarkably low rate we were able to care for this large group for nearly four months.

Many good Japanese traits helped. Their respect for authority and gratitude made discipline easy. They were accustomed to living simply and making good use of their limited resources. They shared the work in cleaning, cooking, laundering, and caring for the grounds. But their lack of respect for womanhood and the mothers' poor English made communication difficult in families whose father was interned. The older boys could not understand their mothers' concern.

Since the older generation was denied American citizenship, it was only natural that they felt a deep loyalty to Japan. They were secretly pleased by Japan's strength and rapid advance. But they were even more pleased that the advance was south and west, not east of Hawaii. Their children on the other hand, were loyal Americans at heart and legally citizens; some were serving in the Army. The attack on Pearl Harbor left them broken-hearted. The Japanese living near Salinas, California were especially unfortunate. A number of Japanese draftees from that area were casualties of the attack on Pearl Harbor. Caucasian truck farmers were nonetheless resentful because Japanese farmers were often more successful than they.

After Pearl Harbor there was public pressure demanding the internment of all Japanese, citizens and aliens alike. The first efforts to intern them resulted in hopeless confusion. Japanese were told they would get adequate warning if their evacuation was ordered, but the first order allowed only two days. Some tried to leave the West Coast voluntarily but few had a place to go. Some of those who left were refused service at gasoline stations, restaurants, and hotels. In the face of these difficulties many families gave up plans to go east. On the other hand, hundreds of Caucasians remained friendly and did all they could to be neighborly. Teachers were especially kind to Japanese children who attended public school up to the day of evacuation.

One little Japanese girl was reported to have told a traffic policeman, "I won't be coming to school tomorrow. We have to go away. Father says 'If it wasn't for those damn Japs, we wouldn't have to go.'" Such sentiments were common. The children considered themselves Americans. Finally, the evacuation of the western half of the Pacific states was ordered. Each family was allowed to take what its members could carry, and their other possessions were to be stored in government warehouses, left with friends, or rented with houses and land owned by Japanese citizens.

Presidio of San Francisco, California
May 3, 1942

INSTRUCTIONS
TO ALL PERSONS OF
JAPANESE
ANCESTRY
Living in the Following Area:

All of that portion of the City of Los Angeles, State of California, within that boundary beginning at the point at which North Figueroa Street meets a line following the middle of the Los Angeles River; thence southerly and following the said line to East First Street; thence westerly on East First Street to Alameda Street; thence southerly on Alameda Street to East Third Street; thence northwesterly on East Third Street to Main Street; thence northerly on Main Street to First Street; thence northwesterly on First Street to Figueroa Street; thence northeasterly on Figueroa Street to the point of beginning.

Pursuant to the provisions of Civilian Exclusion Order No. 33, this Headquarters, dated May 3, 1942, all persons of Japanese ancestry, both alien and non-alien, will be evacuated from the above area by 12 o'clock noon, P. W. T., Saturday, May 9, 1942.

No Japanese person living in the above area will be permitted to change residence after 12 o'clock noon, P. W. T., Sunday, May 3, 1942, without obtaining special permission from the representative of the Commanding General, Southern California Sector, at the Civil Control Station located at:

Japanese Union Church,
120 North San Pedro Street,
Los Angeles, California.

Such permits will only be granted for the purpose of uniting members of a family, or in cases of grave emergency.

The Civil Control Station is equipped to assist the Japanese population affected by this evacuation in the following ways:

1. Give advice and instructions on the evacuation.
2. Provide services with respect to the management, leasing, sale, storage or other disposition of most kinds of property, such as real estate, business and professional equipment, household goods, boats, automobiles and livestock.
3. Provide temporary residence elsewhere for all Japanese in family groups.
4. Transport persons and a limited amount of clothing and equipment to their new residence.

The Following Instructions Must Be Observed:

1. A responsible member of each family, preferably the head of the family, or the person in whose name most of the property is held, and each individual living alone, will report to the Civil Control Station to receive further instructions. This must be done between 8:00 A. M. and 5:00 P. M. on Monday, May 4, 1942, or between 8:00 A. M. and 5:00 P. M. on Tuesday, May 5, 1942.
2. Evacuees must carry with them on departure for the Assembly Center, the following property:
   (a) Bedding and linens (no mattress) for each member of the family;
   (b) Toilet articles for each member of the family;
   (c) Extra clothing for each member of the family;
   (d) Sufficient knives, forks, spoons, plates, bowls and cups for each member of the family;
   (e) Essential personal effects for each member of the family.
   All items carried will be securely packaged, tied and plainly marked with the name of the owner and numbered in accordance with instructions obtained at the Civil Control Station. The size and number of packages is limited to that which can be carried by the individual or family group.
3. No pets of any kind will be permitted.
4. No personal items and no household goods will be shipped to the Assembly Center.
5. The United States Government through its agencies will provide for the storage, at the sole risk of the owner, of the more substantial household items, such as iceboxes, washing machines, pianos and other heavy furniture. Cooking utensils and other small items will be accepted for storage if crated, packed and plainly marked with the name and address of the owner. Only one name and address will be used by a given family.
6. Each family, and individual living alone, will be furnished transportation to the Assembly Center or will be authorized to travel by private automobile in a supervised group. All instructions pertaining to the movement will be obtained at the Civil Control Station.

Go to the Civil Control Station between the hours of 8:00 A.M. and 5:00 P.M., Monday, May 4, 1942, or between the hours of 8:00 A.M. and 5:00 P.M., Tuesday, May 5, 1942, to receive further instructions.

J. L. DeWITT
Lieutenant General, U. S. Army
Commanding

SEE CIVILIAN EXCLUSION ORDER NO. 33.

A relocation order typical of those posted.

The American Friends Service Committee, the Quaker group with which I worked, did not believe the evacuation was necessary and protested it strongly. We tried, however, to help the evacuees in any way we could. We opened the largest of the hostels in Los Angeles in February 1942 for evacuees from Terminal Island. Volunteers acted as advisors and helped arrange for the care of property.

One of the evacuations was scheduled to leave from a park in a town where zoning prohibited Orientals. We tried unsuccessfully to find a church group which would contribute coffee or at least the facilities for making it, so volunteers rose at 3 a.m. in Pasadena, took buttered rolls and milk for the children, and quietly served the 600 departing by bus at 6 a.m. In the park the American Legion had a small hall with huge coffee pots which they gladly loaned for the next morning when another group was scheduled to leave.

The evacuees loaded their possessions onto trucks. One efficient Quaker helped with this, packing carefully so nothing was left behind. Army officers were in charge to direct, not to serve, but the younger men caught the spirit of goodwill and helped lift children into the buses. Neighbors and teachers were on hand to see their friends off. Members of other minority groups wept. One old Mexican woman wept, saying, "Me next. Me next."

Order followed order in March. County fair grounds and horse racing courses were prepared as assembly centers to receive all persons of Japanese ancestry. The groups were to assemble at 5:30 a.m. for 6 a.m. departures. The first to go were brought to the assembly areas by friends. The evacuees found it difficult to close their homes, arrange for their future care, and provide breakfast for their children so early in the morning. Certain church groups quietly arranged to serve hot coffee, bread, and rolls with milk for the children. In spite of rationing, the volunteers somehow provided butter as well as jam.

An army-planned move does not always consider the needs of small children, nursing mothers and the very old. The Santa Anita Race Course was an assembly center near Los Angeles. I took my car to help with four very feeble old men from a home for the aged. As they were too weak or crippled to climb on a bus or army truck, I was allowed to add my car to the procession of buses to the assembly center. People were starting off to 7 o'clock jobs, watering their gardens, sweeping their pavements. Passersby invariably stopped to stare in amazement, perhaps in horror, that this could happen in the United States. People soon became accustomed to the idea, however, and many profited from the evacuation. Japanese mortgages were foreclosed and their properties attached. They were forced to sell property such as cars and refrigerators at bargain prices. Alien bank accounts were frozen, so cash in hand seemed necessary to the evacuees.

I was in the San Joaquin Valley as one of a group of volunteers helping obtain legal aid and other services just after the evacuation orders for Japanese in that area were announced. I was forced to stop in a small town to have my generator repaired. While the work was being done, I lunched in a local diner. The proprietor was urging his customers not to buy anything yet from the "Japs." "Wait 'til a day or two before they have to go and they will sell cheap." He seemed to know those Japanese who owned autos, trucks, valuable farm equipment, and household appliances.

I tried to reassure the Japanese by urging them to believe that the U.S. government would keep its word and return all the property it stored —and the government eventually kept that promise.[1] I think my reassurance convinced a substantial number, but cash in the pocket seemed to be the only security of one woman whose prominent husband was interned.

The officials who actually handled the registration and inoculations were, on the whole, kindly men and women doing their duty. I remember one center in a Mennonite church which was comparatively free of anxious faces. The pastor treated the registrants with friendliness and that inspired confidence in a better future, which, combined with the natural Oriental acceptance of the inevitable, made for a relaxed atmosphere.

The evacuation continued into June 1942. First, Japanese near military installations were taken, then other groups in the western half of the Pacific states and finally those in the eastern half and Arizona. Ten relocation centers were built, each housing from 10,000 to 20,000 people. They were built on marginal land: Manzanar in Owens Valley was built on farm land abandoned following the exercise of water rights by officials in Los Angeles; the Tule Lake Camp in northeast California was built on a dry lake bed too alkaline to use for farming. Others were Minidoka in Idaho; Heart Mountain near Yellowstone Park, where the temperature dropped to 40 degrees below zero in winter; Poston and Gila River in the Arizona desert; Topaz in Utah; Jerome and Rohwer in Arkansas; and Granada in Colorado.

The Army erected black tar paper-covered buildings in blocks each with sixteen barracks, eight on each side of a central dining hall. Common wash rooms were built, army style. Such accommodations were adequate for able-bodied men but they were unsuitable for the old and those caring for small children—the outside, often distant, toilets were especially difficult for the latter to use. It was weeks before partitions were installed. The use of showers was a new experience for many Japanese accustomed to the deep hot baths in their homes.

Barracks built in the first centers were divided into rooms of equal size so that couples without children had to share a room with others. Later centers built barracks with various sized rooms to eliminate such unsatisfactory arrangements.

The Army architects planned the hospitals and the first one erected lacked a delivery room. The Japanese doctor in charge pointed out the need and chose a suitable place, only to find carpenters fixing shelves to receive the delivery of hospital supplies there. Apparently it never occurred to the architects that babies would be born in the camps.

There were many other adjustments that had to be made by the evacuees. Their meals were adequate but uninteresting, with too much starch and canned food. But, considering the transportation problems of wartime and the isolation of the centers, the government deserves credit for providing as well as it did. In time most of the centers developed great truck gardens. Some of the best melons and cantaloupes I have ever eaten were from the gardens of Poston and Gila.

The greatest adjustments were not occasioned by the routines of daily life, rather they resulted from changed living patterns. Communal feeding did not permit children to be fed by their parents. Long lines formed outside the mess halls. Boys of the "gang" age often ate together instead of with their parents. Rarely did fathers and mothers line up with their children to sit together as a family during meals.

Since the government provided all necessities, such as housing, food, and medical services, the problem of paying those who worked took some time to solve. The evacuees were asked to sign up for jobs. Many people were needed to work in the mess halls and to clean the wash rooms and the grounds. Assistance was needed in the offices, the hospitals, the warehouses, the fields, and the community service programs, such as welfare, schools, kindergartens, libraries, and sports.

The government finally decided to pay $14 to $18 a month for workers, and a clothing allowance of $3 a month was provided each member of each family. This allowance of "spending money" was satisfactory for the farm laborer who had earned barely enough to cover his living expenses, but it was almost insulting to businessmen and professionals used to earning $1,000 or more a month.[2]

Nevertheless, hundreds signed up to work. The effect of the crisply neat Japanese secretaries on the government staff was immediate. A day or two before Santa Anita assembly center opened, two of us took the first load of recreational materials in to those in charge. We were received casually by a large man in a plaid lumber jacket, smoking a cigar with his feet up on his desk. Five days later, after the center opened, we delivered a second load. We were received by an attractive Nisei secretary in a fresh white ruffled blouse and the same official, now in a white shirt, rose courteously to greet us.

The standards of these young people raised morale. They insisted that their mothers appear neat and fresh when they went to the mess halls, and that fathers who were not interned continue to represent the family properly. On the other hand, the parents generally insisted upon obedience and respect for authority. They were grateful that they were not separated from their citizen children. Most of them were not as disillusioned as the older children, who resented being treated as alien criminals.

Each center had a store where toilet articles, laundry soap, food, simple clothing, yard goods, and notions were sold. Each ordered hundreds of Montgomery Ward and Sears, Roebuck catalogs which the evacuees called "Wishing Books." The catalogs helped them pass many lonely hours. The evacuees bought wisely and made excellent use of the few materials available to them.

Kindergartens were organized by the evacuees and the government provided education for grades one through twelve, although buildings and teachers were not immediately available. The teachers were accredited, paid government workers and were mostly competent and sincerely interested in their students' development. This was also true of the staff working with community service programs. Relations were good between these government workers and the residents. Some difficulties arose with security, maintenance, and supply personnel. The government staff of these services tended to deal with the evacuees as prisoners.

Protests occurred in several camps and rifts developed among the residents. Some evacuees claimed that others were pro-administration "informers." The protests mostly took the form of strikes against the administration, but violence was threatened and some residents required protection of the administration. One such group was sent from Manzanar to an old Civilian Conservation Corps barracks in Death Valley, where I later made three trips to help arrange relocation.

The centers were called "relocation" centers and the War Relocation Authority began as soon as possible to encourage evacuees to "go out" of the camps. The young people going out had to prove they were loyal citizens, have a definite job adequate to support them, and provide proof of community acceptance and a sponsor. Many of the jobs offered were for farm labor, maid's work or jobs in hotels. Too often the wage offered was low.

During the first year the War Relocation Authority was forced to direct most of its energies to running the centers. Its officials therefore welcomed help from any group which could place persons of Japanese ancestry outside the centers. College students were first to be relocated outside the camps as soon as arrangements could be made. Offices were opened in Los Angeles, San Francisco, Portland, and Seattle to assemble the records of those who wished to go to college. Each record file contained the scholastic record of the applicant, letters of recommendation from university professors and neighbors, information about financial ability and needs, and a health certificate. It took weeks to assemble and evaluate this material. In the Midwest other offices contacted colleges, developed community acceptance, and arranged scholarship aid and jobs for interested students.

I was head of a Los Angeles office organized by the American Friends Service Committee with a full-time YWCA secretary and dozens of volunteers. The character and willing service of the volunteers were of inestimable value. They typed and filed hundreds of letters asking for the necessary recommendations. Experienced registrars and student advisors among them gave hours of their vacation time evaluating the records so that the best openings in colleges could be filled by the most deserving students.

One student received a clearance before leaving the assembly center but his authorization papers lay on the director's desk until only a few hours remained before his pass expired. He was hurriedly found among the thousands roaming about the camp, given an hour to pack, rushed to the Los Angeles railroad station by army jeep, and left dazed and alone in that hostile yet familiar place. He phoned us and a friend hurried to the station to see him off. In his case, a denominational college asked for him specifically because he was a certain pastor's son and consequently clearance came early.

By autumn the trickle of students cleared to leave the camps became a stream, as openings were found in medical, law, and other graduate courses as well as in many undergraduate schools. The student relocation staff placed more than 2,600 students before the evacuation ended. These students won a great deal of respect for the Nisei. They excelled scholastically, worked hard to supplement their scholarships, and wholeheartedly entered into the life of the college communities. Many attended schools in communities where there had been almost no contact with Orientals and where prejudice was strong against Japanese, but most succeeded.

One project that helped the evacuees to know that they were not forgotten by their fellow citizens originated in Pasadena, from where the idea spread. Christmas gifts were collected and shipped to the camps for distribution to the children. In early December I went to Poston to discuss the distribution and found one discouraged pastor who felt that such a project would only make trouble. There was considerable rivalry between Christians and Buddhists and probably between the different sects of each faith. This pastor felt that gifts distributed by the Christian churches might be interpreted as bribes to attract children to their Sunday schools. He could not believe there would be enough for all.

We decided to have the Christmas distribution handled by community services with all treated alike. Truck loads of gifts arrived and to everyone's delight there were many more gifts than children. Each child of school age and below received an inexpensive gift which carried a message of good will. The committees in charge sorted the gifts wisely. Toys went to the kindergartens, books to the libraries, and towels and soap were given to the old bachelors who had no children in their barracks. The supply of five- and ten-cent gifts was distributed in the Sunday schools. Some of the contacts made with the donors helped with relocation later. The recipients and donors exchanged letters, and somehow the evacuees' feeling of being forgotten was lessened.

I shared the pastor's fear that there would not be enough gifts so I bought bargain materials at a "mill-end shop"—pieces big enough to make gay skirts. After Christmas I received enthusiastic letters of appreciation from the recipients addressed "Dear Esther." I wrote back that I planned to stop in Poston and offered to perform errands for them. I also explained that I was on my way east to celebrate my mother's eightieth birthday, suggesting that my age might be guessed. Thereafter I received notes beginning "Dear Miss Rhoads" with apologies and modest requests for bobby pins and other small items. I found that my correspondents were a group of Buddhist girls whose parents were not in favor of allowing their daughters to go to college.

By 1943 the War Relocation Authority began opening offices in such large cities as Chicago. Officials sought to encourage employers to make use of the manpower available in the camps as well as to provide a channel for processing applications from the camps. Before the Authority's first office opened in Chicago, the American Friends Service staff had placed 300 Japanese in satisfactory jobs in that city. The American Friends Service devoted its energies toward the placement of special applicants, i.e., professionals with licenses to practice only in California. For example, the staff found a job in a clinic for a capable optometrist, who had supposed that the only work available to her would be as a typist or maid.

Before long, church groups opened hostels where evacuees could come for a few days and get jobs as a result of personal interviews. The hostels satisfied the requirement that the evacuees had to have jobs before they could be relocated. Many Nisei found far better jobs as a result of the hostels because they were challenged to make good.

Some parents were afraid to let their children go. Two sisters came to me and asked that I permit the younger girl to go with her sister to one of our hostels. Their parents would not give permission. I talked with the younger girl about her relationship with her parents and suggested that a break with them would be tragic. I advised her to wait until she had her parents' permission. The girls insisted that their parents were stubborn and would not understand. Still I refused and urged them to be frank with their parents. In two days the parents consented, apparently feeling they could trust the girl to an organization which stressed the value of good relations with parents.

Later the emphasis changed from relocating individuals, mostly Nisei, to that of arranging for families to leave the camps. The staff found work for many able Issei in nurseries, truck farms, and maintenance jobs at colleges where Japanese students had already proven their worth.

By autumn of 1943 induction of the Nisei into the U.S. Army became a great issue. Some of them wanted to volunteer to prove their loyalty as Americans. Others felt it was unfair of the government to call men from "internment" into service. As a result families were divided, and some boys volunteered and left without telling their parents. Two other events complicated the situation. An exchange ship, I recall, was scheduled to transport expatriates to Japan and the United States Government eventually decided to segregate those to be embarked at the Tule Lake Center.[3] I served on the welfare staff at Poston during this confusion. Japanese nationals who applied for expatriation were considered disloyal and transferred to Tule Lake. A very few subsequently embarked on the repatriation ship and most of them had relatives in Japan who requested their expatriation and helped pay their passage. We had to interpret regulations to the few who left since they were not allowed to take printed matter with them. That regulation was especially tragic for one Boy Scout who was not permitted to take the record of his honors with him—like many others he did not want to leave.[4]

The evacuees' applications for repatriation seldom were related to national loyalties. One man, too old to start over, had all his savings in a Japanese bank, and requested return to Japan to maintain his financial security. Another did not want his daughters to relocate in the Midwest —he elected to take his family to Tule Lake so the daughters would not be allowed to relocate. Still another was a second son whose older brother died, leaving a mother in Japan without support. He sent his mother money until the outbreak of the war and since that became impossible he could see no other course than to take his family back to Japan, try to find work, and support his mother and family there. So, although the list of expatriates grew, loyalty to Japan was not the primary reason for expatriation.

Social workers should not try to change the minds of such people but they can emphasize problems. Two Kibei boys came in asking to be repatriated because they did not want to serve in the U.S. army. Each owned property so they were advised to seek legal advice concerning the disposition of the farms which they would inherit from their parents. Both of those young men remained in the United States and I believe both served loyally and effectively in the army.

As the family relocation increased, fewer capable Japanese were left in the centers. Many American people protested the evacuation from the beginning and "Fair Play" committees were formed to press for a change of policy. Also, the outstanding service of the 442d Infantry Regiment Combat Team, composed entirely of Nisei, in the European Theater of Operations helped to influence public opinion and finally just before Christmas in 1944 it was announced that as of January 2, 1945 persons of Japanese ancestry would be permitted to return to the West Coast.

Again the American Friends Service Committee negotiated with the owners of the school used as a hostel in 1942. During the next two months one hundred volunteers repaired the building, which was left in a sorry state by the U.S. Army. Volunteers painted walls, restored the plumbing and fixtures and placed furniture contributed by friends. When the facility was sufficiently restored the flow of returnees began to increase. They were given board and bed at one dollar a day for ten days while they made arrangements to get back their rented properties and searched for jobs and housing. After ten days the price was raised to discourage returnees lingering with us. Some of the Japanese churches maintained smaller hostels and we helped alien Buddhist priests to obtain permits for use of their temples. By summer, the relocation centers were closed. Many of the remaining evacuees had no plans and public assistance was needed for them. The treatment of applicants by doctors and social workers who certified them for relief was impressive. They trusted the Japanese not to ask for help except when it was needed. Several men well over 75 found work somewhere and never drew on relief funds; it was a comfort to them to know they were eligible if need arose.

As the centers emptied, vacant barracks became a hazard increasingly expensive to police. The last residents were brought back and established in trailer towns recently vacated by war workers. Government and private agencies helped determine the relocation of these final groups.

The war against Japan ended on August 15, 1945 with persons of Japanese ancestry scattered all over the United States. Big cities, Chicago and New York, had the greatest concentrations but almost every state had some. The record of the Japanese was impressive; everywhere those who started with humble jobs advanced rapidly. Many stayed where they relocated; others, especially those with property, returned to the West Coast. During the three years of expulsion from the West Coast the number of Nisei of voting age increased, as those just under 21 made up the largest number of any age group in 1941. The leaders of the Japanese American Citizens League were active; lawyers and civic leaders among them worked for restoration of rights and property. New opportunities for work in professional and business fields opened up. Little by little persons of Japanese ancestry won their rightful place, including the right of the first generation to become citizens.

The evacuation camps left a black mark in the record of American justice, but their tragic effects were ameliorated by the character and determination of the Japanese themselves and the efforts of the Japanese American Citizens League. This organization worked effectively, without hate but with remarkable understanding of the war hysteria, to enrich the lives of Japanese Americans and reestablish their rightful place in American society.

Americans have generally failed to maintain racial equality—our record is not good. Negroes were brought here as slaves; Indians were driven from their land; Orientals were encouraged to immigrate to provide cheap labor; and all these racial groups have been the target of prejudice and discrimination. Now that the American conscience has been aroused great strides have been made in erasing the dismal record of the past. Perhaps no group has done so much for itself and become so much a part of American life as have the Japanese. Despite their treatment which involved discrimination, financial loss, and evacuation, they proved most loyal.

NOTES

1. Editors' note. In some communities the government formally designated places for storing personal goods which were returned undamaged to the evacuees at the end of the war. However, the authorities in charge often made no special effort to inform families of the storage arrangements and some were even

hostile to inquiries. The Tolan Committee of the House of Representatives sharply criticized this failure to protect the property of the evacuees and after the war Congress passed legislation which included provision for paying a percentage of the losses incurred.

2. Editors' note. Obviously the allowances were inadequate for anyone with continuing financial obligations such as taxes, insurance policies and mortgages. The evacuees lost heavily from the resulting defaults.

3. Editors' note. Actually no repatriation of evacuees was scheduled during the war. Only non-resident Japanese, such as diplomats and treaty merchants (that is, employees of such companies as the Mitsui and the Mitsubishi) and their families were repatriated during the war. They were taken via the Swedish ship *Gripsholm* to Lourenco Marques (Mozambique) where they were exchanged for Americans of similar status returning from East Asia. Evacuees who sought repatriation were segregated at Tule Lake late in the war, preparatory to postwar deportation. But very few were actually deported.

4. Editors' note. Children, regardless of their American citizenship and preference for staying in the United States, were required to accompany their parents.

A BIBLIOGRAPHICAL ESSAY ON THE WARTIME EVACUATION OF JAPANESE FROM THE WEST COAST AREAS

The mandatory removal of Japanese, Japanese Americans and Japanese Canadians from the West Coast during World War II has troubled many men and women of principle. Many writers, concerned with the moral and legal issues involved in the actions of their government toward the Japanese Americans, have produced works valuable for examining this aspect of wartime America. The U.S. government also published a series of official reports during the evacuation and resettlement period, which are invaluable aids to understanding the difficulties the government faced and the methods it used to solve problems as they arose.

The government publications produced under supervision of the War Relocation Authority—the agency entrusted with the detention and the resettlement of the Japanese—exhaustively examine the entire undertaking. The *Legal and Constitutional Phases of the WRA Program* treats the constitutionality of the process of evacuation and detention and the legal structure of the agency and its functions. *The Evacuated People—A Quantitative Description* is a collection of more than a hundred statistical tables and charts, covering every aspect of the evacuee population during the "relocation years." *Community Government in the War Relocation Centers* deals principally with the internal administration in the ten relocation settlements. *Impounded People—Japanese Americans in the Relo-*

cation Centers deals with the life of the evacuees at work and at play, problems of social adjustment, and the beginning of relocation to various cities and areas of the country. *The Relocation Program* covers the work of the WRA from the time of forced removal, through the period of detention, and on to the resettlement phase of the evacuation. Other useful pamphlets in this series are: *Administrative Highlights of the WRA Program; Wartime Handling of Evacuee Property; Wartime Exile—The Exclusion of the Japanese Americans from the West Coast,* and *WRA—A Story of Human Conservation,* which contains an appendix on relocation areas and their population figures. Related to these works is *People in Motion: The Postwar Adjustment of the Evacuated Japanese Americans,* produced by the War Agency Liquidation Unit, the successor to the War Relocation Authority. *People in Motion* is the story of the resettlement and readjustment of the evacuees in their new surroundings in the postwar period. *Impounded People* was also published by the University of Arizona Press (Tucson) in 1969, as was WRA Director Dillon Myer's account, *Uprooted Americans,* in 1971.

The report of the Tolan Hearings, which was partly responsible for setting the official mood for the evacuation, is found in *National Defense Migration, Hearings before the Select Committee Investigating Interstate Migration, Fourth Interim Report,* (House of Representatives, 77th Congress, 2nd Session, Report No. 2124, parts 29, 30, and 31, 1942). Appended to the report are copies of the executive orders and proclamations which created the authority and organization charged with the removal of Japanese and Japanese Americans from the West Coast Military Areas.

Three books are especially recommended for reminiscences of life in pre-war Japanese society and for glimpses of evacuee camp life as seen through the eyes of participants: Mine Okubo's *Citizen 12660* (New York: Columbia University Press, 1946) depicts the period of evacuation and the relocation in a series of revealing pictorial sketches with accompanying captions. In a similar vein, Monica Sone's *Nisei Daughter* (Boston: Little, Brown and Company, 1953) and Daisuke Kitagawa's *Issei and Nisei: The Internment Years* (New York: The Seabury Press, 1967) portray scenes day by day through the evacuation, relocation, and resettlement phases. These books sympathetically treat the evacuees' doubts and worries which arose from the shock of their economic losses and uncertain future, compounded by rapidly deteriorating family ties and divided loyalties.

Both works are autobiographical in approach. The earlier pages are devoted to the authors' views of pre-war Japanese society, followed by an account of their personal experiences among the Japanese and Japanese Americans during the years of upheaval and eventual re-integration into the larger society. Kitagawa penetratingly analyzes his subjects from both outside and inside the barbed-wire compounds of a number of relocation centers which he visited on official business as an Episcopalian minister. Monica Sone, in her narration of her early years, gives a good account of the setting of Japanese society in pre-war Seattle. Her reactions to her earlier experiences during a trip to Japan are probably indicative of the general Nisei attitudes toward Japan and its culture.

Bill Hosokawa's *Nisei: The Quiet Americans* (New York: William Morrow & Co., 1969) is the first comprehensive story of the Japanese and Japanese Americans in America. The author, a well-known journalist (associate editor of the *Denver Post*), was evacuated and relocated. His vivid account of the war years, although written for the lay reader, is based on substantial research.

Dorothy Swaine Thomas wrote a graphic account of the plight of the Japanese and Japanese Americans at three crucial periods during the war years in two volumes. The first volume, entitled *The Spoilage* and co-authored by Richard S. Nishimoto (Berkeley and Los Angeles: University of California Press, 1946), analyzes the problems of those groups which sought repatriation and expatriation to Japan. (It should be noted that some social scientists associated with WRA, such as Professor Marvin Opler, disagreed with the work.) The author's description of the removal and resettlement aspects of the evacuation process serves as a convenient comparison with the version given in the official government reports mentioned above. The second volume, *The Salvage: Japanese American Evacuation and Resettlement,* prepared with the assistance of Charles Kikuchi and James Sakoda (Berkeley and Los Angeles: University of California Press, 1952), consists chiefly of representative case histories of a number of evacuees and the course of their lives following removal from the Pacific coast regions. The brief surveys of the economic and cultural history of the immigrant Japanese identifies the pre-war motives and objectives of the Japanese and Japanese Americans in contrast to their sense of indirection during the evacuation and relocation periods.

Carey McWilliams wrote *Prejudice: Japanese-Americans: Symbol of Racial Intolerance* (Boston: Little, Brown and Company, 1944) while the decisive battles were being fought in the Pacific. It indicts American leadership in the Pacific coastal regions and the official government policies toward Japanese Americans. McWilliams' account relates the growth of prejudice against the Japanese and the triumph of anti-Japanese sentiment in the West which culminated in the expulsion of both aliens and United States citizens of Japanese ancestry from their homes. The work also assesses the effect of that biased treatment of the Japanese on the peoples of post-war Asia.

Removal and Return: The Socio-Economic Effects of the War on Japanese Americans by Leonard Broom (also Bloom) and Ruth Riemer (Berkeley and Los Angeles: University of California Press, 1949. University of California Publications in Culture and Society, IV, 1949) is a sociological study of the evacuees and the impact of the evacuation on their economic and occupational status. Case histories provide ample evidence that U.S. government agencies failed to protect Japanese American property and interests. The authors comment on how certain government agencies minimize that failure in their official records.

Case history studies on Japanese families are found in Volume VI of the University of California Publications in Culture and Society, *The Managed Casualty: The Japanese-American Family in World War II* by Leonard Broom and John I. Kitsuse (Berkeley and Los Angeles: University of California Press, 1956). This work includes a brief general survey of the evacuation and relocation. Case histories cite the solidarity of Japanese families prior to the evacuation, family disintegration in relocation, and post-war settlement and reintegration. The study shows clearly that the evacuation undermined the authority of heads of households with a consequent breakdown in family solidarity which resulted in more individualism and independence for the younger members.

Alexander H. Leighton in the *Governing of Men: General Principles and Recommendations Based on Experience at a Japanese Relocation Camp* (Princeton: Princeton University Press, 1945) studies the Poston Relocation Center in depth. The study is based on an investigation of the social and anthropological aspects of camp life. A team of experts analyzed social problems in the camp, such as those which resulted in a strike against the administration. The analysis was the basis of recommendations made to the governmental authorities concerning those features of community management judged to be useful in the administration of "occupied areas" in the Pacific.

Probably the best study on the cultural and artistic activities in the relocation communities is the short work by Allen H. Eaton, *Beauty Behind Barbed Wire: The Arts of the Japanese in Our Relocation Camps* (New York: Harper, 1952). Despite the vicissitudes of camp life, many evacuees brought beauty to their otherwise bleak surroundings, creating works of art by judiciously blending their natural and human resources. The author describes the hobbies and group activities which helped to keep the Japanese constructively occupied. A selection of photographs portrays the range of talent present among the evacuees. The work includes an annotated bibliography helpful to those who wish to pursue the subject further.

Two works by Forrest La Violette provide a meaningful basis for understanding Japanese Canadian as well as American problems during their evacuation from the Pacific coastal areas of the United States and Canada and their eventual resettlement. *Americans of Japanese Ancestry: A Study of Assimilation in the American Community* (Toronto: Canadian Institute of International Affairs, 1945) is a sociological study of the Japanese community in the United States. *The Canadian Japanese and World War II: A Sociological and Psychological Account* (Toronto: University of Toronto Press, 1948), was published under the auspices of the Canadian Institute of International Affairs and the Institute of Pacific Relations. It is a study of the crisis created by the Pacific War and its effects on the Japanese Canadians in the "protected areas" of the Canadian West. The popular agitation for evacuation of Japanese Canadians from these areas and their consequent removal and resettlement are given considerable attention, enabling readers to compare the methods employed by the United States and Canada in solving similar problems.

A unique feature of the official Canadian proposal for the "ultimate resolution" of the Japanese problem was a government order, initiated during the final stages of the war, directing the Royal Canadian Mounted Police to exert pressure on the "Japanese" to accept the terms of "repatriation" to Japan. This was the only instance in which the Canadian policy differed seriously from that of the United States with regard to the evacuated population during and following World War II. The legality of the order itself was contested in the courts after prolonged delays and was, in principle, upheld by a majority ruling of the Supreme Court of Canada. The subsequent change by the government was largely designed to mollify the general moral indignation of a small, but important, segment of the Canadian public. The attempt at a general "repatriation" was thus thwarted.

The story of the leadership of the small but powerful group mentioned above is told in a short pamphlet by Edith Fowke, *They Made Democracy Work: The Story of the Co-operative Committee on Japanese Canadians* (Garden City Press Co-operative, Toronto). The Cooperative Committee, encouraged by support from religious and labor organizations, university and cultural groups, ethnic societies, associations of scientific and social workers, the Canadian Welfare Council, the National Council of Women, and the Civil Liberties Union, sought to uphold the principles of democracy by challenging the Canadian government which was determined "to deport" almost half the Japanese in Canada. The outcome, however, "merely underlined the fact that a nation can never depend upon the laws or constitution to defend its rights: eternal vigilance is always the price of liberty." This statement applied equally to the handling of Japanese Canadian property which is treated in a separate section. It reveals that the Cooperative Committee was instrumental in forcing the government into a re-evaluation of its policy on this property.

The same author discusses legal impediments to the freedom of Japanese Canadians in her article, "Justice and the Japanese Canadians" on page 225 of the January 1947 issue of *The Canadian Forum* (XXVI, 312). The March 1943 issue (XXII, 66, p. 350) of the same journal published a short article by C. Carlson, entitled, "Sugar Ration: Incident in Japanese Road Camp," a whimsical account of the relations between a group of "road camp evacuees" and members of the permanent crew.

What About the Japanese Canadians? written by W. H. Howard Norman and published by the Vancouver Consultative Council for Cooperation in Wartime Problems of Canadian Citizenship, is an excellent handbook explaining the circumstances faced by the Japanese and, particularly, by those among them who sought repatriation. The author was born and educated in Japan and served as a minister of the United Church in Vancouver during the war. He was an advisor to the British Columbia Security Commission (the agency for directing the removal of Japanese Canadians from the "protected areas") in setting up facilities for instruction of the children in accordance with the regulations of the Department of Education of British Columbia. He was therefore familiar with many of the problems which confronted the uprooted people.

Bernard K. Sandwell, editor-in-chief of *Saturday Night*, was one of the most outspoken and influential supporters of justice and fair play for the Japanese Canadians, especially during the most intense period of anxiety over the threat of deportation. In addition to his many speaking engagements and editorials on the subject, Sandwell made space in *Saturday Night* available to other writers to join in his efforts to arouse a lethargic public to the inherent dangers in the government policy. The pressure exerted by *Saturday Night* and its editor on the collective conscience of Canadians helped avert a further blot on the conduct of the Canadian government during wartime and in the following period of adjustment.

In one *Saturday Night* editorial (60:52, September 1, 1945, p. 3) Sandwell cited the unfair deportation procedures, deplored the lack of official information and contrasted Canadian methods with those of the United States, noting the greater American regard for citizenship. A later front-page editorial (61:19, January 12, 1946), dealt with the legal technicalities of depriving the Japanese Canadians of citizenship and deporting them without due process of law and the need for testing the validity of legislation governing these actions. On March 16 in another editorial, "Deportation Orders Can Involve Big Constitutional Problems" (61:28, 1946, p. 9), Sandwell challenged some of the judicial opinions which shaped the post-war ruling on summary deprivation of citizenship and deportation of natural-born and naturalized citizens.

Representative contributions to *Saturday Night* from other sources include the following articles: Jean E. Ferguson's "Adventure in Citizenship" (57:43, July 4, 1942); "What Future for Japanese Canadians?" by Margaret Zieman (59:11, November 20, 1943); "The Problems of Japanese Canadians, and Solution" by Norman Fergus Black (59:22, February 5, 1944); "Why the Japanese Are Against Moving East" by Frank Morrison (62:13, November 30, 1946); and N. M. McDougal's "Gunnery School for Jap-Canadians" (62:42, June 21, 1947).

The United States experience with the Japanese is further treated in Bradford Smith's *Americans from Japan* (Philadelphia: J. B. Lippincott Company, 1948). This work is a comprehensive narrative of the Japanese experience in America from the time of the arrival of castaways to the period following the evacuation. Together with Yamato Ichihashi's work on the background of Japanese society in America, *Japanese in the United States: A Critical Study of the Problems of the Japanese Immigrants and Their Children* (Stanford: Stanford University Press, 1932), it serves admirably as a review of the conditions under which the Japanese came to the United States and made it their adopted country.

Roger Daniels in the *Politics of Prejudice: The Anti-Japanese Movement in California and the Struggle for Japanese Exclusion* (Berkeley and Los Angeles: University of California Press, 1962) studies the anti-democratic agitation against the Japanese which culminated in their evacuation from the West Coast. He reviews the opposition to the Japanese displayed by groups supposedly dedicated to democratic ideals—labor unions, progressives, and the radicals of the left—and the paradox of conservative businessmen, educators, and clergymen who were often less anti-democratic. A new study by Daniels promises to be very significant: *Concentration Camps, USA: Japanese Americans and World War II* (New York: Holt, Rinehart & Winston, 1972).

The historical and political aspects of evacuation and resettlement are covered in the book *Japanese American Evacuation and Resettlement: Prejudice, War and the Constitution* by Jacobus tenBroek, Edward N. Barnhart, and Floyd W. Matson (Berkeley and Los Angeles: University of California Press, 1954). This work is a systematic analysis of the origins and consequences of the orders for the removal and dispersal of Japanese

Americans from the West Coast. It argues the pros and cons of the judicial actions taken and the probable reasons why the courts were not altogether sympathetic toward the Japanese Americans.

Capt. Allan R. Bosworth's *America's Concentration Camps* (New York: W. W. Norton, 1967) is recommended for its penetrating inquiry into the legal and political significance and the moral consequences of Lt. Gen. John L. DeWitt's order for general evacuation of all Japanese and Japanese Americans from the United States Pacific Coast Military Areas. It includes a brief, but illuminating, account of the American heritage of injustice toward racial minorities.

A useful recent study on the evacuation is *The Great Betrayal: The Evacuation of the Japanese-Americans During World War II* (New York: The Macmillan Company, 1969) by Audrey Girdner and Anne Loftis. It is an objective examination of the factors leading to the evacuation and the roles of some prominent individuals involved in the event.

An article by Eugene Rostow, "The Japanese American Cases—A Disaster," in the *Yale Law Review* LIV, 3 (June 1945), pp. 489-533, which is reproduced as Chapter VII in his book *The Sovereign Prerogative: The Supreme Court and the Quest for Law* (New Haven and London: Yale University Press, 1962) is basic to an understanding of the legal aspects involved in the evacuation. An abbreviated version on the same subject appears as "Our Worst Wartime Mistake," in *Harper's Magazine* CXCI (September 1945), pp. 193-201.

Rostow's thesis, strongly supported by Allan R. Bosworth, Jacobus tenBroek, and Carey McWilliams, is that the U.S. government erred in issuing the blanket order for the forced removal of Japanese Americans from the West Coast and that the course of action taken was an unjustifiable affront to American civil liberties. Rostow, however, mistakenly accepted the statement of Lieutenant General DeWitt, chief of the West Coast Military Command, that there was evidence of "radio signaling" from unknown persons within the command area to enemy ships at sea. Other evidence clearly indicates this was a deliberate misrepresentation by the general, who apparently possessed official information which contradicted that rumor. (See Bosworth, *supra.*, p. 56.) The WRA publication, *Wartime Exile,* also refers to the general's deliberate misrepresentation.

The legality of relocation is further discussed by Milton F. Konvitz in his book, *The Alien and the Asiatic in American Law* (Ithaca and New York: Cornell University Press, 1946). Chapter XI of that work discusses a number of Japanese "evacuation cases" taken up by the Supreme Court of the United States. Konvitz's work is an informative source on the legal position of the alien in general and the Asiatic, in particular, in regard to their right to own land, work, share in natural resources, and operate foreign language schools, as well as on our government's right to exclude and expel aliens.

Much has been written about the Japanese American fighting forces during World War II. Among the accounts of exploits of the Japanese in the special units of armed forces is *Ambassador in Arms* (Honolulu: University of Hawaii Press, 1954) by Thomas D. Murphy which is a detailed battle account of the famed 100th Infantry Battalion, composed of Japanese Americans from Hawaii. A more general work is Orville Shirey's *Americans: The Story of the 442nd Combat Team* (MTOUSA, Information-Education Section, 1945). Additional information on that subject appears in the materials already cited above, such as Bosworth's *America's Concentration Camps,* which has a superb section on the Japanese Americans in military service. Bill Hosokawa's book summarizes the less known but vital role of Nisei in the Pacific war which hitherto had been "classified" information. For an account of an individual's contribution, *A Boy from Nebraska* (New York and London: Harper & Brothers, 1946) by Ralph G. Martin on the life of Ben Kuroki, who won fame as an Air Force ace, is informative as well as delightfully entertaining.

Japanese American participation in government and military service is also discussed briefly in the *6th National Nisei Veterans' Reunion* (Los Angeles, 1970). The booklet includes some interesting and hitherto unpublished information. For example, many Japanese Americans served in the Women's Army Corps and a large number served in the Pacific theater in a variety of roles including military intelligence (as many as in the 442nd regiment in the European war). It also notes that there were nine Japanese among the crew of the *USS Maine* when it exploded in Havana Harbor in 1898 and it reveals that a Japanese was employed by the U.S. government over a hundred years ago.

Short articles covering a wide range of topics concerning the Japanese and their removal to the interior of the country are plentiful. For example, John H. Oakie's "Japanese in the United States," in *Far Eastern Survey* XI 2 (January 26, 1942) gives a brief account of the immediate impact of war on the daily lives of the Japanese in the United States. The April 1944 issue of *Fortune,* XXIX, 4 was devoted entirely to Japan and the Japanese and it summarizes Japanese culture and life and the industrial war potential of Japan. One of the articles in that issue is especially pertinent to the evacuation: "Issei, Nisei, Kibei" gives a clear insight into the mass removal with its inherent problems related to the background of the three classes of evacuees.

Frank Miyamoto's "Immigrants and Citizens of Japanese Origins," in the *Annals of American Academy of Political and Social Science* CCXXIII (September 1942), pp. 107-113, is a short commentary on the socio-economic conditions of the pre-war Japanese American population, the rise of antagonism toward them, and the eventual clamor for evacuation. The resettlement of the Japanese in their original communities is treated by William L. Worden in "The Hate that Failed," in *Saturday Evening Post* CCIX (May 4, 1946), a story of the propaganda against the Japanese and the counter-offensive carried on by the War Relocation Authority and the various citizens' committees which made frequent reference to the Nisei military record.

Carey McWilliams' "Moving the West Coast Japanese," in *Harper's Magazine* CLXXXV, 1108 (September 1942), pp. 359-369, praises the conduct of the detainees as well as the dispatch with which the U.S. Army prepared the locations and cleared the West Coast Military Areas of Japanese Americans by moving them to temporary "reception centers" during the inital stages of evacuation. The author, however, makes an erroneous assumption that "Canada, for example, merely evacuated all male Japanese between the ages of 18 and 45, but this policy again resulted in separating families." The initial order, based on sex and age categories, was soon superseded by a general order calling for the immediate evacuation of all Japanese Canadians from the "protected areas" of Canada. (For a special study of the evacuation in Canada, see La Violette's *The Canadian Japanese and World War II*, cited above.)

Commander Kenneth D. Ringle in "Japanese in America: The Problem and the Solution," in *Harper's Magazine* CLXXXV, 1109, (October 1942), pp. 489-497, is a sophisticated account with a keen appreciation of the actual situation and developments during the period under discussion. Charles Iglehart's "Citizens Behind Barbed Wire," in *The Nation* (June 6, 1942) and Forrest La Violette's "American-born Japanese and the World Crisis," in *Canadian Journal of Economic and Political Science* VII (November 1941), pp. 517-527, also merit attention.

We gratefully acknowledge the assistance of Senator Daniel K. Inouye in making available a most useful reference, entitled *Japanese-American Relocation During World War II: A Selected Bibliography*, prepared by Maryann Conway of the Library of Congress. Besides a number of the titles referred to here, Conway's bibliography lists other materials, including: Henry Fukuhara's *Portfolio of 50 Scenes of Relocation Centers* (New York: Plantin Press, 1944); the Japanese American Citizens League's *The Case for the Nisei: Brief of the Japanese-American Citizens League* (Salt Lake City, 1945); R. E. Cushman's "West Coast Curfew Applied to Japanese American Citizens: U.S. Supreme Court Decision," in *American Political Science Review* XXXVIII (April 1944), pp. 266-268;

J. F. Embree's "Relocation of Persons of Japanese Ancestry in the United States: Some Causes and Effects," in *Washington Academy of Science Journal* XXXIII (August 1943), pp. 238-242; "Epilogue to Sorry Drama: Supreme Court Decision on U.S. Debt Owed to Japanese-Americans," in *Life* LXII (April 28, 1967), p. 4; S. Fine's "Justice Murphy and the Hirabayashi Case," in *Pacific Historical Review* XXXIII (May 1964), pp. 195-209; "Racism in the Constitution: Dissenting Opinions of Justices Murphy and Jackson in the Case of F. T. Korematsu," in *Christian Century* LXII (January 3, 1942), pp. 8-9; "Restitution for the Nisei," in *Economist* CCV (October 6, 1942), p. 63; "Supreme Court Orders Repayment to Japanese-Americans," in *Christian Century* LXXXIV (April 26, 1967), p. 525; Larry Tajiri's "Farewell to Little Tokyo," in *Common Ground* IV, 2 (1944), pp. 90-95; and a number of references to Congressional and other governmental papers.

Part Three

From History to Sociology

Introduction

The relatively few overall studies on Japanese immigration to the United States and on Japanese Americans have generally concentrated on West Coast developments. The reasons are quite obvious. The Issei and Nisei were a very small, though significant, minority, and before World War II most of them lived in the Western states. In all East Coast states, the Japanese population totaled only about 2,000 in 1910, 3,800 in 1920, 4,200 in 1930, and 3,600 in 1940, as contrasted to the millions of European immigrants then on the East Coast. Moreover, until the war in the Pacific, most Americans became aware of the Japanese population only when some controversy about them arose in the Western states.

We would like to suggest that as small as their numbers were, the substantial contributions these East Coast Japanese made to America and to Japanese-American relations, as well as the differences in their experiences from those of the West Coast Issei, raise some important questions concerning the accepted views on the immigration of Japanese and their acculturation and assimilation in this country—indeed, concerning these social processes as such. Unlike their West Coast counterparts, the East Coast Issei did not face organized anti-Japanese movements; a number became prominent in the professional and cultural life of the larger society; they were able to participate actively in the promotion of Japanese-American cultural exchange; and they had a major part in founding the now gigantic trade between the two countries. They were occupationally and residentially more urban than the West Coast Issei. Very few went into agriculture or lumbering. They lived in various parts of the cities and did not develop the organized community life found in a number of West Coast cities and analyzed in the next part by Professor S. Frank Miyamoto.

The East Coast Issei, especially those in the New York area, had, as Professor Edwin O. Reischauer has observed, a crucial part in founding and fostering the Japan-America trade, which is now the largest overseas trade for both the United States and Japan. Obviously, no one in the late 1870s dreamed that trade between the two countries would become a major factor in the world economy. The New York Issei had to take the initiative, partly because Western traders residing in Japan monopolized Japan's foreign commerce in the early Meiji era. To begin building the direct trade between the two nations, the pioneer New York Issei had to establish themselves in the city, become familiar with American business practices, overcome inertia and suspicion, and win the confidence of American industrialists. T. S. Miyakawa summarizes aspects of these little-known early developments, and with access to new sources of information, reviews some of the special difficulties these Issei had to overcome.

The East Coast Issei were in a better position than the West Coast Issei to participate in the early efforts to promote Japanese-American cultural and intellectual exchange, again partly because the East Coast was free from organized anti-Japanese movements which inhibited social contacts between the Americans and the resident Japanese. Individually, many became prominent in the arts, scholarship, science, and the professions, as such names as Takamine, Kawakami, Kuniyoshi, Asakawa, Nakano, Tsunoda, and Takami would suggest.

A substantial proportion of the Japanese on the East Coast lived in "two worlds." They resided for varying periods of time in both the United States and Japan. They acted as "bridges" between the two societies; therefore it is possible to classify them either as Issei, despite their frequent stays in Japan, or as Japanese who periodically lived in America. Yasukata Murai, the ranking executive of the Morimura interests in the United States, is said to have crossed the Pacific about ninety times in the days when trans-Pacific trips meant several weeks on the high seas. America was his permanent home and his wife was an American. The Japanese American Research Project would regard him as an Issei. Incidentally, observe that he alone accounted for forty-five Japanese "arrivals" in the immigration records!

Many other trans-Pacific "bridges," however, would be difficult to regard purely as either Issei or Japanese. These can be classified, occupationally and professionally, in two main groups; the first group included international traders engaged in Japan-America commerce and the second included artists, musicians, and intellectuals. Individuals in these groups could list either country as their main residence and could accept appointments or exhibition opportunities in either country. The American academic world is more familiar now with these categories, since some scholars move back and forth between two countries.

In the second essay in this section, Sharlie C. Ushioda examines the conflicting values and cultural heritages that one intellectual had to reconcile. Inazo Nitobe could be regarded as a Japanese scholar and official dedicated to enhancing the welfare of his society, but as Mrs. Ushioda observes, he was a Quaker, a League of Nations official, and always a promoter of peace, anxious to make Japan and the United States more intelligible to each other. As a youth while still in Japan, he became a Christian. Subsequently, while living in the United States, he joined the Society of Friends and married a member of a prominent

Philadelphia family. Consequently, this traveler between the two countries was more Americanized than many Issei. Because these "bridges" had important roles, especially in the modern world, further studies in this broad subject are needed.

Early New York Issei: Founders
of Japanese-American Trade

T. SCOTT MIYAKAWA

Early New York Issei had major roles in founding direct trade between
Japan and the United States and in promoting closer relations between
the two countries. In recent years, the great United States-Japan trade
has been America's largest overseas trade (and second only to its virtually domestic trade with Canada), and the largest for Japan. In 1970
Japanese-American trade totaled over ten billion dollars and was grow-
steadily. In addition to the direct trade between the two nations, Japan
also purchased heavily from American firms located in other countries,
perhaps more than three billion dollars. Although such imports officially come from the countries where these American companies conduct business, they contribute substantially to the income of these firms
and indirectly to the American financial balance.[1]

The sheer magnitude of this trade makes it all the more difficult for
us to understand how discouraging and unpromising its prospects often
seemed to its founders, beset as they were with one obstacle after
another. Nowadays, we can scarcely appreciate what the development
of this trade implied for Meiji Japan at a time when its foreign trade was
monopolized by resident Westerners in Japan and when business firms
in America did not, and in practice could not, deal directly with their
Japanese counterparts.[2]

Most histories of this period understandably emphasize the broader
institutional and impersonal economic factors of Japanese-American
trade, such as governmental policies and commodity trends, rather than
the day-by-day activities and experiences of individual Japanese who
went abroad to build the foundations of direct trade. Many of these
studies also overlook the suspicion and hostility which these overseas
Japanese often encountered at first and their untiring efforts to overcome negative attitudes and establish mutual confidence. Numerous
difficulties arose partly because Japan had not yet developed many of
the basic financial and technical institutions which modern international commerce assumes, ranging from simple availability of reliable

business newspapers to insurance services and exchange banks for forwarding funds at standardized rates.

This account briefly describes the careers of three early Japanese arrivals in New York, Ryoichiro Arai, Toyo Morimura, and Momotaro Sato, who were regarded by their contemporaries as the founders of direct Japanese-American trade. As we shall see, they were interested in three different fields of Japanese-American trade. The difficulties they faced exemplify many that the Japanese had to overcome to trade directly with the outside world.[3]

Arai, Morimura, Sato, and three other Japanese crossed the Pacific to San Francisco on the liner *Oceanic* and arrived by train in New York in March, 1876. The other three members of the *"Oceanic* group," as the six became known in later years, were Chushichi Date, who had come to promote trade in ceramics and art goods for the Mitsuis; Rinzo Masuda, who was seeking markets for Sayama tea, silks, and Japanese merchandise; and Toichi Suzuki of the Maruzen organization, who was concerned with exports of Japanese pharmaceuticals and merchandise. Arai and Morimura were the first known New York Issei. Although it is possible that at least one or more of the pre-1876 Japanese visitors to New York settled elsewhere in the United States, the early Japanese who organized the permanent New York Issei social institutions were not aware of other long-term Japanese residents, as distinct from students and others only temporarily in the city, who might have preceded the *Oceanic* group.[4]

To understand more clearly the roles of Arai, Morimura, and Sato in New York, let us first review briefly the situation in early Meiji Japan. From its beginning in 1868 the Meiji government was confronted with the question of whether Japan could survive intact in the face of expanding European powers. To resist further encroachment, Meiji leaders took steps to strengthen their country militarily, politically, and economically. Their program called for imports of arms and such industrial essentials as machinery, railway equipment, rails, and telegraph wires. With limited specie holdings, Japan could pay for these vital imports only by exporting or by obtaining loans at high interest, the repayment of which would require more exports.[5]

To promote industry and trade, the Meiji reformers had to overcome both the feudal outlook which denigrated commerce and the traditional seclusionism which was opposed to all foreign relations, not merely foreign trade. Such Meiji slogans as "Wealth and Strength of the State through Development of Industry" meant little to many of the old feudal elite. The Japanese had to learn to esteem careers in industry, agriculture, and trade as a patriotic duty. The development of direct foreign trade was extremely difficult, since the officials and merchants who were most convinced of its necessity lacked first-hand knowledge and experience in overseas trade and marketing. Government agencies, particularly the Kansho Kyoku, were on the whole successful in their aim to make Japanese products better known by exhibiting at major international expositions. Nevertheless, in 1875 even the Kansho Kyoku failed in its project under Tomotsune Komuchi to begin exporting raw silk and silk cards directly to the United States. Understandably, resident Western traders in Japan monopolized its international commerce, except for that part of Japan's trade with China which Chinese traders controlled. Unlike the Japanese, these resident foreigners were experienced in foreign trade and had the necessary contacts with overseas firms and banks. Unequal treaties also gave the Westerners special privileges denied to the Japanese.[6]

Western nationals and nations were obviously in a position to exert major influence on the course of Japan's foreign trade. Japanese trading companies merely accepted orders from resident Westerners, collected export goods from local producers, and delivered them to the warehouses of the foreign merchants or received imported products from the Westerners for local distribution. Meiji Japanese feared that the Western merchants would expand their activities to control the domestic economy directly by replacing the Japanese trading companies and producers. The experiences of Asian and Near Eastern peoples under Western dominance clearly illustrated that Japan was in danger of becoming a plantation of the Western powers, a source of materials they wanted and a captive market for their goods. The Westerners' control of Japanese trade accounted for a significant part of the growing imbalance of Japanese international payments. Western traders profited directly from both imports and exports. Above all, a Japan dependent on foreign intermediaries would never be able to exercise normal control over its own domestic economy, promote immediately unprofitable but potentially lucrative products competitive with Western industries, or acquire first-hand familiarity with Western markets and merchandising and with foreign trade.[7]

Momotaro Sato is often considered the immediate founder of direct Japanese-American trade. He conducted a small-scale business in "fancy silks," Japanese handicraft and consumer goods, and tea, some of it retail and the balance wholesale, partly under his Japanese and American Agency. At the same time, he was associated with Toyo Morimura in founding and promoting the Hinode Company. This firm was the predecessor to the Morimura organization which engaged increasingly in substantial imports of mass production-manufactured goods from Japan. Sato also collaborated with Ryoichiro Arai in trading in raw silk, which became the most important single Japanese commodity exported to America before World War II.[8]

Sato was born in 1854 to a family well known in Japanese medicine. He was the eldest son of Shochu Sato, who was once invited to become a physician to the Shogun. Shochu Sato remained in what is now Chiba Prefecture, however, because the Han officials pleaded with him to stay. After the Restoration, he served the Emperor for a time as a physician. Shochu's father, Taizen Sato, was an even better known physician of the late Tokugawa and early Meiji period and an ardent advocate of Western medicine and learning. Taizen Sato founded and was the first director of Juntendo, a famous medical center, school, and hospital at Sakura, which still is a major medical school and center. There he attended Daimyo (feudal lord) Hotta, and also insisted on serving the public and teaching students.

In 1861, Taizen Sato retired from Juntendo and moved to Yokohama. He became an active friend of Dr. and Mrs. James C. Hepburn (Hepburn devised a system of writing Japanese in Roman alphabet), who taught his son, Kaoru, and he also knew many other American, Dutch, and French physicians in Yokohama and Tokyo. A remarkable number of his sons, sons-in-law, grandsons, and other relatives became prominent in Meiji Japan, especially in medicine. (Several sons are better known by their later adopted names, among them Kaoru Hayashi and Ryojun Matsumoto.) Almost every Japanese delegation and student group going abroad included one or two of his relatives. These ties to the West suggest that he had a significant personal role in opening Tokugawa and early Meiji Japan to the outside world.

When he was about eleven, Momotaro Sato came under the care of his grandfather, Taizen, to study English with the Hepburns. His adopted brother, Susumu, was perhaps the first Japanese to receive a regular passport to go abroad and the first Japanese to study medicine in Holland and Germany. In later years, Susumu became the third director of Juntendo and was made a baron for his distinguished service to Japanese medicine and surgery.[9]

Because of the family's strong commitment to Western learning and its personal contacts with Westerners, it is not surprising that young Momotaro also went overseas. At the age of thirteen he crossed the Pacific on the *Colorado* and landed at San Francisco. He attended a "commercial school" (probably a business college). Soon after his graduation, he went to work in a store near the corner of Market and Montgomery Streets which dealt in "general merchandise" (probably household and dry goods, although Toga suggests it was an art shop). Sato was interested in American business methods and merchandising. Some time later, he arranged to sublease one section within the store and opened his own shop to sell Japanese tea and merchandise.[10]

Sato's fellow Japanese passengers on the *Colorado* included some who were to have further contacts with him and other members of the New York group:

> Korekiyo Takahashi, a former fellow student of Momotaro Sato, who travelled by deck steerage. (Takahashi later became President of the Yokohama Specie Bank, now Bank of Tokyo, a distinguished minister of finance, and prime minister. He was one of the victims of the military assassinations in the 1930s.)
>
> Saburo Takagi of Shonai Han, who became the second consul in New York, ranking executive of the Doshin Company, and active promoter of direct foreign trade.
>
> Tetsunosuke Tomita of Sendai Han, who became the first Japanese consul in New York, governor of Tokyo Prefecture, president of the Bank of Japan, and prominent in the organization of the Fuji Textiles.

In January 1871, while in San Francisco, Sato received a Meiji government scholarship to study business and transportation. He was one of the highly selected students whom the Meiji regime sent to study in eastern U.S. schools and universities. Many of this group later became prominent in Japanese public life. Sato moved to Boston to investigate matters of concern to his business. There he attended classes at Massachusetts Institute of Technology and also observed merchandising practices of the various stores. His special interest in business administration, marketing, commercial design, and transportation could be more systematically pursued today at a modern university than at M.I.T. In 1872, he served the Iwakura diplomatic mission as an interpreter. He returned to Japan in 1875 and met Yukichi Fukuzawa, the great leader of the Meiji Enlightenment and founder of Keio Gijuku (later Keio University). Fukuzawa encouraged Sato in his efforts to awaken the Japanese to the vital need to develop their country's trade and economy. Sato apparently wanted to bring together a group to go to America to help promote direct trade. His practical, even if limited, experience in trade and his understanding of American business was unusual in the Japan of that period.[11]

The earlier New York Issei and leaders of Japanese silk industry familiar with the development of the pre-World War II silk trade between Japan and the United States considered Ryoichiro Arai as its founder. No one did more in the face of great handicaps, setbacks, and personal humiliation to initiate the silk trade and nurture its growth.[12]

Ryoichiro Arai was born in July 1855, in Kurohone-Mura, Seta-Gun, Gumma Prefecture, the fifth son of Mr. and Mrs. Shichiroemon Hoshino. He was originally named Ryosuke. His father was the head (mayor) of eighteen villages, and although he was a commoner, the Tokugawa regime granted him the privilege of carrying a samurai sword. The family was engaged in silk production. Ryosuke's older brother, Chotaro Hoshino, was a leading silk producer who introduced modern reeling methods at the Mizunuma Mills. When the Arai family adopted Ryosuke, his name was changed to Ryoichiro. He attended schools in Gumma and Ise Prefectures and in Tokyo where he studied English and modern accounting in addition to such traditional subjects as calligraphy and Chinese literature. The family gave him extensive training in the silk business.[13]

Chotaro Hoshino realized that the only way the Japanese could break the Western traders' stranglehold on Japanese foreign trade was to bypass them and trade directly with America and Europe. The foreign merchants had been extremely helpful when Japan had to establish contacts with the outside world for the first time in the modern era, but as a whole they had acquired a vested interest in maintaining monopolies and strengthening their own economic positions and were not concerned with advancing the Japanese economy. They had no reason to defer their own gains to enhance the long-term benefits of Japanese producers or to train Japanese to take over their businesses. Governor Motohiko Katori of Gumma Prefecture encouraged Hoshino to send Ryoichiro to the United States. Arai met Sato, who had returned to Japan in 1875, and with Fukuzawa's encouragement was actively publicizing his views on Japan's vital need to promote its trade and industry. This meeting reinforced Arai's growing conviction that to go to America to start direct trade in silk was a patriotic duty essential to help strengthen the Japanese economy and a family responsibility as well.[14]

The third member of the trio, Toyo (or Yutaka) Morimura, was born in 1854 and was the only one with a family background in business. The Morimuras were a Yedo (Tokyo) merchant family which had dealt in riding accouterments for samurai, helmets, and related riding equipment for nearly two centuries. Toyo's older brother, Ichizaemon, was the active head of the family business. When Yokohama was designated as a new international port by the *Bakufu* (the Tokugawa government) in the 1860s and concessions were offered to Japanese merchants willing to erect buildings suitable for trade, Ichizaemon Morimura went to inspect the site. Like many others at that time, he did not take full advantage of the opportunity, but he observed that some second-hand stores in Yokohama were selling used Western uniforms, shoes, and

162 / From History to Sociology

other articles which crews of foreign warships and soldiers in Japan sold to obtain cash. When Morimura opened a new *karamonya* (draper's shop) in the Teppozu district of Tokyo (around the present Tsukiji area) where he sold *rasha* (woolens) and similar items, he purchased some of these second-hand Western articles to serve primarily as shop decorations. To his surprise, samurai as well as others wanted to buy them for personal use.[15]

Morimura, in doing business with the family of the Daimyo Okudaira, became acquainted with Noboru (or Hozai) Kuwano, one of the Daimyo's higher officials in Tokyo. Kuwano would often talk at length with Morimura, unlike most upper-class officials who would not see merchants. Kuwano told Morimura that later, when business men held positions of power in Japan, samurai would have to enter through the kitchen door traditionally used by servants and merchants. Morimura demurred, and Kuwano referred to the commerce-oriented American colonists who won their independence from England and the British East India Company's conquest and control of India. Kuwano argued that Japan would have to be able to trade internationally on an equal basis to survive. Japanese businessmen would have to go abroad, negotiate necessary agreements, and conduct trade, and he concluded that when they assumed major economic and national roles, their status in Japan would rise. The conversations with Kuwano were among the influences which eventually led Morimura into foreign trade.[16]

Kuwano introduced Morimura to Yukichi Fukuzawa, the founder of a school which would shortly evolve into Keio Gijuku (and then into Keio University). Fukuzawa was also teaching some members of the Okudaira family. Morimura noticed that despite Kuwano's high rank, he respected and showed considerable deference to the younger Fukuzawa who came from a much lower ranking samurai family.[17]

During the turbulent period prior to the 1868 Meiji Restoration, Morimura made substantial profits by supplying the Tosa Han (anti-Shogunate) forces. He became increasingly aware that Japan was losing its limited specie holding by importing arms and woolens. The country would have to expand its exports to balance its international trade and build up its monetary reserves. At the same time, the special privileges and favoritism often involved in official business with han governments disturbed him, so he became even more interested in the possibilities of selling to foreign residents in Japan and of exporting abroad.[18]

When his brother, Toyo, reached school age, Ichizaemon Morimura wanted him to attend the Keio Gijuku. Ichizaemon told Fukuzawa that he was not trying to make Toyo a scholar or prepare him for politics or the civil service, rather he wanted Toyo to become a better businessman.

Fukuzawa was intrigued by this idea, novel for traditional Japan. Toyo became a Keio student. After graduation he taught there for a while before joining his brother in business. [19]

About 1874, Fukuzawa advised Ichizaemon Morimura to send Toyo to the United States to learn about American business and trade. Later, perhaps influenced by Sato, Fukuzawa expanded his original recommendation to urge that a number of young men in different businesses go to the United States to familiarize themselves with their special fields and to establish trade. Ichizaemon objected to this plan partly because of the cost, about a thousand yen per person for travel alone. (The foreign exchange value of the yen was then slightly above the dollar.) Fukuzawa, however, repeated his suggestion several times, and Morimura finally investigated its practicability. He discovered that it would actually cost only about 270 yen each for economy passage. Consequently, he agreed to send Toyo to New York, especially if others like Arai would go also. Since Sato had been trying to gather a group to go to America, Ichizaemon Morimura's decision made possible the original *Oceanic* group of six, all concerned with promoting trade. Toyo Morimura took with him a substantial stock of merchandise, as did Sato, to judge from the subsequent claims of his creditors mentioned below. The goods constituted a major part of the initial inventories of the Morimura and Sato enterprises.[20]

Shortly after the *Oceanic* group arrived in New York in March, 1876, Sato began his personal business at 97 Front Street. It later became known as the Japanese and American Agency. He also collaborated with Toyo Morimura to open a store handling such general Japanese merchandise as china, lacquer and metal wares, parasols, fans, scrolls, silk goods, and tea. The distinction between the two businesses depended, at least in part, on the two inventories, Sato's and Morimura's. Sato apparently had some wholesale business while the joint firm (Hinode) was dependent on retail sales. Morimura briefly left his shop under Sato's supervision to attend short-term courses at the Eastman Business College in Poughkeepsie, New York. The Morimura-Sato firm was formally established in November 1876, as the Hinode Company, which later moved to Fulton Street.[21]

Sato hired Richard von Briesen as his assistant. Von Briesen was a German migrant who had served in the Union navy during the Civil War. He soon assumed active responsibility for much of Sato's business. In later years, von Briesen was well known among New York Japanese through his association with the Morimura Brothers, Morimura Arai Company, and the Takamine organizations.

In the spring of 1878, Morimura temporarily returned to Japan to confer with his brother about their future plans. That same year, Arai and Sato established the Sato Arai Company to conduct trade in raw silk. This firm was separate from both the Hinode Company and Sato's personal business.[22]

Sato's business had scarcely begun when his creditors in Japan began to demand payments for the goods they had advanced. By 1878, they insisted on conferring personally with him in Japan and sent Mr. Tachibana to New York to persuade him to return. Since Toyo Morimura was not yet back from Japan, Sato placed von Briesen in charge of the New York business, partly on a profit-sharing basis. In San Francisco, en route home, Sato purchased some mercury for the Kobusho in Japan. The few Japanese shops in the city now looked far more attractive than they had before, he wrote Arai in New York.[23]

Once in Japan, he conferred informally with helpful friends and with his creditors. Together they considered ways in which Sato could meet his obligations and protect his family assets. The participants at these meetings included several who have already been mentioned and were to rise to prominence in subsequent years:

> Tomotsune Komuchi, who was in charge of the unsuccessful 1875 attempt to begin direct trade in raw silk with the United States; Tetsunosuke Tomita, the first Japanese consul in New York and one of Sato's fellow passengers on the *Colorado* in 1867; Chotaro Hoshino, the older brother of Ryoichiro Arai and a leading silk producer; Susumu Sato, Momotaro's adopted brother.

Other participants at the meetings, Yukuro Niwa, Asahina, and Tachibana, were businessmen. The group agreed that Sato should organize a new firm, Sato and Company, to take over his personal business. Sato and Company was to export primarily "fancy silks" and consumer goods, preferably on a commission basis. These items moved readily and promised quicker returns to liquidate Sato's obligations. The creditors retained prior claims on the company's profits in proportion to their original advance. The conferees estimated that Sato's liabilities totalled 29,000 yen with assets worth 14,000, leaving a debt of 15,000 yen. The Sato family assets were pledged as security to the two largest creditors, the Kangyo-Bu and Sayama.[24]

Officially, Sato and Tachibana were the active members of Sato and Company, but Niwa and Asahina effectively controlled it, as representatives of the creditors. Niwa and Asahina had little knowledge of the export business, yet their prior interest prevented Sato from exercising any initiative. Unfortunately, he was in no position to protest, since the Sato family assets were at stake. Sato predicted that Asahina and Niwa would be too preoccupied with their own business to devote more than a few hours per month to Sato and Company or even to seek additional funds to take advantage of new export opportunities.[25]

Sato wanted to return to the United States, but his creditors objected. In his opinion, they assumed that he would live too extravagantly in New York and thus increase the operating cost of the New York business. After living abroad for ten years, Sato felt more comfortable in the United States. His wife's continuing ill health in Japan also made them eager to return to the utilities and conveniences of American homes. Even more basically, Sato wanted to be active in trade, but despite these desires, he apparently never returned to America. The Sato Arai Company, with Arai in New York and Sato in Japan, continued in business until 1880 when it suspended operations after Arai became the New York representative of a new silk export organization. The company was formally dissolved in 1881.[26]

In 1880, Sato joined Yukuro Niwa and Eijiro Ueno in organizing a new firm, the Nihon Shokai, to export ceramics, chinaware, silks, and other merchandise on a commission basis for Bumpei Takagi of Kyoto. Niwa was one of the two active representatives of the creditors who controlled Sato and Company. He took advantage of the government's growing interest in expanding Japanese exports to approach Count Okuma and the Ministry of Finance for aid. Okuma approved a 30,000 yen loan. When the Nihon Shokai was first organized, Sato planned to return to the United States to open the company's New York branch, but he resigned before travel arrangements were completed. He suffered from a heart condition and was hospitalized at Juntendo. Although his ill health was a decisive factor, he may also have had second thoughts regarding the company's financial backing. The 30,000 yen loan was about the same as the gross liabilities of his original business, and he may have feared experiencing similar difficulties again, even though the new trade was to be on a commission basis.

Niwa finally went to New York, but failed to establish the business on a profitable basis. He curtailed his remittances to Takagi, who then asked Ueno to go to New York to help. Ueno investigated the situation in New York and concluded that the firm's prospects were not good. He liquidated the New York branch by selling about $20,000 of the stock in England, France, and Holland and the balance in New York, and returned to Japan in 1883.[27]

Momotaro Sato recovered from his illness and retained his active interest in commercial and cultural relations with the West. In the subsequent years, he founded the Sandai Shoten in Kyoto, which conducted business, including exports, in Uji tea, raw silk, Kiyomizu ceramics, and chinaware, and also became active in cotton textile

OAKLAND PUBLIC LIBRARY
OAKLAND, CALIFORNIA

manufacturing and exports. Besides compiling and publishing a commercial dictionary, he helped to promote Yukichi Fukuzawa's *Sekai Kokujin* (a series of five volumes and index), translated various publications, and supported international cultural exchanges. In later years, he lived in the Fushimi Momoyama district of Kyoto and died December 24, 1910.[28]

The reverses Sato experienced in his attempt to start a small-scale export-import business in finished consumer goods and handicrafts were typical of those which his successors in this field encountered for many years. Some were, of course, more successful or more fortunate than he was. All had to find readily marketable products.

There were at least three specific problems which plagued Sato and later affected many other Japanese. His two major creditors, "Kangiobu" and "Sayama," were supposedly industry and trade promotional organizations and hence better informed about American conditions than individual Japanese producers. Their officers, however, apparently had little practical understanding of the Western markets or were afraid to make long-term commitments.

Whatever the reason, they first made almost no allowance for the time Sato needed to find a suitable location for his business, make necessary contacts, and begin active business. He did not arrive in New York until March, 1876, and yet a little more than a year later they were already pressing him for settlement. Perhaps they viewed Sato's business as a speculative trade, a series of discrete transactions on a commission basis. Given a year or two more, Sato conceivably might have established his business solidly enough to satisfy his creditors and produce further orders. The Hinode Company, which Sato helped to organize, prospered under Toyo Morimura. By 1880, it was grossing over $100,000 and growing steadily.[29]

Secondly, Sato's creditors apparently placed little or no value on the capital worth of his New York business. In reporting to Arai, Sato did not mention its capital worth in his creditor's estimate that his assets were worth only 14,000 yen compared to his liabilities of 29,000 yen. Curiously, even a profitable New York concern was probably worthless to Japanese creditors in Japan at this stage of the Meiji economy, unless by some miracle an individual in Japan happened to be interested in buying the company. Yet, such a New York outlet was valuable for promoting trade. Sato's creditors also objected to the financial arrangements he made with von Briesen to run the business on his return to Japan, although without a competent manager, the New York firm would have collapsed.[30]

The third problem that Sato faced was a lack of capital. His net obligation of 15,000 yen, when the yen was slightly above the dollar in value, was a modest total for a small New York trading firm but it represented a sizable fortune at that time for individual Japanese who could live well on the income from that amount. The minimum capital needed to start a small-scale business in America and Europe was substantially larger than the capital with which most individual Japanese businessmen customarily operated. Since Issei traders in New York could not obtain credit from American banks, this limitation in the capital available in Japan was a serious obstacle.[31]

Toyo Morimura, who went back to Japan in the summer of 1878 to consult with his brothers and associates, returned to New York and assumed full responsibility for the Hinode Company. He moved it from Fulton Street to 238 Sixth Avenue. It was reorganized in 1879 as Morimura Brothers and Company (having no further association with Sato). In 1880 the company moved once more to 221 Sixth Avenue. Here, Morimura rented a three-story building for $300 per month. The retail shop occupied the first floor and the wholesale display and store rooms the second floor. The third floor served as the living quarters for several of the staff. It proved to be a fortunate location for the firm's retail business which doubled from roughly $50,000 in 1879 to $100,000 in 1880 and continued to grow substantially after that. In 1880, Morimura opened a summer branch in Saratoga Springs, although by then the wholesale business already constituted about thirty percent of the total.[32]

Even after the Hinode Company was doing well the Morimuras encountered difficulties because Japan lacked many basic requisites of modern international trade. For example there was no word for "insurance" in the Tokugawa era Japanese, and there were no insurance companies. Yukichi Fukuzawa coined a Japanese word to mean insurance in 1867. One of Morimura's immediate problems was his inability to send the proceeds of the business routinely to his brother in Japan. He experienced excessive discounts and delays in transferring funds comparable to those which Arai and Sato also faced in their silk trade. The Yokohama Specie Bank and its overseas branches were not yet organized. Western traders and banks had no reason to go out of their way to help Japanese intent on breaking the Westerners' monopoly over the trade unless the transactions were very lucrative.

Ichizaemon Morimura discussed this problem with Fukuzawa, who promised to consult with the Foreign Office. The officials told Fukuzawa that the New York consulate needed over $1,000 per month for operating expenses and that Toyo could deposit at least that much with the consulate each month. He was then to send the consular receipt to

Fukuzawa, who personally went to the Foreign Office each month to obtain the yen equivalent for Ichizaemon Morimura. (The Foreign Office apparently did not fully trust Morimura, a merchant, and specified that the higher-ranking Fukuzawa bring the receipt. It is ironic that within a few years Morimura became an officer of the Bank of Japan.) Although the deposit of $1,000 a month did not solve the problem of transferring money, the regularity of these remittances enabled the Morimuras to send the balance through the usual channels at more opportune moments.[33]

Fukuzawa also recommended to the initially reluctant Ichizaemon Morimura that he employ Yasukata Murai, a Keio Gijuku graduate the same age as Toyo. Murai went to New York in 1879 to help Toyo Morimura, who at first was disappointed that his new assistant was not qualified in English or accounting. Toyo had specified competence in both as prerequisites of anyone to be sent to New York, but he soon learned to appreciate Murai's wit, enthusiasm, and competence. The newcomer was a driving force in the company's expansion, especially into wholesale and direct import business. In time he became the ranking executive of the Morimura organization in America. His leadership was especially important to the American business of the firm, since Toyo Morimura died in 1899, while still a comparatively young man of forty-five.

When Murai left for the United States, Fukuzawa advised him to live there permanently and to become an American citizen if American naturalization laws permitted Japanese to do so. In any case, Fukuzawa urged Murai to become a constructive, law-abiding resident of America. Fukuzawa may have counseled Toyo Morimura in a similar vein when he encouraged him to go to the United States. Murai became one of Ryoichiro Arai's closest friends and was for many years Arai's next-door neighbor in Riverside, Connecticut.[34]

In addition to overcoming these obstacles, the Morimuras had to find domestic products which would create a substantial and sustained foreign demand without costly promotion. While visiting Japan Toyo Morimura wrote to Arai in New York, in despair of discovering any commodity worth serious attention, except raw silk:[35]

It is getting very hard to make money by Jap(anese) business because as you know, in Japan there is not much necessary thing (staple article) that we can export profitably, except raw silk and I do not know even myself what kind of thing is most saleable or what kind of thing to make. Your business is only business bet(ween) Am(erica) and Jap(an) that we can call staple article and at same time we can carry on with profit I think.

Over the next several decades, however, the Morimuras found marketable goods and also developed Japanese products to export in substantial quantities, especially manufactured goods which were often modernized outgrowths of traditional crafts, such as ceramics, chinaware, and mats. By 1882, with the help of Yasukata Murai the Morimura organization in New York moved into the import and wholesale business. Where the company was able to create adequate demands, as in chinaware, Ichizaemon encouraged and organized mass production plants in Japan (such as the Nihon Toki for making Noritake ware). Many Japanese entering larger-scale foreign trade faced similar challenges.[36]

Raw silk, which Toyo Morimura considered an important staple, became Japan's largest pre-World War II export to the United States, the most important domestic source of Japanese foreign exchange, and a leading basis for employment in Japan. Yet, up to the time the *Oceanic* group arrived in New York, not even the resident Western traders in Japan exported silk directly to the United States. Although silk was a major Japanese export from the beginning, the Western merchants in Japan shipped it only to European dealers. Indeed, many present-day readers would not realize from the accounts of this period in the economic histories of Japan that all international silk trade activities were controlled by Westerners and that the Japanese had virtually nothing to do with the actual transactions and shipping. As noted before, however, several Japanese government agencies helped to create Western public interest in Japanese silks by exhibiting at international expositions.

The United States imported most of its silk from European producers and from China in the 1870s. The negligible amount of Japanese silk used in this country came indirectly through European houses. American importers and manufacturers had no contact with Japanese producers. In 1874, when Tetsunosuke Tomita, then Japanese consul in New York, showed American manufacturers some sample reels of Japanese silk, they told him that the threads were too thin and too uneven to be used in high-speed American machinery.[37]

When twenty-year-old Ryoichiro Arai arrived in New York in March, 1876, he carried samples of the silk threads reeled at the Mizunuma mills, with which his brother was associated. Arai's initial experiences in New York would have crushed a less resolute and resilient person with less faith in his objectives. He was determined to "stick to it," even if he had to hang on by "biting on rock" *(ishi wo kajiritsuku)*. In common with most of the *Oceanic* group, Arai lived frugally to conserve his limited funds. His search for a reasonably priced place to live was discouraging. When he tried to look at rooms for rent, some owners said "Chinaman, go away," and slammed the door in his face. Several called him worse names. He at first lived in a rather "dirty" rooming house near the corner of Third Avenue and Ninth Street. As a further economy he walked to his 97 Front Street office, where Sato conducted business for himself and the Hinode Company. During his walks, Arai was often called derogatory names, insults usually applied to Chinese. Hoodlum gangs occasionally attempted to beat him or throw stones at him. Most Issei had similar experiences.[38]

These unpleasant experiences may seem strange in contrast to the welcome that Japanese students at that time received from fellow students, faculty members, and their families. One reason for the difference was that Japanese students were known in the American college communities to be Japanese, whereas the first Issei who arrived in New York were regarded as Chinese at a time when the West Coast anti-Chinese campaigns were beginning to arouse prejudices among some people on the East Coast. The variation in attitudes probably also reflected American ethnic and class differences. At that time a high proportion of the American college students, faculty members, and their families were of middle- and upper-class background. The New York Issei, however, were forced to live in areas of New York occupied by lower-class, less educated and immigrant people who were more directly influenced by the anti-Chinese movements. The incipient labor unions were also strongly anti-Chinese.[39]

During his first year or two in New York Arai economized on food as well as rent. He typically had Japanese noodles and tea for breakfast and lunched on three one-cent cookies purchased from a peddler who had a stand near the Front Street Office. He ate dinner at low-cost restaurants which purchased only the cheapest and toughest cuts of meat. Arai and his Japanese associates consequently assumed that American meat was always tough. Arai felt that he had dined exceptionally well when he had some salted salmon and rice which he prepared himself and a glass of beer. Later he could afford to move to Mrs. Delia A. Dudley's boarding house at 55 West 9th Street. Toyo Morimura, who occupied Arai's room while the latter was visiting Japan, wrote Arai that he was paying eight dollars per week, with "lunch extra." The Dudley boarding house became popular with the Japanese.[40]

Momotaro Sato's creditors thought he lived too extravagantly in New York and would do so again if he returned to the city. Sato, we may assume, actually lived rather plainly, if somewhat more comfortably than most New York Issei. His creditors probably did not take into account the higher cost of living in New York than in contemporary Tokyo. In the 1880s, when the resident manager of the Yokohama Specie Bank, Teisaku Takagi, and Mrs. Takagi first lived at the Hotel Chelsea, their comparative luxury aroused considerable discussion among the local Japanese. From the opening of the Japanese consulate in 1872 until almost the end of the century, even the Japanese consuls lived in boarding houses; some of them at Mrs. Dudley's. The consulate did not have an official residence until around 1896, and even then, it was at first a rather modest apartment. The early resident Japanese in New York scarcely practiced "conspicuous consumption," but lived more closely to the simple style of life associated by Max Weber with ascetic Protestantism. In more recent years the Japanese government has maintained substantial official residences for its representatives abroad, as have the major private Japanese firms for their senior overseas employees.[41]

Arai had to visit various importers and manufacturers to establish contacts with potential silk buyers. Some fluency in English was required, so shortly after his arrival in New York, he enrolled in the evening program at the then well-known Plymouth Institute of Brooklyn to improve his command of English. Some members of the original *Oceanic* group corresponded at least occasionally in English with each other, perhaps to maintain their facility in that language. This use of English among themselves was apparently more common during the Meiji era than at present. In those years, many university and higher school classes in Japan were taught by Westerners in English, less often in French and German, and not in Japanese.[42]

Even business calls were occasionally disagreeable to the first Issei. Many American importers had a very poor opinion of Japanese silk and its producers. Their impressions were not based on personal contacts or direct business with Japanese producers, since they never dealt directly with the Japanese. The wide circulation of derogatory Japanese stereotypes constituted another major block to normal trade relations which early Issei in New York had to overcome. Officials and merchants in Japan were not aware of the situation and its consequences and certainly did not appreciate the New York Issei's efforts. Formal histories of this period in Japan almost invariably overlook the Issei's vital contribution to the development of mutual confidence and the foundations of trade in the face of disagreeable personal experiences.[43]

We do not know to what extent the negative stereotypes held by some American importers were based on actual experiences, differences in standards of silks used by the domestic industry in Japan and by the American mass production industry, and mere repetition of hearsay.

Obviously, among the Japanese producers were those who were as unscrupulous and unreliable as some producers in any other country. Yet resident Western traders in Japan monopolized silk exports, and they also controlled shipments to the European agents. Japanese producers had no way of knowing or controlling what happened to silk deposited at the Westerners' Yokohama warehouses at the convenience of the Western merchants—at times when the price was most profitable to the Western trader and least favorable to the Japanese producer. According to their own rules, the Westerners "inspected" each bale deposited in their warehouses and "compensated" themselves for this "service" by taking one bundle of silk per bale, in addition to their profit on each bale.[44]

It is doubtful that all these Westerners confined their take to only one bundle per bale. When Japan was opened to the outside world, many Western adventurers seeking quick fortunes came to Japan. So did reputable traders interested in founding permanent businesses. Extraterritorial treaties gave all Westerners greater freedom of action and privileges than the Japanese had. Unlike the legitimate traders, the Western adventurers cared little about ethical standards and only wanted quick profits. In any case, they, rather than the Japanese producers, were more directly responsible for the quantity and quality of each bale of silk shipped abroad.[45]

Arai understood the problem. He realized that he and other Japanese representatives, and indeed the entire Japanese silk industry, were faced with the enormous task of overcoming the New York importers' negative impressions in order to establish a reputation for integrity and reliability. A few importers had genuine complaints, since some Japanese silk they had bought from European sources was adulterated, perhaps by the Western traders and possibly by Japanese producers. At any rate, Americans commonly assumed that the Japanese producers were responsible for the adulteration.

Arai called on one industrialist who received him coldly and led him to a cabinet in the rear of his office. There he showed Arai hanks of silk mixed with pieces of metal and other impurities. The manufacturer vigorously denounced such trickery, blamed it on the Japanese producer, and concluded the visit by saying, "Young man, get out!" Arai obviously failed to obtain an order at that time, but later this particular industrialist became one of Arai's best customers and whenever Arai called he greeted him cordially, "Hello '70s," referring to their first encounter. This New Yorker's acceptance reflected the change produced by Arai's personal integrity, sense of responsibility, sustained effort, and the continuing pressure he put on the Japanese producers to improve the quality and uniformity of the silk exported to New York. Doubtless, the manufacturer's changed attitude also reflected his better understanding of the Japanese export trade situation.[46]

At first Arai found almost no buyers, but he was still able to help his family and other silk producers by sending them samples of silks used by American manufacturers and accurate information on the American silk industry. Americans preferred European silks because their mass production machinery required heavier threads of greater uniformity than those used by Japanese craftsmen.[47]

Arai finally obtained an order from a leading New York silk importer, B. Richardson & Son, but far from being profitable for the Hoshinos, the order almost bankrupted the entire family. He had used the Yokohama silk market prices and trends mailed from Japan as the basis of his contract with the New York buyer. By the time his order was returned to Japan by mail, the prices in Yokohama were about eighty percent higher than the New York delivery price he had quoted. Such setbacks occurred because Japan did not have telegraphic links with the Western world. About two years would pass before even Asian cables reached Japan. The trans-Pacific cables were scarcely dreamed of at that time and were decades in coming. Because of slow communications, the New York trade journals did not regularly publish news of Japanese markets. Besides, with direct trade almost nonexistent, the New York commercial press had no incentive to obtain the latest Japanese quotations even by mail. Therefore, Japanese traders in New York had no way of following day-by-day trends.[48]

In Japan, friends advised Chotaro Hoshino, Arai's older brother, to ask Arai to appeal to Richardson and seek redress by renegotiating the contract. Arai flatly refused and insisted on upholding the agreement as it stood, despite its almost disastrous consequence for him and his brother. Hoshino agreed that the contract should be fulfilled. To survive the loss, he had to pledge all of his personal and family assets, including the family tombstones, despite emergency financial aid from the government.

Regardless of its initially adverse repercussion on the Hoshino family, this transaction began a new day for the Japanese silk industry and Japanese foreign trade as a whole. It was: (1) the first direct silk export of any significance from a Japanese producer to an importer in the United States and hence it was a step toward a break in the resident Western traders' monopoly over Japanese foreign trade; and (2) the beginning of direct silk shipments to America. In this case, Hoshino sent the consignment by ship to the West Coast and by train to New York. He thus anticipated the twentieth century silk ships and silk trains.

Until then, as noted, the negligible amount of Japanese silk used by American manufacturers came entirely from secondary sources in Europe.[49]

This fulfillment of a nearly disastrous agreement favorably impressed Richardson and his associates, who in turn voluntarily paid an additional dollar per pound to lessen the Hoshino family loss. More important for Arai and the Japanese silk producers, Richardson and other silk importers who were influential in the New York silk trade had dealt directly with the Japanese representative of an industry in Japan for the first time. They appreciated Arai's forthright integrity and they found they could rely on Arai and other Japanese. With considerable justification, the early Issei regarded the following letter from Richardson as the beginning of the New York business leaders' new attitude toward the Issei and the eventual establishment of direct trade with Japanese firms:[50]

B. Richardson & Son
Silk Brokers
No. 5 Mercer Street
(Opposite Howard Street)

New York, Sep 26 1876

Mr. R. Arai

Dear Sir

I have your note of the 21*st.* I am glad you have filled the order we gave you altho prices advanced on your hand You have acted like an honest merchant and you will not hereafter be sorry that you did so After your doing as you have done I beg to assure you that I will do my best to improve the prices for you

Yours faithfully

(Signed)   B Richardson

c/o Mr M Sato
97 Front St

Arai continued a lifelong activity in developing mutual confidence and understanding between Americans and Japanese, especially traders and manufacturers. He and other early Issei and representatives of Japanese producers played a significant role in establishing a reputation for integrity, and in personally assuming responsibility for maintaining the quality and delivery dates of Japanese goods shipped to the United States. Arai was the first, and the most prominent, Issei involved in the growth of the silk trade, but others who followed also contributed to the growing confidence American importers acquired in Japanese products. Oriye Kai came several years after Arai to represent the Asabuki interests in Japan and he insisted on taking back silk consignments which did not fully meet the detailed specification of the original order. Kai lived for a time in Paterson, New Jersey, then the major center of the American silk industry, to establish better contacts and to maintain better control over the quality of the incoming shipments.[51]

Arai met regularly with American manufacturers and the importers. Industrialists gave him first-hand information on changes in machinery, processes, and products, and on changes in the silks they needed. He forwarded this information to Japanese producers, including his brother and later to members of the Doshin Company. He thus contributed significantly to the continued improvement in the quality and uniformity of Japanese silks for several decades. This improvement was a major reason why American manufacturers and importers who once deprecated Japanese silks began to prefer the Japanese product. In time, Japan became the largest source of raw silk used by the American silk industry.[52]

Although Sato himself had to return to Japan, he continued for more than two years to collaborate with Arai. By the time he went back, the Far Eastern cable was extended to Japan. Because of the long route (via Europe and Asia), however, the rates were high and messages were subject to frequent delays and errors. Sato attempted to prepare a special code for the Sato Arai Company business, but despite his efforts for over a year, he was unsuccessful. He should have obtained advice from American foreign traders before leaving New York and possibly made use of code books. However, an important initial deterrent was the attitude of the Japanese telegraphic agency, which frankly did not want to have anything to do with foreign cables, which its officials regarded as nuisances *(urusai)*. The bureau was reluctant to consider registering cable addresses or help Sato with practical suggestions on composing a suitable cable code.[53]

Sato reported to Arai that the telegraphic agency withdrew five percent from the cabled dollar remittances and determined the amount in yen only after the mailed copy of the order arrived and then at the rate prevailing on that day. When Sato asked the agency to pay according to the exchange rate of the day the cablegram was received, the officials hesitated and eventually countered with a proposal to deduct one and a half percent surcharge on telegraphic orders (in addition to the usual exchange rates). Sato objected to this extra cost. As he wrote to Arai, at that time (1878–1879) the exchange value of the yen was fluctuating, and the delays and various obstacles that Japanese traders encountered in trying to obtain funds remitted by their overseas dealers increased their risks appreciably. The situation probably favored parasitical exchange speculators, but it was detrimental to legitimate traders.[54]

Considering the limited capital available to these early traders, the adverse effects of cable delays become clear. The government telegraphic agency did not take full advantage of the potentialities of the cable service to facilitate trade by the Japanese. It therefore worked at cross purposes with the trade promotion objectives of the finance and commerce ministries.

In 1879 Sato wrote to Arai about his difficulties in keeping abreast of the Yokohama trade market. "It is quite hard thing for Japanese silkmen to get good and reliable report from foreigners in Yokohama and what they are doing," he reported, since "even the ablest silkman who is not accustomed in foreigners' way of business can hardly ascertain the full report." The "inscrutable Westerners" said little of value about the trade to the Japanese. Indeed, it was virtually impossible to find out what their nominal commission rates were. The Westerners, with their nearly complete monopoly over foreign trade, preferred to keep information on market transactions to themselves. A few years earlier, Kenzo Hayami of Maebashi Han, a pioneer in the modernization of the Japanese silk industry, saw a copy of the London *Times* and suddenly realized how much higher the silk prices on the Western markets were than the figures the Western traders in Japan gave the Japanese. Consequently, he became an advocate of the direct export of silk.[55]

Following a major silk fair in Yokohama in 1879, such Meiji leaders as Ito, Kawase, Matsukata, and Okuma began to stress the importance of expanding silk exports. Under Hayami's initiative, a number of Japanese silk producers met to consider the possibilities of further developing direct silk exports. In November, 1879, they organized a jointly-owned concern, the Doshin Company, initially capitalized at 300,000 yen. In addition, the company had access to substantially larger credit. Hayami became its first president; Saburo Takagi, who as the second Japanese consul in New York had actively promoted trade, became vice president; and Kiyoshi Fujii of the Yokohama Specie Bank (now Bank of Tokyo), manager. In 1880 it opened a branch in New York (with Arai as the representative) and one in Paris. It had far greater financial resources than the Sato-Arai Company which suspended active business when Arai joined the Doshin Company. As a joint organization of the leading silk producers, the Doshin Company had extensive contacts in Japan and could keep Arai better informed on the industry in Japan. Conversely, Arai's reports on American trends and his continuing emphasis on better quality and uniformity had greater impact in Japan. For Arai personally, it also meant competent assistants to help him in New York.[56]

In 1893, Arai returned to Japan and resigned from the Doshin Company. During this visit, he spent some time at a brush factory at Fukushima, near Osaka, which he had helped to organize in 1887. The plant marketed its products primarily in the United States and continued in active business until 1914, but was apparently not financially successful. Arai also met with Shinjuro Arakawa, Nagata Sato, Matsusaburo Yoshida, and several Yokohama silk leaders to plan for a new silk export company. They organized the Yokohama Kiito Gomei Kaisha in September, 1893, with an initial capital of 5,000,000 yen. In 1916, the firm became a public stock corporation known as the Yokohama Kiito Kabushiki Kaisha. Arakawa, Sato, and Yoshida were previously associated with the former Asabuki trading interests which had a New York affiliate, the Yamato Company, under the management of Oriye Kai.[57]

Ichizaemon Morimura and Arai then formed the Morimura Arai Company to represent the Yokohama Kiito Kaisha in the United States and to conduct business of its own. The Morimura Arai Company established agencies in Canton and Shanghai, China, in France, and in Italy, and traded in Chinese, French, Italian, and Japanese silks. By 1908, the firm's direct silk imports from Japan surpassed the total silk trade still handled by resident Western traders in Japan and represented over one-third of the Japanese silks imported by the United States as a whole. The company was one of the first to export American cotton to Japan on a substantial scale and contributed significantly to the rapid growth of the modern Japanese cotton textile industry, which depends entirely on foreign cotton. The firm also handled Egyptian, Indian, and Peruvian cotton.[58]

In 1901, Arai was elected to the board of governors of the Silk Association of America. The board membership symbolized the personal respect he had won from the American silk industry through his integrity and active efforts and with it a new attitude of American manufacturers toward Japanese silks.[59]

This summary of the activities of the three early Japanese traders has referred briefly to the characteristic setbacks which they (and other Japanese who entered foreign trade shortly afterwards) experienced at first. Their reverses varied in extent and origin. Some were relatively personal and specific. Other problems were broader in scope and reflected at least partly the cultural and institutional differences between the two countries. To some degree, even seemingly personal or specific difficulties usually involved differences in national traditions. For example, Sato's creditors might not have acted as they did had they understood the situation in New York, such as the time and capital needed to start a small trading concern, the capital value of an established firm, and the potential promotional role of such an outlet.

These three Issei arrived in New York before Meiji Japan had developed many of the technological bases and institutional services which modern trade requires. Arai's first major order led to near disaster for him and the Hoshinos, because they had to rely on inadequate and outdated information on market trends sent by mail, since cable services had not yet been extended to Japan. Even after Japan was linked to the existing Asian cables, the Japanese telegraphic agency at first failed to provide the services that their new technical facilities theoretically permitted.

Although Meiji-period Westerners often spoke of the predictable quality of products in terms of business morality, the development of mutual commercial confidence and mutually acceptable standards involved the more basic differences found in the prevailing practices of a traditional handicraft economy compared with an industrialized society. To make silk threads suitable for American machinery, the Japanese silk producers had to build relatively modern reeling mills and rationalize household silk raising. Both steps involved basic cultural and economic changes, which in turn needed sustained well-directed guidance by responsible leaders, aided by a continuing flow of reliable information on the specific requirements of foreign consumers.

Even more basically, since Tokugawa Japan had no direct international commerce and no experienced traders, the three early Meiji tradesmen had to find their way through the thickets of the unknown world of foreign trade. They could not look to any Japanese reference group as models for proper action or as guides. Not even Sato had much background or adequate range of experience in trade; he merely had more than other Japanese. Through inquiry, observation, risk taking, and hard experience, they learned how to conduct their businesses.

The founders of Japanese-American trade were Issei—permanent or long-term residents of New York. Members of their generation had to reside in the city long enough to learn how to live in an American community and to establish successful businesses. Temporary visitors and traveling salesmen could not have changed the strongly negative stereotypes about Japanese products widely prevalent in New York trading circles. It took dedication, patient effort, and personal assumption of responsibility for the quality and prompt delivery of Japanese products to create mutual confidence and their growing acceptance.

The Issei's restraint and faith in America in the face of the prejudices unconsciously held by many Americans are worth continuing notice, especially since this was a period of triumphant Western imperial expansion and marked ethnocentrism. Aside from a tiny minority of East Asian culture enthusiasts, most Americans assumed without question that only Western cultures were significant and only Western ways of doing anything were right. For the most part, objective studies on comparative cultures and cultural anthropology came decades later. Even now, some critics point out that "international" law and rules of "international" trade are primarily Western in their origin, assumptions, and practices.

In recent years, several American anthropologists and sociologists have investigated the adjustment of post-World War II Japanese students in American universities. Although present-day Japan is a relatively industrialized, urbanized, and modernized nation with many institutional features similar to those in other industrialized countries, these American scholars found that these Japanese students experienced at least some difficulties in adjustment before they were able to carry on their studies successfully. If post-World War II Japanese students find American life puzzling and disturbing within the relatively favorable environs of university communities, we can only imagine how perplexing and more difficult American society and business must have seemed to the early Meiji Issei, who came to the United States from traditional, quasi-feudal Japan, especially when at the same time, they were expected to establish trade with America. As Fukuzawa recalled, the most elemental needs of daily existence troubled Meiji visitors to the West. They knew, for example, how electroplating was done and how steam engines worked from their study of Western textbooks, but such immediate personal problems as the use of Western bathrooms, the routine governing daily social contacts, and the ordinary workings of a commercial bank troubled them the most.[60]

Early Meiji education included teachings of direct relevance for the *Oceanic* group. Their simple mode of living, orderly personal conduct, strong determination to overcome obstacles, patience, and emphasis on legitimate established trade rather than speculation undoubtedly helped them in their efforts to found Japanese-American trade. Observers have already commented on the similarities between some traditional Japanese values and traits and those traced by sociologists to the Weberian Protestant Ethic. Partly because they emphasized rational legitimate trade, Arai, Morimura, and Sato found many unpredictable features of economically traditional Japan vexing—for example, the confusion of personal and business relations, complications in transmission of funds, and lack of adequate trade news services.[61]

Some historians have been impressed by the high proportion of young men from samurai and village head families who became leaders of Meiji economic reform and industrialization. With a few notable exceptions, established traditional merchants were not involved as often as one might expect. None of the three early traders had speculative mercantile training. Toyo Morimura, the only one with a Yedo business family background, was a product of Keio Gijuku and personally close to Yukichi Fukuzawa, the great Meiji leader of intellectual modernization and rationalization. His older brother, Ichizaemon Morimura, disliked the official han business because of its speculative and political quality, even though he profited substantially from it, and he deliberately moved into foreign trade and modern industry. He had many contacts with Fukuzawa and with the Japanese Protestant leaders. In his later life, he became a Christian convert. Readers may see in these personal experiences some developments suggestive of the Weber thesis.[62]

In the light of the contrast between early Meiji Japan and the United States of the 1870s which these three founders of modern Japanese-American trade had to bridge, their contributions to a completely new field for Japan and to the American economy are all the more impressive.

NOTES

*This paper is based on a section of an unpublished preliminary report on a continuing study of the Japanese and Japanese Americans on the East Coast of the United States. The East Coast research was originally a part of the nationwide study of the Japanese and Japanese Americans by the Japanese American Research Project at the University of California, Los Angeles. The Project has been supported by grants from the Carnegie Corporation of New York, the Japanese American Citizens League, and the National Institute of Mental Health. The highly appreciated financial assistance for the preliminary East Coast field work came primarily from the original Carnegie Corporation and Japanese American Citizens League contributions to the Project. The East Coast study is now a separate project, supported by the Japanese American Citizens League and located at Boston University. I also wish to thank Boston University Graduate School for financial aid to carry on a part of the documentary research and to type this manuscript.

I should like to express my deep appreciation to Mr. and Mrs. Yoneo Arai, for making available certain valuable records of Mr. Arai's parents, the late Mr. and Mrs. Ryoichiro Arai, and for answering many questions about them. Among the documents were some informative letters from Toyo Morimura and Momotaro Sato to Ryoichiro Arai (referred below as "Morimura to Arai" and "Sato to Arai"), a biographical outline requested by the Japanese silk organization when the Japanese government conferred a medal of distinction in recognition of his outstanding contribution to Japanese-American trade (cited as the "Arai sketch"), notes, photographs, and articles. The information from the interviews (August 5-7, 1966 and January 2-4, 1970) is identified as "Arai interviews."

For thoughtful assistance on this part of the East Coast study, I wish to thank Mr. Ken Matsumoto of Tokyo, Mrs. Ann Staffeld Mendez, Yasuo Sakata, Dr. and Mrs. Mochinobu Shimo, Miss Fusako Takemasa of Tokyo, formerly of the Harvard Yenching Library staff, Mrs. Chiyo Itanaga, Mrs. Mitsu Yasuda Carl, and Dr. Miwa Kai and Frank Yorichika of the East Asian Library, Columbia University. M. M. Masaoka, Shigeo Wakamatsu, and Dr. Mary Watanabe actively helped the East Coast research as a whole in many ways, as did Professor Robert A. Wilson and the late Joe Grant Masaoka of the Japanese American Research Project at UCLA.

1. In recent years, several agencies, both official and private, especially the United States-Japan Trade Council, have periodically been publishing data on the trade of various sections of this country with Japan. Among others, Gerde Wilcke comments on the Japanese purchases from American overseas firms, which are not included in the United States-Japan trade data, in "Mitsui's U.S. Chief Urges Cooperation Among Resources Producers," *The New York Times,* March 30, 1969. The Japanese American Research Project of the University of California, Los Angeles, defines the pre-World War II Issei as the long-term or permanent Japanese residents who migrated to the United States before 1924.

2. Keizo Shibusawa, ed., *Japanese Society in the Meiji Era* (Tokyo: Obunsha, 1958), pp. 106-109, Chapter 10; Keishi Ohara, ed., *Nichibei Bunka Koshoshi,* Volume II: *Tsusho Sangyohen* (Tokyo: Yoyosha, 1954), pp. 225-237. See also G. C. Allen, *A Short Economic History of Modern Japan* (New York: Frederick A. Praeger, 1963), pp. 35, 46, 69, 95-96; Yukimasa Hattori, *The Foreign Commerce of Japan Since the Restoration,* 1869–1900 (Baltimore: The Johns Hopkins Press, 1904), pp. 28-29; and W. W. Lockwood, *The Economic Development of Japan* (Princeton, N.J.: Princeton University Press, 1968), pp. 329-330.

3. Shozo Mizutani, ed., *New York Nihonjin Hattenshi* (New York: Japanese Association of New York, 1921), Parts 1, 2, and 3, Chapter I, and pp. 724-728; also Yeiji Anraku, *Japan in New York* (New York: Anraku Publishing Company, 1908), *passim* (especially the Japanese section); and *New York Shimpo (The Japanese Times),* No. 1290 (October 16, 1926), No. 1291 (October 20, 1926), and No. 1296 (November 6, 1926). Other references include: Shinichi Kato, *Beikoku Nikkeijin Hyakunenshi: Zaibei Nikkeijin Hatten Jinshiroku* (Los Angeles: New Japanese American News, Inc., 1961), pp. 1332-1334; Matsuzo Nagai, ed., *Nichibei Bunka Koshoshi,* Volume V: *Ijuhen,* pp. 17, 22, 25, 31, 55, 297, 339 (Volume VI: *Index,* p. 83, lists the scattered references to Sato); Yoichi Toga, *Nichibei Kankei Zai Beikoku Nihonjin Hattenshiryo* (Oakland, California: Beikoku Seisho Kyokai Nihonjin-Bu, 1927), pp. 25-27, 40-42; *Zaibei Nihonjinshi* (San Francisco: Zaibei Nihonjinkai, 1940), pp. 28-29, 1053ff.

4. See footnote 3. The few Japanese in New York before 1876 were mainly visitors and temporary residents, among them students, sailors, and members of acrobatic and theatrical troupes. According to Mr. Martin Cohen, theatrical

notices of 1862 mention a "Japanese Tommy," who apparently was a juggler. He is not to be confused with a popular young member of the 1860 diplomatic mission whose American friends also called him "Japanese Tommy." Over the next few years, several Japanese troupes visited New York, which by 1867 experienced a minor boom of interest in things Japanese, as reflected in the various theatrical programs: Martin Cohen, "Meiji Period Vaudeville in New York," *The New York Nichibei,* May 23, 1963. Mr. Cohen has kindly sent a summary of the references to the Japanese in New York in the pre-1876 press. Dr. Robert S. Schwantes summarizes the experiences of earlier Japanese students, as does Nitobe more briefly: Robert S. Schwantes, *Japanese and Americans: A Century of Cultural Relations* (New York: Harper and Brothers, 1955), Chapter VI, and Inazo Nitobe, *The Intercourse Between the United States and Japan* (Baltimore: The Johns Hopkins Press, 1891), p. 158 *et passim.*

5. Shibusawa, *loc. cit.* See also Allen, *op. cit.,* pp. 31-39; Hattori, *loc. cit.;* Lockwood, *op. cit.,* Chapters 1, 6, and 7; Ohara, *loc. cit.*

6. Mizutani, *loc. cit.;* Nagai, *loc. cit.;* Ohara, *loc. cit.;* Shibusawa, *loc. cit.;* Toga, *loc. cit.;* and *Zaibei Nihonjinshi,* pp. 27-29. Senzo Mori, ed., *Meiji Jimbutsu Itsuwa Jiten* (Tokyo: Tokyodo Shuppan, 1965), Vol. I. p. 354, contains a brief biographical sketch of Tomotsune Komuchi.

7. See footnote 6. See also Allen, *loc. cit.;* Hattori, *loc. cit.;* and Lockwood, *op. cit.,* pp. 329-330.

8. Anraku, *loc. cit.;* Ken Matsumoto, ms (see footnote 28 below); Mizutani, *loc. cit.;* Nagai, *loc. cit.; New York Shimpo, loc. cit.;* and Toga, *loc. cit.* For references to Sato in *Nichibei Bunka Koshoshi,* see Vol. VI: *Index,* p. 83. Ichiro Murakami has included a brief history of the Sato family as a whole in his biography of Taizen Sato, *Ran-I Sato Taizen* (Chiba-Shi: Boso Kyodo Kenkyukai, 1941). In addition to the various scattered references, for Momotaro Sato, see pp. 200-201 and for Shochu Sato, pp. 183-185.

9. See footnote 8. Senzo Mori, *op. cit.* contains biographical sketches of Susumu and Taizen Sato to supplement Murakami's longer account in Volume I, pp. 425 and 426-427, respectively.

10. See footnote 8.

11. See footnote 8. Momotaro Sato's scholarship was apparently intended for studying in Germany, but if so, he or his family persuaded the educational officials to let him use it to investigate American merchandising, business methods, and transportation. Although Sato is said to have enrolled for some courses at Massachusetts Institute of Technology, the Institute's alumni office has no record of Sato as a student (Letter, June 25, 1968). It should also be observed that even Sato did not have an adequate background in foreign trade, although he had a better understanding than almost any other Japanese had at that time —Sato to Arai, November 25, 1878, October 4 and 10, and November 1 and 21, 1879.

12. Arai interviews; Arai sketch; Mizutani, *op. cit.,* pp. 60-68, Part 3, Chapter I, and pp. 726-728; Ohara, *op. cit.,* pp. 225-228, *et passim;* Shibusawa, *op. cit.,* p. 484.

13. See footnote 12.

14. See footnote 12.

15. Kanmei Ishikawa, ed., *Fukuzawa Yukichi Den,* Volume II (Tokyo: Iwanami Shoten, 1932), pp. 807-816 (quoting from *Fukuzawa Sensei Jiseki Tanmonroku,* edited by Yoshio Takahashi). See also Unosuke Wakamiya, *Morimura-Oh Genkoroku* (Tokyo: Diamond-sha for the Morimura Homeika, 1969) for some personal recollections of this period by Ichizaemon Morimura.

16. See footnote 15.

17. See footnote 15. It was Hikozo Okami, a prominent han official and advocate of Western learning, who earlier called Fukuzawa to Yedo (Tokyo) to start a han school which included Western studies: Eiichi Kiyooka, ed., *The Autobiography of Yukichi Fukuzawa* (New York: Columbia University Press, 1966), pp. 93-94. (For his rejection of feudal status system, see pp. 18-19, 243-247.)

18. Ishikawa, *loc. cit.;* Mizutani, *op. cit.,* pp. 143-156, 796-797; and Wakamiya, *op. cit.,* pp. 83-106. See also Yasuzo Horie's brief reference to Ichizaemon Morimura in "Modern Entrepreneurship in Meiji Japan," in *State and Economic Enterprise in Japan* (Princeton, N.J.: Princeton University Press, 1965), edited by W. W. Lockwood, pp. 191-192.

19. See footnote 18.

20. See footnote 18; and also Momotaro Sato to Arai, October 11 and November 25, 1878. The average exchange value of the yen declined from slightly above the American dollar in 1874 to approximately 51 cents in 1895; W. W. Lockwood, *The Economic Development of Japan,* p. 257.

21. Arai sketch; Morimura to Arai, July 13, 1878; Mizutani, *op. cit.,* pp. 60-68, 143-155, Part 3, Chapters I and VI, pp. 724-733; Sato to Arai, November 25, 1878; and *Zaibei Nihonjinshi,* pp. 27-29, 1053ff.

22. See footnote 21.

23. Morimura to Arai, July 13, 1878 and Sato to Arai, September 14, October 11, and November 25, 1878.

24. Sato to Arai, September 14, October 11, and November 25, 1878. For a brief account of Tomita's career, see Senzo Mori, *op. cit.,* Volume II, pp. 116-117.

25. See footnote 24.

26. Mizutani, *loc. cit.;* Morimura to Arai, *loc. cit.;* Sato to Arai, September 14, October 11, and November 25, 1878 and October 4 and 10 and November 1 and 21, 1879.

27. Mizutani, *op. cit.,* pp. 60-68, 151-152, 724-725. Anraku, Kato, Mizutani, Toga, and others who wrote on the early Issei and Japanese residents in America regarded Sato as the immediate founder of direct Japanese-American trade. Yet they said very little about him and almost nothing about his activities with the Sato Arai Company after his return to Japan in 1878, and with the partial exception of Mizutani, very little about his subsequent life, aside from erroneously implying in passing that he died shortly afterwards. This neglect is a poignant commentary on the extent to which this pioneer in Japanese-American trade has been overlooked. This oversight could be another case of the nationally prominent members of an outstanding family overshadowing the one who

ventured into a new field at that time with little prestige and whose contributions are more difficult to assess.

28. Murakami, *op. cit.,* pp. 200-201; Ken Matsumoto, "Momotaro Sato" (an
unpublished manuscript sketch); Mizutani, *loc. cit.;* and Sato to Arai, *loc. cit.* Mr.
Ken Matsumoto kindly took the initiative to make further inquiries on
Momotaro Sato's career after his return to Japan.

29. Mizutani, *op. cit.,* pp. 60-68, 143-155, Part 3, Chapters I and VI, pp.
724-725; Sato to Arai, *loc. cit.*

30. Sato to Arai, *loc. cit.*

31. *Ibid.* and Mizutani, *loc. cit.* Typically, in *Kuwayama Senzo Oh Monogatari*
(Kobe: Tankoshinsha, 1963) by Masataka Kamide, Kuwayama refers many
times to the inability of Issei and Japanese small traders in New York to obtain
any American bank loans. At the same time, before World War II, Japanese bank
branches in New York did not conduct local business, and hence, did not lend
to the Issei.

32. Mizutani, *op. cit.,* pp. 147-169, Part 3, Chapters I and VI; and Morimura
to Arai, April 22, May 13, and July 23, 1880.

33. Ishikawa, *loc. cit.;* Kiyooka, *op. cit.,* pp. 358-359; Mizutani, *loc. cit.*

34. Ishikawa, *loc. cit;* Mizutani, *loc. cit.* and pp. 727-733; Takao Morimura,
letter, June 10, 1970; Rihei Onishi, *Murai Yasukata Den* (Tokyo: Zaidan Hojin
Murai Yasukata Aigo Kai, 1943), pp. 46-130; and Arai interviews.

35. Mizutani, *loc. cit.;* Morimura to Arai, June 13, 1878 (except for the
reference to "staple article," the parenthetical inserts in the quotation are mine
—TSM); *New York Shimpo, loc. cit.*

36. To supply the growing overseas markets, the Morimuras organized such
manufacturing firms as the Nihon Toki, the makers of the well-known Noritake
ware. For a summary of some of the basic problems they faced in the beginning,
see Takehira Okabe, *Tsuchi no Honoho: Nihon Toki no Ayunda Michi* (Nagoya:
Chubu Keizai Shimbunsha, 1968).

37. Shichiro Matsui, *The History of the Silk Industry in the United States* (New
York: Howes, 1930), p. 62; Mizutani, *op. cit.,* Parts 1 and 2, and Part 3, Chapter
I; Ohara, *op. cit.,* pp. 225-237; Schwantes, *op. cit.,* pp. 51-52; Shibusawa, *loc. cit.*

38. Arai interviews; Arai sketch; Mizutani, *op. cit.,* pp. 60-68, Part 3, Chapter
I, and pp. 726-728; and Shibusawa, *op. cit.,* p. 484.

39. Arai interviews; Arai sketch; Mizutani, *op. cit.,* pp. 60-68, Part 3, Chapters I, IV, and IX, pp. 726-728, 757-761, 786, 805-809; Nitobe, *loc. cit.;*
Schwantes, *op. cit.,* Chapter VI.

40. Arai interviews; Mizutani, *loc. cit.* (numerous scattered references to
Arai); Morimura to Arai, April 22, 1880. As a small child, Mr. Yoneo Arai
managed to walk out of Mrs. Dudley's boarding house by himself and was
immediately lost on nearby Fifth Avenue. A lady passing by realized that the
boy was lost and brought him back to Mrs. Dudley's. She had correctly guessed
that he was a child of one of the Japanese who lived there: Arai interviews.

41. Arai interviews; Mizutani *loc. cit.,* especially Part 3, Chapter IX;
Morimura, *loc. cit.* Veblen discusses his views on "conspicuous consumption"
in *The Theory of the Leisure Class* (New York: The Modern Library, 1931). For

an analysis of the "Protestant Ethic," see Max Weber, *The Protestant Ethic and the Spirit of Capitalism* (New York: Charles Scribner's Sons, 1958).

42. Arai interviews and papers; Ethel C. Ince, "Pioneer Japanese Silk Dealer Had Job To Win American Confidence," *The Christian Science Monitor*, March 9, 1932; Taizo Ishizaka interviews; Matasaku Shiobara, ed., *Takamine Hakase* (Tokyo: Shiobara, 1926), pp. 10-12.

43. Arai interviews; Ince, *loc. cit.*

44. Arai sketch; Ince, *loc. cit.*; Ohara, *loc. cit.*; and especially Shibusawa, *op. cit.*, pp. 107-108, Chapter 10.

45. See footnote 44.

46. Ince, *loc. cit.*; Mizutani, *loc. cit.*

47. Arai sketch; Ince, *loc. cit.*; Matsui, *loc. cit.*; Mizutani, *op. cit.*, pp. 60-68, Part 3, Chapter I, pp. 726-727; Schwantes, *op. cit.*, pp. 51-52; Shibusawa, *loc. cit.*

48. Arai interviews and papers; Ince, *loc. cit.*; Mizutani, *op. cit.*, pp. 60-68, Part 3, Chapter II, *et passim;* Shibusawa, *loc. cit.*

49. Arai interviews; Ince, *loc. cit.*; Mizutani, *loc. cit.*; Nagai, *loc. cit.*; Ohara, *loc. cit.*; Shibusawa, *loc. cit.* Ince, of course, is mistaken about the amount of the loss. It was apparently closer to 200,000 yen.

50. See footnote 49. Mizutani has included a photocopy of the Richardson letter between pages 64 and 65.

51. Mizutani, *op. cit.*, pp. 60-75, Part 3, Chapter I, pp. 767-775, (numerous scattered references).

52. Arai interviews; Ince, *loc. cit.*; Matsui, *op. cit.*, Chapter VI; Mizutani, *loc. cit.* For a summary of the role of silk in the economic growth of Japan, see Allen, *op. cit.*; W. W. Lockwood, *The Economic Development of Japan;* and E. B. Schumpeter, ed., *The Industrialization of Japan and Manchoukuo* (New York: The Macmillan Company, 1940); and other standard references.

53. Arai interviews; Mizutani, *op. cit.*, pp. 60-68, Part 2, Chapters I and II-2, Part 3, Chapters I, II, and VI, and Part 4, Chapter IV; Sato to Arai, November 25, 1878, October 4 and 10 and November 1 and 21, 1879.

54. See footnote 53.

55. See footnote 53 and also Ohara, *op. cit.*, pp. 225-228.

56. See footnote 53, and also Arai sketch.

57. See footnote 53 (especially Arai sketch and Mizutani, *loc. cit.*).

58. Anraku, *Japan in New York*, p. 19; Arai interviews and sketch; Mizutani, *loc. cit.*; *New York Shimpo, loc. cit.* (on the fiftieth anniversary of the founding of Hinode Company, the predecessor to Morimura Brothers, and on Arai's association with Toyo Morimura and Yasukata Murai).

59. Arai interviews and sketch.

60. Kiyooka, *op. cit.*, Chapters VI and VII. For studies of Japanese students in American universities, see, for example, John W. Bennett, Herbert Passin, and Robert McKnight, *In Search of Identity* (Minneapolis: University of Minnesota Press, 1958).

61. Among the many recent treatments of certain traditional Japanese values, see Robert J. Smith and Richard K. Beardsley, eds., *Japanese Culture: Its Development and Characteristics* (Chicago: Aldine Press, 1962) and Ronald P.

Dore, *Education in Tokugawa Japan* (Berkeley: University of California Press, 1965). Ezra F. Vogel, *Japan's New Middle Class: The Salary Man and His Family in a Tokyo Suburb* (Berkeley: University of California Press, 1963) examines the close relations between achievement orientation and recent education in Japan. Momotaro Sato believed, as did Arai, in the economic importance of the sharper American distinction (as compared with the Japanese) between personal friendships and impersonal business relations: "I agree with you concerning the distinction to be made between a friendship and a *businesship* [*sic*]. That is what the sensible Americans are all making the abruptest distinction. I hope the Japanese will make that distinction": Sato to Arai, October 4, 1879.

62. On the non-merchant origins of Meiji economic reformers and industrial leaders, see among others, Allen, *op cit.,* p. 29; Lockwood, *op. cit.,* p. 10; and for the broader background of industrial entrepreneurs, Johannes Hirschmeier, *The Origins of Entrepreneurship in Meiji Japan* (Cambridge, Mass.: Harvard University Press, 1968). Wakamiya, *op. cit.,* pp. 140-190, refers to some of Morimura's religious concerns.

Man of Two Worlds: An Inquiry into the Value System of Inazo Nitobe* (1862-1933)

SHARLIE C. USHIODA

Most traditional studies of Japanese immigrants in the United States assume that the main problem the Japanese faced was assimilation. This is an oversimplification. Most first-generation immigrants wanted to live in two worlds, Japanese and American, but the psycho-cultural problem involved was beyond their ability to articulate. Some businessmen and intellectuals showed greater awareness of the need for a fusion of cultural values.

Inazo Nitobe was a particularly articulate and sensitive individual, equally at home on both sides of the Pacific. He was a modern samurai of nationalist-internationalist and pacifist Quaker leanings. The contradictions in his life and thought are worthy of study for themselves and as an example of the sort of value conflicts faced by "Americanized" Japanese of his generation, 1862–1933.

Nitobe never became an American citizen and he always considered Japan his permanent home. He was, however, very much a part of the American world because of his conversion to Christianity, an American graduate school education, frequent, often lengthy visits to the United States, his marriage to an American woman, and his lifelong contacts and friendships with Americans in Japan and the United States. He dedicated his life to the realization of a youthful dream of becoming a "bridge across the Pacific."[1] He has been lauded as a true reconciler of East and West and for being at one time a Japanese patriot, a true internationalist, a defender of *Bushidō* (the "way of the warrior"), and a model member of the Society of Friends. On the other hand, that synthesis of opposing value systems has also been viewed as completely unstable and his actions and writings explained so as to picture him a traitor to all of his Japanese, Bushi, Quaker, and international causes.

*In this paper Nitobe's name is given in the Western order, but the names of other Japanese appearing in the story are given Japanese fashion, with the family name first.

Both interpretations seem to have merit. Nitobe's activities reveal his sincere devotion to Japan, Christianity, and international understanding. However, his reactions to certain events in which the objectives of these causes conflicted seem inconsistent with his pronouncements and raise doubt concerning his fundamental loyalties. Was he, as Dorothy Gilbert has stated, "a Japanese patriot first, a citizen of the world second, and a Quaker third?"[2] Or was Christianity the most important value in his life, as Kiyoko Takeda Cho suggests?[3] In the latter case he might have been a Quaker first, citizen of the world second, and Japanese patriot third. Perhaps his devotion to international understanding was paramount and his order of values should read: world, Quaker, Japan. Was he a true reconciler who fused all of these values, or was his synthesis so precarious that he had to delude himself to force its elements into an equilibrium? This essay will discuss his life in order to provide some insight into these paradoxical questions.

Inazo Nitobe was born in 1862 into a high-ranking samurai family of the Morioka fief. His early years, delightfully described in his *Reminiscences of Childhood in the Early Days of Modern Japan,*[4] were steeped in samurai training and discipline. His father died when Inazo was five but his mother, grandfather, and uncle continued to remind him of his samurai heritage, and Bushido values were well ingrained in him. From a very early age, however, Nitobe sensed the importance of the changes in Japanese society which followed the Meiji Restoration and he was always interested in learning about Western culture. His interest in the United States dates from 1872 when he first began to study English. Nitobe decided on a career in agriculture and in 1877 entered Sapporo Agricultural College. There he was influenced by American missionaries and became a Christian.

He was graduated from Sapporo in 1881, and entered Tokyo Imperial University to study English literature and economics. In 1884 he went to the United States to study economics, history, and literature at Johns Hopkins University. He went to Germany in 1887 to study statistics and agricultural economics. In 1891 he returned to the United States and married Mary Patterson Elkinton, a Philadelphia Quaker he had met during his earlier stay in America. He returned to Japan with his wife that same year.

During the next thirty years Nitobe held many posts and performed many services. One of his primary interests was education: between 1891 and 1918 he taught at Sapporo Agricultural College, Kyoto Imperial University, and Tokyo Imperial University; served as president of the First Higher School (Daiichi Kōtōgakkō, possibly the most prominent higher school in Japan), and Tokyo Women's Christian College;

and wrote many widely read books and articles on such topics as ethics, life in the United States, and Western literature.

Since his wife was an American he was naturally interested in improving United States-Japanese relations. Consequently, he wrote books on Japanese culture and society for Western readers and books on American culture and society for Japanese readers. His publications during this period include *Bushido: The Soul of Japan* and *The Japanese Nation: Its Land, Its People and Its Life* in English, and *Zuisōroku* (Thoughts and Essays) and *Kigan no Ashi* (Student Days Abroad) in Japanese.

From 1900 to 1903 he used his agricultural background as head of the industrial development and sugar bureaus of Formosa. Throughout his early career he worked diligently "with the strength of ten men,"[5] and as a consequence his work was interrupted by periods of illness and convalescence. He had great recuperative powers, however, and managed to continue his many activities.

Nitobe was appointed under-secretary-general of the League of Nations in 1920 and in this post became one of Japan's leading spokesmen for internationalism. He resigned in 1927 to work with the Institute of Pacific Relations, and to act as advisory editor of the *Ōsaka Mainichi* and the *Tōkyō Nichi Nichi*. He spent the last years of his life attempting to improve Japanese-American relations by writing and lecturing in Japan and the United States on various aspects of Japanese and American culture, history, and politics. His publications during this period include *Japanese Traits and Foreign Influences* and *Japan: Some Phases of her Problems and Development* in English, and *Tōzai Aifurete* (Contacts Between East and West) and *Taiheiyō Mondai* (Problems of the Pacific, which he edited) in Japanese. He died suddenly in 1933 after attending a conference of the Institute of Pacific Relations at Banff, Canada. His posthumous publications include two volumes of *Editorial Jottings* and a book of collected *Lectures on Japan*.

Nitobe's life spanned the turbulent and unstable years following the Meiji Restoration when Japan transformed itself into a modern state. He was active in some of the most progressive aspects of that era, the educational and international aspects, not the narrow nationalistic ones. However, he published books and articles defending various elements of Japanese culture, and justified Japanese military actions in the face of foreign criticism. These activities have been interpreted to indicate that he was strongly gripped by his Japanese heritage despite his devotion to progress, and felt some inner psychological need to defend his nation's policies and actions. Despite his American wife and his internationalism, he apparently could not escape the "Japanese particularism" which was his heritage. This perplexing psychological dilemma made it impossible for him to promote progressivism in the full sense. There were several key instances in which his samurai, national, Quaker, and international values conflicted.

The first major inconsistency in Nitobe's life centered around the publication in English of his best-known work, *Bushido: The Soul of Japan* in 1899. In that book he attempted to analyze and assess the Japanese value system, and to his surprise, it became a best seller when world interest in Japan soared after Japan's victory over Russia in 1905. Nitobe's work on the "soul of Japan" was thought of as a key to understanding the reason for Japan's strength. *Bushido* was translated into many foreign languages and read by scholars and statesmen all over the world.

Soon after publication book reviewers hailed *Bushido* for its timely exposition and invaluable insights into the "inscrutable" Oriental personality. Nitobe was noted for being "wise not only in the philosophy of his own land but well grounded in the history and philosophy of the English race."[6] Americans marveled at his excellent command of the English language. "A more scholarly, finished, poetic, and lucid exposition of an abstract and subtle philosophy would be difficult to find," lauded one reviewer.[7]

Japanese readers were also interested in this little book. In fact, the book was copyrighted in the United States and before Nitobe could return to Japan, a Japanese publisher secured a copy, forged the Nitobe seal, and printed nine editions, making a large profit. The influence of the book grew and it was eventually adopted as a textbook in Japan.[8]

Because of Nitobe's Christian and pacifist Quaker leanings, it is strange that he wrote a book extolling the "way of the warrior." Statements from this book explain the moral precepts which he alleged were the basis of the Japanese personality. Nitobe's book discussed those virtues commonly associated with the behavior of the samurai warrior. Chapters on courage, honor, loyalty, self-control, suicide, and the all-important sword were included.

The text explained the concept of *giri*, that "vague sense of duty which public opinion expects an incumbent to fulfill."[9] He noted the importance of suicide (*seppuku*) and revenge as legal and ceremonial institutions in a land which had no criminal court, where "only vigilant vengeance of the victim's people preserves social order."[10] In discussing the "training and position of women" he stated that "the woman's surrender of herself to the good of her husband, home, and family was as willing and honorable as the man's self surrender to the good of his lord and country."[11]

Nitobe was fully aware of the profound influence that Bushido had on the Japanese people. Samurai ideals filtered down to the lower classes, Nitobe explained, because "the samurai grew to be the beau ideal of the whole race. . . . There was no channel of human activity which did not receive in some measure an impetus from Bushido. Intellectual and moral Japan was directly or indirectly the work of knighthood."[12]

After considering the beneficial influence of Bushido in molding the Japanese personality, however, Nitobe noted that "on the other hand it is fair to recognize that for the very faults and defects of our character Bushido is largely responsible."[13] Thus *giri* as a vague sense of duty "in time degenerated into a vague sense of propriety called up to explain this and sanction that . . . ," and in his opinion it "often stooped to casuistry."[14] Likewise, suicide and revenge as legal and ceremonial institutions "lost their *raison d'être* at the promulgation of the criminal code"[15] of the Meiji period. And the "ascending scale of service" in which woman sacrificed herself for man, "that he might annihilate himself for the master, that he in turn might obey heaven"[16] was, according to Nitobe, definitely inferior to the Christian doctrine that "requires of each and every living soul direct responsibility to its Creator."[17] In fact, "universal and natural as is the fighting instinct, fruitful as it has proved to be of noble sentiments and manly virtues, it does not comprehend the whole of man."[18]

"Bushido, and all other militant types of ethics, engrossed doubtless with questions of immediate practical need, too often forget to duly emphasize" that "beneath the instinct to fight there lurks a diviner instinct—to love."[19] Thus Bushido, despite its more glorious aspects, in comparison with Christianity was like "a dimly burning wick."[20] Nitobe concluded that although Bushido was perhaps adequate in the past, "when the conditions of society are so changed that they have become not only adverse but hostile to Bushido it is time for it to prepare for an honorable burial."[21]

Nitobe clearly pointed out the weaknesses of many of the institutions which the Bushi ethic fostered. In a letter to an American reader of the book who commented on his attitude toward Christianity, Nitobe made his own position even more explicit:

> Without being oblivious to the legacy left by our dead (I am alluding to the Japanese forefathers) I see in Jesus the far higher type of life and of living than can be found in Bushido. I am glad to notice that thee recognized between the lines in my book where I stand.[22]

Perhaps because the book was written in a flowing, ornate style and stressed the "higher ideals" of the samurai, however, it has often been considered to be an idealization of the Bushi ethic and a defense of the Japanese value system based on it. That the book was misused and misinterpreted can be seen by the appearance in 1936 of an edited Japanese translation of the essay published in a book containing other articles and proverbs which extolled Bushido and its associated values as the highest system of morality.[23] Omissions in that translation consisted mainly of Nitobe's references to Christianity, including the "dimly burning wick" comparison quoted above.

Nitobe knew that the ethics of Bushido could become a powerful weapon of militarists and ultranationalists. In later writings he continued to praise some of the high ideals of the samurai, their dignity, self-respect, and self-discipline,[24] but did not hesitate to say, "let obsolete forms of Bushido lie with the bones of their followers."[25] Although through Bushido Japan was victorious in the Sino-Japanese War and the Russo-Japanese War, he said Japan would need "something better than Bushido"[26] in the future.

In an eloquent speech delivered at Stanford University in 1911 he made that even more explicit:

> I confess that the two great wars in which we came out triumphant have turned the head of some of our weaker brethren. They believe that our success was due expressly to the spirit of Bushido, the remnant of the excellent teaching which formed the samurai's code of honour. I myself feel partly responsible for disseminating this idea. I do not regret I wrote regarding it and in behalf of it, . . . but I do not share the views of the Chauvinists that the spirit of Bushido is the peculiar monopoly of our people; neither do I share the view that it is the highest system of morality that man can conceive or construct. I know its weakness. I know all its temptations to misinterpretation and degeneration, and I should feel a regret too deep for words, if my people failed to see that the new wine requires a new wine-skin. I should be most sorry if the noble ethics of Bushido were converted by bigots into an anti-foreign instrument.[27]

Thus it is clear that Nitobe did not intend to defend or idealize Bushido. Furthermore, he knew its strengths and weaknesses as a system of morality for the modern world. He admired many of the elements of Bushido; personal courage, a sense of honor, loyalty, and self-discipline, yet he was not blind to its limitations. A Quaker who knew Nitobe suggested that it was the Quaker emphasis on self-discipline which first attracted him to the Society of Friends.

His book *Bushido* exemplifies an eclectic approach to differing value systems as it accepts one value and discards another in the search for a higher morality. Nitobe's samurai-Quaker synthesis, equating the samurai sword of the warrior with the Quaker sword of the spirit, is here quite convincing.

The primary aim of the Meiji leaders in their drive to modernize Japan was to achieve equality for their nation and security from the threat of international colonial rivalries. Thus early Meiji foreign relations were primarily directed toward keeping Japan independent. As the era progressed, however, and the islands themselves were no longer in direct danger, the Japanese government became increasingly concerned about the countries surrounding Japan and their relation to Japan's security. The European powers' success in scrambling for colonies influenced the Japanese who began to feel that real equality with European countries required Japan to expand.

Thus, when they felt their security was threatened in neighboring Korea, first by the Chinese and then by the Russians, they decided it was necessary to resort to war. The Sino-Japanese War (1894–95) resulted in a crushing defeat for China which ceded Formosa, the Pescadores, and the Liaotung Peninsula to Japan. The Triple Intervention of Russia, France, and Germany, however, forced Japan to return the Liaotung Peninsula to China, and Russia occupied it. The Russo-Japanese War of 1904–05 again found Japan victorious. Her defeat of China in 1895 clearly revealed Japan's superiority over other Asian nations, and the defeat of Russia put Japan on a level with world powers.

During the war years between 1894 and 1905 Nitobe engaged in various activities. He taught at the Sapporo Agricultural College, he wrote books and articles, and he served as head of the industrial development and sugar bureaus of Taiwan. He was appointed professor at Kyoto Imperial University in 1903.

Nitobe's reaction to these wars, as a Japanese Quaker devoted to the cause of international understanding, needs clarification. He could have, like some other Japanese Christians, opposed the wars and espoused pacifist views. He could have supported the views of most Japanese nationalists trained in the Bushi ethic by loyally encouraging his country in its military endeavors. A study of several sources is needed to clarify Nitobe's thoughts regarding the Sino-Japanese and Russo-Japanese Wars.

Letters written by Nitobe and his wife during this period indicate that the Nitobes preferred peace, but they did not hold a strong pacifist position. They supported these wars because they considered them necessary to maintain Japanese security. Nitobe discussed the Sino-Japanese War in a letter written to his brother-in-law, Joseph Elkinton, in 1894. The first section of the letter extolled the great samurai spirit of the soldiers and noted many instances of personal bravery which characterized Japanese fighting men. He then described his own feelings:

> As for ourselves, we have kept quiet. Nobody questions us about our peace principles neither have we attempted any public declaration of peace, for such a course will do no good but more harm. The utmost I can do is to call the attention of the public to the other side of the war than its mere jubilance. So . . . I try to emphasize the evils and terrors of war. We are also interested in relieving the sufferings that attend war.[28]

Mary Nitobe similarly discussed the Russo-Japanese War in another letter to Joseph written in 1904. "The nation did not want war," she explained to her disturbed Quaker relatives. "Japan would have been thankful to arbitrate if she had felt Europe would sincerely make an effort to see fair play. . . . However, she had no reason to think that such would be done." Thus, because of the "persistent deadly glacier movement of Russia . . . it is a struggle for Japan's very life." Mrs. Nitobe also noted the samurai spirit of the soldiers, their determination and willingness to die, and concluded by saying:

> It may sound egotistical, but the tremendous sincerity of Japan's sense of the importance of her mission in the development of the Far East is at once interesting and striking and elicits one's respect. . . . Yes, there is intensity of feeling but deep gravity and determination. If only the struggle may be brief and thoroughly victorious for Japan. Pray for us all when thee can.[29]

The Nitobes' comments about Uchimura Kanzo also reflect their position during the Russo-Japanese War. Uchimura, another important Christian of pacifist leanings (though not a Quaker) was strongly opposed to the war and tried to convince the Nitobes to aid him in advocating peace. Mary Nitobe discussed his ideas as follows:

> Clearly as we love Uchimura san we can not follow him in all of his ultra phases of thought and we must warn thee that he paints *black* the other side from that which he has taken and his judgement can not be considered as infallible. . . . This is no time to hamper the government. Horrible as the war is, there is no way in the present stage of civilization for Japan to win the place which she feels she deserves except by fighting.[30]

Thus the Nitobes' correspondence of the period reveals their conviction that the wars were just and unavoidable.

Essays written during and immediately following the Russo-Japanese War, however, temper this view slightly. In an essay written in 1904 Nitobe revealed that he felt the wars were necessary for Japanese security.[31] However, he was profoundly disturbed by some of the war's effects on the mentality of the Japanese people. In June 1905, near the end of the war, he enumerated the enormous tasks which remained for Japan as "the deafening sound of *banzai* dies into the distance and the glaring torches pale away."[32] He said care of bereaved families, careful settlement of Korea, diplomacy, commerce, and communication with the rest of the world must follow the war or the greatness won would not endure.

In an essay written in 1905 he was even more direct. He warned that pride goes before a fall, by writing, "if we go on singing our own praises, if we beguile ourselves into the belief that we are superior . . . we may rue the day most awfully."[33] And he continually stressed Japan's "new duties and responsibilities."[34]

Nitobe's position was revealed even more clearly in discussions and reflections on the war written later. Although he adhered to the idea that both wars were "just and justifiable,"[35] his distress at many of the effects of the wars increased. He argued that the Sino-Japanese War was fought "not for altruistic reasons, but for the sake of her [Japan's] own national safety"[36] since "Korea's weakness jeopardized the very existence of Japan."[37] However, as a result of Western attitudes and the Triple Intervention, the Japanese were taught that "only in armament lay security."[38] Patriotism was intensified and the way was paved for the Russo-Japanese War.

Similarly he felt the Russo-Japanese War was necessary to protect Japan from the Russian menace and to save Japan's honor. Because of Russia's arrogant behavior "there was no other alternative for a proud people than to take the only course left,"[39]—war. Nevertheless, he noted that Japan's success in the war had undesirable effects. One "unfortunate consequence of the war with Russia was the malicious propaganda of a Yellow Peril"[40] which made foreign opinion unfriendly and even hostile to Japan. The "most lamentable effect" of the Russo-Japanese War, however, was "the demoralization of the national mind."[41] He deplored the fact that "militant ideas flowed into every channel of the nation's life,"[42] government policy, civil policy, and even children's toys, and stated that there is "nothing so demoralizing as a war spirit."[43]

As with Bushido, Nitobe was opposed to idealizing the Sino-Japanese and Russo-Japanese Wars. Although he believed in the initial righteousness of the wars and did not adhere to a strict pacifist position, he was aware of the difficulties which the war climate brought. He again tried to rationalize the conflicting nationalist, internationalist, samurai, and Quaker points of view.

A third crisis in Nitobe's values came with the Manchurian incident of September 1931, one of the first steps which eventually led to the Pacific War. Japan, following the Russo-Japanese War, considered Manchuria its "sphere of influence" but made little attempt to reduce the area to an actual colony. In 1931, however, the Japanese Army staged an incident which was used as an excuse to take over Manchuria completely, and by early 1932 Manchukuo was established as a puppet state. The rest of the world was outraged.

At the outbreak of the Manchurian crisis, Nitobe was retired from his formal teaching duties and had resigned from his position as under-secretary-general of the League of Nations. However, he had not forgotten his youthful dream of "building a bridge across the Pacific" and was actively working for international understanding. He was still serving as an editorial counsellor for the *Ōsaka Mainichi* and *Tōkyō Nichi Nichi* English sections; as a member of the House of Peers; and as director of the Institute of Pacific Relations. He continued to lecture and write to further East-West understanding. During this period his publications included *Japanese Traits and Foreign Influences* and *Western Influences in Modern Japan* (edited by Nitobe) in English, and *Tōzai Aifurete* (Contacts Between East and West) in Japanese.

The United States' passage of the 1924 Japanese Exclusion Act was a serious blow to Nitobe's hopes regarding Japanese-American understanding. He believed this act was a primary cause for the increasingly tough and unconciliatory nature of Japanese foreign policy, and resolved that he "would not step upon the shores of the United States until this law was repealed."[44] The seriousness of the Manchurian situation, however, prompted him to reverse this decision. After nine years' absence from the United States, he and his wife came to America in 1932 to lecture and try to explain Japanese actions to indignant Americans.

Following that lecture tour he returned to Japan. In 1933 he came to the Banff Conference of the Institute of Pacific Relations. He died soon after this conference, while still in Canada. Since the Manchurian crisis extended many years beyond his death, Nitobe's attitudes toward it did not develop as fully as in the case of the Sino-Japanese and the Russo-Japanese wars. Yet his speeches and writings, as one of Japan's leading spokesmen for internationalism, reveal his distress over the Manchurian situation and world reaction to it.

Nitobe's radio address of May 20, 1932 summarized his general view of Japan's actions in Manchuria. "The so-called Manchurian issue is not a wanton desire for territory. What we want and insist upon is recognition of our treaty rights, and in these rights is involved the question of whether Japan can carry on her existence."[45]

In a lecture given November 11, 1932 he went into more detail. He first described the "fundamental issues underlying the present situation in the Far East,"[46] namely the interests and claims of China, Japan, and Russia in Manchuria. Russia, he said, had a territorial interest in Manchuria "on account of geographical contiguity"[47] and its need for an ice-free port. China based its claim on "her territorial sovereignty, which in turn is based on prescription."[48] Japan's claim was "founded on the economic interests she has secured"[49] through treaties which the Chinese were trying to repudiate, and its interest was both strategic and economic. He said Manchuria was of strategic importance as a buffer between Japan and Russian Communism; economically Manchuria was the industrial and agricultural "life line of Japan."[50]

Nitobe pointed out that because the United States was far away and not deeply affected, Americans were understandably indifferent to the Japanese situation. However, Manchuria was as important to Japan as Nicaragua or El Salvador to the United States. Then, making clear that he had "presented only the Japanese side of the situation,"[51] he concluded by expressing hope for "a just and reasonable settlement between the two countries at the earliest possible moment."[52]

In another of Nitobe's writings concerning the Manchurian crisis, he made four significant points. First, he emphasized the need for the "spirit of good will and conciliation"[53] in the deliberations between China and Japan, and the necessity for Sino-Japanese friendship in the future.

Second, he reiterated his distress at the "propaganda" regarding the Manchurian incident circulating at the League of Nations, in the United States, and throughout the world. He noted there was a general lack of knowledge about the situation. He stressed that therefore many people failed to understand Japan's motives and condemned his country without good reason. He also pointed out the failure of nations to see Japan's movements in the perspective of their own national actions. "Japan's advance in search of a life line," he stated in a radio address on August 20, 1932, "is as irresistible an economic force as the westward march of the Anglo-Saxon empires."[54] Furthermore, he declared, it is perfectly comparable to Western actions in Central and South America and Africa. Why should such actions be "right in one place and wrong in another?"[55]

Third, Nitobe pointed out that the Japanese army was keeping order in Manchuria and constructing an economically prosperous nation which could become a melting pot of opportunity for all. This attitude was shared by many prominent Japanese liberals who believed "the creation of the new state of Manchukuo filled the air with new hope:

industry started humming; unemployment disappeared; young men and women rushed to Manchuria."[56]

Fourth, he argued that Japan's national honor was at stake as it had been in the Sino-Japanese and Russo-Japanese Wars.[57] He emphasized that Japanese actions fell under the category of "self-defense," and stated that "should the League fail to recognize the justice of our claim which involves our honor and our very existence as a nation, will the world blame Japan for feeling herself obligated to withdraw from the League?"[58] Honor also explained the attitude of Japanese liberals. "The liberals were not in favor of military operations in Manchuria, but when menace came from abroad they turned against it in defense of their country's honor, giving up the pettier conflict with their militaristic countrymen."[59] Once again Nitobe tried to reconcile his background with his position on the Manchurian situation. His samurai heritage made him proud of the acts of Japanese soldiers in defending their territory. His Quaker teachings brought him to seek a peaceful resolution of the difficulties. His Japanese nationalism patriotically justified what he considered to be Japanese rights. His role as an internationalist led to his attempt to make the nations of the world understand the situation and see it within the perspective of their own actions.

Nitobe was apparently convinced of the fairness of Japanese actions in the international arena. However, as in his discussions of Bushido and the Sino-Japanese and Russo-Japanese Wars, he did not hesitate to criticize aspects of the Manchurian policy with which he did not agree. In June of 1929 during General Tanaka's term of office as prime minister, he indicted Japanese policies in a speech delivered in the House of Peers. He accused Tanaka and his cabinet of abusing the imperial prerogative to save their positions and sharply criticized Tanaka's bold policies. Tanaka was ousted several months later and Nitobe's speech was a contributing factor to his fall.[60]

In 1932, at the height of the controversy over Manchuria, Nitobe became even bolder. In a newspaper interview he was reported as saying, "Two insidious dangers confront Japan today—militarism and communism."[61] This remark was extremely irritating to the military and ultra-nationalists and Nitobe's life was threatened. The situation was reported in the magazine *The Friend* as follows:

> Dr. Nitobe is lying in the hospital under the constant fear of bodily violence. ... His enemies are a powerful nationalist organization. This is a consequence of remarks made by him recently which were interpreted as insulting to the army and because of which he received a number of threatening letters denouncing him as a traitor. Subsequently the Zaigogun Jin-Kai [*sic*] Reservists Association, which has a membership of 3,000,000 demanded an

apology from Dr. Nitobe. Though the papers asserted that an apology was actually made, Reuter's special correspondent is assured on good authority that Dr. Nitobe declined to apologize but that "he gave an explanation which the higher officials readily accepted." However reactionary elements among the Reservists continue to demand an unqualified apology and back up their demands with threats of personal violence.[62]

Nitobe's "explanations" of Japanese actions were apparently for the benefit of foreign audiences and not to be interpreted as unequivocal endorsements of Japanese policies.

His criticisms of Japanese policies were radical enough to incite militaristic elements in Japanese society, but they were not pacifist enough to convince his American friends and admirers of his peaceful intent. In fact his "explanations" dismayed his Quaker friends and relatives, for it seemed to them that he had abandoned the principles which they supposedly held in common. In 1932 when he reversed his decision and came to the United States to explain the Manchurian situation, many Americans questioned his motives.

One Christian journal headlined its story the "Bankruptcy of Dr. Nitobe" and denounced him as a "comprador of the militarists."[63] Other newspapers accused him of being "a propagandist and protagonist for what he could not endorse."[64] In his postwar study Robert S. Schwantes says that Nitobe was forced to retract earlier statements critical of military policy and to defend Japanese actions in Manchuria.[65] And Harold Wakefield states that because Nitobe became popular as a representative of Japanese liberalism "he was used after 1931 as an apologist in America for the crimes of Japan against China."[66]

Those closest to him, however, refused to consider Nitobe a traitor to the Quaker and international causes, and they explained his actions in other terms. One relative of his wife quoted Nitobe, that "if he decided to criticize his government he would do so at home and not in a foreign country, and that his responsibility in the United States in 1932 was simply to recite the injustices received by Japan from China and to explain why his government felt they had to take the action they did."[67] Another friend wrote that Nitobe's explanation of his country's reasons for invading Manchuria was a duty which "it was impossible for him to shirk."[68] Both attributed the strength of Nitobe's determination to "the teachings of Bushido which still rested in his life"[69] and the "depths of loyalty of a Japanese to his emperor."[70]

The New York *Herald Tribune* reported Nitobe's death by stating he had a change of view early in 1933 and "as his faith in Japan's inherent righteousness waned . . . he admitted that his native country was failing to cooperate in the international scheme of things."[71] An article by the famous Quaker friend of Japan, Gilbert Bowles, written in 1944, corroborates this statement:

> The determination of Dr. Nitobe to visit America at this time was felt by some of his best Japanese friends to be a mistake. Many Americans who heard his explanations of Japan's policies shared in this sorrowful judgement. It was therefore a great relief to his friends to see that during the end of this American visit he changed from a defensive to an interpretive and educational emphasis concerning his own country.[72]

Nitobe's Japanese followers also felt it necessary to "clarify for the world at large his position against the Japanese military,"[73] and one wrote that "Dr. Nitobe did not go to the United States at the instigation of the government, much less of the military. On the contrary he went out of his own deep concern."[74] His friends emphasized that in being a "genuine internationalist" he was not un-Japanese, by stating "it has been generally agreed that very few Japanese have ever been so patriotic and loyal as he."[75] Probably because of the frantic efforts of his American and Japanese friends to explain his motives, newspaper articles both in English and Japanese reporting his death on October 15, 1933 pictured him as a true champion of international brotherhood.

Four value systems—Bushido, nationalism, Quakerism, and internationalism—influenced Nitobe's thinking. He could not be completely loyal to any one of them when confronted with a difficult situation. After considering Nitobe's reactions to several significant events, it is still not clear where his ultimate loyalty lay. Instead, it seems that in Nitobe's reactions to these events all of the four values merged into a practical philosophy, uniquely Nitobe's. Probably that practical philosophy, rather than any one of the discrete value systems, caused him to respond as he did.

After reading virtually all of Nitobe's books, articles, and letters available in English, and delving into many of his Japanese works, the author conceives Nitobe's philosophy as consisting of three main elements. First, Nitobe sincerely desired to promote Japanese-American understanding. Second, he insisted on maintaining honor or face. Third, he strictly observed and admired self-discipline.

Because he never lost hope that he would build a bridge across the Pacific, he devoted most of his life to creating tools for understanding, in public service as an educator in Japan and the United States, as a delegate to the League of Nations, as a director of the Institute of Pacific Relations, and on a more intimate level, through informal lectures and discussions with Japanese and Americans. Because of his keen concept of honor and dishonor he insisted on adhering to principles which he considered fair and right for himself, his family, and his nation. And because of his great faith in self-discipline as necessary to a full and productive life, he admired many aspects of Bushido and lectured widely on morals and ethics.

Honor and self-discipline as practical values suggest a strong legacy of Bushido. In Nitobe's case the two were tempered by his Quaker training which taught that both were dependent on one's "Inner Light" rather than on external values. His emphasis on East-West understanding indicates that he was aware of and sensitive to the excitement of the Meiji-Taisho eras when Japan opened its doors to the world and became a powerful member of the community of nations.

The creation of East-West understanding and friendship was a main ingredient in Nitobe's philosophy. From his first statement on wanting to be a bridge across the Pacific through his years as a student in Western universities, his marriage to an American, his books on Japan for Americans and on America for Japanese, his term as under-secretary-general of the League of Nations, and his leadership of the Institute of Pacific Relations, his whole career was pointed toward building the tools for East-West understanding.

Nitobe approached the problems of East versus West with the following spirit:

> It is not by mutual fault finding or by exaggerating each other's peculiarities that we can arrive at understanding or appreciation. Not by antipathy but by sympathy, not by hostility but by hospitality, not by enmity but by amity, does one race come to know the heart of another.[76]

He was keenly aware of the dissimilarities in national sentiment and diversities of culture which divide people, yet he was convinced that if "one be scratched only deep enough he will show common humanity."[77] His prescription for studying an alien people was "firstly to understand their temperament and secondly to consider them from their own angle."[78]

In the introduction to *Tōzai Aifurete* he argued that it was Japan's duty to connect East and West and to understand the psychology of the West by saying that "this volume does not contain any new or especially interesting material ... my only contribution is the thesis that all men are the same at heart although they differ greatly on externals."[79] Similarly his writing for American readers was intended to shed light on different aspects of the Japanese mind. He said, "my sole plea is the cultivation of a sympathetic understanding between peoples trained at opposite poles of tradition."[80] Nitobe was also convinced that truth could be found by combining the best features of both cultures. He said:

Not in the Occident and not in the Orient, but in the union of both will be revealed many of the secrets of Divine dispensation as yet hidden from our sights.[81]

He seemed to realize that religion is one of the most important areas of life to be benefited by East-West eclecticism. Unlike many Japanese Christians Nitobe criticized those aspects of Christianity with which he was dissatisfied, and he stated:

If the West is dissatisfied with Christianity as it seems to be, will it not find a fresh clue to some of its teachings in the East?[82]

His Quaker beliefs are evident in his statement that "that mysterious Love, the man Jesus Christ, can be appreciated better by intuition and mysticism—capacities oriental."[83] Furthermore, "though at the foot of the hill the ways are far apart, as we ascend higher and higher the nearer approach our paths, until they meet at the summit to share the view of the plains below from the height of the same divine wisdom."[84]

Nitobe's strong sense of honor and face was a bit more nebulous than his desire for East-West friendship, although just as evident in his career and writing. He criticized the Bushi concept of honor which demanded the warrior's ultimate sacrifice for the honor of his family, lord, and nation, and said it "not infrequently deteriorates into mere sensitiveness."[85] However, his own concept of honor was highly important in his scheme of things. He equated samurai honor with the Inner Light of Quakerism, stating that:

The samurai standard of right and goodness was too often decided by outward human relations than by the inward voice of the spirit.[86]

The word honor often entered his discussions of Japanese history and culture and was of utmost importance in his view of warfare, nationalism, and international relations. About war he stated:

In medieval warfare the sense of honor often robbed it of its horrors.[87]

Regarding the remarkable progress of Japan after the Meiji Restoration he said:

The sense of honor which can not bear being looked down upon as an inferior power—that was the strongest of motives.[88]

Honor played a primary role in his view of international relations. In fact, Nitobe tended to explain nearly all Japanese actions in the international arena in terms of honor. The Triple Intervention following the Sino-Japanese War threatened Japan's honor and taught her that "only in armament lay security."[89] The Russo-Japanese War was fought because there was no other alternative for a proud country to take. The Japanese Exclusion Act of the United States was a serious affront to Japan's honor, sowing seeds of suspicion and resentment, and "each year that passes without amendment or abrogation sharpens our sense of injury."[90] He also regarded the Manchurian crisis as a direct result of infringements on Japanese honor. In fact, in the final analysis, Nitobe stated, "Japan will be internationally minded unless provoked by hostile acts that may wound her pride."[91]

Although Nitobe was aware that "in the name of honor deeds were perpetuated which can find no justification in the code of Bushido"[92] he believed, as Mencius taught, that "anger at a petty offense is unworthy of a superior man but indignation for a great cause is righteous wrath."[93] Therefore in "great causes" he did not condemn his country for her "righteous wrath" and insisted on her right to defend her honor.

The third important ingredient in Nitobe's philosophy was his respect for self-discipline. Because of his admiration for this trait he believed in much of the samurai ethic even though it conflicted in aim with Quaker ideals. Besides trying to discipline his own life, he was full of praise for others who did so.

Nitobe's writings on Bushido and *shūyō* (self-improvement) reveal his conviction concerning the importance of self-discipline. Among his works on the subject are *Yowatari no Michi* (The Art of Living) and *Shūyō* (Self-Improvement) in Japanese, and various essays on such topics as self-mastery, cheerfulness, common sense, and loneliness[94] collected in *Thoughts and Essays* and *Editorial Jottings*. It is important to note, however, that Nitobe's concept of *shūyō* differed sharply from what one writer calls the "moral educationalists" of the 1910s and 1920s.[95] He conceived of *shūyō* not as submission to some "external order or discipline," but as "a way for an individual to shape his personality."[96]

There are many examples of Nitobe's personal self-discipline. Throughout his life he adhered to his principles even in the face of the pressures imposed on him as a result of the Russo-Japanese War, the Japanese Exclusion Act, and the Manchurian crisis. Those events threatened his ideals of peace and world friendship but he maintained his principles—aided by his Bushido training which imbued him with high standards and the capacity to disregard hardship. He was undeterred by personal problems, illness, nationalism and international events. His remarkable ability to recover from physical and mental traumas enabled him to believe and continue to espouse four value systems without physical and mental collapse despite their contradictions.

In sum, Nitobe expounded principles of internationalism and nationalism, Quakerism and Bushido, to Americans and Japanese alike. His actions were based on a practical philosophy composed of Japanese-American understanding, personal and national honor, and self-discipline.

This essay has examined the efforts of a brilliant and sensitive Japanese to erect a cultural and philosophical bridge across the Pacific. In the immediate sense he failed. The improvement in Japanese-American relations which he hoped to see did not materialize during his lifetime. Indeed Japanese-American relations were deteriorating at the time of his death in 1933, and World War II for a time completely destroyed his "bridge." He was not totally successful in reconciling the value systems he espoused. Nationalism did not yield to internationalism, nor Bushido to Quakerism, even in his own psyche. Yet, his life and efforts were not failures. Despite the submergence of his comparatively liberal ideas during the war, Nitobe eventually won a respected place in modern Japanese history. Some of his students and followers attained important positions in the leadership of postwar Japan, especially in the field of education. Among them are Maeda Tamon, who served as minister of education; Yanaihara Tadao, former president of Tokyo University; Takagi Yasaka, emeritus professor of American history at Tokyo University; and the well-known international labor expert, Ayusawa Iwao.

Deplorably, Japan experienced a terrible war and defeat before it could appreciate the worth of Nitobe's ideas.[97] In 1952 a "cultural stamp" bearing Nitobe's picture was issued to commemorate him as an educator who "throughout his life espoused the cause of humanity and international goodwill against the forces of prejudice of which there were no lack."[98]

An examination of Nitobe's statements on the four themes which characterized his political and cultural philosphy indicates that he failed to achieve a convincing synthesis. On the other hand, he maintained his psychological stability and kept faith with his heritage while working for Japanese-American friendship. His hope for resolution of the larger problems was expressed in his writing:

> What seem to our limited vision as contradictions or opposing elements on our level find harmony in a higher, and the higher we ascend, the fewer the contradictions which distract us.[99]

Finally, the "stress of conflicting idealisms"[100] which Nitobe felt so keenly was not the monopoly of Japanese intellectuals trying to reconcile their traditional values with those of the West. It was a common problem faced by Japanese businessmen in America and immigrants of every social and occupational level, whether they could articulate the problem or not. Nitobe and those Japanese who moved to the United

States found that to become a "man of two worlds" or to "bridge the Pacific" was not an easy thing.

NOTES

1. Inazo Nitobe, *The Japanese Nation: Its Land, Its People and Its Life* (New York, 1912), p. vii.

2. Dorothy Lloyd Gilbert, *Dr. Inazo Nitobe and Mary P.E. Nitobe* (produced for private distribution, 1955), p. 81.

3. Kiyoko Takeda Cho, "The Christian Encounter with the Traditional Ethos of Japan: A Study of Nitobe Inazo's Ideas," *Asian Cultural Studies*, No. 5, October 1966.

4. Inazo Nitobe, *Reminiscences of Childhood* (Tokyo, 1934).

5. Gilbert, p. 69.

6. *The Public Ledger*, Philadelphia, February 15, 1900, quoted in appendix of Inazo Nitobe, *Bushido: The Soul of Japan* (Tokyo, 1904), p. 14.

7. *Ibid.*, p. 15.

8. Gilbert, p. 73. This fact is also mentioned in Tadao Yanaihara, *Bibliography of the Writings in Japanese of Inazo Ota Nitobe* (Tokyo, 1936), which states that the secondary school textbooks *Chūto dai Nippon Shūshin* [Ethics for Middle Schools] (Tokyo, 1931) and *Jitsugyō dai Nippon Shūshin* [Ethics for Technical Schools] (Tokyo, 1931) were based on writings of Nitobe.

9. Inazo Nitobe, *Bushido: The Soul of Japan* (Tokyo, 1935), p. 26.

10. *Ibid.*, p. 133.

11. *Ibid.*, p. 154.

12. *Ibid.*, p. 169.

13. *Ibid.*, p. 183.

14. *Ibid.*, p. 27.

15. *Ibid.*, p. 135.

16. *Ibid.*, p. 154.

17. *Ibid.*, p. 154.

18. *Ibid.*, p. 194.

19. *Ibid.*, p. 194.

20. *Ibid.*, p. 199.

21. *Ibid.*, p. 195.

22. Unpublished letter from Inazo Nitobe to Elizabeth C. Dunn, January 30, 1900, included in Nitobe Papers, Record Group 5, Series 2, Friends Historical Library, Swarthmore College, Swarthmore, Pa.

23. Inazo Nitobe, *Bushido* (Tokyo, 1936). This book includes an article by Ishii Kikujiro entitled "Bushidō to Hōjō Tokimune" [Bushido and Hojo Tokimune], an article by Matsuoka Yōsuke entitled "Ikkoku no Kōhai" [The Destiny of a Country], and various "Bushidō Kakugen" [Bushido Proverbs].

24. See, for example, Inazo Nitobe, "Ascent of Bushido," in *Thoughts and Essays* (Tokyo, 1909).

25. *Ibid.*, p. 143.

ASIAN COMMUNITY LIBRARY
1934 PARK BLVD.
OAKLAND, CA 94606

26. *Ibid.*, p. 179.

27. Nitobe, *The Japanese Nation,* p. 316.

28. Unpublished letter from Nitobe to Joseph Elkinton, November 15, 1894, Nitobe Papers, Record Group 5, Series 2, Swarthmore College.

29. Unpublished letter from Mary P.E. Nitobe to Joseph Elkinton, January 6, 1905, *ibid.*

30. Unpublished letter from Mary P.E. Nitobe to Joseph Elkinton, December, 1904, *ibid.*

31. "The Slav Peril Versus the Yellow Peril," in Nitobe, *Thoughts and Essays.* Nitobe's conclusion to this essay reads, "if there is any menace to Europe and the rest of the world from one dominant race it is from the avowedly enslaving power of the Slav." (p. 79).

32. *Ibid.*, p. 119.

33. *Ibid.*, p. 127.

34. *Ibid.*, p. 138.

35. Nitobe, *The Japanese Nation,* p. 297.

36. Inazo Nitobe, *Japan: Some Phases of her Problems and Development* (New York, 1931), p. 127.

37. *Ibid.*, p. 128.

38. *Ibid.*, p. 129.

39. *Ibid.*, p. 142.

40. *Ibid.*, p. 145.

41. *Ibid.*, p. 146.

42. *Ibid.*

43. *Ibid.*

44. Sukeo Kitasawa, *The Life of Dr. Nitobe* (Tokyo, 1953), p. 73.

45. Inazo Nitobe, "Japan's Hopes and Fears," a radio address over station WOK on May 20, 1932. Typewritten copy in Nitobe Papers, Record Group 5, Series 3.

46. Inazo Nitobe, *Lectures on Japan* (Chicago, 1938), p. 242.

47. *Ibid.*

48. *Ibid.*, p. 243. "Prescription" in this context means "custom or title continued until it has acquired forces of law."

49. *Ibid.*, p. 245.

50. *Ibid.*, p. 251.

51. *Ibid.*

52. *Ibid.*, p. 252.

53. Inazo Nitobe, *Editorial Jottings,* Volume 1 (Tokyo, 1938), p. 342.

54. Nitobe, *Lectures on Japan,* p. 268.

55. *Ibid.*, p. 271.

56. Kitasawa, p. 83.

57. It might be of interest to note here that Nitobe's four themes (the necessity for Sino-Japanese friendship, the unfairness of anti-Japanese propaganda, the opportunities in Manchuria, and the saving of Japan's honor) are familiar themes in discussion of the Manchurian situation by other Japanese liberals in the early 1930s. See, for example, Kikujiro Ishii, "The League and the Chinese

Problem," *Contemporary Japan,* June 1932; Iyesato Tokugawa, "Peace in the Pacific," *Contemporary Japan,* September 1933; and Hatsutaro Haraguchi, "War Clouds in the Pacific," *Contemporary Japan,* March 1934.

58. Nitobe, *Lectures on Japan,* p. 258.

59. *Ibid.,* p. 269.

60. There seems to be some discrepancy as to the exact contents of this speech which, unfortunately, I have been unable to resolve, due to my inability to find the text of the talk. Several Philadelphia Quakers who knew Nitobe personally are of the opinion that this speech directly criticized Japanese military actions in Manchuria; however, according to Nitobe's biographer, Sukeo Kitasawa, the speech was concerned with abusing the imperial prerogative.

61. Kitasawa, p. 76.

62. A reprint of this article was found in Nitobe Papers, Record Group 5, Series 5.

63. Kitasawa, p. 79.

64. Mary P.E. Nitobe in her foreword to Inazo Nitobe, *Lectures on Japan.*

65. Robert S. Schwantes, *Japanese and Americans* (New York: Harper and Brothers, 1955), p. 32.

66. Harold Wakefield, *New Paths for Japan* (London, 1948), p. 56.

67. Unpublished letter from J. Passmore Elkinton to Dorothy Gilbert, December 15, 1948, Nitobe Papers, Record Group 5, Series 2.

68. Howard W. Elkinton, "Inazo Nitobe," ms., typewritten, October 17, 1933, Nitobe Papers, Record Group 5, Series 1.

69. *Ibid.*

70. J. Passmore Elkinton to Dorothy Gilbert, *ibid.*

71. *New York Herald Tribune,* October 15, 1933, in Nitobe Papers, Record Group 5, Series 5.

72. Gilbert Bowles, "The Peace Movement in Japan," *The Friend,* December 7, 1944, p. 184.

73. Yasaka Takagi, "A Tribute to the Late Dr. Inazo Nitobe," ms., typewritten, no date, Nitobe Papers, Record Group 5, Series 1.

74. *Ibid.*

75. "Dr. Inazo Nitobe," translation of article in Japanese *Friend,* no author mentioned, 1933 (?), Nitobe Papers, Record Group 5, Series 1.

76. Nitobe, *The Japanese Nation,* p. 9.

77. Inazo Nitobe, *Japanese Traits and Foreign Influences* (London, 1927), p. 9.

78. *Ibid.*

79. Inazo Nitobe, *Tōzai Aifurete* (The Contacts Between East and West) (Tokyo, 1928). Translation of part of introduction in Tadao Yanaihara, *Bibliography of the Writings in Japanese of Nitobe.*

80. Nitobe, *Japanese Traits and Foreign Influences,* p. viii.

81. Nitobe, *The Japanese Nation,* p. 10.

82. Inazo Nitobe, ed., *Western Influences in Modern Japan* (Chicago, 1931), p. 23.

83. *Ibid.*

84. Nitobe, *Lectures on Japan,* p. 158.

85. *Ibid.*, p. 315.
86. Nitobe, *Japan*, p. 354.
87. Nitobe, *The Japanese Nation*, p. 67.
88. Nitobe, *Bushido*, p. 175.
89. Nitobe, *Japan*, p. 131.
90. Nitobe, *Lectures on Japan*, p. 288.
91. Nitobe, *Japanese Traits and Foreign Influences*, p. 210.
92. Nitobe, *Bushido*, p. 46.
93. *Ibid.*, p. 77.
94. This essay on loneliness is especially significant. In it Nitobe character-izes loneliness as "the soul's confession of its own greatness . . . the assertion of that divine nature within us which the world does not silence nor satisfy." He urges youths to "drain to its last drop . . . the cup of loneliness . . . (for) the moments when you feel it most are the moments when your spirit is growing." (*Thoughts and Essays*, pp. 85, 86).
95. See Kiyoko Takeda Cho, "The Christian Encounter with the Traditional Ethos of Japan," *op. cit.*
96. *Ibid.*, p. 133.
97. For example, Tamon Maeda says in his article "Dr. Nitobe Inazo," (Nitobe Papers, Record Group 5, Series 1) "I can't help complaining when I recall memories of Dr. Nitobe that if Japan had followed his teachings she would not have suffered as she did." Furthermore, in connection with Nitobe's influence on the generation of postwar adult Japanese, one of Nitobe's relatives by mar-riage told me that a group of Nitobe's followers were greatly influential in the inclusion of Article 9, the "Peace Clause" in the postwar Japanese Constitution. However, I have as yet been unable to confirm this from other sources.
98. Stamp and introductory remarks found in Nitobe Papers, Record Group 5, Series 5. Other Japanese who have been honored by "Culture Stamps" in-clude Fukuzawa Yukichi, Tsubouchi Shōyō, Uchimura Kanzō, and Mori Ōgai.
99. Nitobe, *Thoughts and Essays*, p. 45.
100. Gurney Binford, "As I Remember It: Stories About Dr. Inazo Nitobe," ms., typewritten, Nitobe Papers, Record Group 5, Series 1.

BIBLIOGRAPHY

Unpublished Primary Sources

Nitobe Papers. Record Group 5, 2 Boxes, Friends Historical Library, Swarthmore College, Swarthmore, Pa.
    Series 1   Biographical material regarding Dr. Inazo Nitobe and his wife Mary P.E. Nitobe (ms. mainly typewritten), includes reminis-cences by Tamon Maedi, Tadao Yanaihara, and Yasaka Takagi.
    Series 2   Correspondence 1890-1962, includes
           Nitobe, Inazo letters sent 1890-1926.
           Nitobe, Mary P.E. letters sent and received 1891-1938
           Miscellaneous letters by various authors to various recipients.

Series 3 Radio addresses by Dr. Nitobe (Typewritten copies)
Series 4 Writings by Dr. Inazo Nitobe. Printed.
Writings by Mary P.E. Nitobe. Printed magazine articles.
Series 5 Printed materials about Dr. Nitobe and Mary Nitobe. Includes
memorials, newspaper clippings, articles.
Series 6 Pictures.
Series 7 Reference Material.
Interviews.
David C. Elkinton. Great-nephew of Dr. and Mrs. Nitobe. February 1967.
Esther B. Rhoads. Former head of Quaker projects in Japan. Personally
acquainted with the Nitobes. July 1967.
Howard Brinton. Eminent Quaker professor and author. Younger contem-
porary of Dr. Nitobe. October 1967.
Dr. Joseph Stokes. Honorary Japanese Consul of Philadelphia. Related by
marriage to Dr. Nitobe. November 1967.

Published Primary Sources

Nitobe, Inazo "Beikoku no tai-Nichi taido ni tsuite" [Comments on the Atti-
tudes of the United States Toward Japan]. *Kaizo,* May 1933.
Bushido: The Soul of Japan. Tokyo, 1904.
Bushido: The Soul of Japan. Tokyo, 1935.
Bushidō (in Japanese). Tokyo, 1936.
Editorial Jottings. Vols. 1 and 2, Tokyo, 1938.
Japan: Some Phases of Her Problems and Development. New York, 1931.
The Japanese Nation: Its Land, Its People, Its Life. New York, 1912.
Japanese Traits and Foreign Influences. London, 1927.
"Kokusai remmei ni okeru Man-Mo Mondai" [The Problem of Manchuria
and Mongolia as Seen by the League of Nations], *Chuō Kōron,* February
1932.
Lectures on Japan. Chicago, 1938.
(ed.) *Manshū Mondai Kenkyū* [Studies of the Manchurian Question]. Tokyo,
1929.
Nitobe Hakase Bunshū [Selections from Dr. Nitobe's Writings], ed. Yanaihara
Tadao. Tokyo, 1936.
Reminiscences of Childhood. Tokyo, 1934.
(ed.) *Taihei-yō Mondai* [Problems of the Pacific]. Tokyo, 1930.
Thoughts and Essays. Tokyo, 1909.
Tōzai Aifurete (Contacts Between East and West). Tokyo, 1928.
(ed.) *Western Influences in Modern Japan.* Chicago, 1931.

Unpublished Secondary Works

Gilbert, Dorothy Lloyd. *Dr. Inazo Nitobe and Mary P.E. Nitobe,* produced for
private distribution, 1955. An 86-page pamphlet on the Nitobes' life until
1909.

Published Secondary Works

Blacker, Carmen. *The Japanese Enlightenment: A Study of the Writings of Fukuzawa Yukichi.* New York: Cambridge University Press, 1964.

Bowles, Gilbert. "The Peace Movement in Japan." *The Friend,* December 7, 1944.

Cho, Kiyoko Takeda. "The Christian Encounter with the Traditional Ethos of Japan: A Study of Nitobe Inazo's Ideas." *Asian Cultural Studies,* No. 5, October 1966.

Haraguchi, Hatsutaro. "War Clouds in the Pacific." *Contemporary Japan,* March 1934.

Ishii, Kikujiro. "The League and the Chinese Problem." *Contemporary Japan,* June 1932.

Jansen, Marius (ed.). *Changing Japanese Attitudes Toward Modernization.* Princeton: Princeton University Press, 1965.

Kitasawa, Sukeo. *The Life of Dr. Nitobe.* Tokyo, 1953.

Schwantes, Robert S. *Japanese and Americans.* New York: Harper and Brothers, 1955.

Seminars at Harvard University. *Papers on Japan,* vols. 1, 2, 3. Cambridge, 1961, 1963, 1965.

Tokugawa, Iyesato. "Peace in the Pacific." *Contemporary Japan,* September 1933.

Wakefield, Harold. *New Paths for Japan.* London, 1948.

Yanaihara, Tadao. *Bibliography of the Writings in Japanese of Inazo Ota Nitobe.* Tokyo, 1936.

Part Four

Sociological Essays

Introduction

The systematic study of Japanese immigrants and their American-born descendants is important for its own sake. It is also important as a check on the widely accepted generalizations about immigration, acculturation, assimilation, and ethnic groups and communities, which have largely been developed from the data on European minorities and Afro-Americans.

According to Professor William Petersen and others, the Japanese American experience differs sufficiently from that of other minorities to raise questions about the universality of some of these generalizations. For example, it has been assumed that a smaller percentage of the second-generation descendants of immigrants were in white-collar and professional occupations than of the "old-stock" Caucasian Americans, since the American-born children of most European immigrants have had on the average fewer years of education than the old-stock Caucasian Americans. Similarly, the children of European immigrants supposedly had on the average higher delinquency rates than the established Caucasian Americans, partly because of the intergenerational cultural conflicts the former had with their parents. Neither of these generalizations holds for second-generation Japanese Americans.

Professor Calvin Schmid and his associates have shown that Japanese Americans average more years of schooling than the Caucasian Americans. By 1960, about 56 percent of the Japanese Americans were in white-collar occupations, compared to 42 percent of the Caucasians. Of this total, more than 26 percent of the Japanese Americans were in the professional and technical classification, and 12.5 percent of the Caucasians. Despite the enormous differences between the early Meiji culture of the Issei and the American culture of their Nisei children, the Japanese Americans have had far lower delinquency rates than the Caucasian Americans. Obviously, we need more inclusive and more sophisticated generalizations to account for the exceptions revealed by the available research on Oriental Americans. The following essays will help us to understand several aspects of the Japanese American experience.

Frank Miyamoto analyzes the Japanese community in Seattle and outlines the institutions and functions of such communities to meet the needs of the Japanese immigrants and their children. According to Professor Edwin O. Reischauer, "no immigrant group encountered higher walls of prejudice and discrimination than did the Japanese—the denial on racist grounds of the right to naturalization, the denial in the areas where they largely lived of the right to own land or enter certain professions, and eventually complete exclusion." European immigrants did not face such legal and institutional barriers. The Japanese, however, in common with all immigrants, had to find employment and housing (and the Japanese were restricted by racial covenants); they had to learn the rudiments of the English language and American ways of living; and they had to find ways of helping each other.

The development of the ethnic community enabled the better-educated, middle-class Issei to assume the leadership in adjusting to America, even as they also upheld Japanese values and patterns of conduct useful in encouraging the upward mobility of the Japanese and Japanese Americans in the economic life of the nation. On the whole, the ethnic community, it now seems, enhanced the Japanese American's educational and occupational aspirations. Professor Miyamoto shows how the Issei survived and advanced despite their own cultural handicaps and the organized barriers to their full participation in American society. The Nisei absorbed from their parents, the community, and the American schools the most meaningful values of their parents and the American society—for example, their esteem for education and achievement. As a consequence, the Japanese Americans (who some European immigrants and American racists insisted were unassimilable) became mostly middle-class within a single generation. Although the ethnic community and some of its institutions and organizations were branded as "un-American" by some racist groups, the very groups which played so large a role in attempting to segregate the Japanese, the ethnic community in reality was an important influence in the Americanization and acculturation of both the Issei and the Nisei. The strength of Japanese family ties, the relationship of the family to the larger institutions, and the community itself minimized delinquency and sustained Japanese aspirations, despite the sharp cultural and age differences between the Issei and the Nisei. In retrospect, we can see how delicate was the balance between potentially positive or negative roles in acculturation that the ethnic community had. In this case, it helped its members to advance into the larger society. As the history of several other ethnic groups would suggest, given a different balance of factors, it could have delayed the Japanese Americans.

The next essay, by Minako Kurokawa, is also concerned with the processes of acculturation and Americanization of the Japanese Americans (as well as the Chinese Americans). In contrast to Miyamoto's paper which focuses on the community—that is, on relatively large-scale processes, Professor Kurokawa concentrates on some influences that these processes have on the personality and more directly on the patterns of bodily motion and physical behavior of the acculturating individuals. What may be regarded as an inquiry into the relations between cultural heritage and accidents as an important public health and medical sociology problem is equally a study of acculturation.

Travelers and students frequently observe the cultural and national differences in the patterns of bodily motion of peoples. Instead of discussing impressionistically, Kurokawa has systematically examined the relations between acculturation and accident rates which here can partly be regarded as convenient quantifiable indices of these patterns. She found a direct correlation between the degree of acculturation of the Japanese American (and Chinese American) child and his parents on the one hand and on the other hand the frequency of accidents that he has. It is not surprising that many Issei complained at first of prolonged fatigue which they could not shake off. Many patterns of bodily motions to which they were conditioned as children were no longer appropriate in their new American environment. They literally had to recondition themselves. This study should encourage further inquiries into the relations of the more abstract or external aspects of a culture and the "gut reactions" they involve.

We previously commented that studies on the Oriental Americans could contribute information useful in testing the universality of some widely accepted generalizations about immigration and acculturation, which were largely derived from the experiences of the European minorities or Afro-Americans. George Kagiwada's essay applies several of these theories in a study on the primary relations between the Los Angeles area Nisei and Sansei (third generation) and the Caucasian Americans. Primary relations constitute a basic factor in Milton Gordon's distinction between acculturation and structural assimilation. Using Gordon's concepts, Kagiwada applies to the Japanese Americans the well-known third-generation thesis of the historian Marcus Lee Hansen that the grandchildren of immigrants, secure in their status as Americans, are concerned with their ethnic heritage. The Los Angeles area Nisei and Sansei data show some evidence that a minority are developing ethnic affiliations, as the Hansen thesis would suggest. Kagiwada, however, finds that on the whole the differences in the primary relations of the Nisei and Sansei are less than we might expect. Education and occupation, for example, are among other factors which directly influence the degree of integration.

Investigating further, Kagiwada then applies Karl Mannheim's theory which distinguishes subgroupings in each generation. It proved to be more useful than Hansen's thesis in bringing out some differences between the Nisei and Sansei. Mannheim's analytical concepts, with some modifications, should be helpful in a variety of further research on the Nisei, Sansei, and indeed Issei. Kagiwada, it should be noted, has compared the primary relationships between Japanese Americans and Caucasian Americans and other Japanese Americans; he did not aim at a systematic comparison of cultural or personality traits.

In the last of these four essays, Stanford Lyman examines the Issei heritage in Japan, their experiences in America, and the cultural and social differences among the Issei, Nisei, and Sansei. He then takes a bold leap to formulate what he regards as the typical Nisei personality. Many will, of course, take exception to the profile he draws and the causal explanations he gives. Some will question the specific traits he emphasizes, the combination he suggests, and the frequency with which they appear in the Nisei personality. Others will prefer to place greater stress on the nature of the ethnic community in which the Nisei grew up. They include even such demographic factors as the unusual history of the Japanese immigration, the restrictions soon placed on further immigration, and the peculiar age and generational composition of the ethnic community. The three previous essays mention a few of the other influences. We also should note that many Nisei grew up in non-ethnic communities or associated primarily with Caucasian peer groups. In calling our attention to the interaction between the social forces and the ideal typical patterns of individual personality, however, Dr. Lyman gives us still another perspective on Nisei (and also Issei and Sansei) experiences.

These essays illustrate some of the diversity and range of the necessary research on the Japanese immigrants and their descendants and the possible insights which may come from such studies. They should help us to understand more fully the unique experience and contributions of the Issei and Japanese Americans and in so doing also contribute further insight into the life of other ethnic and racial groups, in the United States and a number of societies undergoing rapid change.

An Immigrant Community in America

S. FRANK MIYAMOTO

In a study entitled *Nonwhite Races: State of Washington,* Calvin F. Schmid and collaborators compare the socioeconomic status—using as indexes education, occupation, and income—of Japanese, Chinese, Filipinos, Negroes, American Indians, and Caucasians in the state of Washington, from 1940 to 1960. Following their detailed comparisons of the groups, they state in summary:[1]

> There is a distinct separation in the hierarchical position on all three dimensions—education, occupation, and income—between Japanese, Caucasians, and Chinese, on one hand, and Negroes, Filipinos, and Indians, on the other. The Japanese . . . are far above any other group in educational status . . . Chinese and Japanese, with almost identical scores, rank first and second, respectively, in occupational status, and Caucasians are in third place . . . As indicated previously, Caucasians rank highest on income, followed in order by Japanese and Chinese.

Elsewhere, with reference to Milton Gordon's criteria of assimilation, the authors conclude:[2]

> Chinese and, especially, Japanese show a higher degree of cultural and civic assimilation than any of the other minority races. Moreover, in terms of the other dimensions of assimilation, they have made some headway. As the Tauebers point out, the disappearance of ethnic colonies and increased residential dispersion of the Japanese, in comparison to the relatively pronounced spatial segregation of Negroes, are indicative of the higher degree of Japanese assimilation.

These findings for the state of Washington apply equally well to Seattle, the community studied in this essay. A similar "favorable" adaptation to American society can be shown for the Japanese minority in the United States as a whole.[3]

The purpose of this study is to explain the achievements of the Japanese minority. This group, compared to other minorities, enjoyed unusual success in achieving many values favored in American society. What conditions contributed to this success? The answer is suggested in two general hypotheses. First, the Japanese immigrants brought from Japan and transmitted to their children cultural values, consistent with and complementary to the middle-class values emphasized in American society, which motivated status achievement. This proposition, although important to an explanation of the Japanese minority's success, has been previously studied[4] and will be examined only incidentally in this article. Second, the Japanese minority maintained a high degree of family and community organization in America, and these organizations enforced value conformity and created conditions and means for status achievement. The second proposition provides the focus of this study.

The data, taken primarily from a study of the Seattle Japanese community at the time of its maximum organization in the years before World War II,[5] will not permit a genuine test of the hypothesis, but a description of the highly organized Japanese community life will show how the organization facilitated status achievement. Because the strengths of a group are often its weaknesses as well, the dysfunctional consequences of the organized community life will also be examined.

The historical circumstances of Japan during the second half of the nineteenth century had an especially important bearing on the Japanese migration to the United States, more than is usual in international migrations, and significantly influenced the communities which the immigrants established. The accession of Emperor Meiji in 1868 marked the end of Tokugawa feudalism and of Japan's centuries of isolation. The Meiji era that followed was one of dramatic changes in Japan: a period of rapidly rising interest in Western ideas and technology; a phenomenal modernization of the country's institutions, especially its economy; and a growing desire to compete in the world market. The expansionist psychology thus generated an attitudinal base for the migration to America that subsequently developed. On the other hand, the feudalistic tradition could scarcely be expunged by a single act of national will, and even as the social revolution proceeded, manifestations of a counter-revolution also emerged. These contradictory facets were engrained in the character of the generation from which Japanese immigrants to America were drawn.

Once Japan opened its doors to foreign commerce, it became obvious that its science, technology, industry, and social system were backward compared to the West. The popular belief arose that by borrowing from Western methods and ideas, the nation could quickly rise to contending status among the world powers.[6] This belief in Japan's capacity for successful competition provoked widespread interest and curiosity about the West. The American shores on the Pacific, as the nearest major extension of Western civilization, became a magnet to those caught up in the glamor of the Western world.

The force in Japan that mobilized the migration to America was a discrepancy between the hope for advancement, aroused by national reforms and economic expansion, and the rigid system of stratification inherited from feudalism which frustrated the dream of upward mobility for all but a small minority.[7] Access to opportunities for advancement continued to be rigorously regulated by social custom and the economic structure, which increased the disadvantage of those further down the social class scale. Curiously, the legitimacy of this stratification system was not fundamentally questioned.

Economic advancement was at best slow for the middle and lower classes. On the other hand, the expanding economy had excited their interest in advancement despite the stratification structure. America, with its vast resources, offered opportunity. Those who looked across the Pacific believed that with industry and perseverance in that new country, there could be no barrier to economic success.

The revolutionary transformation of Japan in the nineteenth century could not have been achieved under the diffuse controls of a feudalistic state. One of the accomplishments of the Meiji regime was the elimination of feudal autonomy and the consolidation of controls under a constitutional monarch.[8] Unlike the English constitutional monarch, however, the Japanese emperor was deified, and national conscience was solidified around a symbolic identity with this imperial figure. The resurgence of nationalism that followed the initial relaxation of the traditional anti-foreign attitude led to a strong emphasis on Japanese principles in the ethical and humanistic training incorporated into the new system of compulsory education. Moreover, despite the termination of feudalism, an idealized memory of the *samurai* and his code persisted. Youths trained under the system were steeped in the sense of their Japanese heritage.

The immigrants from Japan who arrived on American shores near the turn of the century reflected the contradictory facets of their background. They were eager to learn Western methods and take advantage of the opportunities offered in the new world, but they were more self-consciously identified with their native land than most immigrant groups.

When the flow of Japanese immigrants to Seattle began near the turn of the century, the city was in the throes of spectacular growth—from a frontier town into a major urban center. In 1880, the town had a population of slightly over 3,000, in 1900 it had grown to 81,000, and by 1910 it numbered 230,000.[9] Today, the metropolitan area has a population of well over a million.

The town originally centered around Yesler's sawmill which stood on the shores of Elliott Bay, a beautiful natural harbor on Puget Sound.[10] A logging skidroad came down to the mill off a high wooded hill to the east. Lumberjacks, millhands, sailors, fishermen, and others of a teeming frontier humanity chose the foot of the skidroad as a rallying place, and, consequently the area and its cluster of hotels, shops, and saloons came to be known as "Skidroad." As the town grew and took on the aspects of a city, the better homes were built high on the logged-over hills to the east and north, business moved in the same direction, and Skidroad became a center for transients, prostitutes, and honkey-tonks. The early Japanese arrivals, mostly men, found a natural place of first residence in Skidroad.

There were 125 Japanese in Seattle in 1890, 3,000 in 1900, and 6,000 by 1910.[11] The rate of immigration probably would have continued at a high level, but beginning in 1907, because of anti-Japanese agitation on the West Coast, the United States increasingly restricted the entry of Japanese. Finally, the Immigration Act of 1924 terminated all Oriental immigration. Although the Japanese population of Seattle increased from 7,900 in 1920 to 8,500 in 1930, growth after 1924 was mainly attributable to an increase in American-born children, whereas the foreign-born Japanese steadily declined in numbers. By 1940, the population had decreased to 8,000. However, the post-war boom of third-generation offspring raised the census to over 10,000 by 1960.[12]

The growth of the Seattle Japanese community occurred in three stages.[13] The first stage, from about 1890 to 1907, is called the "frontier period" because of the rough-and-ready quality of life in a community composed largely of working-class males, most of whom were sojourners eager to make money quickly and return to Japan. There were few families and only the bare framework of institutions for normal community life. The second stage from 1907 to 1924 was a "settlement period" in which families were established and institutions were stabilized. In 1907, because of concern in the United States over the rate of Japanese immigration, a Gentlemen's Agreement was concluded with Japan which restricted the further entry of Japanese laborers, but did not prohibit the immigration of women or better-educated males.[14] The emphasis in the community therefore shifted to the establishment of families, the building of an economy to meet family needs, the search for better homes, and the establishment of churches.

The passage of the Immigration Act of 1924 ended the immigration and the establishment of new families, and produced another shift in the community's orientation. Japanese immigrants, who already were excluded from citizenship and from ownership of land by the Anti-Alien Land Law of 1921, saw the Immigration Act as ultimate evidence of white hostility toward the immigrant Japanese.[15] Thereafter, the future of the Japanese minority in this country increasingly appeared to rest in the American-born children, who at least held the rights of citizenship. Because of the emphasis given to the role of the latter generation in the period from 1924 to World War II, we have called this phase the "second-generation period." However, authority in both the family and the community remained primarily in the hands of the parental generation throughout this phase.

The cessation of immigration by the Act of 1924 had a notable effect on the age composition of the Japanese community. Graphically, the age distribution of a normal population is a relatively symmetrical pyramid, with the largest numbers at the youngest age levels and steadily decreasing numbers at increasing ages. The graph for the Japanese community, on the other hand, appeared more like two pyramids, one set atop the apex of the other. The immigrant generation, the older group, constituted the upper pyramid, while the American-born generation composed almost wholly of children and youths represented the pyramid underneath.[16] This abnormal population distribution, which was caused by the sudden stoppage of immigration, dramatizes the social cleavage that existed between the foreign- and native-born generations in the community, a generational gap found in any community but aggravated in this case by the absence of intermediate age groups.

The Japanese terms for the generations thereby held special meanings. The *Issei* (first generation) are immigrants born and raised in Japan, who generally came to the United States in the first two decades of the century. They were principally Japanese speaking, and reflected their Japanese cultural background. The *Nisei* (second generation) are American-born, therefore citizens, and primarily American in their cultural orientation. The *Kibei* (literally, "returned to America") refer to Nisei who for various reasons were sent to Japan for their upbringing, and returned to America where they often found themselves aliens in their own families and community. The *Sansei* (third generation) are children of the Nisei who generally have few ties with their Japanese background and are fully Americanized. The Issei were finally granted the right of naturalization in 1952, and many of them became naturalized, but their change of status has not perceptibly modified the differential conceptions of the generations.

From 1900 to 1920, as the community grew and families increased, the Japanese community established a business center around Sixth

Avenue and Main Street, southeast of Skidroad and adjoining China-town. Hotels and rooming houses, groceries and fish markets, drug stores, cleaners, furniture stores, clothier shops, general merchandise stores, newspaper offices, doctor and dental offices, in short, all the enterprises required in an immigrant community mushroomed in this center. Because Seattle never developed a tenement district, families typically made their first homes in flats and old clapboard houses, often with small but carefully cultivated gardens, but in an area, also, where children grew up aware of the activities in houses of prostitution and Chinese lotteries. The residences spread eastward up First Hill and mingled with those of Jews, Italians, and groups who had settled earlier. Subsequently, the residences spread into better residential areas, partic-ularly east and southeast of the first area of settlement. Since World War II the Japanese business center has become a shadow of the busy center it once was, but the people's identity with "Japanese town," although markedly weakened today, still persists.

The ethnic community of the Seattle Japanese reflected different characteristics in various periods of its history. This paper will concen-trate on the mid-1930s when the community achieved its most mature form, but will also touch on its earlier history and its present characteristics.

Most of the male immigrants found their first employment in the typical industries of the Pacific Northwest such as railroading, logging and lumbering, fishing, and farming, in which unskilled labor was much in demand. The Chinese, who preceded the Japanese by at least twenty years in these occupations, evoked the antagonism of the whites and moved into other fields, or left these jobs in search of more lucrative work. The Japanese moved into the vacated areas. They spoke no En-glish and were ignorant of American customs. To aid their initial em-ployment, a pattern similar to the padrone system of the Italian immigrants was instituted. A Japanese boss contracted all the workers and himself conducted all negotiations with employers.

The Japanese regarded these unskilled jobs as temporary stopping points, for their compelling motivation was to advance as quickly as possible to individual entrepreneurship. They leased farms or opened shops and offices in the city as their savings and opportunities permit-ted. The acquisition of farmland was typical of their method. In the river valleys and other areas in the hinterland of Seattle, Japanese farmers searched out lands which were fertile but of marginal use because of their undeveloped state. For example, where the land was marshy, they employed the drainage methods learned in the paddy fields of Japan. Where the land was covered with stumps, thickets, and other growth, the would-be farmer cleared the land using enormous industry and perserverance, and often the help of all his family and of members of the community.[17]

Their interest in entrepreneurship was more evident in the city. In 1930 a business census of the Seattle Japanese community reported more than 900 separate establishments, including professional offices, under Japanese proprietorship—i.e., there was a separate Japanese-owned enterprise for every nine persons in the Japanese community. An estimated three out of four persons in the labor force were engaged either as proprietors or employees in the operation of small businesses.[18]

An occupational census taken in 1935 gives a detailed account of the types of business operated by the Japanese minority in Seattle.[19] The ten most frequent trades and their numbers indicate the character of Japanese-operated businesses: there were 183 hotels, 148 groceries, 94 cleaners and dyers, 64 public market stands, 57 produce houses, 42 gardeners, 36 restaurants, 36 barber shops, 31 laundries, and 24 fruit and vegetable peddlers. Those trades which grew did so by extending into the city's larger economy. Thus, Japanese-operated groceries and cleaners were scattered throughout the city, the hotels and restaurants were generally of the second- and third-class variety catering to white trade, and the Japanese produce houses competed against white companies on the wholesale produce market. On the other hand, most shops and offices in the Japanese business district sought the patronage of both the Japanese and the poly-ethnic residents of the so-called Central Area, while others were oriented almost exclusively to Japanese customers.

The economy clearly reflected the strong organizational base of the community. Most trades were first learned in the Japanese business center or on Skidroad during the early years of heavy immigration when hotels, groceries, laundries, and other similar services were much in demand. The patterns of mutual assistance, characteristic of town and village life in Japan, played a significant role in these early economic adjustments. One old-time resident remarked:[20]

> There was a tendency toward the concentration of people from the same prefectures in Japan at the same places and in the same lines of work. For example, the barbers in Seattle, at least in the old days, all tended to be people from the Yamaguchi-ken, for Mr. I. came first and established himself in that line, and then helped his friends from Japan to get started. Then again, in the restaurant business, the majority of them are *Ehime-ken,* for men like Mr. K. first got into this, and then aided his ken friends to follow in the same field. Homes like those of Mr. I. were places where young men congregated who were eager to learn things and discuss them, and in the course of their association, they learned such trades as their friends knew.

The *ken* and *kenjinkai* (prefectural association), which will be discussed more fully later, not only served as a means of drawing workers into particular businesses and training them, but also provided a network of relations that sustained the economy and determined its patterns. A man in need of financial support, if he could not call upon his family or relatives for assistance, was likely to seek aid from a *ken-jin* (prefectural member), and the latter was obliged, in a way different than for outsiders, to give aid. On the other hand, a merchant or salesman could expect a *ken-jin* to trade with him rather than with those from other *ken*. One insurance agent explained that he was giving up his business because he came from a small *ken* group and could not compete successfully against agents from large prefectural associations.

Even more than the prefectural groups, the family and the network of relatives were the bases of the small business economy of the Japanese community. In economic competition, the Japanese minority faced serious handicaps—prejudice and discrimination, a lack of fluency in English, and a limited knowledge of American customs. The one advantage enjoyed by the minority was the cohesion of the family and assurance that the wife and children would assist in the family enterprise. Enterprises, such as hotels, cleaners, and restaurants, succeeded because wives and often children contributed substantially to the work. The resulting reduction of labor costs added greatly to the competitive power of Japanese businesses.

Still other patterns of social relationship supported this economy. The success of the Japanese in their groceries, public market stands, produce houses, fruit and vegetable peddling, and restaurants was in no small part the result of ties which they maintained with Japanese truck farmers in areas surrounding Seattle. The network of personal relations with farmers assured these tradesmen better quality vegetables, cheaper prices, and prompter service than their white competitors. The Japanese tradesmen also enjoyed special treatment when a shortage of crops or other limitations reduced the supply of needed items.

Business financing was also aided by social relations. The immigrant tradesmen adapted mutual assistance patterns learned in Japan, such as the arrangement known as the *tanomoshi-kō,* an informal money-raising group.[21] In Seattle the *tanomoshi-kō* was usually constituted by calling a dinner meeting of a dozen or so friends, each of whom would agree to subscribe a set amount to a financial pool. By bidding or by agreement, the pool would be lent to one member at a set rate of interest, and upon repayment the pool might be lent to another.

In addition to these informal arrangements, entrepreneurs used formal means to facilitate their operations. Proprietors of hotels, groceries, cleaners and dyers, and restaurants, where sizable groups were in the trade, separately organized into business associations which regulated competition, provided mutual assistance and protection, and transmitted information. For example, the Cleaners and Dyers Association established rules prohibiting Japanese operators from invading an area occupied by an established Japanese cleaning firm. This system of control effectively used informal controls, such as social ostracism, to exert pressures on violators.

All the business associations, as well as other independent Japanese businessmen, were members of the Seattle Japanese Chamber of Commerce. The Chamber conducted the usual promotional activities, but also, because of the close ties within the Japanese business community, functioned more than usual as a regulatory agency.

An economy based upon a system of interpersonal claims has advantages, but it also has problems. The problems of extending credit and collecting debts were especially acute. In all commercial relations with the white community, the Japanese minority maintained an enviable record of honesty and promptness in paying bills. Within the Japanese community, however, discount rates were commonly expected in trade between friends, transacted through a special etiquette that masked and yet made evident the favor that was being granted. Credit was often forced from merchants on the principle that such favors were to be expected in relations between countrymen.

In the classical system of rural Japan, there was a tradition of accumulating debts through the year and making full payment at the New Year's season. That pattern was successful where the family was linked to the same plot of land for generations and the importance attached to the family name gave assurance that debts would be paid. However, in the transplanted immigrant community, which lacked the traditional bases of family stability, the use of similar patterns of credit extension resulted in defaults on payments often enough to create considerable strains in the business community.

The economy of the Japanese community was thus built upon a mixture of Western commercial rationalism and Old World traditional mutualism. Businessmen in the community were acutely conscious of their dilemma, that Japanese patronage was essential for their business but the need to grant special treatment in every transaction threatened businesses with disaster. Business success, in other words, depended very much on the art of persuading each customer of his privileged treatment, without violating the profit-making requirements of the enterprise.

A few early immigrants came with their wives or sent for them after making initial economic adjustments, but the bulk of immigrants at first were single males whose dominant aim was to save toward establishing a business in Japan. The migrants soon realized, however, that wealth is not accumulated quickly even in America. Moreover, bachelorhood was regarded as an unnatural state, while the family was held in special esteem. Thus, the idea of establishing families in the United States soon became popular.

The Japanese practice of arranged marriages greatly eased the problem of finding wives for male immigrants. Men who had obtained stable jobs and sufficient means to think of starting a family wrote to their relatives or friends in Japan to ask that a suitable wife be found. The friends would search for eligible girls, and a *baishakunin* (go-between), usually a person of standing who commanded the respect of both families, was solicited to assist in negotiating the arrangement. Family backgrounds were investigated, negotiations were conducted, and with most of the preliminary arrangements settled, the young men returned to Japan to consummate their marriages and bring their brides to the United States.

A variant of the traditional arranged marriage known as the "picture-bride marriage" was also employed. The prospective bride and groom exchanged photographs and reached agreement by this means. Following agreement, the usual pattern of arranging a marriage was ordinarily followed, except that the girl immigrated to the United States to be met at the dock by her prospective husband. The marriages then took place in this country. A folklore has emerged concerning the deceits which were perpetrated under this arrangement. Homely men and women sent photographs of more photogenic substitutes. There were instances in which a betrothed fled from the dock after one sight of the prospective spouse. Nonetheless, the "picture-bride marriage" was a practical device used by grooms to avoid an inconvenient trip to Japan.

The hotels and rooming-houses around Main and Jackson Streets and the backrooms of shops were the first homes for most of these immigrant couples. As one old-time resident relates:[22]

> In 1900 there were only three families with what might be called private homes; all the rest lived in rooming-houses or in hotels. Even as late as 1910 people lived in rooming-houses, and the backrooms of shops. Of course, there weren't so many of the latter at that time. They didn't even have apartment rooms in any great numbers. During the years from 1910 to 1918, many of the people leased large houses and rented several of their rooms to other families or to single men.

This was a strange world for newly arrived brides. A woman arriving from Japan dressed in her traditional kimono would be rushed to a hotel and met by a dressmaker and shoe salesman who would fit her in Western attire. The furnishings, equipment, and supplies of the American household often bewildered those unaccustomed to chairs, tables, cooking ranges, and beds. Shopkeepers were not merely tradesmen; they often served as household consultants. One grocer reported, "In the old days, I frequently furnished the whole kitchen for a woman." Relatives, friends, even strangers, assisted in establishing new households. As in other matters, there was a noticeable tendency to collectivize the problems of individuals and make them problems of the neighborhood, if not of the community.

The Japanese household in the Seattle community, whether in a Skidroad hotel room or in a middle-class residence, invariably had a Japanese quality, which in some degree persists today. The house, furniture, and appliances were Western, but the details were Japanese. The fabrics characteristically were of Japanese patterns. Traditional Japanese cushions were used to cover all the chairs. (Even on chairs, women often preferred to sit on their knees, Japanese style, rather than in the Western manner.) Lacquered bowls and containers were used as decorations. Japanese princess dolls adorned in graceful gowns, encased in paulownia wood boxes with glass windows, were displayed. Japanese wall hangings and prints graced the walls. In Buddhist homes, especially, the family shrine occupied a space where ritual acts could conveniently be performed. The hybridization was true of the diet as well. An American cuisine would often be served at breakfast and lunch, followed by a Japanese dinner. A mixture of both often appeared at the same meal. The mood created by the day-to-day presence of familiar items tended to preserve and reinforce a sense of Japanese identity.

The immigrants' pattern of family relations was integrally related to the highly organized and cohesive character of their community. The patriarchal structure of the traditional Japanese family was transplanted to Seattle, but in modified form. In Japan, the family system is composed of a *honke* (main family) and *bunke* (branch families). The primary male head dominates the overall family structure, and the other lineal male descendants are subordinate to him but dominant in their own families. The main and branch families generally live near each other, and intimate ties characteristically are maintained among members of the great family.[23]

In America, the detachment of the immigrant's family from the main family in Japan tended to reduce the system to the nuclear family, but the conceptions of the traditional family system persisted. For example, in the absence of a genuine *honke-bunke* system in this country, the traditional conception was introduced into employer-employee rela-

ASIAN COMMUNITY LIBRARY
1934 PARK BLVD.
OAKLAND, CA 94606

tions. Male employees of a firm often attached their families to that of the employer, as though theirs were *bunke* families subordinate to the employer's *honke,* and carefully observed the rights and obligations of the traditional system.

The male head of immigrant families generally assumed the role of authority traditionally ascribed to that position. He made major family decisions, although the wife probably exerted more influence here than in Japan, especially when she played a significant part in the family's business. Male dominance was reinforced by the community's expectation that a man, not a woman, would represent the family in any external relations. Local circumstances also contributed to this dominance: e.g., Issei women rarely spoke English as the men did, and the women rarely learned to drive a car.

The wife's role in the family was subordinate and submissive, and it often called for a stoical endurance of hardships. Nisei children may not have understood the system of authority in which they were involved, but they recognized the father's authority and the mother's role as a surrogate of the father. It was a code of this community that parents had a right to control children's behavior and that children should yield to parental demands.

The internal relations of a family were sometimes marked by distinct deviations from community norms. Some women, by virtue of their superior intelligence or greater aggressiveness, occasionally dominated a family. Children occasionally rebelled against parental authority or asserted their independence. Nevertheless, the prevailing influences worked powerfully against deviations. However much a family's internal patterns varied from the norms, the family tended to preserve the expected roles in external relations with the community.

These traditional patterns of family relations were reconstructed in the immigrant community because they fulfilled a number of functions highly valued in Japanese society. Male primogeniture, apart from its economic function, assures continuity of the family name and status. The hierarchy of authority through the male heads, and the interdependence of family members, assures control over the members. Representation in important community activities by the male head of the family assures its involvement in community affairs and reinforces its community standing. This condensed description of the immigrants' family system necessarily ignores its complexities, but it does suggest the importance immigrant families attached to such concepts as family continuity, male dominance, interdependence of family members, family control, and the role of the family in the community.

The transmission of these family values to Nisei children was seriously hampered by linguistic barriers, but it nevertheless was accomplished effectively. Few Issei acquired a comfortable fluency in English, and the characteristic language of parent-child communications was Japanese. On the other hand, few Nisei ever learned to speak Japanese well, and parent-child conversations therefore tended to be confined to a crude basic Japanese interspersed with English. Yet, the paratactic mode sufficed to transmit many parental attitudes, sentiments, and values.

The primary parental lesson was a respect for etiquette. The Nisei child was taught the proper greeting in the morning, the proper farewell on departure for school and greeting upon return, and the proper words of thanks before and after meals. He learned to thank another for any favor received, and also learned the need to acknowledge the obligation again at the next encounter. And he learned the formalities observed at New Years, the ritual expressions for occasions of bereavement, and the ritual performances expected in sundry other situations.

The training in etiquette served as a basis for more subtle aspects of socialization. Etiquette requires a regard for others, and a sensitivity for the feeling and attitudes of others. In turn, sensitivity for others induces a coordinate self-awareness and self-control. Although the Nisei, trained and socialized in the direct and informal patterns of America, were by Issei standards lacking finesse in social relations, they nevertheless acquired some basic Japanese features in their habits of interpersonal relations.

Japanese etiquette also maintains an implicit regard for status and authority. It requires that parents be addressed respectfully, and with regard for form. Eldest sons, as heirs apparent, likewise are accorded due respect, and eldest sisters only less so. Teachers and other persons of recognized status are spoken to with respect, except that if one's own status is higher, the role relationship may be reversed.

The most persistent efforts at training were devoted to teaching the Nisei the age-old Japanese principles of *kō* (duty to parent), *on* (filial obligation of reciprocity), and *giri* (duty and responsibility). The Japanese sense of these values was difficult for Nisei to comprehend, but the insistent emphasis on them left some impression of their meaning on the Nisei.

Related to the principles of social obligation, duty, and social responsibility is the tendency amongst Japanese to refer important individual decisions first to a collective judgment. The obligation to concern oneself with the welfare of friends implies, also, the obligation to call on friends to exercise such concern. Critical points in the family cycle—birth, marriage, and death—were occasions for collective expressions of joy or sorrow. Births were followed by gift exchanges, in which the proud father distributed boxes of *mochigashi* (rice flour confectionary) bearing appropriate symbols of gratification on the cover. Marriages were expected to involve relatives and close friends in consultation and preparatory activity. Weddings often were so lavish they indentured the bridal couple and their families with burdensome debts. At funerals, the status of the deceased and his family was measured by the number of mourners attending and the amount of *kōden* (funeral gift) received.

Festivals and holidays occasioned the convivial implementation of reciprocity principles. The New Year's festivities, especially, were carefully observed. Housewives and daughters became hyperactive days in advance preparing traditional foods and setting out the traditional decorations. On New Year's day, male family heads started rounds of visiting early in the day, exchanged traditional acknowledgments of past obligations at each household, and were wined and dined. Other Japanese holidays, such as the Emperor's Day, Girls' Day and Boys' Day festivals, and the like, were observed either as family or community functions. American holidays, especially the Fourth of July, Thanksgiving, and Christmas, also had a significant place in the immigrant community.

This discussion of the organizing influence of the Japanese family fails to treat departures from traditional patterns sufficiently. Such deviations were inescapable in an immigrant community. The bases of the traditional system could not be reproduced exactly. The assimilative influences of American society were at work in all families. From the Issei point of view, the Nisei children, by their constant exposure to American influences and their lack of regard for Japanese traditions, were losing the values offered by their Japanese heritage. The Nisei, in turn, considered their Issei fathers to be unduly authoritarian, distant, and conservative. Mothers were thought to be overly anxious about their children and given to endless preaching. And the community was viewed as parochial in its concerns.

Despite these potentially disorganizing influences, however, the social controls were extremely effective. This is evidenced by the low rates of criminality and juvenile delinquency which characterized the Japanese minority population.[24]

A number of factors functioned to sustain effective controls. First, the values emphasized in the immigrant family were generally consistent with those of middle-class American society.[25] Success at school, work, or play were doubly reinforced by the immigrant community and the American society. Second, despite the Issei's apparent slowness of assimilation into American life, they eventually absorbed many American tastes and attitudes. This assimilation of the Issei may have been affected by a third factor, their high degree of concern for their children. According to Japanese principles, the children have filial obligations *(kō)*, but parents in turn have responsibilities to their children *(on)*. Issei parents generally devoted a great deal of attention to their children, to the point of over-protection by Western standards. The effect on the parents' assimilation was twofold: to absorb them in their children's interests and attitudes, and to increase their willingness to strike compromises with their children, if for no other reason than to preserve the solidarity of the family.

The *ken* (prefectures) in Japan are governmental units roughly corresponding in their functions to our states, although in area they are much smaller, averaging only about half the size of Connecticut. Because 85 percent of Japan is mountainous and the arable lands are concentrated in the narrow coastal plains, the population is also concentrated near the coast line. The immigrants from any given *ken*, therefore, were likely to be drawn from a localized region, and people from the same *ken* usually had much in common on which to base their relationship. The conversation of two strangers, meeting for the first time, often began with a polite inquiry regarding the other's *ken;* and the discovery that both were from Hiroshima-ken, for example, started an animated exchange of information regarding the ward or village from which each came. Their common geographic background served as an important basis of group identification, for Japanese attach high significance to the ancestral home and its locality.

The majority of Japanese immigrants to Seattle came from prefectures *(ken)* in southern Japan. The largest group was from Hiroshima-ken, and the next largest groups were from two adjacent prefectures, Okayama and Yamaguchi. Fukuoka, Kumamoto, and Kagoshima-ken on the southern island of Kyushu, and Wakayama, Shiga, and Ehime-ken also had sizable groups. Most of the prefectures of Japan were represented in the Seattle community by groups of varying sizes, and an immigrant's range of social and trade relations within the community tended to be directly correlated with the size of his *ken* group.

The larger prefectural groups were organized into *kenjinkai* (prefectural associations). Their functions were primarily social, directed toward the promotion of certain events such as a New Year's banquet or annual picnic. These organizations were merely formal extensions of the community's informal associational patterns, based on *ken* identity. A family's closest friendships usually were with persons from the same *ken*, and given the system of obligations among friends, the *ken* identity also affected other relations such as employment, trading, consultation, weddings, funerals, and club affiliations. Parents preferred their sons and daughters to marry within the prefectural group. The smaller prefectural groups were not as formally organized, but the same informal patterns were evident among them.

The *kenjin* (prefectural people) tended to be the group with which the closest ties were felt, after the family and relatives. The church was the only other organization which exerted a comparable influence on patterns of association, but even frequent and intense activity in church functions seldom resulted in relationships as personal as those based on *ken* identity. Each *kenjin* shared a common dialect, a fact of some importance because of the variations to be found in Japan, and also shared common practices such as in food preparation and ritual observances. They shared prejudices about the peculiarities of those from other *ken*. In short, there was a basis for identity, founded on common experiences in Japan and common sentiments, that was only a step removed from kinship identity.

The *ken* group thus served as an intermediate link between the immediate family, relatives, and the ethnic community. It is likely that the cohesiveness of any community depends upon the development of vigorously functioning intermediate associations to link smaller units, such as the family, with larger community organizations.

Buddhism is the dominant religion of Japan. Christianity has attracted only a small minority. Therefore, most Japanese immigrants at first were Buddhists and few were Christians. Yet, a count of memberships in the Seattle Japanese churches in 1936 revealed 1,200 members of Christian churches and only 800 Buddhists.[26]

The low membership in earlier years in the Buddhist churches (only 10 percent of the Japanese population) reflects the character of Buddhism as an organized religion and also its role in the immigrant community. Unlike Christianity, Buddhism in Japan is not organized around weekly church functions. Rather, it is closely articulated with the family system; and although faith may be renewed by occasional visits to the temple, it is usually reinforced by day-to-day observances within the family, especially by rites performed at a family shrine. Therefore, any count of Buddhist church members tends to under-represent the number of adherents.

On the other hand, considering the immigrants' lack of a Christian background, there is a question of why the Christian churches—including Baptist, Congregational, Episcopalian, Methodist, Presbyterian, and Catholic denominations—enjoyed such vigorous growth during the early days of the community. The growth of these churches, which initially required heavy recruitment, again points to the immigrants' readiness to adopt any organization for which functions could be recognized. The Christian churches fulfilled a number of useful purposes.

In the "frontier period," when the main goal of the immigrants was to find employment, a number of Christian missions served as employment agencies. In particular, they recruited and sent out a large number of "mission boys" (houseboys) and found the immigrants other positions suited to individuals with minimal knowledge of the American language and customs. Moreover, many immigrants perceived that acquisition of American culture was important to their economic advancement, and the Christian missions, eager to attract new members, organized classes to give the desired instruction. Even Christian weddings were more simply managed than the elaborate Buddhist rites. The missions' care for the sick and help to those in difficulty, which in Japan would have been rendered by the family, was perhaps the service most appreciated by the young immigrants.

As the Japanese community grew the Christian churches established kindergartens popular among immigrant families. The children received pre-school care and were taught by white teachers those lessons in American ways of behavior which the parents were unable to provide. Moreover, the parochial kindergartens offered ethical training. The Japanese, accustomed to formal ethical training in the public schools of Japan, appreciated the training in honesty, kindness, humility, and brotherly and filial love even when offered within the context of Christian instruction. It sufficed that the right virtues were being taught. Through the children, parents were often won over to the Christian faith.

The structure of the Japanese Christian church was fitted to the requirements of an immigrant community. Japanese ministers, usually trained in both Japanese and American seminaries, led the Issei program. White missionaries and Sunday School teachers directed the Nisei's program until the latter were old enough to develop leaders of their own. In all the churches, there were intense schedules of activity for both the Issei and Nisei. In addition to the usual church services and Sunday Schools, prayer meetings, choir practices, young people's groups, church socials, church bazaars, and holiday events, many churches promoted auxiliary organizations for the Nisei such as Boy Scout and Girl Scout troops and basketball teams. An annual Northwest Young People's Christian Conference brought together youths from all the Christian churches of Northwest Japanese communities. This was one of several bases on which a network of relations was developed among the Nisei of the Northwest.

In contrast, the Buddhist churches suffered during the early years of growth. They were adapted to a society in which the family and the village community served most of the needs accommodated in America by the church, and they were slow to develop the functions successfully used by Christian churches to proselytize members of the immigrant community. The Buddhist churches also suffered an inherent disadvantage since they were initially unable to facilitate Americanization.

In time, however, they adapted to their environment, evolved a church organization similar to that of the Christian churches, and developed the same range of activities as the latter. Moreover, the Buddhist churches eventually enjoyed three unique advantages over the Christian churches. First, as the Nisei grew, Issei parents became less concerned about their children's Americanization than about their retention of Japanese values and heritage. Buddhism served to maintain the Nisei's awareness of Japanese culture. Second, because the Issei have aged and their mortality increased greatly during the years since World War II, they now show a renewed interest in the Buddhist faith learned in their childhood. Third, the increased tendency of American society since the war to tolerate ethnic variations and to show an active interest in Japanese culture has assured the Buddhist churches of their acceptability in America. As a result, in a period in which Seattle's Japanese Christian churches have lost members because of the decline of the ethnic community, the Buddhist churches have gained in popularity.

The public schools which the Nisei attended in and around the Japanese community were the one aspect of the community's institutional life beyond the direct control of the residents. Nevertheless, the community exerted influence even here.

The earliest Nisei groups attended an elementary school in the heart of the Japanese business district known as the Main Street School. The principal was a vigorous woman of Irish background, Miss Ada Mahon, who supervised the school's 400 Oriental pupils, mostly Japanese, and staff of white female teachers with iron control. In the mid-1920s the school became inadequate and a handsome new structure was erected some distance from the original site, with Miss Mahon as principal. The clapboard main building of the old school still stands, but the neon sign of a Chinese restaurant now flashes over its front.

The Nisei children attended other elementary schools as the population grew and residences moved outward, but Miss Mahon's school deserves special comment because of the number of Nisei children who attended it and because her teaching philosophy won community approval. She allowed vigorous play in the schoolyard during recess, but once the school bell rang, she imposed a "no nonsense" strictness in the classrooms and emphasized drillwork in all basic subjects. During her two decades or more as principal of the two schools, Miss Mahon symbolized educational leadership in the community. She commanded respect not only for her intellectual efforts but as much for her moral influence on the students. The community honored her on many occasions, and on her retirement expressed its gratitude by giving her an elaborate tour of Japan.

The Issei's appreciation of Miss Mahon is understandable considering the authority and devotion with which she ran her school. To the Issei, education required disciplined attention to teachers, diligent study of books, and careful preparation of lessons. Teachers were regarded as founts of knowledge and authority. Success in school was to be won by conscientious application and a willingness to exert oneself. And honor or shame to the family name would be brought according to the success or failure of the child in school. The Issei lost no opportunity to impress these views upon the children.

The formula worked from the standpoint of the community, at least as measured by the Nisei's success in the public schools. The community had an unusually low rate of school dropouts. There also was an unusally high percentage of Nisei valedictorians and salutatorians, and of honor students, in the three Seattle high schools which most Nisei attended during the 1930s.[27] By 1960, the median number of school years completed and other measures of educational status were higher for the Japanese minority than for whites or other non-white groups.

The Issei's emphasis on the formal aspects of schooling also had dysfunctional consequences. The Nisei often were better trained in textbook learning than in the broader aims of education; they acquired less capacity for integrating general concepts than might be desired or expected. Originality, too, may have been sacrificed by the emphasis on conventional learning. Yet the average level of intelligence produced by this community has proved high, and a number of outstanding scholars and artists are among its products.

In addition to the public schools, there was also a Japanese Language School. Community opinion at first was divided on the question of building a large language school, for some felt that Japanese language proficiency was unnecessary for citizens. Once the structure was established with a capacity of almost 1,000 students, however, hundreds of Nisei completed its eight grades. Each day after the regular public schools, the Nisei youngsters reluctantly spent an additional hour and a half studying the Japanese language. Despite this schooling, few Nisei acquired more than an elementary knowledge of the language. The Issei, however, persisted in the belief that this knowledge was important for the Nisei's future employment, and for an appreciation of their ethnic

ASIAN COMMUNITY LIBRARY
1934 PARK BLVD.
OAKLAND, CA 94606

heritage. On the other hand, the social effect of the school was more pronounced. It expanded the range of friendships and strengthened group identity among Nisei.

In addition to the economy, families, churches, and schools, a large number of other organizing influences strengthened the community's social fabric. The Japanese consulate in Seattle, although not a part of the community, was highly influential. As an office of the Japanese government, its main functions were to certify Japanese visas and promote trade relations between the Pacific Northwest and Japan. It had little administrative control over the immigrant community, especially Nisei American citizens. However, as aliens ineligible for United States citizenship, the local Issei tended to look to the Japanese consulate for leadership in combating anti-Japanese agitation and legislation. The consulate had little power to alter the course of these events, but because the Issei lacked other means of leverage, they continued to feel dependent on the Japanese government for protection.

The Japanese consul was accorded more respect than any member of the local community. He was certain to be the central figure at any community affair which he chose to attend. But his significance for the community was more symbolic than real. As the symbol of the Japanese government, the consul represented for the Issei the last bulwark against discrimination, the ultimate means of protection, given their lack of legal status in America.

The Seattle Japanese Association provided the main leadership within the community. In the early years when immigration and adjustment were the dominant concerns, the association helped the consulate to handle passports and immigration problems, and by providing information to new arrivals. During the 1920s when anti-Japanese agitation on the Pacific Coast reached its peak, the organization launched its major political efforts. The association gave financial support and attempted to mobilize community support when one of its members, K. Ozawa, in an effort to win the right of franchise, took his case unsuccessfully to the Supreme Court. It similarly aided efforts to circumvent the Anti-Alien Land Law which prohibited ownership of property by alien Japanese.

The lack of success in these political ventures shaped the main activities of the organization during the 1930s. With an annual budget of about $8,000, largely from contributions, the association's financial means were inadequate to develop programs of its own. However, it functioned as a planning body to promote community programs, acted as a coordinating agency to mobilize existing community groups behind the activities, and represented the community in relations with outside groups. The Issei, who could not engage in politics in the larger community, found an outlet for their political ambitions in the association.

Leaders of the Japanese Association who perceived the Issei's lack of citizenship as a severe limitation were instrumental in creating a Nisei organization, the Japanese American Citizens League (JACL). This group was organized to arouse political consciousness among the Nisei and protect the interests of the Japanese minority. A national organization of the same name was also established with which the local group affiliated.

Although the JACL became the leading Nisei organization during the 1930s, it was not an effective political group at that time because its leaders lacked experience and there were too few Nisei of voting age.[28] It functioned as the Nisei's counterpart of the Japanese Association, kept the Nisei informed of political developments affecting the Japanese minority, combated prejudice and discrimination, and dealt with such community problems as education and social welfare. Above all, the JACL served as a social medium for bringing Nisei together in conferences, banquets, and dances, and thus further reinforced the relations among the Nisei.

In this small community of 8,000, less than half of whom were Issei, there were two Japanese-language afternoon dailies. Each devoted one page to an English language section for the Nisei. There also was an English-language weekly, the *Japanese American Courier,* whose editor-publisher was a leading figure in the JACL. All the papers combed the regular news services for items pertinent to the Japanese community. The Japanese language papers, in addition, took items from the newspapers of Japan and hired Nisei radio hams to take wireless news from Japan. The main function of these papers for the local residents, however, was to keep them informed of the events in the community. Because the community was highly organized and intimately integrated, there was much of interest to be reported.

The Nisei were especially interested in news regarding recreational activity. Competitive sports and games were a great attraction, and boys started playing baseball, basketball, and football at an early age. A boy who did not acquire at least some skill in these sports was an oddity in the community, and many acquired considerable skill. By the 1930s, the English-language weekly organized leagues in all sports, known as the Courier Leagues, and as many as two dozen baseball and football teams and twice as many basketball teams were engaged in almost continuous competitive activity. Thus, long before the appearance of the Little Leagues and Babe Ruth Leagues on the American scene, Nisei youths were intensely involved in organized competition.

The Issei maintained interest in their own sports. Judo clubs were organized and their competitions attracted large audiences. Issei fishermen won a considerable reputation in the Puget Sound area, especially at salmon fishing, and again competition was organized in fishing derbies. Fall mushroom hunting drew hundreds of families into the foothills of the Cascades and Olympics. The community's recreation included Japanese chess and *go* clubs, poetry clubs, singing groups, dramatics groups, and *odori* (Japanese dance) groups.

From their first years in America, the Japanese minority faced prejudice and discrimination from white majority groups. The various restrictions on immigration, the denial of enfranchisement, and the Anti-Alien Land Laws were but formal manifestations of a more generally pervasive rejection of the Japanese minority by West Coast communities. Many of the discriminatory practices imposed upon other colored minorities in the United States were experienced by the Japanese. They were victimized by name calling (i.e., "Japs" and "Skibbies"); exclusion from hotels, restaurants, and barber shops; suspected Jim Crowism in movie theaters and other places of entertainment; residential segregation; and restrictions of economic opportunity. To be sure, some persons in the white communities supported the Japanese and some became staunch friends, but the predominantly hostile reactions of many organizations and most politicians set the dominant tone.[29]

The hostility of the majority group contributed to a tendency of the Japanese community to turn inward, and it minimized the individual's effort to seek contacts outside the community. Thus, discrimination intensified the tendency of the Japanese community to organize, and increased community cohesiveness.

The evacuation experience of the Japanese minority incident to the military order of March 2, 1942 has been fully documented in several books, and is described elsewhere in this volume. One aspect of that event, however, requires comment here. The solidarity of the Japanese community was a factor that contributed to the evacuation. First, if any one general factor explains the evacuation better than any other, it is the persistent climate of hostility against the Japanese minority that prevailed on the Pacific Coast for a half century before the war. Once the war between Japan and the United States began, this climate strongly disposed the majority group to perceive the Japanese minority with extreme doubt and suspicion. Second, the persistent external hostility intensified the tendency of the Japanese minority to seek relations within their own community. The extensive organizational network created by the Japanese minority, which may have had admirable consequences for their adjustment to America, had a disastrous effect in the context of a wartime crisis.

The Japanese minority's social self-sufficiency erected a barrier against the majority group's understanding, and ultimately led to the kind of doubt and suspicion epitomized by General John L. DeWitt's pronouncement, "Once a Jap, always a Jap." Thus, majority group prejudice and the minority's self-sufficiency created a dialectic that led almost inevitably to a rupture between the two groups under the tension of wartime.

At the conclusion of the war, several thousand evacuees who remained at the Minidoka Relocation Center were transported back to Seattle. Others who earlier had resettled eastward also drifted back to their former community, but the censuses of the Japanese population in Seattle in 1940 and 1950 showed a net loss during that period of more than 1,000 persons. Some initial opposition to the return of the evacuees was counteracted by actions of the mayor and religious groups, and the return was effected with a minimum of incidents.

The evacuation losses of the evacuees, measured by dollar costs, were large, but the greatest loss was the pre-war economic organization of the community. It required considerable effort to re-establish the former patterns. Yet within a few years, many of the old shops reappeared in their former locations or in the same neighborhood, some new shops appeared, many hotelmen were again in business, and the general features of the former business community were restored.

For important basic reasons, however, the business community never regained its pre-war level of activity. Most important among these was the aging of the male Issei population, whose median age in 1950 was about 62.5 years, and the maturation of Nisei males. Because of their age, many Issei men lacked the energy to re-establish themselves in business, or the opportunity to regain their former employment. The Nisei, on the other hand, reached their most employable age in large numbers at this time. Unlike the Issei who characteristically sought self-employment, the Nisei generally chose professional work, or salaried and wage positions in the employment of others. The opening of employment opportunities which in pre-war years had been completely closed to the Japanese minority contributed to this trend toward professional and salaried employment. The Japanese could now obtain employment as engineers or skilled workers in the Boeing Aircraft Company, as federal and municipal office workers, and as clerks, secretaries, and salesmen in white companies and offices.

These improved opportunities for employment came as a part of generally improved conditions for all racial minorities in the United

States after the war, but they were also the result of an unanticipated consequence of the war. Because of the military occupation of Japan following its defeat, many Americans were exposed to the Japanese people and returned with an appreciation of Japanese culture. A sentiment also developed that the Japanese evacuees had been subjected to unjust treatment and should be recompensed. As a result, the pre-war climate of anti-Japanese feeling was substantially modified. Although prejudice and discrimination were not absent, the lowering of the barriers encouraged members of the Japanese minority to move into white residential areas and increasingly establish relations with majority group members. The decline in the number of Issei and the residential diffusion of the Japanese minority reduced the need for the Japanese business district.

The evacuation and the changing age composition of the population had another important effect on the Japanese community. In 1940, despite the increasing maturation of the Nisei, community and family authority still rested predominantly in the hands of the Issei. At the outbreak of the war, however, Issei organizations with any capacity for political leadership were immediately abolished, and most of them were not reorganized following the war. Although the kenjinkai, poetry clubs, singing groups, and other similar organizations were re-established, their numbers were fewer and their range of functions narrower than before. Because community and family authority shifted to the Nisei, the Issei organizations had a much more circumscribed role in the community than in the pre-war years.

Today, the Nisei are mostly in their forties and fifties and parents of Sansei children, and they have established a Nisei community life. The Japanese American Citizens League is now the central organization of the community, and the Nisei Veterans' Association exerts influence in another sphere. The ethnic churches persist, but those least successful in maintaining a Nisei membership are on the brink of closure. The sports leagues and bowling, basketball, fishing, and golfing clubs are again active. Unlike the Issei, however, the Nisei's interests are not circumscribed by the life of the local ethnic community, and there is today neither the extent nor the intensity of social organization which characterized the community during the era of Issei dominance.

Despite the decline of the local community, however, there is a surprising persistence of the community's influence. The JACL and other organizations which have been arguing the issue of integration since the end of the war still draw a membership, even from the Sansei. The churches which have been talking for twenty years about dissolving likewise persist. Most persistent are the bonds of friendship and identity which draw the Nisei back to the community or into their old circles of association, and there is a noticeable carry-over of this influence into the third generation.

As suggested at the outset of this paper, the status achievement of the Japanese minority in Seattle, indicated in the study by Calvin F. Schmid and his associates, can be explained by the high degree of community organization which this group established, the opportunities for advancement which the organization created, and the controls over the population which the organization made possible.

The basis of the organizational tendency probably lay in collective action practices learned in the rural villages of Japan, which in turn were based on the Japanese tendency to deal with problems on a collective basis. The immigrants tended to reconstruct this familiar pattern of life in the American setting, and because of its adaptiveness to the American scene, it was the basis for some measure of personal success in advancing in this society. The Nisei, in turn, were trained by their Issei parents in the same underlying values and principles of action, and the fact that no great breach arose between these two generations suggests the effectiveness of the socialization process that was employed.

Two characteristics of the Japanese community were emphasized as particularly influential in providing a basis for a strong community organization. First, not only was the Japanese family in America generally a close and well-unified entity, but the family tended to be involved in fairly extensive quasi-familial relations, notably with relatives and with prefectual associates. These intermediate groups served as a bridge between the individual or family and the more impersonal associational units in business, religion, education, recreation, and social welfare. In addition, because one was likely to be drawn into these activities by relatives and *kenjin*, the individual tended to enter the associations with a basis in established intimate relations. The effect was to create for each individual and family a network of bonds more extensive, but also more intimate, than is usually found in American urban communities.

A second feature of the community was the strong emphasis on the principle of social obligation and responsibility, expressed by such traditional Japanese concepts as *on* and *giri*. The cohesiveness of the family, the relative group, the *kenjin*, the neighborhood, and community organizations was built upon the principle, and the amount of group activity required to fulfill the principle had the effect of further extending the network of relations.

Finally, we observed that family and community organization often provided the means and opportunities for status advancement. The motivation for status achievement came from the values which were imported as a part of the Japanese heritage, but the social structure offered the means for achieving the value aspirations.

NOTES

1. C. F. Schmid, C. E. Nobbe, and A. E. Mitchell, *Nonwhite Races: State of Washington* (Olympia, Wash.: Washington State Planning and Community Affairs Agency, 1968), p. 127.

2. *Ibid.*, p. 131.

3. Harry H. Kitano, *Japanese Crime and Delinquency in the United States* (Unpublished manuscript, School of Social Welfare, University of California, Los Angeles). See also William Petersen, "Success Story, Japanese-American Style," *The New York Times Magazine,* January 9, 1966, pp. 20-21 ff. and Bill Hosokawa, *Nisei: The Quiet Americans* (New York: William Morrow & Company, 1969).

4. William Caudill and George De Vos, "Achievement, Culture and Personality: The Case of the Japanese Americans," *American Anthropologist* 58 (December 1956) 1102-26; William Petersen, *op. cit.*

5. S. Frank Miyamoto, *Social Solidarity among the Japanese in Seattle* (Seattle: University of Washington Press, 1939). Other sources of information on this community are Forrest E. LaViolette, *Americans of Japanese Ancestry: A Study of Assimilation in the American Community* (Toronto: The Canadian Institute of International Affairs, 1945); and Monica Sone, *Nisei Daughter* (Boston: Little, Brown & Company, 1953).

6. E. Herbert Norman, *Japan's Emergence as a Modern State: Political and Economic Problems of the Meiji Period* (New York: Institute of Pacific Relations, 1940), pp. 46-47.

7. *Ibid.*, pp. 70-103.

8. *Ibid.*, p. 68.

9. Calvin F. Schmid, *Social Trends in Seattle* (Seattle: University of Washington Press, 1944), p. 2.

10. *Ibid.*, pp. 43-45.

11. *Ibid.*, pp. 131-137.

12. Schmid, Nobbe, and Mitchell, *op. cit.,* p. 55.

13. Miyamoto, *op. cit.,* pp. 65-68.

14. Yamato Ichihashi, *Japanese in the United States* (Stanford: Stanford University Press, 1932), pp. 243-60.

15. *Ibid.*, pp. 298-318.

16. Miyamoto, *op. cit.,* p. 92.

17. John A. Rademaker, *The Ecological Position of the Japanese Farmers in the State of Washington* (Ph.D. dissertation, University of Washington, 1939), pp. 113-211.

18. Miyamoto, *op. cit.,* p. 71.

19. *Ibid.*, p. 72.

20. *Ibid.*, p. 72.

21. R. K. Beardsley, J. W. Hall, and R. E. Ward, *Village Japan* (Chicago: University of Chicago Press, 1959), p. 261.

22. Miyamoto, *op. cit.*, p. 93.

23. Beardsley, *et al.*, *op. cit.*, p. 262ff.

24. Norman S. Hayner, "Delinquency Areas in the Puget Sound Region," *American Journal of Sociology* 39 (November 1933) 314-28.

25. Caudill and De Vos, *op. cit.*

26. Miyamoto, *op. cit.*, p. 99.

27. *Ibid.*, p. 108.

28. LaViolette, *op. cit.*, pp. 153-61.

29. Ichihashi, *op. cit.*, pp. 392-400. See also Hosokawa, *op. cit.*, Part One.

Acculturation &
Childhood Accidents

MINAKO KUROKAWA

Children of Oriental ancestry in California have fewer injuries than Caucasian or Afro-American children, according to a study made by the California State Department of Public Health.[1] Statistics indicate that each year one out of 3.7 Caucasian children went to a hospital for treatment of injuries, compared with one out of 6.7 children of Oriental ancestry.

Having come to the United States from Japan, I was fascinated by these contrasting figures and reminded of the great differences in the child-rearing practices of traditional Oriental and modern American families. A question which came to my mind was, "As children of Oriental ancestry in this country become Americanized, will they have more accidents than before?" This paper summarizes some of the findings of my research on childhood accident experiences among Chinese American and Japanese American children in California. As we shall see, the changes in accident rates are indeed related to the degree of acculturation to the American way of life by Orientals and Oriental Americans in this country.

Previous research suggests that the two basic determinants of accident rates are *exposure to hazards* and *ability to cope with hazards*.[2] Social systems in which individuals live in a complex state of interdependence inhibit individual initiative and independent action and correspondingly influence the child-rearing practices and the socio-psychological traits of the child. An outstanding characteristic of the traditional East Asian family in its original setting was the formal structure which dedicated the lives of individuals to the continuity and welfare of the family group.[3] A child's emotional dependence, especially on the mother, was accepted and even encouraged; the emphasis on descent group placed the parent-child relations above that of husband and wife.[4]

A child with limited independence was less exposed to hazards than the child whose parents encouraged him to take initiative, act independently, and explore his environment. The child taught to be relatively passive, however, lacked the opportunity to learn how to cope with hazards.[5] Once exposed to hazards, a child exercises some control over the risk of injury by his response to the situation, the degree of his alertness, and his motivation to avoid injury. If a child is tense because of a conflict, he may not be alert. Or if some unresolved need causes the tension, it may be more important to him to reduce the tension at some risk of injury, as in the case of an Oriental American child who is anxious to be accepted by a Caucasian peer group and thus motivated to do risky things in order to show his courage.

Research indicates that second-generation Americans, whether European or Oriental, experience considerable normative conflict.[6] Parental discipline loses its effect as the American-born child is more and more influenced by his peers. The traditional values of the alien parents no longer serve their children, who can see other standards of conduct which contradict those taught at home. Thus, Americanized children of non-acculturated parents face normative conflicts which may affect their ability to cope with hazards.

The first phase of our research extends the childhood accident project of the California State Department of Public Health. The previous study included 444 children of Oriental ancestry under eighteen years of age living in Berkeley and Oakland and enrolled in the Kaiser Foundation Health Plan for two or more two-year periods. As our study population, we used 355 of these children of Chinese and Japanese ancestry, who were still living in the area when the research was conducted.

The Kaiser Foundation Health Plan is a prepaid medical service program which encourages members to use the medical facilities at Kaiser rather than at other hospitals. Its members come from various social classes, although upper and lower classes are underrepresented. In racial composition, the Kaiser membership and the population of Berkeley and Oakland do not differ by more than 3 percent, but the Kaiser membership does not reflect the national racial distribution. The Berkeley and Oakland area is an atypical urban area where the proportions of Afro-Americans and Orientals are much higher than in most other parts of the country. The occupational distribution of the Kaiser membership does not differ substantially from that of the Berkeley and Oakland area, or from urban areas in general, or from the total population of the country, although the Kaiser membership underrepresents semi-skilled and unskilled workers.

Because service is readily available, one might suspect that children belonging to a prepaid health plan, such as the Kaiser Plan, have higher medically attended injury rates than do children in the country as a whole. It was found, however, that the injury rates among members of the Kaiser Plan are not very different from those shown in the National Health Survey.[7] In fact, injury rates of young girls are lower in the

Kaiser population than in the national population. Thus, the Kaiser membership provides a study population that is reasonably representative of urban children in terms of social class and use of medical facilities.

In selecting the sample of 151 children of Oriental ancestry from the population, the following criteria were used:

a. Ethnicity.

To compare the Chinese and Japanese, we attempted to draw equal numbers of children from the two groups.

b. Sex.

To separate the effects of sex on accident involvement from the effects of acculturation, we sought to draw an equal number of boys and girls.

c. Accident rate.

This study operationally defines "accident" as "medically attended injury." Based on the description of accidents in the medical records, we chose three sub-groups to represent low-, medium-, and high-accident rate children. The subgroups consisted of children having zero, two, and three or more medically attended injuries.

d. Time span between child's accidents.

Although we should have given priority to children whose accident experiences were consistent in successive periods, this choice was not always possible. An accident is a relatively rare event, particularly among Oriental-American girls. The two major objectives in setting up the sample were: (1) to have sufficient cases to allow simultaneous analysis of the variables included in the study, and (2) to define samples which would represent the extreme range of children's accident experience.

To obtain a sufficient number of high-accident rate cases, we included nearly all in the population. Even so, we did not get the desired total of ten girls. The selection of the medium-accident rate group gave priority to those who had two accidents within the shortest period of time.

e. Length of time enrolled in Kaiser.

In selecting the low-accident rate group, we considered the length of time the children belonged to the Kaiser Plan, whereas the high accident rate sample was chosen without reference to the duration of enrollment, because of the limited number in this category. It was assumed that the longer the child was enrolled in the Kaiser Plan, the more likely he was to have a record of medically attended injuries.

f. Age.

We selected our sample from children aged ten through fifteen, because this is a retrospective study in that it relates the child's accident history during the period covered by his medical records to his behavior and to parental child-rearing practices. It is obviously unrealistic to ask a mother to report in detail about such matters over an eight- to twelve-year period. A compromise was made by holding the referral age constant in order to avoid partitioning the already small sample by another variable. In interviews, questions on a specified age of the child concerned the period when he was about ten.

The reasons for selecting this particular age were: (1) the Oriental children in our study population were mostly born between 1947 and 1955 and were thus between eight and sixteen years old; and (2) the difference in accident rate between white and Oriental children is greater for school-age children than for those younger.

g. Number of families.

The unit of the sample was the child rather than the family. At times more than one child was selected from the same family, with a total of 151 children from the 130 families in the sample.

In summary, it should be noted that the high-accident rate children were over-sampled to obtain sufficient cases and the medium-accident rate cases were selected from those who were first to have two accidents. That is, the basic criterion of the number of accidents was modified by these additional factors.

To cover a wide range of materials in minimum time, we used a combination of mailed questionnaires and interviews. The questionnaire which was mailed to the respondents with a letter of introduction included all the factual questions. Within a week after the respondent received the questionnaire, an interviewer telephoned to make an appointment. During the visit, the interviewer collected the questionnaire, checked whether all questions were answered, and then proceeded with the interview, which took approximately an hour. Under this procedure, the mailed questionnaire helped to orient the parents to what was to follow. Only one percent of the mothers refused to cooperate because of physical or mental illness.

Our study employed four experienced interviewers, including the writer. They all had Oriental backgrounds: a Japanese with a Caucasian husband, a Chinese with a Caucasian husband, and a Caucasian with a Japanese husband. They could speak Japanese or Chinese, but did not have to use either language since all respondents spoke English adequately.

Since the small size of the sample precluded elaborate analyses to produce statistically significant results, a "reasonably scoring approach" was used.[8] The original theoretical framework provided the basis of reasonableness for combining a set of questions. The degree of reasonableness can show how well the content of the questions bears on a central issue.

In this study, a cross-tabulation of responses served to test reasonableness quantitatively. For instance, to develop a scale of the child's aggressiveness, we cross-tabulated responses to the questions on the following four topics to see whether the respondents who scored high on one question would do so on the other questions.

(a) How the mother describes the child's personality (open ended)
    (i)   aggressive
    (ii) sometimes aggressive, or aggression not mentioned
    (iii) seldom or never aggressive
(b) How often child acts aggressively to mother
    (i)   very often
    (ii) sometimes
    (iii) rarely
(c) How often the child fights with siblings
(d) How often the child fights with other children

The questions on these four factors seemed to cluster reasonably well, and we totaled the scores of each respondent for the four questions as a measure of aggressiveness. In this particular case the total score ranged from 4 to 12.

The independent variable of this study, acculturation, is a complex process and any distinction between the acculturated and the nonacculturated is artificial and should be treated with caution. Based on the literature[9] on acculturation and family system and on a pretest of the results, we constructed two scales of acculturation, one referring to the mother and the other to the child.

Maternal acculturation indices included:
    The mother's knowledge of an Oriental language
    The racial composition of her group of friends
    Her membership in Oriental organizations
    Her subscription to an Oriental newspaper
    Her opinion on the ideal number of children
    The arrangement of her marriage
    Her habit of leaving her children with a baby-sitter
Child acculturation indices included:
    The child's knowledge of an Oriental language
    The racial composition of his group of friends
    His interest in Oriental games
    His preference for Oriental food

To simplify the results, on the basis of these indices we classified the mothers as either "acculturated" or "unacculturated." The children were grouped into three types, however, since unacculturated mothers could have relatively acculturated or unacculturated children. The children of acculturated families were placed in Type 1. Type 2 included the acculturated children of unacculturated mothers, and Type 3, the unacculturated children of unacculturated mothers. A comparison of the acculturation scores of the mothers of the three types of children showed that the scores of the mothers of Type 2 children came between those of the mothers of Type 1 and Type 3 children, rather than approximating the scores of the mothers of Type 3 children.

Interviews with the mothers of the 151 sampled children provided the data analyzed in the first phase of this study. The data supported almost exactly the hypothesis that acculturated children are more likely to have accidents than are nonacculturated children. Particularly among girls (Types 2 and 3) there was perfect correlation between accidents and acculturation. It is unusual that a crudely indexed scale of acculturation is able to predict the accident rate without an error. Of course, other factors were examined in the first phase, including the mother's predisposition to medical service. The mother was asked such hypothetical questions as what she would do if her child had a high fever or were injured. There was some correlation between accident frequency and the mother's willingness to use medical facilities, but there was no objective way to measure medical predisposition.

We also suspected that the coding of open-ended questions might have been inaccurate. The use of the same answers to measure more than one variable may contaminate the variables. Consequently, to identify the problems encountered in the first phase, the following follow-up was conducted in the second phase.

In Phase 1, we gathered data only on accidents, without considering other available information, such as illnesses. To measure the degree of the mother's predisposition to medical care, it was important to have an almost complete medical history of each child. Therefore, the medical charts of all the Oriental study population (444) were re-analyzed. Out of the original 444 cases, only 400 charts were available, since some children had moved away or dropped their membership. Two nurses analyzed and coded the medical charts: the superintendent of the medical chart room and a worker in the clinical administration. Both were experienced in reading and summarizing medical charts. Phase I covered the time period to 1960; Phase II included the next five-year period, 1961–1965. Hereafter, these two time periods will be called Time 1 and Time 2.

Since we now had two periods for analysis, accident persistency in each child could be studied for a longer time span. Through examination of the accident patterns of each child in Times 1 and 2, a new classification of accident group was developed. Those who had one or no accident in both Times 1 and 2 were classified in the low-accident rate group, and those with three or more accidents in the two periods were placed in the high-accident rate group.

The number of routine check-ups and immunizations was used to develop the scale of medical predisposition. The Kaiser Plan recommends that every child be brought to the hospital for a routine check-up at least once a year. Some mothers who are overcautious may bring the child for check-ups and immunizations quite frequently. On the other hand, if a mother is reluctant to use medical care or thinks that the child can be well cared for at home, she may bring the child far less frequently for this check-up.

We divided the numbers of check-ups and immunizations by the number of years the child was enrolled in the Kaiser Plan to produce the following scale:

Medical predisposition scale =

$$\frac{\text{Nos. of check-ups} + \text{Nos. of immunizations} \times 100}{\text{Nos. of years enrolled}}$$

Numbers of immunizations and check-ups were added because we found them to be correlated with the coefficient of .572.

The major hypothesis of this study is that acculturated children of Oriental ancestry in the United States are more likely to have accidents than non-acculturated ones.

The first group of more specific hypotheses is concerned with accident determinants per se. Previous accident research has suggested two variables in accidents; the child's exposure to hazards and his ability to cope with hazards once exposed to them. Our concern with the exposure variable focuses on the scope of the child's activities as affected by the parental child-rearing practices and his personality traits. Our main interest in the coping variable is the effect of the child's psychological tension, as determined by family relations, child-rearing practices, and his behavior patterns.

Group I Hypotheses:

H_1:   A child reared by parents who take egalitarian and permissive attitudes toward him tends to have many accidents (i.e., be a high-accident rate child), since such child-rearing practices increase his exposure to hazards.

H_2:   A child who is gregarious, independent, venturesome, and athletic tends to have many accidents (be a high-accident rate child), since such a child is more exposed to hazards.

H_3:   A child whose parents repress his aggression and take a detached, authoritarian attitude toward him tends to be a high-accident rate child.

H_4:   A child who is overtly or covertly aggressive and disobedient tends to be a high-accident rate child.

The second group of hypotheses is concerned with the relationships between acculturation and exposure and between acculturation and coping ability.

Group II Hypotheses:

H_5:   The acculturated mother is more likely to take egalitarian and permissive attitudes toward the child than is the nonacculturated mother.

H_6:   The acculturated child is more likely to be gregarious, independent, and venturesome than the nonacculturated child.

H_7:   The nonacculturated mother of an acculturated child tends to prohibit the child's aggression, take authoritarian attitudes, and have a relatively detached relationship with the child because of the acculturation conflict.

H_8:   The acculturated child of a nonacculturated mother tends to be overtly or covertly aggressive and disobedient toward parental authority because of the acculturation conflict.

The third group of hypotheses extends the first two. It is concerned with the joint effects of exposure and acculturation on accident frequency and the ability to cope with hazards. The sample is divided into types of acculturation to examine the various relationships within each type.

Group III Hypotheses:

H_9:   Within each acculturation type, mothers of high-accident rate children are more likely to score high on child-rearing exposure scales (see p.252 for definition) than are mothers of low-accident rate children.

H_{10}:   Mothers of boys are more likely to score high on the child-rearing exposure scales than are mothers of girls.

H_{11}:   Within each acculturation type, high-accident rate children are more likely to score high on the child-behavior exposure scales (see p.254 for definition) than are low-accident rate children.

H_{12}:   Within each acculturation type, boys are more likely than girls to score high on the child-behavior exposure scales.

H_{13}: Within each acculturation type, mothers of high-accident rate children are more likely to score high on child-rearing scales that measure the inability to cope with hazards than are mothers of low-accident rate children.

H_{14}: Within each acculturation type, high-accident rate children are more likely to score high on the child-behavior coping scales than are low-accident rate children.

The first group of hypotheses to be tested is, as noted before, concerned with accident determinants per se.

The first hypothesis in Group I stated that the child reared by parents who take egalitarian and permissive attitudes toward him tends to be a high-accident rate child. It is assumed that such child-rearing practices increase the child's exposure to hazards.

The mother's independence, her preference for an egalitarian role, and her permissiveness toward the child's activities are interacting factors which affect the child's exposure to hazards. These three factors correspond successively to the mother's general value orientation to the family, her influence on the psychological orientation of the child, and her control over the physical activities of the child.

The mother's permissiveness toward the child's risk-taking most explicitly affects his exposure to hazards. Her preference for an egalitarian role influences the child's mental attitudes more subtly than does permissiveness. An egalitarian mother treats the child as an equal and encourages him to be self-reliant and to explore his surroundings. The mother's independence has still less direct influence on the child's exposure to hazards than her permissiveness since it primarily involves her own life-orientation. The assumption is that the scope of a child's physical activities is affected by his mental attitudes, which in turn are influenced by the mother's value system as well as by her direct control of the child's physical activities.

The first variable to be considered was the mother's independence, which was evaluated according to her attitudes toward (1) work outside the home; (2) her outside activities; and (3) her self-expression and self-assertion. Many questions were asked in open-ended form. A content analysis of the responses made possible a rank-ordering of the respondents on the scale of independence. Independent mothers usually feel that, if feasible, women should work outside the home, or at least should have positive interests in outside activities. Many women think that through this contact with society such outside interests will help them to understand the needs of their husbands and will insure their own social and intellectual growth.

Our findings show that a high-accident rate for boys is associated with a high degree of independence on the part of the mother. The difference in the mother's scores on the independence scale between high- and low-accident rate boys is significant (at the .05 level), but the mother's independence and the daughter's accident rates are not significantly related.

The mother's preference for an egalitarian role—that is, the degree to which she prefers to treat her child as an equal rather than as a relatively helpless child—was assessed through her responses to questions concerning the pleasure and pains in child rearing, the amount of assistance the mother gives the child in homework and other matters, and attitudes toward career and child-rearing roles. Analysis of these open-ended questions revealed a dichotomization of mothers into the categories we have labeled "maternal" and "egalitarian." The egalitarian mother usually enjoys sharing activities with the child and feels uncomfortable when disciplining him. She commonly encourages the child to resolve problems concerning homework, clothing, and other matters himself without much dependence on her. The maternal mother typically enjoys having the child depend on her and makes it clear to the child that she is superior.

According to the data, the egalitarian mother is likely to think that a woman can improve herself as a mother if she works outside the home or at least has positive outside interests. Through outside activities she can widen her perspective and can better understand any problems confronting the child. Some mothers whose scores were very high on the scale of egalitarianism expressed ambivalent feelings about child-rearing; they seemed frustrated at having to sacrifice career opportunities because of the child. At the same time, because they held this view, they felt guilty and were likely to consider themselves as inferior mothers. The maternal mothers were content to stay at home, and to concentrate on their children, and were less likely to leave their children with baby-sitters.

The results indicate that egalitarian mothers are more likely to have high-accident rate children than are the maternal mothers. The scores of high- and low-accident rate boys differ significantly (at the .05 level) on this scale.

Permissive mothers allow the child, at an earlier age, to take risks such as riding a bicycle, going swimming, or handling a chemistry set. In general they do not impose many restrictions on the child's conduct in such matters as bedtime, watching TV, or being noisy in the home. The permissive mother is more likely to have a high-accident rate child. The difference in scores on the permissiveness scales between high- and low-accident rate groups is significant at the .01 level for boys.

This study defines the total exposure variable as the sum of the three previously discussed variables—the mother's independence, preference for egalitarian role, and permissiveness toward the child's activities. The difference in the total exposure variable between high- and low-accident rate boys is significant at the .01 level.

The second hypothesis in Group I states that a child who is gregarious, independent, venturesome, and athletic tends to have many accidents. It should be remembered, however, that we classified behavioral characteristics of the children according to parental description, rather than by strictly objective evidence.

The mother described the gregarious child as outgoing, extroverted and friendly, the nongregarious one as shy, introverted and reserved. The latter type of child usually has few friends, spends most of his time alone, and engages in quiet activities, such as watching TV or playing with dolls.

According to our data, the high-accident rate boy is slightly more gregarious than the low-accident rate one, but the difference is not significant. Among girls, the medium-accident rate group scores highest on the gregariousness scale, and there is little difference between high- and low-accident rate groups. Thus, gregariousness and accident rates are not clearly related.

By our definition, an independent child, as described by his mother, does things on his own without relying on others. This concept includes independence from convention, i.e., searching for new things. An independent child often initiates actions and suggests them to his peers and family members instead of doing what other people propose. He expresses his own personality through his activities rather than playing the family-ascribed role of a child.

In our study the high-accident rate child scores higher on the independence scale than the low-accident rate child. The differences are greater for the girls than for the boys (at the .05 level of significance for boys and at the .01 level for girls).

Mothers described the venturesome child as daring and prone to do things that seem, at least in her eyes, to be dangerous. He is likely to have many more accidents than one who is not venturesome. The difference in scores on venturesomeness between high- and low-accident rate children is significant at the .01 level. Particularly among the boys, the accident rate groups differed significantly on venturesomeness (at the .05 level even between high- and medium-accident rate groups).

When the scores for gregariousness, independence and venturesomeness are combined to produce the child's total exposure score, differences in scores between high- and low-accident rate children are significant at the .01 level.

For boys, exposure variables in child-rearing practices and in child behavior are equally important in determining the child's involvement in accidents. In the case of girls, however, the exposures arising from the child's own behavior are more frequently associated with accident experience than are those associated with parental child-rearing practices.

The mothers' evaluation and description of their children's activities were the bases for assessing athletic ability. A child who scored high on this scale was reported by his mother to be good at sports, physically well coordinated, the outdoor type. The nonathletic child, on the other hand, spent time indoors, reading books or playing with toys, and was described as clumsy and slow.

A child who likes to participate in outdoor sports is presumably more exposed to hazards than a child who spends his time indoors. However, low-accident rate children scored significantly higher (at the .05 level for boys) on the scale of athletic interest than did high-accident children. It would appear, then, that athletic ability, because it implies competence, may be regarded as a coping variable rather than an exposure variable. In each group, boys were reported to be more athletic than girls.

One might expect that athletic orientation is related to venturesomeness, but the data show that this is true only with girls. In our sample, nonventuresome boys are as likely as venturesome boys to be athletic, while nonventuresome girls are unlikely to be athletic. Being athletic may be considered venturesome for girls, since more boys routinely engage in athletic activities.

A venturesome child who is athletic may be better able to cope with hazards, and may have fewer accidents, than a venturesome, nonathletic child. The number of cases is too small for the data to be conclusive, but when venturesomeness is controlled, athletic ability and accident involvement are negatively correlated.

Any of the previous exposure factors may suggest competence as an aspect of coping, if we assume that a child learns to cope with his environment as he is exposed to it. For example, as we have seen, the data on athletics indicate that the athletic child is more competent in coping with hazards and sustains injury less frequently than the non-athletic child.

We now shall focus on the psychological antithesis of the coping variable. Previous research indicated that a small number of children were accident prone. These children had many accidents in spite of limited exposure to hazards.[10] The data showed a positive correlation for these accident-prone children between psychological maladjustment and accident rates. In this study, we shall attempt to identify factors in child-rearing patterns and in family relations that may produce anxiety, frustration, and tension. The third hypothesis in Group I was that a child whose parents prohibit his aggressiveness and take a detached authoritarian attitude toward him tends to have many accidents.

A child feels strongly frustrated when he cannot, or is not allowed to, express dissatisfaction or anger or protest against another.[11] The traditional Oriental society teaches children to control their emotions and to inhibit impulsive behavior, particularly aggressiveness toward their seniors. The nonacculturated child who has been socialized in this tradition can survive without too much frustration, but the acculturated child of nonacculturated parents may consider such an Old World norm intolerable.

The prohibition of aggression scale reflects the mother's attitude to the child's aggression toward her, to his fighting with siblings, and to his fighting back when picked on.

The authoritarianism scale concerns the decision-making process between mother and child, the punishment patterns, and the mother's ideas concerning respect for parents.

Nonauthoritarian mothers in our sample are likely to say that they listen to the child and try to negotiate an agreement with him, when they disagree about such issues as the week-end activities and TV viewing. Authoritarian mothers may listen to their children, but they alone decide what is best for the children and tell them what to do. They are likely to feel that children show little respect for parents, that parents are always right, that children should respect what their ancestors have achieved.

Traditional Chinese and Japanese families often punished their children by telling them that they had brought shame to the family as well as to themselves. An acculturated child who no longer holds this family orientation may feel frustrated when he is blamed for bringing shame to the family.

The first two variables in child rearing, prohibition of aggression and mother's authoritarianism, appear to be negatively, although not significantly, correlated to accident rates. It is possible that the child of authoritarian parents who is not allowed to be aggressive may be more cautious, because of inhibition, than other children.

The child's perception of parental authority varies and is affected by parental affection. The child may not feel frustrated even under strict discipline, if he has a close, warm relationship with family members.

The literature on this subject indicates that the combination of parental restrictiveness and hostility foster considerable resentment, which can lead to self-punishment, suicidal tendencies, accident proneness, or more generally, internalized turmoil and conflict.[12] For these reasons, we hypothesized that high-accident rate children come more often from families without close emotional integration.

We evaluated the closeness of family interaction on the basis of the time the fathers spent with their children, on the extent to which the family as a whole did things together, and on the degree of sympathetic understanding of the children's needs demonstrated by the mothers.

High accident-rate children are significantly (at the .01 level) more likely to have cold, detached family relations than are low-accident rate children.

The child having a conflict is presumably frustrated, and according to the frustration-aggression theory, is likely to be aggressive. The fourth hypothesis in Group I stated that a child who is overtly or covertly aggressive and disobedient tends to be a high-accident rate child. Such a child may be less capable of coping with hazards when exposed to them than children who are not aggressive or frustrated. In general, there is a positive correlation between these coping variables and accident frequencies.

The mothers' description of their children's personalities and their reports on their children's fights with siblings and peers, and their aggression toward their mothers determine the scale of aggressiveness. High-accident rate children are significantly (at the .01 level) more aggressive than low-accident rate children. The former fight with siblings and peers frequently and show an aggressive attitude even toward their mothers.

The scale of disobedience was based on the mothers' reports of their children's disobedience toward mothers and fathers, their displeasing behavior, the frequency with which they had to be punished, and their reaction to punishment.

Our study disclosed that the disobedient child is more likely to have accidents than the obedient one, indicating that the degree of disobedience and the accident rate are related. Not only are differences in scores between high- and low-accident rate groups significant at the .01 level, but the differences between high- and medium-rate and between medium- and low-accident rate groups are also important.

The frequency with which the children sulked or pouted, whether or not they hurt themselves when angry, the mothers' description of their children's personalities, and medical records on emotional problems determined the scale of covert aggression. The high accident-rate boy is more likely (significant at the .05 level) than the medium-accident rate one to be covertly aggressive. These differences are not noticeable among girls.

When the three preceding scales are combined to produce the total coping scale, the high-accident rate children score significantly (at the .01 level) higher than the low-accident rate children.

In general, exposure and coping variables in child behavior in this study are closely related to accident rates, although some of the indices originally thought to measure coping factors in child rearing were found to be primarily exposure factors.

In order to avoid repetition, we are not presenting the data which, however, support the second group of hypotheses that exposure and coping variables are related to the process of acculturation. An acculturated mother (of Type 1 children) is more likely than a nonacculturated one to rear a child so as to permit his exposure to hazards. Acculturated children (Types 1 and 2) are more likely than the nonacculturated (Type 3) to be independent and venturesome, which increases the exposure to hazards. Unlike Type 1 children, Type 2 children are not very gregarious and are thus relatively sheltered from hazards arising through human interaction.

As hypothesized, coping variables are related to accidents among Type 2 children, who have acculturation conflict at home. Because of tension and frustration, they are likely to be overtly or covertly aggressive, and less capable of controlling hazardous situations. Variables that tend to lower the ability to cope with hazards are also found to some extent in Types 1 and 3.

The third group of hypotheses concerns the joint effects on accident frequencies of exposure and acculturation and the ability to cope with hazards.

The first hypothesis in Group III (H_9) stated that within each acculturation type, the mothers of high-accident rate children are apt to score higher on child-rearing exposure scales than the mothers of low-accident rate children to the extent they permit their children to be exposed to hazards.

In the case of Type 1 children, most exposure variables are related to accident rates; that is, the child is likelier to have accidents because his mother's nature permits him to be exposed to hazards. The relationships between the mother's preference for an egalitarian role and her child's accident experience are significant (at the .05 level). The independence of the acculturated mother shows low correlation with the accident rates of boys or girls, except that the effect of the mother's independence on girls is opposite of our hypothesis. However, we have too few cases for results to be conclusive.

In Types 2 and 3, the relations between exposure variables and accident rates are very slight. From the sample studied, the possible conclusion might be that exposure variables affect the accident experience of children differently depending on acculturation type.

The second hypothesis of Group III (H_{10}) stated that mothers of boys are likely to score higher on the child-rearing exposure scales than are mothers of girls. Scores on the scale of the mother's independence should have no relation to the child's sex, since the scale should indicate the mother's independence of traditional norms. Both Types 2 and 3 follow this trend, but in Type 1 the differences in scores between mothers of boys and girls are fairly large, though not significantly so, and the patterns of differences are not consistent. Possibly, other factors, such as the sex composition of the children in the family as a whole, affect the scores.

With regard to the egalitarian role, the scores of mothers of boys and of mothers of girls do not differ significantly except in Type 3 where mothers of boys are more likely to prefer egalitarian roles than are mothers of girls.

Except in Type 1 medium- and low-accident rate groups, boys' mothers scored higher than girls' mothers on the scale of permissiveness. In Type 1, differences in permissiveness scores between high- and low-accident rate groups are greater for mothers of boys than for mothers of girls.

Nonacculturated mothers (of children of Types 2 and 3) are somewhat more likely to allow boys to be exposed to hazards, but when mothers become acculturated (Type 1), they do not necessarily try to shelter girls more than boys. The sex difference in the degree of exposure by then is no longer clear-cut. Most sex differences reported are slight and not statistically significant.

The third hypothesis of Group III (H_{11}) stated that within each acculturation type, high-accident rate children are likely to score higher than low-accident rate children on the exposure scales based on child's behavior.

For Type 1, our data indicated scarcely any relation between gregariousness and independence on the one hand and accident rate on the other. Venturesomeness is positively related to accidents, while athletic ability is negatively related. A venturesome child is prone to have accidents, while an athletic child is less likely to sustain injury. Among

Types 2 and 3 in general, athletic children have fewer accidents than nonathletic ones. We have already mentioned the relation of athletic ability and venturesomeness and the consequent accident rates. Other relations among the exposure variables in the child's behavior and accident experience are negligible.

The fourth hypothesis of Group III (H_{12}), that boys are more likely to be exposed to hazards than girls, is not well supported when acculturation is controlled. Sex differences are almost negligible except that boys are reported to be more athletic and venturesome though less gregarious than girls in Type 3. In the Type 1 low-accident rate group, boys are reported to be more athletic but less venturesome than are girls.

Acculturated children are more likely to be exposed to hazards, but when acculturation is controlled, we found that the relations between the degree of exposure and the frequency of the accidents were not consistent. For instance, independence in Types 1 and 3 seems to have different effects on the child's involvement in accidents. An independent child in a group that holds the norm of independence is accustomed to being independent, whereas if he is in a group that denies independence he may feel more strongly about it. Combinations of variables must be considered. Exposure factors can become coping factors in that a child exposed to hazards learns to cope with them more easily than one shielded from danger.

Finally, we investigated the degree of association between the mother's attitude toward child rearing and child behavior. The correlation coefficients obtained are not extremely high; but the mother's reports of the child's independence are related to the mother's independence ($r=.370$), her preference for an egalitarian role ($r=.418$), and her permissive attitude toward the child's activities ($r=.478$). Also a permissive mother is more likely to have a venturesome child ($r=.473$).

When the sex and acculturation of the child are controlled, the association between the mother's attitude and child's behavior becomes extremely slight except in a few cases. Among the nonacculturated girls, the mother's permissiveness is related to the daughter's independence ($r=.505$) and venturesomeness ($r=.416$) while among boys the relations are almost nil. This may suggest that girls, particularly when nonacculturated, are under a stronger maternal influence than are boys.

It has been found that mothers of Type 2 high-accident rate children are less inclined to let their children be exposed to hazards than mothers of Type 1 high-accident children, but that, as far as child behavior is concerned, Type 2 high-accident children are almost as likely as Type 1 high-accident children to expose themselves to hazards. This section is concerned with Type 2 children who are expected to suffer from acculturation conflict; it examines the relations between conflict, frustration and accident involvement. The focus is on frustration, anxiety, and defense involved in the coping variable rather than on competence.

The fifth hypothesis of Group III (H_{13}) stated that within each acculturation type mothers of high-accident rate children are more likely to score high on the coping scales than mothers of low-accident rate children. In other words, mothers of high-accident rate children tend to permit environments in which children are unable to cope with hazards. Such environments are examined in terms of the frustration, aggression, and anxiety dimension of the coping variables.

In Type 1 cases, mothers of low-accident rate children are more apt to prohibit aggression and to be less egalitarian than mothers of high-accident rate children. It seems that encouragement of aggressive behavior and egalitarianism contributes to the accident rate as much as exposure variables. If the child is encouraged to express his feelings freely and is treated as a responsible individual, he is likely to be free and hence more exposed to hazards. However, as hypothesized, the third variable, detached family relations, does have a bearing on accident rates. Where the family relations are detached and cold, the child is more likely to suffer accidents than a child in a family enjoying close interaction. This relation is significant at the .01 level among boys and at the .05 level among girls.

Type 2 cases supported the hypothesis that high-accident rate children are more likely to come from a family in which parents take an authoritarian attitude (significant at the .05 level among boys) and are aloof and detached. Only in Type 2, however, do the accident rates and coping variables have consistent relations.

Type 3 cases show no clear relations. Mothers of low-accident rate children are more likely than mothers of high- and medium-accident rate children to prohibit aggression by boys, to be authoritarian to boys, and to take a detached attitude to boys and girls. The association between the mother's prohibiting aggression or her authoritarian attitudes and the absence of the child's accident involvement may be explained by the restrictive child-rearing practices which inhibit the child's exposure to hazards. However, we find the relationship between the low-accident rate and detached family relations among Type 3 girls difficult to explain. A possible reason may be that nonacculturated mothers who have close interaction with their daughters are likely to be over-protective and will not allow them the opportunity to learn to cope with hazards.

In short, when acculturation is controlled, only Type 2 cases show consistent relations of coping variables to accident rates. Even in this group the differences are not statistically significant except in the one case of authoritarianism.

Since parental authoritarianism and the child's accident experience were distinctly related in Types 1 and 2, authoritarianism will be investigated in greater detail.

One of the indices of authoritarianism is the punishment pattern. Mothers of Type 1 high-accident rate children often resort to yelling. These mothers are acculturated and evidently feel freer to release tension by overt expression, as shown by the content analysis of their responses to open-ended questions. Mothers of low-accident rate children seem to employ more reasoning in disciplining. Among Type 3 boys, shaming is used frequently. The data support the hypothesis to the extent that mothers of Type 2 high-accident children tend to adopt the shaming method. Whether this induces anxiety and frustration as claimed by Gorer and others requires further investigation.

Fathers of Type 1 children, as described by the mothers, are disinclined to participate in child discipline because they are away from the children much of the time and often engage in social activities outside the home. A sizable proportion of the fathers of Type 3 children do not share with their wives the task of disciplining, but their reason is different from that of Type 1 fathers. Mothers say that Type 3 fathers consider child rearing as a mother's job and maintain an unexpressive, detached, although not necessarily authoritarian, attitude.

Fathers of Type 2 children, their wives report, are stricter disciplinarians than the wives, and tend to be authoritarian. This emphasizes the hypothesis that Type 2 children may harbor frustration and aggression against their fathers.

The fathers of both Type 2 and Type 3 children are traditionally oriented and have similar attitudes toward training. The question is whether a substantial difference actually exists in the disciplinary methods of these fathers or whether it is the child's perception of the discipline which differs. Some Type 2 acculturated children may be rebellious against the image of a traditional father even if he is not dictatorial. The mother may perceive this father-child relationship as a conflict and may report the father as being authoritarian. Further, the educational levels of the parents may affect the mother's report on the father's discipline methods. Highly educated fathers are somewhat more likely to be nondisciplinarian than poorly educated fathers, because they may be away more often from home or are unexpressive, or regard discipline as a mother's responsibility. This explanation is based on their wives' reports.

If the mother is better educated than the father, she is likely to view him as authoritarian toward the child. Since a poorly educated mother is much less likely to report her husband to be authoritarian than a highly educated mother, the evaluation of their poorly educated husbands by highly educated women may contain a bias.

The greater percentage of authoritarian fathers, as reported by the mothers of Type 2 children, may be explained in three ways. First, these fathers in fact may be more likely to be authoritarian than fathers of Types 1 or 3 children; second, the fathers of Type 2 children may more likely be classified by the mothers as being authoritarian because their children tend to be more aggressive and rebellious; or third, the fathers' authoritarianism may be a function of the educational discrepancy between the fathers and mothers rather than a function of acculturation type.

Our results do not show any consistent pattern of sex differences except in a few cases. Mothers of girls are likely to score higher than mothers of boys on the prohibition of aggression and authoritarianism scales in Type 3 and on the detached family relation scale in Type 1. Where a difference exists, the girls always score higher than the boys, as parents are more likely to prohibit aggression in girls than in boys, to be more authoritarian to girls than to boys, and to take a more detached attitude to girls than to boys.

It was found that families tend to have an environment conducive to frustration and tension for the Type 2 child. Within this type, accident rates are related to this environment. We shall now consider whether or not the children in such an environment harbor frustration and turn it into aggression and whether or not such frustration and aggression are related to accident involvement.

The sixth hypothesis of Group III (H_{14}) stated that in each acculturation type, high-accident rate children are more likely to score higher on the coping variable scales than low-accident children, that is, have difficulties in coping with hazards. We shall examine the coping variables in terms of frustration, aggression, anxiety, and defense rather than in terms of the competence. As far as aggression and disobedience are concerned, it is hypothesized that boys are more likely to score higher than girls.

In Type 1, except in the case of the female medium-accident rate group on the scale of covert aggression, the data support the hypothesis that high-accident rate children are more likely to be overtly or covertly aggressive and disobedient than low-accident rate children. The differences in disobedience scores among boys and in aggressiveness and disobedience scores among girls are significant at the .01 level.

Among Type 2 boys, the relations are almost in the hypothesized direction, but the magnitude is slight except on the disobedience scale.

In Type 3, the relations between coping variables and accident involvement are negligible.

The hypothesis that boys are more likely to be overtly aggressive and disobedient than girls is supported only in Type 3, whereas among the Type 1 acculturated children there is little difference between the sexes and in Type 2, the relation is reversed.

The correlation coefficients between the mother's encouragement of aggression and the child's aggression, and between the mother's encouragement of aggression and the child's disobedience are not large (r=.375 and r=.261 respectively); nor are they large between the mother's attitude and the child's aggression and the mother's attitude and the child's disobedience (r=.197 and r=.228). It appears, however, that the disobedient child is more likely to come from a family in which the interaction is characterized as cold and detached (r=.510).

Covert aggression is correlated with the mother's prohibition of aggression (r=.308) and with an authoritarian attitude (r=.403). The more prohibitive the mother is toward aggression and the more authoritarian she is, the more likely the child is to be covertly aggressive. Correlations between overt aggression and covert aggression and between overt disobedience and covert aggression are very small (r=.137 and r=.110). Those who do not, or cannot, express their aggression and disobedience overtly seem to do so covertly.

At the beginning of this paper, observing the appreciably lower than average accident rates of the children of Chinese and Japanese ancestry in this country, the author was led to ask whether as these children became Americanized their accident rates will rise. The results of this study indicate that their accident rates indeed rise with increasing acculturation. To carry out the research, we selected several variables associated by previous research scholars with acculturation and related such factors as supervision vs. training for independence in the family and intergenerational cultural conflicts. The correlation of each of these factors was generally consistent with the overall results.

The artificial device of acculturation types fits the accident rates so neatly that some doubt may arise about the validity of the indices. The most crucial factor which may have a spurious effect on the correlation is the mother's attitude toward medical service. A high-accident rate may simply mean that the mother is more ready to take the child to the doctor for minor injuries. That is a particularly important consideration for Oriental peoples who are noted for their reluctance to go to the hospital, although we have, to a degree, considered mothers' predisposition to use the medical facilities.

One way to examine the predisposition to use medical service is to compare racial groups by their ratios of severe injuries against all medically attended injuries. If parents make frequent visits to the hospital for minor injuries, the ratio should be small. However, no statistically significant nor consistent difference in ratios according to race and occupation was discovered. Next, a scale of predisposition to medical care was developed based on the following hypothetical questions: "What would you do: if your child were six years old and had a rash on the face and neck? swallowed a smooth glass bead? had a bad stomach ache? Would you: take the child to a doctor at once? treat it yourself?" There was no significant correlation between medical predisposition and accident rate in any of the subgroups divided by sex and acculturation except in the female non-acculturated group. The non-acculturated mothers (of Types 2 and 3 children) who are predisposed to medical services are more likely to have high-accident rate daughters. This partly explains the high correlation between acculturation type and accident rate. It means that the high-accident rate in Type 2 girls is not entirely accounted for by the acculturation of the children, but is in part the result of their mothers' greater willingness to take them to a doctor.

NOTES

Professor Kurokawa's paper originally included a longer introduction describing certain characteristics of the traditional Chinese and Japanese families and child-rearing practices, the cultural differences between these two traditions, and the acculturation of Orientals in the United States. Several other contributors to the present volume, however, examine some of these topics, although in different contexts. Sections of her introduction were consequently deleted from this version to retain a larger part of her findings. We deeply appreciate the invaluable editorial assistance and suggestions of Mrs. Ann Staffeld Mendez.

Readers interested in a fuller account of the research and the statistical details may refer to Minako Kurokawa, "Acculturation and Childhood Accidents Among Chinese- and Japanese-Americans," an unpublished doctoral dissertation, University of California, Berkeley, 1967 and available as University Microfilm Number 68-5754. —The editors.

1. Epidemiology of Childhood Accidents Project of the Bureau of Maternal and Child Health, California State Department of Public Health, Berkeley, California, 1962–1965.

2. "Epidemiology of Childhood Accidents," directed by Dean I. Manheimer, Bureau of Maternal and Child Health, California State Department of Public Health, Berkeley, California, 1960–1963.

3. Irene B. Taeuber, *The Population of Japan* (Princeton, N.J.: Princeton University Press, 1958), Ch. 6, pp. 100–122; R. P. Dore, *City Life in Japan* (Berkeley:

University of California Press, 1958), Section III, pp. 91-190; Yoshiharu Scott Matsumoto, "Contemporary Japan," *Transactions of the American Philosophical Society,* Vol. 50, Pt. 1, 1960; Takeyoshi Kawashima, *Nihon Shakai no Kazokuteki Kozo* [The Familial Structure of Japanese Society] (Tokyo: Gakusei Shodo, 1948); Hajime Tamaki, *Nihon Kazoku Seido-ron* [A Theory of the Japanese Family System] (Kyoto: Horitsu Bunkasha, 1953); and Takashi Koyama, *Gendai Kazoku no Kenkyu* [A Study of Contemporary Family] (Tokyo; Kobundo, 1962).

4. Ezra F. Vogel and Suzanne Vogel, "Family Security, Personal Immaturity and Emotional Health in Japanese Sample," *Marriage and Family Living* XXIII:2 (May 1961) 161-65; and Charlotte G. Babcock, "Reflections on Dependency Phenomena as seen in Nisei in the U.S.," in Robert J. Smith, ed., *Japanese Culture: Its Development and Characteristics* (Chicago: Aldine Press, 1962).

5. The relationship between the quality of maternal care and child's accident involvement has been studied by many researchers: E. Maurice Backett and A. M. Johnston, "Social Patterns of Road Accidents," *British Medical Journal* (February 14, 1959) 409-13; Vita Krall, "Personality Characteristics of Accident Repeating Children," *Journal of Abnormal and Social Psychology* XLVIII (1953) 99-107; S. B. Birnbach, "Comparative Study of Accident Repeater and Accident Free Pupils," Center for Safety Education (New York, 1949); A. A. Fabian and L. Bender, "Head Injury in Children," *American Journal of Orthopsychiatry* XVII (1947) 68-79; Irwin Marcus, "Research with Children Showing Repeated Accidents by Family Study Unit," (unpublished paper), New Orleans, Tulane University, n.d.; and Harold Jacobziner, "Causation, Prevention, and Control of Accidental Poisoning," Section on Pediatrics, A.M.A. Annual Meeting, Atlantic City, N.J., June 9, 1959.

6. As Matza points out, the image of these people is one of "drift," "an actor neither compelled nor committed to deeds nor freely choosing them." Their basis is an area of the social structure in which control has been loosened, coupled with the abortiveness of adolescent endeavor to organize an autonomous subculture: David Matza, *Delinquency and Drift* (New York: Wiley, 1964).

Normative conflict caused in the process of acculturation, resulting in crime or in neurosis, has been discussed by many people: Thorsten Sellin, *Culture Conflict and Crime* (New York: Social Science Research Council, 1958); and Arnold W. Green, "The Middle-Class Male Child and Neurosis," in Seymour Lipset and Reinhard Bendix, eds., *Class, Status and Power* (Glencoe, Ill.: Free Press, 1953).

7. *Health Statistics,* U.S. Health Survey, Series B., Nos. 3, 8, 16, 39, July 1959–June 1961; U.S. Dept. of Health, Education and Welfare.

8. M. W. Riley, et al., *Sociological Studies in Scale Analysis* (New Brunswick: Rutgers University Press, 1954).

9. P. Campisi, "A Scale for the Measurement of Acculturation," Ph.D. dissertation, University of Chicago, 1947; K. M. Kwan, "Assimilation of the Chinese in the United States," Ph.D. dissertation, Berkeley: University of California, 1958.

10. See footnote 2 above.

11. W. C. Becker, "Consequences of Different Kinds of Parental Discipline,"

Review of Child Development Research I (Russell Sage Foundation, 1964), pp. 169-208.

    12. K. A. Menninger, "Purposive Accidents as an Expression of Self Destructive Tendencies," *International Journal of Psychoanalysis* XVII (1936) 6-16.

Assimilation of Nisei in Los Angeles*

GEORGE KAGIWADA

This paper will examine intergenerational changes in the assimilation of Japanese Americans, using certain hypotheses of generational changes which have been applied in research on European ethnic minorities.

The term *Nisei* has both a generic and a specific meaning with reference to the Japanese American population. In its broad sense, it is applied to all American-born descendants of Japanese immigrants to the United States, while in its limited Japanese American usage, it designates only the second-generation offspring of the first (immigrant) generation. This limited meaning corresponds to the literal Japanese (*ni* = second, and *sei* = generation). In like manner, *Issei, Sansei,* and *Yonsei* refer to the first, third, and fourth generation, respectively. These terms, used in everyday conversation by the Japanese and Japanese Americans in the United States, suggest the extent to which the concept of generations is an integral part of their frame of reference in interpreting their experience in America.

From a sociological perspective, generational distinctions have long been important in viewing acculturation, assimilation, and accommodation processes of immigrant groups in American society. Few would deny that such distinctions have played an indispensable part in the work of Robert E. Park and his associates. More recently, however, two distinct trends have reemphasized the concept of generations. One movement originated with the historian Marcus L. Hansen, who sug-

---

*This is a revised version of a paper originally presented at the annual meeting of the Pacific Sociological Association, March 1968. Since the Third World Strike at San Francisco State College and the University of California, Berkeley in 1968 and the subsequent rise in ethnic consciousness, it has become evident that ideology, conflict, and power are crucial variables to be considered in understanding patterns of assimilation among Third World as well as other ethnic groups. This observation further underscores the basic conclusions suggested by this paper that the experience of a minority group is a highly complex phenomenon that remains to be adequately conceptualized.

gested that "what the son wishes to forget, the grandson wishes to remember."[1] He saw the second-generation offspring of immigrants as anxious and insecure about their ethnicity, as well as their identity as Americans. The third generation, grandchildren of the immigrants, however, were considered secure in their American cultural identity and thus able to look to their ethnic past with pride and interest.

Hansen's hypothesis has stimulated a number of scholars interested in ethnic life in general, as well as religious life in particular. These studies have resulted in somewhat conflicting conclusions, and at best, seem to give relatively weak support to the third-generation hypothesis. Other studies have concluded that the alternative hypothesis, positing steadily greater assimilation over successive generations, appears to be more consistent with the experiences of most ethnic groups in America. Still other writers have argued that minorities have maintained a pattern of continued pluralism over time after an initial period of accommodation. Although studies on the assimilation of Oriental immigrants have assumed or considered the last two hypotheses, they have seldom applied the third-generation thesis.[2] This omission is understandable, since Hansen originally formulated his views on the basis of his work on European immigration. One of the purposes of this paper, therefore, is to consider further the relevance of Hansen's hypothesis in interpreting assimilation patterns of an Asiatic group.

Milton Gordon has made a conceptual distinction between "structural assimilation" on the one hand, and "behavioral assimilation," or what is more commonly referred to as acculturation, on the other.[3] Although the third-generation hypothesis has been primarily interpreted as a reversal, in a sense, of acculturation, perhaps a resurgence of ethnic interest may also be revealed in the recultivation of contacts with other individuals who share a common ethnic heritage. Studies of the third-generation hypothesis regarding religious life have implied that comparative church attendance over successive generations may be interpreted as a preference for worshiping with those of similar backgrounds.

It should be noted that the ethnic community to which the third generation may return is not the same community as that known by its grandfathers. Of course, the cultural features of the ethnic heritage are not completely gone, but the Americanization process has greatly modified them. The question to be considered here is whether the Sansei, in contrast to the Nisei, seek to renew participation with others who share the common ancestry. Perhaps this is more unlikely to occur than a return in cultural terms, but this very limitation makes it a much more crucial test of the Hansen hypothesis.

A second source of recent scholarly interest in generations comes from Karl Mannheim.[4] In *Essays on the Sociology of Knowledge,* he conceptualizes and distinguishes between generations in terms of: (1) the generation location, (2) the generation as actuality, and (3) the generation unit. Generation location refers to those who are born and live in the society during the same historical period. The sociological relevance of this concept is limited, since they do not necessarily share "in the same destiny." Generation as actuality exists where exposure to the social and intellectual currents of a society and era has created a concrete bond among members of a generation. Under specific conditions, an actual generation may be subdivided into several generation units when individuals experiencing common social and intellectual influences respond to them differentially. In Mannheim's view, generation units have a much more concrete bond than actual generations. Mannheim further postulates that two or more generation units may be separated into a dominant and one or more opposing types. The former will likely have its effect upon those included in the latter, particularly upon individuals within the opposing unit who happen to "be rising in the social scale."

Most studies have considered generations without the sophistication offered by Mannheim's conceptualization. To designate all foreign-born as "first generation" and label the other generations relative to this initial definition does not take into account the possibilities of wide variations in age, time of arrival, previous differential experiences in the mother country, and other variables among those who make up such generations.

Several recent studies of assimilation have utilized Mannheim's generational distinction as a common analytic framework, but have differed somewhat in the procedures used to designate generations as actuality as well as generation units. What these studies have in common is their utilization of age or a combination of age and generational differences (as commonly understood with reference to immigrants and their successive offsprings) in designating generational segments.[5] Defining generations by such procedures may be viewed essentially as crude attempts to use Mannheim's conception of generation as actuality.

In spite of the seeming limitations of these procedures, we have attempted to follow a similar approach in a secondary analysis of data gathered as a part of a study on structural assimilation among Japanese Americans in the Los Angeles area. It soon became apparent that the data would be inadequate as a true test of the third-generation hypothesis. Nevertheless, the hypothesis has served as a basis for developing interpretive framework to analyze patterns which were observed in the data.

One hundred and forty eight American-born residents of Japanese ancestry who were male heads of household in Los Angeles responded to a mailed questionnaire in January, 1967.[6] The original mailing list was randomly drawn from two Japanese American directories, one covering what might broadly be characterized as "Central Los Angeles" and the other covering the San Fernando Valley. The percentage of returns was poor.[7] Although the age distribution appeared fairly representative, there was a sharp bias toward the higher socio-economic levels. For these reasons, no claim can be made that the sample is representative.

Three structural assimilation variables are used. "Primary assimilation" is defined as the degree to which ethnic Japanese have relinquished close friendship with other Japanese in preference to establishing friendship ties with majority (Caucasian) individuals. Similarly, "residential assimilation" refers to the degree to which Japanese Americans have moved from areas with other Japanese neighbors and reside in neighborhoods which are predominantly Caucasian. The third variable originally involved a similar conceptualization of "voluntary associations assimilation." The data, however, did not reveal a significant relationship between reduced participation in Japanese (or Japanese American) association and increased involvement in non-Japanese association. Since Hansen's thesis, interpreted in structural terms, implies that the third generation will more readily participate in ethnically circumscribed activities rather than focusing on assimilation into non-Japanese organizations, the emphasis has been placed upon what is referred to as "Japanese associational participation." This variable was defined as the degree to which ethnic group members participate in associations of which the members are predominantly (75 percent or more) Japanese or Japanese American. It does not measure assimilation directly, but rather, reflects a component of continued pluralism. Furthermore, it should be noted that this variable considers the make-up of the membership rather than the cultural content of the organizational activity.

Following the precedent set by other studies, we divided the respondents into "generations as actuality" by taking into account age and generation. The ages of Nisei respondents ranged from 25 to more than 60, an age span greater than that usually considered a generation. Hence, the Nisei were separated into two segments, those under 45 years of age and those 45 and older. This cutting age was selected because greater opportunities for Japanese Americans began to open in the larger community for the first time shortly after World War II. Given the high educational background of the respondents, most of the younger Nisei had just finished college and were beginning to establish themselves economically and socially, particularly in their family life. Their experiences were likely to differ markedly from the older Nisei who went through this period of their life cycle under much more adverse conditions of outright prejudice and discrimination.

The Sansei respondents, on the other hand, were all under 45. They were, therefore, considered to be a single (actual) generation. Admittedly, these are very crude procedures for designating generations as actuality, but given the nature of the data, it was one of the more feasible approaches consistent with Mannheim's conception of actual generations.

Following the research design of previous studies, the third-generation hypothesis would be considered supported if the Sansei showed significantly lower structural assimilation than the Nisei. Such a conclusion would be particularly applicable in comparison with the older Nisei who had experienced the full impact of the earlier historical period. Table 1 indicates the comparison of these three actual generations on the three structural variables.

Contrary to expectation, age difference among the Nisei showed no meaningful differences. Older and younger Nisei showed virtually identical percentages on all three assimilation variables. More importantly, comparisons between the older Nisei and the Sansei, the groups for whom we might have anticipated the greatest difference, showed no statistically significant differences. Thus, the data gave little support to the third-generation hypothesis, but rather, indicated a pattern which appears to be consistent with the hypothesis of continued pluralism. At best, the data showed weak support for Hansen's thesis in terms of residential assimilation.

What is more, other data not presented here revealed a significant positive association between increasing assimilation and rising socioeconomic status, as measured by education and occupation. Furthermore, education and occupation tend to rise over generations. No such relation existed, however, between assimilation and generation on the one hand and income on the other. This lack of association can be largely accounted for by age difference, with older respondents tending to have higher incomes but exhibiting a lower degree of assimilation.

The respondents included a sizable number born and raised in Hawaii. The proportion among the three successive actual generations varied greatly—17, 35, and 41 percent respectively. In general, Hawaiian respondents in our sample showed a greater tendency toward patterns of assimilation than those from the mainland. Although the limited size of the sample precluded any systematic statistical control, the tendency is for any pattern toward a third-generation return to be somewhat obscured by status differences as well as by Hawaiian origin.

TABLE 1
STRUCTURAL ASSIMILATION BY GENERATION AND AGE

GENERATION AGE (in years)	*Nisei*		*Sansei*
	Older (45 & over)	*Younger* (21 - 44)	*Total* (21 - 44)
Primary Assimilation [1]			
High	32%	34%	39%
Intermediate	41%	38%	25%
Low	27%	28%	36%
(N)	(37)	(76)	(28)
*Gamma = -0.00, x^2 = 1.74, df = 2, p .50			
Residential Assimilation [2]			
High	77%	71%	55%
Low	23%	29%	45%
(N)	(35)	(75)	(29)
*Gamma = -0.29, x^2 = 2.55, df = 1, p .20			
Japanese Associational Participation [3]			
Low	56%	56%	67%
High	44%	44%	33%
(N)	(36)	(71)	(27)
*Gamma = 0.12, x^2 = 0.40, df = 1, p .50			

*Whether any statistical measures of association or tests of significance should be used for this data is questionable. Nevertheless, Gammas and chi squares have been presented to provide information which may serve as additional basis for speculative interpretation for readers who may choose to do so.

1. High: Respondents who indicate more than 25% of their close friends are Caucasian.
   Intermediate: Respondents who indicate less than 25% of their friends are Caucasian, but less than 90% are Japanese.
   Low: Respondents who indicate that more than 90% of their friends are Japanese.
   Note: Friendships with Jewish, Mexican, and other racial minorities are *not* included.
2. High: Respondents who indicate 50% or more of their neighbors are Caucasian and less than 10% are Japanese.
   Low: Respondents who indicate more than 10% of their neighbors are Japanese and claim to live in a Japanese neighborhood.
   Note: Jewish, Mexican and other racial minority neighbors are *not* included.
3. This is not a direct measure of assimilation, but of weakening ethnic ties.
   Low: Respondents who lack Japanese associational membership or maintain only nominal membership.
   High: Respondents who participate occasionally or regularly in Japanese associational activity.

Given these limitations in the analysis, it would seem dubious to conclude simply that the data tended to support a pattern of continued pluralism. Furthermore, such a conclusion would contradict the generally accepted view that the present trend for the Japanese in the United States is one of increasing assimilation over successive generations.[8] Admittedly, by continuing the discussion we become involved in sheer speculation. Nevertheless, we have found that Hansen and Mannheim have provided the basis for extending our analysis even though at best it can only lead to suggestions for further research. We hope that this discussion will illustrate the complexities involved in the process of assimilation.

Hansen's hypothesis contains a crucial feature that is often assumed rather than empirically substantiated. Studies which have attempted to verify the thesis have not been concerned with determining if the third-generation respondents are actually "secure in their Americanness." Unfortunately, the present data do not give us this information. It may be argued, however, that such a sense of security is largely a function of the degree of discrimination which the minority individual perceives. As indicated in Table 2, the Sansei do show a significantly lower degree of "perceived discrimination," especially in comparison with the older Nisei.[9] Whereas 78 percent of the older Nisei are categorized as perceiving high discrimination, only 48 percent of the Sansei are so classified.

TABLE 2
PERCEIVED DISCRIMINATION BY GENERATION
AND AGE

GENERATION	Nisei		Sansei
AGE	Older	Younger	Total
(in years)	(45 & over)	(21 - 44)	(21 - 44)
Perceived			
Discrimination			
High	78%	69%	48%
Low	22%	31%	52%
(N)	(40)	(78)	(29)

Gamma = -0.57, x^2 = 5.11, df = 1, p .025
(Between Older Nisei and Sansei)

In light of this observation, a more meaningful way to consider the relationship implied in Hansen's theory may be the association between generations and primary assimilation with perceived discrimination held constant. The hypothesis would suggest that second-generation individuals who are insecure (i.e., with high perceived discrimination) would exhibit greater assimilation than third-generation individuals who are secure (i.e., with low perceived discrimination). Table 3 shows that the expected relationship does not hold when comparing the older Nisei and the Sansei. The modal category for the older Nisei with high perceived discrimination is an intermediate degree of primary assimilation (46 percent), whereas 60 percent of the Sansei with low perceived discrimination are classified as high in primary assimilation.

TABLE 3
PRIMARY ASSIMILATION BY PERCEIVED
DISCRIMINATION AND GENERATION

GENERATION	*Older Nisei*		*Sansei*	
PERCEIVED	High	Low	High	Low
DISCRIMINATION				
Primary Assimilation				
High	18%	78%	15%	60%
Intermediate	46%	22%	46%	7%
Low	36%	0%	39%	33%
(N)	(28)	(9)	(13)	(15)
	Gamma = 0.89		Gamma = 0.42	

If a sense of insecurity is largely a product of discrimination, the very factor that causes the insecurity may prevent any extensive degree of assimilation. Hence, the data do not reflect the expected pattern, but rather support our view to the degree that those perceiving low discrimination are more likely to be assimilated than those who perceive high discrimination. What is of particular interest, however, is the tendency for the Sansei with low perceived discrimination to be somewhat polarized in their primary assimilation. Although 60 percent are highly assimilated, another 33 percent are considered low in primary assimilation. This latter figure contrasts sharply with the pattern among the Nisei with low perceived discrimination, where no cases show low assimilation. Furthermore, it should be noted that the Nisei and Sansei with high perceived discrimination exhibit almost identical patterns. Because of the small number of cases, it cannot be claimed that these contrasts are significant. Nevertheless, they are striking.

One implication of the foregoing discussion may be that when the Sansei who are secure and show low primary assimilation are compared with their Nisei counterparts, they reflect a pattern of third-generation return. This possibility is merely speculative because of the limitation in the size and character of the sample. Furthermore, the research design of the study which provided the data was static or cross-sectional in nature, comparing generations at a given point in time. The Hansen hypothesis, on the other hand, is longitudinal in nature. Apparently a more crucial test of the hypothesis would require information which would show whether or not the Nisei parents of these particular Sansei were more structurally assimilated than their offspring. Perhaps the Sansei merely mirror the pattern of their parents. In other words, we need to know the generational sequence of specific families.

Even if the third-generation hypothesis was considered to hold true for some of the Sansei, they would constitute only a small segment of the total generation.[10] To a degree, these individuals are reacting to socio-cultural forces in a particular historical period in a contrasting manner from the modal pattern. This point is precisely what Mannheim conceptualized in his definition of a generation unit. Thus, in pursuing the discussion, we have shifted from a view of the third-generation hypothesis within the context of generations to a perspective assuming generational units.

Mannheim has suggested that the concept of generation unit, rather than generation as actuality, is likely to lead to a more fruitful sociological understanding of the impact of the changing socio-cultural forces upon a person's experiences. The convergence of his view and the outcome of our discussion suggests that the context within which the third-generation hypothesis has been viewed needs to be modified. Rather than considering whether successive generations of ethnic groups exhibit modal patterns consistent with this or that hypothesis, we should grant the existence of varying generation units within any actual generation. Each unit may exhibit a pattern consistent with a hypothesis, but several hypotheses may be relevant simultaneously. We then need to determine the structural and cultural variables which are associated with these different patterns.

Mannheim furthermore suggested that within each actual generation, one of the units becomes more dominant and influences the opposing types. By focusing on generational units, it may be possible to consider the complexities and intricacies of various combinations of dominant and opposing types under varying conditions in successive historical periods and to determine the degree of dominance of the strongest unit.

We have come a long way from our initial focus on structural assimilation of Japanese Americans. It seems appropriate, therefore, to recapitulate what has been implied about them. The limited data, from a viewpoint of actual generations, suggest caution in assuming a rapid trend toward greater structural assimilation over successive generations, as some writers have suggested. At the same time, the data do not clearly support the third-generation return hypothesis, as it is commonly interpreted. We have also speculated, however, that to assume the continuity of a pattern of pluralism for Japanese Americans, at least on the basis of our data, may be an over-simplification. Rather, we have proposed the interpretation of the data by modifying the Hansen hypothesis within the context of generation units.

The view developed here, however, obviously requires further investigation, using adequate sampling and a more sophisticated research design, before we can consider it as even partially verified. Furthermore, since the three dimensions of structural assimilation discussed in this study have not shown consistent patterns, the process of assimilation, it would seem, is a highly complex phenomenon. Scholars should strive to develop a conceptual framework which will adequately explain the intriguing subtleties and intricacies which underlie the process. This study has merely suggested some of the complexities of assimilation among the Japanese Americans.

NOTES

1. Marcus Lee Hansen, "The Third Generation in America," *Commentary* 14 (November 1952) 492-500.

2. Two papers by Leonard D. Cain, Jr. refer to the third-generation hypothesis. See his "Japanese-American Protestants: Acculturation and Assimilation," *Review of Religious Research* 3 (Winter 1962) 113-121; and "The Integration Dilemma of Japanese-American Protestants," paper presented to the Pacific Sociological Association, Sacramento, California, April, 1962.

3. Milton M. Gordon, "Assimilation in America: Theory and Reality," *Daedalus* 90 (Spring 1961) 263-285.

4. Karl Mannheim, *Essays on the Sociology of Knowledge,* edited by Paul Kesckemeti (London: Routledge and Kegan Paul, Ltd., 1952), Chapter VII.

5. See, for example, Noel Iverson, *Germania, U.S.A.* (Minneapolis: The University of Minnesota Press, 1966); Judith Kramer and Seymour Leventman, *Children of the Gilded Ghetto* (New Haven: Yale University Press, 1961); and Alex Simirenko, *Pilgrims, Colonists, and Frontiersmen* (New York: The Free Press, 1964). The techniques used in these studies are reminiscent of those in W. Lloyd Warner and Leo Srole, *The Social System of American Ethnic Groups* (New Haven: Yale University Press, 1945).

6. Actually, 180 respondents returned adequately completed questionnaires, but for the purposes of this article, those of four Kibei (American-born but educated in Japan) and of 28 mixed generational parentage were eliminated from consideration.

7. The 180 respondents represented approximately a 30 percent and a 40 percent return for the two areas respectively.

8. Charles Marden and Gladys Meyer, *Minorities in American Society,* 2nd ed. (New York: American Book Company, 1962), p. 464.

9. Perceived discrimination was measured by a four-item Guttman-type scale using the Goodenough technique. Coefficient of reproductibility = .92, minimum marginal reproductibility = .71, coefficient of scalability = .72.

10. Although discussing within the context of cultural, rather than structural, assimilation, Herbert J. Gans deemphasizes the third-generational effect by considering it as a phase of a more or less straight-line trend toward assimilation. He notes that whatever "return" may be perceived involves a small number of individuals. See his "American Jewry: Present and Future" (a two-article series), *Commentary* 21 (May 1956 and June 1956).

Generation & Character:
The Case of the Japanese-Americans

STANFORD M. LYMAN

When the first Japanese embassy arrived in the United States in 1860, the *Daily Alta Californian,* a San Francisco newspaper, reported with mingled approval and astonishment that

> Every beholder was struck with the self-possessed demeanor of the Japanese. Though the scenes which now met their gaze must have been of the most intense interest for novelty, they seemed to consider this display as due the august position they held under their Emperor, and not one of them, by sign or word, evinced either surprise or admiration.[1]

Thus, with their first major debarkation in the New World, the Japanese appeared to Americans to lack emotional expression. Indeed San Francisco's perceptive journalist went on to observe: "This stoicism, however is a distinguishing feature with the Japanese. It is part of their creed never to appear astonished at anything, and it must be a rare sight indeed which betrays in them any expression of wonder."[2]

In the eighty-five years which passed between the arrival of Japan's first embassy and the end of World War II, this "distinguishing feature" of the Japanese became the cardinal element of the anti-Japanese stereotype. Characterized by journalists, politicians, novelists, and film-makers as a dangerous enemy, the Japanese were also pictured as mysterious and inscrutable.[3] Supposedly loyal to Japan, cunning, and conspiratorial, most of the Japanese Americans were evacuated and incarcerated throughout World War II. This unusual violation of their fundamental civil rights was justified in the minds of a great many ordinary Americans by the perfidious character they imputed to Japanese.[4]

The anti-Japanese stereotype was so widespread that it affected the judgments of sociologists about the possibilities of Japanese assimilation. Thus, in 1913 Robert E. Park was sufficiently depressed by anti-Japanese legislation and popular prejudice to predict: "The Japanese . . . is condemned to remain among us an abstraction, a symbol, and a symbol not merely of his own race, but of the Orient and of that vague ill-defined menace we sometimes refer to as the 'yellow peril'."[5] Although Park later reversed his doleful prediction, his observations on Japanese emphasized their uncommunicative features, stolid faces, and apparently blank character. The Japanese face was a racial mask behind which the individual personality was always hidden. "Orientals live more completely behind the mask than the rest of us," he wrote. "Naturally enough we misinterpret them and attribute to disingenuousness and craft what is actually conformity to an ingrained convention. The American who is flattered at first by the politeness of his Japanese servant will later on, perhaps, cite as a reproach against the race the fact that 'we can never tell what a Japanese is thinking about.' 'We never know what is going on in their heads'."[6]

Since the end of World War II, the recognition of the evils of racism has reduced the pejorative effects of racial stereotypes, but it has not brought about an end to their popular usage or academic study. Recent scholarship, while avoiding negative stereotypes, has begun to emphasize the role of character and character formation in achievement and assimilation. Thus, in one study, the success of Jews in America is attributed in part to their belief "that the world is orderly and amenable to rational mastery"; to their willingness "to leave home to make their way in life"; and to their "preference for individualistic rather than collective credit for work done."[7] Another study points out that the child-rearing practices of Jews, Greeks, and white Protestants emphasize independence and achievement, while those of Italians, French-Canadians, and Negroes encourage cooperation and fatalistic resignation.[8]

The remarkable record of achievement by Japanese Americans has often been reported by journalists and sociologists. As early as 1909 Chester Rowell noted their refusal to accept unprofitable contracts, their commercial advancement beyond the confines of the ghetto, and their geniality and politeness.[9] Seventeen years later Winifred Raushenbush, Park's assistant in his race relations survey of the Pacific Coast, admonished the Japanese of Florin, California, for their impatience with racial restrictions and praised the Japanese community of Livingston, California, for its propriety.[10] More recently Rose Hum Lee vividly contrasted the Chinese Americans with their Japanese counterparts, noting that the Nisei "exhibit greater degrees of integration into American society, than has been the case with the Chinese, whose settlement is twice as long."[11] Broom and Kitsuse summed up the impressive record of the Japanese in America by declaring it to be "an achievement perhaps rarely equaled in the history of human migration."[12] The careful statistical measures of Schmid and Nobbe indicate that present-day Japanese have outstripped all other "colored" groups in America in occupational achievement and education.[13]

Analyses of Japanese American achievement stress the same character traits which once made up the notorious stereotype. Thus, Caudill and de Vos pointed out that the Nisei appear to be more acculturated than they are because of "a significant compatibility (but by no means identity) between the value systems found in the culture of Japan and the value systems found in American middle-class culture."[14] "What appears to have occurred in the case of Japanese-Americans is that the *Nisei*, while utilizing to a considerable extent a Japanese set of values and adaptive mechanisms, were able in their prewar life on the Pacific Coast to act in ways that drew favorable comment and recognition from their white middle-class peers and made them admirable pupils in the eyes of their middle-class teachers."[15]

The experiences of prewar California were repeated in Chicago during World War II. Personnel managers and fellow workers admired the Nisei. "What has happened here," wrote Caudill and de Vos, "is that the peers, teachers, employers and fellow workers of the *Nisei* have projected their own values onto the neat, well-dressed, and efficient *Nisei* in whom they saw mirrored many of their own ideals."[16] What were these ideals? They included patience, cleanliness, courtesy, and minding their own business,[17] the same ideals capable of distortion into negative characteristics. Thus, Japanese patience has been taken to be silent contempt; cleanliness and courtesy as matters for comic ridicule or dark suspicion; minding their own business as unwarranted aloofness and clannishness.[18] What was once caricature is now recognized as character.

The fact that the same or nearly identical traits can be used to denigrate the Japanese as well as account for their unprecedented success suggests the possibility that a unique character structure exists behind these traits. Indeed, the Japanese Americans themselves believe this, and, as we shall presently show, they believe each generation of Japanese Americans is possessed of a unique character. The existence of a correspondence between racist stereotype and culturally-created character should not cause great concern. A stereotype survives through time and other changes by distorting a kernel of fundamental truth. Recently a great advance in the understanding of the nature of slavery and Negro personality was made by recognizing true personality elements in the Sambo stereotype and attempting to discover just how such a personality could arise.[19] Progress in the social analysis of culture and personality might be enhanced by assuming for the sake of research that the worst statements made about a people have their origins in some fundamental truth which needs first to be abstracted from its pejorative context and then subjected to behavioral and cultural analysis.

In sociology, the ideal types exaggerate the actual social characteristics for analytical purposes. Therefore, no Nisei individual is expected to personify all the attributes delineated below. The typology may also be less applicable to the Nisei who grew up outside the Japanese communities or who associated primarily with non-Nisei peer groups. It should, however, be useful in understanding some basic features of the Nisei personality.

A conceptual framework first developed by Alfred Schutz[20] and effectively employed by Clifford Geertz to study the Balinese[21] is used in this paper to analyze Japanese American character. A somewhat similar formulation of concepts by Florence Kluckhohn has been applied to Japanese character by Caudill and Scarr.[22] Although this paper relies heavily on Schutz, the conceptual schema of Kluckhohn and the findings of Caudill and Scarr will be noted when appropriate. In addition the findings of numerous researchers on Japan and Japanese Americans have been employed and interpreted throughout.

In every culture and in many subcultures there is a predominant time-person perspective. This perspective organizes the relevant temporal and personal categories in order to structure priorities with respect to past, present, and future and to structure orientations with respect to intimacy or impersonality. Consequently, any culture may be viewed with respect to its priorities of predecessors, contemporaries, consociates, and successors.[23] *Predecessors* are all those who have lived in some past time and of whom no contemporary can have direct subjective knowledge. *Successors* are all those who shall live in some future time, with whom no contemporary can share a mutual inter-subjective identity. *Contemporaries* are all those fellow men who share the same spatiotemporal environment. Contemporaries include those about whom one has only categorical but not personal knowledge, and those whom one knows intimately and in regular association. The latter are *consociates*.

In any culture or subculture these distinctions appear, not merely as analytic features, but also as members' understandings of their own world. It is possible for members to perceive any one of these time-person perspectives as prior to, having precedence over, or exclusive from any one or group of the others. The relative subjective weight placed on any one or more of these perspectives has profound consequences for the organization of behavior and in turn is reciprocally related to other elements of culture and the institutional order.

In the case of the Japanese in America, time and person are perceived in terms of geographic and generational distance from Japan. The Japanese are the only immigrant group in America who specify by a linguistic term and characterize with a unique personality each generation of descendants from the original immigrant group.[24] In contrast, for example, to the U.S. census[25] and the Chinese,[26] the Japanese do not merely distinguish native-born from foreign-born but count geogenerationally forward or backward with each new generational grouping. Moreover, from the standpoint of any single living generational group, the others are imputed to have peculiar and distinctive personalities and attendant behavior patterns which are evaluated in positive and negative terms. Each generation removed from Japan is assumed to have its own characterological qualities as a result of its spatiotemporal position which can not be voluntarily adopted or rejected. And each generation is thus living out a unique, temporally governed lifetime which shall not be seen again after it is gone.

Prof. Frank Miyamoto's essay in this book explains the meaning of the terms *Issei, Nisei, Sansei,* and *Kibei.* The definition can be continued to two additional generations. The great-grandchildren of the Issei are called *Yonsei,* literally "fourth generation," and include all born to Sansei parents. The great-great-grandchildren of the Issei are known as the *Gosei,* literally "fifth generation," and refer to the children of Yonsei parents.

While some persons' age and situation might informally reassign them to a group to which they do not belong by virtue of geographical or generational criteria, the *idea* of the groups remains intact as a working conception of social reality. Thus, a young Japanese American friend who enjoys the social status of a Nisei jokingly refers to himself as an Issei since he was born of Nisei parents during their temporary residence in Japan. Older Nisei whose social and personal characteristics are similar to those of Issei are sometimes treated as if they are the latter.[27] Sansei age peers of Nisei are treated as the latter if they behave accordingly. But Nisei who appear to their fellow Nisei as "too Japanesy" are sometimes associated in the minds of their more Americanized friends with Kibei, while those who are "too American" are associated with Sansei. Finally, the offspring of geogenerationally mixed parentage, e.g., Issei-Nisei, Nisei-Sansei, Nisei-Yonsei, etc., and of racially mixed parentage are not easily classifiable. In practice they tend to demonstrate the sociological rule that "status is as status does;" that is, they enjoy the classification which social relations and personal behavior assign to them and which they assign to themselves.[28]

In terms of the temporal categories with which we began this discussion, the Japanese in America lay great emphasis on contemporaries. Their ideas about predecessors and successors are vague and diffuse, or in the case of consociates, de-emphasized and deprecated.

This paper will examine the Nisei's perspective. While all individuals live through an age-demarcated life cycle with rites of passage to mark birth, marriage, death, and certain ceremonies, for the Nisei it is the common life-time of the whole generational group that circumscribes social and personal orientations. The generational group has a life cycle of its own internally indicated by its appropriate behavior patterns and externally bounded by the temporal duration of the whole group.

The Nisei know the world of their predecessors through whatever their parents have told them about old Japan and what they have learned in afternoon language schools, college history courses, and Japanese movies. Nisei parents are concerned about their own children in particular and the Sansei and Yonsei successor generations in general, partly in terms of achievement and advancement; but more significantly, they are worried about the character of future generations. Sansei and Yonsei do not exhibit Nisei character, and Nisei regard this fact as both inevitable and unfortunate.

However, it is as contemporaries and with contemporaries that Nisei feel both pride and apprehension. The basic conception of the Nisei phenomenon depends ultimately on the objective existence of their own generational group. The Nisei geogenerational group inhabits time and space between that of the Issei and the Sansei. The Japanese community in general and the Nisei group in particular provide a Nisei with emotional security and a haven from the turbulence and unpredictable elements of the outer world.[29]

But the Nisei group is threatened by both centripetal and centrifugal forces, by individual withdrawal and acculturative transcendence.[30] If the collective identity were dissolved by atomized individuals, dyadic relationships, or small cliques, then Nisei would lose both its objective existence and its subjective meaning. If individuals transcend the generational group by moving out into the world of their non-Japanese contemporaries, by "validating their acculturation,"[31] then too both the objective and subjective senses of Nisei identity would lose their compelling force.

Thus, Nisei must worry about the risks of intimate association in two directions. Inwardly, the close contacts in the Japanese community allow for intimate association below the level and hence outside of the generational group; outwardly, the breakdown of prejudice and discrimination threatens to seduce the Nisei individual away from the confines of his racial group.[32] Hence, Nisei social and interpersonal relations are governed by a permanent interest in maintaining an appropriate social distance, so that individuals do not escape into integration or withdraw from group solidarity.

Nisei do not speak of their social and personal life in this fashion. Rather, they exhibit in numerous ways a quiet but deep and pervasive pride in their Nisei identity. This pride is not rooted in their material success, as it might be among other ethnic groups in America, but instead in their character. Nisei believe that they combine in themselves a perfect balance of Japanese and American traits. They are not "too Japanese," as are the Issei by definition and the Kibei by virtue of imposed culture and education; they are not "too American," as are their white American contemporaries and the Sansei. Nisei character at its best is exhibited in cathectic management, by control over and suppression of spontaneity, emotionalism, and inappropriate expressiveness. It is this character itself, in which the Nisei take so much pride, through which the Nisei group maintains its objective existence. It is this character which operates to orient behavior in such a manner that contemporaries are not converted to consociates, that fellow men are not brought into too close an intimate circle.

For the Nisei to preserve the objective identity of their own generational group, to deemphasize biological aging in favor of preserving the single moment-to-moment simultaneity of the generational group, it is necessary to remove interpersonal relations from the intimate or consociate level and push them back toward the formal or contemporary plane. In behalf of this objective, the Nisei have a built-in aid, Japanese culture, especially as it had developed by the late Meiji-early Taisho eras, when the bulk of Issei came to America. Although this culture had its origins in an environment far different from that which the Nisei experienced, it served the goal of anonymization of persons and immobilization of individual time through its emphasis on etiquette, ceremony, and rigid status deference.

The emphasis on etiquette in Japanese culture hardly needs further demonstration here.[33] The Japanese language itself is one of social forms, indicative politeness, and status identifiers.[34] Moreover, the Japanese language is indirect, permitting the removal of the subject (speaker) in a sentence from direct relation to the predicate, and utilizing stylistic circumlocutions so that the intended object of the particular speech is reached by a circular rather than a linear route.[35] The net result of these forms is that individuals are held at arm's length, so that potential consociates remain contemporaries—quasi-strangers, quasi-friends.

The Issei were able to transmit the basic ideas of this culture to their offspring, but it was manifested in an American idiom. Thus, Japanese etiquette appeared in the form of a sometimes Victorian politeness. Although the bow, whose rigid rules the Japanese imposed upon themselves while exempting all foreigners,[36] did not survive the generational passage except in a limited vestigial form,[37] other forms, especially verbal ones, could be translated into English. Japanese Americans are thus likely to pay careful attention to titles, to employ the terms of genteel propriety, to avoid obscenity, and to use the passive voice.[38] In all this the Nisei succeed simultaneously in keeping associations under management and in keeping emotions under control.

The primary concern of a Nisei male is the economical management and control of his emotions. To him the ideal human state is that of inward quiescence and an outward appearance of emotional equanimity. Any emotional expression that is boisterous, passionate, fearful, vain, or shows excessive embarrassment is distasteful and shameful.

"Etiquette," as Clifford Geertz has pointed out in his study of Java, provides its user "with a set of rigidly formal ways of doing things which conceals his real feelings from others. In addition it so regularizes behavior, his own and that of others, as to make it unlikely to provide unpleasant surprises."[39] The manner in which Nisei employ tonal control, euphemisms, and circumlocutions in speaking English illustrates the role of etiquette in language.

Although English-speaking Europeans and most native-born Americans employ tonal change for emphasis and object indication, the Nisei strive for a flatness of tone and an equality of meter in their speech. Individuals unfamiliar with this style, as are a great many white Americans, find it difficult to distinguish the important from the insignificant items in any verbal encounter. It provides the Nisei a continuous demonstration to themselves and others who understand the proper state of emotional equanimity; the uninitiated "foreigner" perceives the Nisei as a blank slate. Since no one believes that a fellow human is in fact a blank slate, the Nisei's tone creates a doubt about what is really being said and in some instances a suspicion of ulterior motives.[40]

Nisei employ euphemisms whenever the simpler and more direct form might indicate a state of emotional involvement or evoke an undesirable emotional response from others. When there is no English euphemism or the use of one is so awkward it could be embarrassing, a Japanese term may be employed. This is especially the case in using nouns to designate racial or ethnic groups. Nisei rarely say "white man," "Negro," "Chinese" or "Jew" in their everyday speech. Nisei understand that race is a touchy subject in America with ambiguous meanings and ambivalent feelings deeply embedded in the value structure. To avoid possible emotional entanglements Nisei substitute terms derived from Japanese. This is the case despite the fact that Nisei tend not to speak Japanese to their peers. They replace "white man," with the term "Caucasian" on occasion, but they are likely to use *hakujin,* literally "white man," or the pejorative *keto* (literally a "hairy person" but freely translated as "barbarian"). The Nisei combine a culturally derived mild antipathy to blackness[41] with some American Negrophobia but they rarely employ such vulgar terms as "nigger," "coon," "jigaboo" and "black boy." Rather, for "Negro" they use the denotatively pejorative *kuron-bo,* literally "black boy," usually in a neutral and unpejorative sense, at least on the conscious level. The Nisei are also ambivalent toward the "Chinese" and they commonly use the mildly pejorative Hawaiian term, *pakē.*

The terminology used for "Jew" is especially interesting and provides an unusual example of linguistic transmogrification. Anti-Semitism was almost unknown in Japan at the time the Issei came to America, and neither they nor their offspring readily adapted to this essentially European prejudice.[42] However, while growing up, Nisei learned of the special attitude some Americans held toward Jews, and in their own inimitable way invented a term which expresses the anti-Jewish stereotype without using such emotion-laden English terms as "kike." Nisei employ the "Japanese" neologism *ku-ichi* to express the idea of the Jewish stereotype, i.e.; stinginess, miserliness, a "cheapskate." The etymology of *ku-ichi* combines the Japanese numbers "ku," meaning nine, and "ichi," meaning one. Nine plus one is ten, and the Japanese term for ten is "ju," the homonym for the English word "Jew." This Nisei linguistic innovation is not used or widely known in Japan. The denotative word for Jew in Japan is *yudaya-jin.*[43] Nisei do not apply *ku-ichi* exclusively to Jews, but rather to fellow Nisei or to anyone who openly displays an attitude of cheapness or stinginess.

Circumlocutions and indirect speech are regular features of Nisei conversations, serving to mute one's own feelings and prevent the eruption of other's. In the Chicago researches employing the Rorschach test Nisei males resorted to a significant amount of "confabulatory" responses when faced with a perplexing or emotionally troubling perception.[44] Indirect speech is a regular feature of conversations in Japan and is matched there by the circular placing of household furniture and the uses of open space in streets and homes.[45] It also affects the quality of translations from Japanese to another language.[46] Among Nisei English is preferred, except when propriety dictates otherwise,[47] and circumlocution and indirections are easy to develop. Abstract nouns, noncommittal statements and inferential hints at essential meanings are regular features.

Indirection is also effected by the use of go-betweens to mediate delicate matters. Anthropologists have emphasized the role of the marriage-arranger *(nakodo* or *baishakunin)* in traditional Japan, and some Nisei are prevailed upon to employ a *baishakunin* to ceremonialize an engagement after it has been effected in the American pattern.[48] Intermediaries may also be employed to inform one friend that another wishes to borrow money from him and to question his willingness to lend it. In this manner the would-be borrower is prevented from having to go through a direct face-losing refusal, and the creditor is saved from the mutually embarrassing situation that would arise if he had to refuse his friend the money. Intermediaries are also employed occasionally to warn individuals of impending invitations to social affairs and to inform someone quietly that a surprise party is planned for him. In the former case the affective linkage hinted at by the extension of an invitation is blunted, the embarrassment of a refusal to attend is reduced, and the invitee is given an opportunity to prepare himself for the receipt of the formal invitation. In the latter case the "surprise" will not provoke an excessive emotional display.

In Japan there is a high tolerance for lengthy monologues and a polite indifference to complete comprehension.[49] The Nisei also do not immediately approach the main point of a conversation. Moreover, as mentioned earlier, the monotonal flatness of affect confuses those who are accustomed to tonal cues which indicate that what is being said now is more important than what has preceded or will follow. Indeed, conversations among Nisei almost always are an information game between persons who maintain decorum by seemingly mystifying one another.[50] It is the duty of the listener to ascertain the important point from the context and his knowledge of the speaker.

Violations of this tacit ritual speech relationship occur fairly often, sometimes among Nisei themselves, but more often in Nisei's encounters with Caucasians, Sansei, and other *gaijin* (foreigners). Exasperation with the apparent pointlessness, frustration with vain attempts to gauge the meaning of sequential utterances, and the desire to reach a conclusion often lead non-Nisei to ask a pointed question directed at the heart of the matter. Nisei are troubled by direct questions; they may refuse to answer, change the subject, or subtly redirect the conversation back to its concentric form. The aim of correct conversation is to maintain the appropriate ritual and the calm state of speaker and audience. Potentially affective subjects are buried beneath a verbal avalanche of trivia, and, in idealized conversations they are never brought to the surface at all; instead they are silently apprehended by the listener.

The emphasis on calmness and composure lends itself to unstated but widely held norms of conversational propriety appropriate to different social occasions. Since it is at informal social occasions, seemingly just the ones for intimacy and spontaneity, that people are vulnerable to conversion from contemporaries to consociates, it is precisely such occasions that require careful monitoring for excessive affect.[51]

Thus, Nisei "rules" for social gatherings include 1) emphasis on "democratic participation" in speech; i.e., no one should speak too long or too much and everyone should have an opportunity to speak; 2) circulation; i.e., small clusters of conversationalists are permissible but these should regularly break up and reform with new elements; lengthy dyadic conversations among large gatherings are discouraged; 3) the content of conversations should be restricted to trivial matters that do not reflect directly on either the speaker's or listener's inner life. The most fruitful items for conversation are sports, stocks and bonds, and technical subjects, for all of these can be kept outside the inner domain of the individual person, and every speaker can be fairly confident that he is not likely to be importuned or embarrassed.[52]

Further exemplification of Nisei emotional management is seen in their emphasis on form over function in their handling of erotic matters which are potentially discomfiting. Two examples, wedding receptions and pornographic movies, illustrate their mode of mitigation and neutralization of the erotic. One rural custom of Japan which survives among Nisei is the employment of a master of ceremonies at wedding receptions. Originally this role was usually enacted by the *baishaku-nin*,[53] but among Nisei a good friend of the groom is often requested to assume this post. At the banquet or reception following the wedding, the master of ceremonies formally introduces the bride and groom and their families to the assembled company, presents toasts to the newly-wed couple, calls people out of the audience to perform as comedians, storytellers, or singers, and tells jokes and droll anecdotes about the groom. In the rural prefectures of traditional Japan, this part of the reception was often accompanied by ribald jokes and risque stories.[54] When Issei participate in such a reception they sometimes introduce humorous obscenities into them. However, Nisei usually instruct their appointed master of ceremonies to "keep it clean" and to refrain from drolleries which would embarrass bride, groom, or company.

Watching pornographic films is not governed by ubiquitous norms.[55] When Nisei watch such films two kinds of responses are prevalent. On the one hand, jibes and catcalls will tease one or another of the assembled company about his excessive interest in the films, alleged similarities or dissimilarities in his behavior and that depicted on the screen, or his remarkable quietness in the presence of an obviously stimulating event. On the other hand, it sometimes happens that a Nisei will verbally transform the meaning of the activities on the screen, emphasizing their form irrespective of content. Thus, the nude bodies copulating on the movie screen are treated in terms of their anatomy, aesthetic quality, or gymnastic innovations.

Emphasis on form over content is not only a protective device against possible emotional disturbance in the presence of the erotic but also a generally utilized mechanism in the presence of anticipated or actual performance failure. Thus, Nisei golfers and bowlers who are performing poorly or who believe they will do so may justify their bad scores by pointing out that they are working on their stance, body form, or follow-through. Since it is widely accepted that form and content are analytically separable but related aspects of a variety of activities, the claim to be emphasizing the former rather than the latter is an acceptable account.[56] Moreover, it prevents any effective referral of the poor scores to the inner or actual state of the performer. Thus, inner equanimity may be maintained and outer calmness may be exhibited even in the presence of apparently contradictory evidence.

The ideal Nisei has mastered the art of personal control and this requires management of body, mind, and feelings.[57] If he is properly under control his outward appearance is that of a calm, collected, blasé sophisticate.[58] The ideal state is rarely reached in fact, but Nisei employ mechanisms of impression management and mutual monitoring to keep any appearance which approximates the ideal from being damaged too much by emotional breakdowns. These mechanisms include face controls, dissimulation, and avoidance.

The face, as Simmel observed long ago,[59] is the most significant communicator of the inner man. This is especially true of facial features; eyes, nostrils, mouth, and color.[60] To a Nisei the face is the most vulnerable object in any interpersonal encounter. An uncontrolled expression met by the searching gaze of another may lock two people into a consociative relationship from which extrication would be both difficult and embarrassing. Nisei tend to "set" their faces at the expressionless level or at least to strive after that effect. In America this can be more easily achieved because of the stereotypical interpretation of Japanese faces, and because the epicanthic eye fold and smooth skin make face "readings" difficult. Some Nisei, however, are disturbed over their vulnerability to facial disclosure; they avoid facing others for any length of time or they erect barriers to shield them from involvement with another's gaze.[61] Newspapers and magazines are used for scanning during conversation, and, although too close attention to them might be considered rude, their deft employment serves to reduce eye contact. Finally, the Nisei's common concern over face management facilitates the mutual avoidance of staring and fixed gazes, and the tendency to avert one's eyes.

Dissimulation is a regular feature of everyday life among Nisei. Its most elementary form is the self-imposed limitation on disclosure. Nisei tend not to volunteer any more information about themselves than they have to. To a listener the Nisei's statements about himself appear as a series of incomplete episodes separated by voids which will not be filled in with events or information unless it is unavoidable. Beyond silence the half-truth or little white lie is used to bridge the gap between information requested and personhood protected. Thus, the Nisei sometimes will not talk about an important event, or he will casually dismiss it with denials or partial admissions, suggesting by style and tone that it was not important at all. Direct questions are usually answered with vague or mildly deceptive replies.[62]

Still another element of dissimulation is the concealment of feelings, opinions, or activities, especially in the presence of employers, colleagues, and guests. As Nisei have been promoted into middle-management and other decision-making posts, their colleagues and superiors are sometimes astonished at their silence during conferences and executive meetings. And, as with the Javanese practice of *etok-etok,* (pretense),[63] the Nisei do not feel a need to justify omissions, white lies, or evasions; rather the burden is on the listener to demonstrate why such tact should not be employed.[64]

Nisei attempt to avoid persons and situations that are likely to evoke embarrassment, personal disorganization, and loss of self-control. When they undertake a new line of endeavor, especially if it requires learning a new skill or taking a risk, it is usually entered into in secret or with people whom the Nisei does not know well or wish to know. When the new task has been mastered, or when risk is evaluated as worthwhile, or the endeavor has already begun, the Nisei will inform his close associates in a casual manner that he thinks he might be about to undertake the line of action in question. Fellow Nisei will understand that the statement is absolute, not probablistic, and they will understand that all preparations, rehearsals, and calculations have already been made. If they later see the subject perform the new skill, they remain silent, aware that it is an exhibition of a perfected ability.

Persons who demand a display of interpersonal commitment or violate norms of emotional propriety are a threat to the cathectic equanimity of a Nisei. A concept usually employed with respect to Japanese child-rearing practices is relevant here.[65]

Japanese speak of *amaeru,* an intransitive verb which means "to depend and presume upon another's benevolence." Children and adults suffer from too much *amae,* and their behavior toward those to whom they express affection is often regarded as overly demanding and excessive. Persons suffering from too much *amae* feel themselves to be *kodawaru,* i.e., inwardly disturbed over personal relationships. A recognition of one's own feeling of *kodawari* leads to *sumanai,* or guilt over the failure to do as one should. Behind many Japanese people's feeling of *sumanai,* as Professor Doi has pointed out, lies "much hidden aggression engendered by frustration of their wish to *amaeru."*[66] Nisei do not employ this terminology generally, but several studies have pointed to a complex of dependency needs and consequent personal difficulties in Nisei individuals which have their roots in the wish to be loved, and the guilt over this wish or the shame over its expression.[67]

The entire complex of *amae-kodawari-sumanai* is rarely admitted among Nisei to be a personal problem; rather, it is most frequently perceived to be a problem in someone else's interpersonal relations. When a Nisei recognizes a close associate's excessive *amae* toward him, he may become upset, retreat further behind a facade of etiquette, and attempt to establish a greater social distance. Or he might even request that a third party tactfully explain the problem to the offending person and urge him to be less demanding and not display excessive *amae.* Alternately the offending party may be gently but firmly teased until he realizes that he has overstepped the bounds of propriety. Another tactic is to ensure that contacts with the offending party take place in the presence of other friends, so that the offender's excessive affection will be diffused among the whole body of friends rather than centered on just one person.[68]

The fundamental source of Nisei character is the samurai ethic which developed from the Tokugawa through the Meiji eras. This ethic is expressed in the brilliant epic films made in Japan to celebrate the feats and character of warriors of that period.[69] At one time shown in basements and church social halls in *Nihonmachi* (the Japanese quarter of American cities), these movies are now known to many non-Japanese Americans because of their general popularity and exhibition at public theaters. *Chambara* (samurai) stories always emphasize the stoic character of the solitary and often tragic warrior. Though beset on every side by enemies, political misfortunes, and natural disasters, he nevertheless retains an outward appearance suggesting inner psychic strength and emotional equanimity.[70] Such characters, poignantly portrayed on the screen in recent years by such actors as Toshiro Mifune and Tatsuya Nakadai, serve as ideal character models and reminders of the appropriate presentation of self.

The patterns of hierarchical society, rigid formalism, etiquette, and shame were routinized features of the early life of the Issei, who grew up in a time of great technological and political but little ethical or interpersonal change in Japan.[71] The modernization of Japan begun in the Tokugawa period was achieved, not by overturning the old cultural order, but rather by adapting Western industrial, educational, and military forms to the framework of that order. "Within this general context," writes Reinhard Bendix, "the samurai were transformed from an estate of independent, landed, and self-equipped warriors into one of urbanized, aristocratic retainers, whose privileged social and economic position was universally acknowledged. They remained attached to their tradition of ceremonious conduct, intense pride of rank and the cultivation of physical prowess."[72]

Few Issei were of samurai rank,[73] but in the 200 years before emigration began a complex melding process helped to "nationalize" the samurai ethic. First, after 1601 many samurai became displaced *ronin* (masterless warriors), obliged to sell their services to other lords, to cities as policemen or magistrates, even to commoners on occasion. As a last resort short of suicide they gave up official samurai status entirely and became merchants.[74] All of these acts caused a certain filtering of the samurai ethic through the social order.

Second, the educational system founded in the Tokugawa period, and universalized in the sixth year of the Meiji era (1873) admitted increasing numbers of commoners to the schools, thus affording them direct access to samurai indoctrination.[75] The educational system fostered the study of classics and later more technical subjects, and more important, it directed major attention to the development of virtue, humble modesty before superiors, self-control, and etiquette.[76]

Third, samurai status itself was muddied by the practice, begun after 1700, of selling commoners the right to wear a sword and bear a surname (i.e., the status symbols of samurai).[77] Finally, a significant portion of America's Issei came from prefectures in southeastern, central, and western Japan in which the democratization of ethical education was well advanced at the time of emigration.[78]

In addition to the samurai ethic, elements of the rural farmer's outlook helped forge the child-rearing orientation of the Issei. The *ie* system, by which Japanese farmers represented both the contemporary physical house and the permanent family household, operated through a notion of preservation and continuity to forestall the development of individualism.[79] In Japan's rural villages the *honke-bunke* (stem-branch family system) allowed nuclear families (i.e., father, mother, and children) to split off from one another in a partial sense, so that nothing like the extended Chinese clan system developed,[80] but atomization below the *ie,* or household, level was strongly discouraged. Village people spoke of the *iegara* or *kakaku,* i.e., the reputation or standing of a family, rather than the *hitogara* or *jinkaku,* the personality or social standing of individuals.

The *ie* "was also far more important than the individuals who at any one time composed it, and hence, if 'for the sake of the *ie*' the personal wishes and desires of those individuals had to be ignored or sacrificed, this was looked on as only natural."[81] The *ie* "required its members each to keep their proper place under the authoritarian direction of the househead, resigning themselves to the suppression of personal desires unbecoming to their position. Thus, order within the *ie* was preserved and its harmony guaranteed—a harmony not of liberated cheerfulness, but of smouldering reserve and the frustration of still incompletely repressed desires."[82]

In America Issei men were often married by proxy to women whom they had only seen in pictures *(shashin kekkon)* and their wives were sometimes quite a bit younger than they were.[83] The Issei applied the principles of late Tokugawa-early Meiji child rearing to their Nisei offspring. In certain respects child rearing was harsher than in Japan. There were no bath houses and geishas to serve as outlets for the Nisei who were thus restrained from physical expression and open sensuality —and the Nisei did not have indulgent grandmothers to assuage the harshness of parental authority.[84]

Issei-Nisei families rarely resort to physical punishments. The use of ridicule and teasing is much more likely.[85] Several reports on Japanese child rearing have emphasized the role of ridicule.[86] A common theme is that boys who are noisy, emotionally upset, or otherwise obstreperous are teased for "behaving like a little girl." Japanese biographies frequently express the idea that a young man should be ashamed of emotional expressions lest they remind him of behavior associated with women.[87] Nisei boys were also reprimanded by their parents for acting like little girls.[88] In addition they were reminded that they were Japanese and therefore obligated to avoid being *arai* (crude); to speak good Japanese and not *zuzu ben* (the dialect characteristic of northern Japan)[89]; and to avoid any association with or even mention of *Eta* (Japan's pariah caste, some of whose members had unobtrusively settled in Florin, California and a few other places).[90]

Moreover, emphasis was placed on individual superiority, achievement, and education as criteria for both individual and group maturity.[91] Thus, Nisei children were not invited to discuss family matters at the dinner table but rather prevented from participating until their age and achievement demonstrated their worth. Nisei children and adolescents were admonished with the statement *Nisei wa mada tsumaranai;* that is the Nisei generation was still worthless. The Nisei were treated as immature but developing children. Manhood was not merely coming of age; it was, more importantly, demonstrated by independent status achieved through steadfastness, determination, and single-minded purposefulness. Self-control was central to the demonstration of maturity among growing Nisei. Although independence and real achievement could not be actually demonstrated until adulthood, emotional management was always worthy of exhibition and often tested for its own sake. Issei tended to be oriented toward their children in terms of the latter's position in the birth order and their sex.[92] A line of direct authority extended down from the father through the mother to the first-born, second-born, and so on. A line of obligation extended upward from the youngest to the eldest. The authority system was frequently tested by elder brothers who harshly rebuked younger brothers, sometimes for no apparent reason. Younger brothers learned that if they could take these rebukes with outwardly calm detachment they would ultimately be rewarded with a recognition of their maturity. First-born sons received similar treatment from their fathers, and daughters sometimes found that they had to live up to both the precepts of manhood maturity and womanliness.[93] Brothers who threw tantrums or gave way to violent emotional expression were regarded as immature and were teased and advised until they became conformative and quiescent.

In the case of the Nisei, teasing and ridicule are characteristic not only of parent-child discipline but also of intra-group relations. They function to monitor behavior. Among Nisei, peer groups begin to share authority over the individual with parents with the onset of adolescence, and they begin to supersede parental authority, though not parental respect, in late adolescence and early young manhood. Persons who have been intimately associated with adolescent second-generation Japanese groups can testify to the remarkable atmosphere and social effect of ridicule among Nisei teenagers. A veritable barrage of "cuts," "digs," "put-downs," and embarrassing stories are the stuff of their verbal life. Nisei youth, like their Japanese forebears across the sea, have a facility and interest in the organization of clubs, cliques, and gangs.[94] These associations are the units through which Nisei character is manifested, sustained, and reinforced.

Nisei teasing is not randomly directed. Targets for verbal cuts are those fellow Nisei and other close friends who exhibit outward signs of tension, embarrassment, excessive emotional display, or boisterousness. Persons who frequently blush, tremble, give way to tears, or raise their voice in anger or for emphasis are the recipients of jibes and cajolery designed to bring them back into line. Many Nisei are self-consciously aware of the didactic purpose of this teasing, and have expressed their heartfelt gratefulness for it.

In addition to its teaching and control functions, two other rules appear to govern Nisei teasing. First, the status position of any particular Nisei vis à vis his fellow Nisei may render him either ineligible or preferable for teasing. As Takagi and others have noted,[95] there are several dimensions of Nisei life in which prefectural background, rural-urban origins, or intra-group status have consequences for social behavior. One of these dimensions is the joking relationship, so that there is a tendency for Nisei whose parents are from peasant and poor prefectures to avoid teasing those whose parents are from urban and higher socio-economic areas. Similarly, Nisei from rural parts of California tend to be somewhat awed by those from San Francisco or Los Angeles; and clique leaders seem to be less eligible for cuts than ordinary members.

These Nisei of inferior status are the butt of jokes which relate offensive behavior and gauche ways to poor, peasant, and rural origins. Thus, Nisei whose parents came from Shiga or Kagoshima, or from Okinawa and Hokkaido are often teased mercilessly about their rustic background, or are perceived to be incapable of realizing the Nisei characterological ideal. The ridicule and humor directed at Nisei from rural America by their urban compatriots is more mild in form but no less felt. Informal avoidance and segregation sometimes is used to set boundaries between Nisei of different status groups and to prevent confrontations that would be mutually embarrassing.

Nisei ridicule and joking steers a careful course between ineffectiveness and associative break-up. Jokes and cuts which are too mild, too obscure, usually misunderstood, or always mitigated by apologies and explanations frustrate the intended objective and the offending party is not brought to heel. On the other hand if the jokes are too pointed, if they cut to the very heart of a person and leave him no room for maneuver or retreat, then the offending party may withdraw from the group in unredeeming shame or anger and lose its benefits and protections. To indicate that a person has gone too far in his teasing, a Nisei target may warn him of his offense by directing a telling remark at a third party in earshot of the two. Thus, watching two youthful Nisei friends of mine escalate their reciprocal cuts, I became the third party in such a situation. The offended party turned to me and said, "Man, he's a chilly dude, isn't he?" The warned person recognized the rebuke and deescalated his humorous assaults on the other, and so the appropriate relationship, not too close, not too distant, was maintained.

The characterological ideal of any Nisei is best realized when others do not know his emotional state. To achieve this he must, as one Nisei put it to me, build a wall around his emotions so that others cannot see what they are. Their authoritarian upbringing and the samurai code of stoicism and endurance helped them to construct this social and psychic edifice. The functions of this wall have been described by Geertz in his study of Java, where he found an identical ideal:

> If one can calm one's most inward feelings ... one can build a wall around them; one will be able both to conceal them from others and to protect them from outside disturbance. The refinement of inner feeling has thus two aspects: the direct internal attempt to control one's emotions ...; and, secondly, an external attempt to build a [wall] around them that will protect them. On the one hand, one engages in inward discipline, and on the other in an outward defense.[96]

The character displayed or aimed at by Nisei in everyday life is not unfamiliar to other Americans. Indeed, while at one time it was thought to be the peculiar possession of aristocrats, Orientals, and urbanites, today mature industrial societies seem to require it of everyone.[97] Ordinary men describe it by such adjectives as "blasé," "sophisticated," and, in more recent times, "cool." Other related terms describing aspects of this character are "self-possessed," "detached," "aloof," "sang-froid" and "savoir-faire." What is referred to is the "capacity to execute physical acts, including conversation, in a concerted, smooth, self-controlled fashion in risky situations, or to maintain affective detachment during the course of encounters involving considerable emotion."[98] For the Nisei this means, ideally, combining courage, that is, willingness to proceed on an anticipated dangerous course of action without any manifestation of fearfulness; gameness, that is, sticking to a line of action and expending energy on it despite set-backs, injury, fatigue, and even impending failure *(Yamato damashii)*;[99] and integrity, that is, resisting temptations which would reduce the actor's moral stance. Finally, Nisei character places its greatest emphasis on composure, including all its ramifications of physical and mental poise during any act, calmness in the face of disruptions and embarrassing situations, presence of mind and the avoidance of "blocking" under pressure, emotional control during sudden changes of situation, and stage confidence during performances before audiences.[100]

In fact, Nisei find it difficult to live up to this ideal. However, there are strategies and tactics whereby its appearance can be generated and its failures avoided or hidden. Thus, courage is balanced by a realistic appraisal of risks and opportunities. Studies of Nisei estimates of first salaries, for example, show that they almost always guessed the salary to the nearest dollar,[101] suggesting, perhaps, a face-saving procedure to prevent rejection of an incorrect estimate of self-worth. Gameness is partially mitigated by choosing lines of action, such as jobs, sports, and games, in which one has secretly tested one's ability. Violations of absolute integrity are neutralized by the practice of situation ethics and the invocation of a layman's version of the international legal principle *rebus sic stantibus* ("things continuing thus"). Composure is guarded by self-discipline, protected by barriers and involvement shields, and tested and supported by teasing and ridicule. Finally, disasters and misfortunes, either personal or collective, may be accepted with equanimity by assigning them to the *shikataga nai* category or fate.[102]

The everyday practice of the Nisei way of life has certain consequences which reflect its essential nature and feed back to Nisei as sources of pride or problems. These consequences include perception and projection, communication confusion, stage fright, and real and imagined illnesses.

The everyday discussions between Nisei would impress any non-Nisei listener by their pointed perceptions and shrewd observations of others. These perceptions and observations are never uttered in the presence of the party under discussion. Nisei pay surprisingly keen attention to the minute details of interpersonal situations, place brackets around particular sets of events, and interpret words and gestures in light of the general theory of Nisei character. Most analyses of fellow Nisei concentrate on the degree to which they fail to carry off an appropriate presentation of self and attribute any failings to some inner-lying maladaptation or maladjustment. Parlor Freudianism is quite common in these analyses, and one Nisei may speak of another's essential inability to mask his inferiority complex, fear of failure, or feelings of inadequacy.

It is my impression that these perceptions are in fact projections. Nisei tend to function as one another's mirror images, showing up these defects in each other's character. This is possible because the wall which Nisei have built to prevent others from seeing their own emotions is actually a set of personal blinders which keep the individual from introspection. To put it another way, the Nisei have attempted to separate personal feeling from particular action and in doing so have alienated their emotional from their behaving selves.[103] This alienation gives Nisei a peculiar advantage of self-detachment and an angular vision of their fellow men not shared by those not so detached from self. But the angle of perceptive advantage, reinforced by the similarity of life styles among Nisei, results, as I see it, in the perceiver imputing to others his own partly recognized failings. Thus, the Nisei's common life and general self-alienation permit projections and perceptions to coincide without the latter necessarily being seen as having derived from the former.

Few Nisei ever feel they have realized the ideal of Nisei character. Moreover, in trying to live up to it, many Nisei find they are confused or confuse others. These confusions occur over mutual misreadings of intentions or meanings, misunderstandings of jokes and ridicule, and problems arising out of the episodic nature of Nisei life. Because tonal cues are not used as indicators of significance, Nisei sometimes fail to grasp the relevant item in a conversation; more often their non-Nisei colleagues or friends miss the important point and fail to act appropriately. Since Nisei often take it for granted that those with whom they converse will be able to separate trivia from the significant, they are frustrated and exasperated when this fails to happen.[104]

The role of jokes and ridicule in Nisei social control has already been mentioned. Despite their importance, or perhaps because of it, cuts and digs create problems. In discussing the problem of what a humorous jibe at another *really* means, a Nisei friend and I distinguished three kinds of barbs: 1) those that are given solely in fun, i.e., pure humor having neither intent nor consequences beyond the ensuing laughter; 2) those that are didactic, i.e., having as their objective the redirection of another's behavior so that it is no longer embarrassing or inept; and 3) those that are intentionally destructive, having as their object another's degradation.

Nisei tend to disbelieve that many jokes can have no object at all, preferring instead to believe that some intent must be behind the ostensibly humorous utterance. However, they experience difficulty in ascertaining whether a jibe is didactic or destructive, because in fact the line between them is difficult to draw. Witty repartee is a well-developed and highly prized art among Nisei, but precisely because skill at it is differentially distributed, no Nisei can feel entirely comfortable about it. Beyond adolescence, Nisei occasionally confess discomfiture about being permanently locked into a system of competitive relations with fellow Nisei. Social visits are occasions for the reciprocal giving and receiving of humorous remarks calling attention to invidious distinctions in such matters as birth, sex, and growth of children, richness and style of furniture, occupational advancement, and skill at leisure time activities. Indeed, a young Nisei told me that one reason Nisei oppose the continuation of a Japanese residential ghetto is that they "just know" that they would be constantly "looking in each other's windows."

Nisei encounters with friends and colleagues tend to be episodic rather than developmental. Among non-Nisei Americans a sequence of social encounters usually proceeds upon the assumption that each new encounter will begin at the emotional level or feeling-state reached at the end of the last meeting. Among Nisei, however, there is a limit in expressed feeling-states that is quickly reached and may not be deepened without loss of inner equanimity or outer poise. Hence, Nisei tend to treat each encounter almost as if the participants were meeting for the first time. This permits the limited range of feeling-states to be reached all over again each time but not transcended. For those content with a permanently established line beyond which interpersonal relations may not go, this pattern may go unnoticed. However, those who expect that each new encounter will bring increased depth, or those who expect to open any second encounter with a Nisei with a reciprocated expression of the warmth typical of Occidental friendships, may be startled or exasperated by an apparent coldness of response. Episodic encounters function to keep potentially consociative relationships at the contemporaneous level, and thus, ultimately, to protect the integrity of the Nisei group.

Unlike many middle-class Occidentals in America, Nisei are more conscious of being on display, so to speak, before a hypercritical audience:

> A simile is useful in pointing up the similarities and differences between Japanese-American and white middle-class achievement orientations: the ultimate destinations or goals of individuals in the two groups tend to be very similar; but Japanese-Americans go toward these destinations along straight narrow streets lined with crowds of people who observe their every step, while middle-class persons go toward the same destinations along wider streets having more room for maneuvering, and lined only with small groups of people who, while watching them, do not observe their every movement.[105]

People who believe that their every move is under scrutiny are liable to suffer from stage fright.[106] In the case of Nisei this would appear to be an inevitable consequence of their need to exhibit an appearance of poise and equanimity in the face of a constantly intrusive and challenging world. Moreover, for the Nisei the exhibition of stage fright is itself a flaw in character management and must be avoided if the illusion of composure is to be maintained. Nisei fear that an encounter will be spoiled by a collapse of formality and a revelation of the actual personality hidden behind the facade of etiquette. Nevertheless, Nisei support the belief system that generates this fear by observing in quite ordinary conversations, and insisting in their reprimands given to fellow Nisei, that the entire community is watching them, and that therefore they must behave with circumspection.[107]

Sometimes ceremony and etiquette collapse and Nisei find themselves locked in the mutually embarrassing relationship of consociates. More often one person in an encounter is unable to sustain appropriate emotional equipoise. When this occurs the other people present will try to repair the psychic bridge which has kept them all at the proper social distance from one another by studied non-observation of the other's embarrassment, or by averting their eyes from the other's discomfiture in order to allow him time to repair his social front. They also may give a warm but unmistakably triumphant grin signalling simultaneously a victory in the ever-played game of social testing and also the social reinstatement of the losing player. For Nisei, social life is a contest something like tennis: a single faux-pas is a game victory; an evening full of them may be a set, but it takes a whole lifetime to play out the match.

Many observers of character in Japan have noted hypochondria among the Japanese,[108] and at least one observer has stated that it indicates a remarkably compulsive personality.[109] The occurrence and extent to which hypochondria is a feature of Nisei life is questionable and for a sociologist the question is difficult, if not impossible, to answer.[110] But disease or its outward signs threaten the equanimity cherished by Nisei. On the other hand, admission that one has a disease is also potentially damaging. In traditional Japan a familial history of disease was sufficient reason to cancel a marriage, and it was the task of the *nakodo* to discover if such a history existed.[111] Shame of illness is found among Nisei and sometimes occurs with any involuntary loss of control as in the case of vomiting or intoxication. A Nisei is vulnerable to attacks from his body, which gives him something of the sociological status of the stranger as conceived by Simmel:[112] it is ever with him but mysterious, and not quite subject to perfect control.

It is my impression that the psychosomatic diseases—ulcers, colitis, psoriasis, and falling hair—occur with unusual frequency among Nisei as a result of their permanently unresolved tensions.[113] That the tensions are real should be clear not only from this paper, but also from the findings of clinical studies.[114] It is more difficult to prove the existence of these diseases because of the Nisei's desire to conceal and deemphasize their sickness, and because of the structural arrangements in current America which aid them in their efforts.

Many of my Nisei friends have informed me that they silently suffer abdominal pains. Others are startled and ashamed of seemingly incurable mottled finger nails and falling hair. However, few Nisei visit doctors to have their symptoms analyzed. Instead, they rely on Nisei pharmacists to diagnose their symptoms and prescribe a remedy or a relief. A visit to a Nisei pharmacist friend is apparently not threatening since the information is localized and requires a less elaborate explanation by either patient or pharmacist than would be required by visiting a physician. The suffering Nisei need only hint at his ailment, and pharmacists who may suffer from the same problem will know what not to say and what medicine to prescribe. By eliminating the middle-man, in this case the physician, the Nisei patient preserves his poise and at the same time protects his health. Moreover, he eliminates the doctor or psychiatrist as a source of potentially embarrassing or frustrating information. They might show him that such pain and discomfort arise directly out of unresolved problems created by his subcultural outlook. That revelation might be too much for the Nisei to bear. One logical conclusion to be drawn from this pattern is that abandonment of the Nisei way of life is the price for a permanent relief from pain.

The geogenerational conception of time and person which predominates Nisei life evokes the recognition that any generation with its attendant character structure will decline and eventually pass away. Although the Issei generation has by no means passed out of existence, its influence began to decline after 1942 when the enforced incarceration of all persons of Japanese ancestry on the West Coast propelled the Nisei into positions of evacuation camp and community leadership.[115] The Nisei group is now beginning to sense its own decline and eventual disappearance as the Sansei generation approaches maturity and establishes an independent existence and special group identity in America. The 1960 census reported that 82 percent of all Japanese in thirteen western states were born in the United States, its territories or possessions. In other words a little more than eight-tenths of the persons of Japanese descent in that area are Nisei, Kibei, Sansei, Yonsei, and Gosei. The manner of taking the census prohibits a further breakdown of these figures into their respective geogenerational groupings. However, we can arrive at a crude approximation by looking at age distribution. In California, where 159,545 persons of Japanese descent live, the 1960 census recorded 68,015 of these between the ages of zero and twenty-four. Most of these are the children, grandchildren, or occasionally great-grandchildren of Nisei, and thus will soon equal and then outstrip the latter in number. The Nisei can clearly see the end of their generational existence in the near future.

As mentioned earlier, no particular Nisei incorporates all the traits described, least of all the Nisei who was raised outside the Japanese community. The typology has proved its value, however, if it has contributed to an understanding of Nisei personality patterns.

The inevitable end of the Nisei group has provoked a mild crisis in the *Lebenswelt* (life-world) of the Nisei.[116] Nisei are beginning to realize with a mixture of anxiety and discomfort, but primarily with a sense of fatalistic resignation, that the way of life which they are used to, and the arts of self-preservation and impression management which they have so assiduously cultivated will soon no longer be regular features of everyday existence among the Japanese in America. The Sansei, and for that matter, the other successor generations, will be different from the Nisei in certain fundamental respects. Moreover, contemporary Nisei view some of these differences with considerable misgivings.

Nisei have always seemed to recognize the socio-cultural and psychic differences between themselves and the Sansei. Some of these differences are based on clearly distinguishable generational experiences. Few of the Sansei experienced or even remember the terrible effects of imprisonment during World War II. Most Sansei have grown up in homes unmarked by a noticeable cultural division between America and Japan and most of them have benefited from the relative material success of their parents and have received parental support for their educational pursuits without difficulty. Finally, very few Sansei have felt the demoralizing agony of anti-Japanese prejudice. In all these respects Nisei recognize that the Sansei are the beneficiaries of Issei and Nisei struggles and perseverance, and therefore, if the Sansei behave differently than an immigrant or oppressed people, it is only right and proper for them to do so.

However, the lack of an appropriate Nisei character in the Sansei worries and disappoints the Nisei: some Nisei see this characterological loss as a product of increased urbanization and Americanization; others emphasize the decline of Japanese culture among the third generation. To illustrate this point, Nisei often use the term Sansei in a pejorative sense to indicate the existence and cause of social impropriety. Thus, they may explain an individual's continued social error by saying "What can you expect? He's a *Sansei*."

Ironically, Nisei child-rearing and parental practices create the same Sansei characteristics that disappoint them, just as their own Issei parents helped to lay the groundwork for Nisei character.[117] Despite the general respect and personal deference paid their parents by Nisei, they tend to see their parents as negative role models when it comes to rearing their own children. The isolation, harshness, and communication difficulties of their own childhoods are vividly recalled, and a great many Nisei have vowed that their children will not experience any of that. As a result, Nisei parents rarely emphasize the ethics of samurai stoicism and endurance and the discipline associated with them. Rather they choose to follow the white middle-class ethos of love, equality, and companionship. The principles of *Bushido* have given way to those of Dr. Spock; the idea of age-graded obligation is supplanted by Gesell's age-cohort theory; and the social distance that separated parent and child is replaced by the idea that parents and children should grow up together.

The children brought up by Nisei are quite different from their parents, and from the point of view of most Nisei, the result is disappointing. Nisei complain that Sansei seem to lack the drive and initiative which once was a hallmark of the Japanese; that they have no interest in Japanese culture, especially its characterological elements; that they are prone to more delinquency and less respect for authority than were the Nisei; and that they are provincial and bound to the provincialisms of Los Angeles, the city that encloses the single largest aggregate of Sansei.[118]

Nisei often complain of the lack of psychological self-sufficiency and independent capacity for decision making among Sansei. Thus, a Nisei scoutmaster pointed out that his scout troop, mostly Sansei, became emotionally upset and homesick when away for a week's camping trip, and that their projected weiner roast would have been ruined if he had not stepped in and directed the planning for food purchases. He attributed these failings to their Sansei background, and he admitted that his own intervention was a distinct departure from what his own parents would have done in a similar situation during his childhood. Issei parents would probably have let their children fail in such an endeavor in order to help them cultivate responsibility and initiative. But to many Nisei such a seemingly cold and unfeeling response to their own children is anathema.

Sansei indicate an ambivalence and a mild anxiety over their own situation. They do exhibit a certain "Hansen effect" (that is, a desire to recover selected and specific elements of the culture of old Japan),[119] but in this endeavor itself they discover that their own Americanization limits the possibility of effective recovery. If juvenile delinquency among them is on the rise, and in fact the evidence is inconclusive,[120] they attribute it in small part to parental misunderstandings and in greater part to the effects of great social changes taking place in America.

Their parents often appear old-fashioned to them, unprepared to understand their "hang-ups" and unwilling to offer them sufficient love and understanding.[121] Finally, they seem ready to claim the right to dissolve their own geogenerational identity and that of their successor generations in favor of deeper intimate associations below the level of the generational group and interracial intimacies transcending it.[122] Yet, they also wonder how and in what manner they can or should retain their Japanese identity.[123]

Unlike many groups, the Nisei do not stand at a cross-roads. Their demise is certain, their fate sealed by the moving hands of the generational clock. They have not merely survived the hatred and oppression of America's racism; they have triumphed over it. In nearly every objective measure they outstrip their minority competitors, and they have surpassed the white majority in education.[124] In all their adversities and accomplishments their own subcultural character has been an invaluable aid and a source of pride as well. Now they see the coming of the end of their own generation and of this character, and they can only wonder what psychic supports will sustain future generations.

In one sense the Nisei are the last of the *Japanese*-Americans; the Sansei are *American*-Japanese. As Jitsuichi Masuoka observed over two decades ago, "It is the members of the *Sansei* who, having been fully acculturated but having been excluded by the dominant group because of their racial difference, really succeed in presenting a united front against exclusion by the dominant group. A genuine race problem arises at this point in the history of race relations."[125]

NOTES

This paper could not have been written without the assistance of a great many Japanese Americans who opened their homes to me in my dual roles as friend and researcher. I am especially indebted to the following: The entire Fukuda family of San Francisco, Rev. and Mrs. Taro Goto, Mr. and Mrs. Leo T. Goto, Mr. and Mrs. Hideo Bernard Hata, Mr. and Mrs. Harry S. Suzuki, Mr. Donald Sakuma, and the *Nisei* group known as "the Barons."

An early version of this paper was presented at the University of California Medical School in 1966. I am indebted to Fred Davis and Egon Bittner for advice and criticism. My colleague Dr. Marvin B. Scott read each draft of the manuscript and advised me throughout. Professor T. Scott Miyakawa encouraged me to revise an earlier version for this volume. Naturally, I am fully responsible for all errors and shortcomings.

1. Quoted in Lewis Bush, *77 Samurai: Japan's First Embassy to America* (Tokyo and Palo Alto, California: Kodansha International, 1968), p. 132. (Based on the original manuscript in Japanese by Itsuro Hattori). Bush does not give

the date of this newspaper article. It would appear to be April 2, 1860 or thereabouts.

2. *Ibid.*

3. See Jacobus ten Broek, Edward N. Barnhart and Floyd Matson, *Prejudice, War, and the Constitution: Japanese American Evacuation and Resettlement,* Vol. III (Berkeley: University of California Press, 1954), pp. 11-98.

4. See Anne Reeploeg Fisher, *Exile of a Race* (Sidney, British Columbia: Peninsula Printing Co., 1965); Morton Grodzins, *Americans Betrayed: Politics and the Japanese Evacuation* (Chicago: University of Chicago Press, 1949), pp. 1-230, 400-422. For a typical example of the rhetoric of that period see Alan Hynd, *Betrayal From the East: The Inside Story of Japanese Spies in America* (New York: Robert M. McBride & Co., 1943).

5. Robert E. Park, "Racial Assimilation in Secondary Groups with Special Reference to the Negro," in *Race and Culture* (Glencoe, Ill.: The Free Press, 1950), p. 209. *(The Collected Papers of Robert E. Park,* Vol. I, edited by Everett C. Hughes *et al.)*

6. Robert E. Park, "Behind Our Masks," *Survey Graphic* LVI (May 1, 1926) 137. This essay emphasized its point with photographs of *Noh* masks on each page.

7. Fred L. Strodtbeck, "Family Interaction, Values, and Achievement," in Marshall Sklare, ed., *The Jews: Social Patterns of an Ethnic Group* (New York: The Free Press, 1958), pp. 162-63.

8. Bernard C. Rosen, "Race, Ethnicity, and the Achievement Syndrome," *American Sociological Review* 24 (February 1959) 47-60.

9. Chester Rowell, "Chinese and Japanese Immigrants—A Comparison," *Annals of the American Academy of Political and Social Science* XXIV (September 1909) 223-30.

10. Winifred Raushenbush, "Their Place in the Sun," *Survey Graphic* LVI (May 1, 1926) 141-45.

11. Rose Hum Lee, *The Chinese in the United States of America* (Hong Kong: Hong Kong University Press, 1960), p. 425.

12. Leonard Broom and John I. Kitsuse, "The Validation of Acculturation: A Condition of Ethnic Assimilation," *American Anthropologist* LVII (February 1955) 45.

13. Calvin F. Schmid and Charles E. Nobbe, "Socioeconomic Differentials Among Nonwhite Races," *American Sociological Review* 30 (December 1965) 909-22.

14. William Caudill and George de Vos, "Achievement, Culture, and Personality: The Case of the Japanese Americans," *American Anthropologist* 58 (December 1956) 1107.

15. *Ibid.,* p. 1116.

16. *loc. cit.*

17. Alan Jacobson and Lee Rainwater, "A Study of Management Representative Evaluations of Nisei Workers," *Social Forces* 32 (March 1953) 35-41.

18. See, e.g., Wallace Irwin, *Letters of a Japanese School Boy* (New York: Doubleday, Page, 1909), pp. 172-73.

19. Stanley M. Elkins, *Slavery: A Problem in American Institutional and Intellectual Life* (Chicago: University of Chicago Press, 1959), pp. 81-139.

20. Alfred Schutz, *The Phenomenology of the Social World* (Evanston: Northwestern University Press, 1967), pp. 139-214 (translated by George Walsh and Frederick Lehnert).

21. Clifford Geertz, *Person, Time, and Conduct in Bali: An Essay in Cultural Analysis* (New Haven: Yale University Southeast Asia Studies, Cultural Report Series No. 14, 1966).

22. William Caudill and Henry A. Scarr, "Japanese Value Orientations and Culture Change," *Ethnology* I (January 1962) 53-91.

23. Schutz, *op. cit.*, pp. 142-43, 194-214.

24. Cf. Edward Norbeck, *Pineapple Town, Hawaii* (Berkeley: University of California Press, 1959), pp. 5, 86-104.

25. See the interesting discussion in Clyde V. Kiser, "Cultural Pluralism," *The Annals of the American Academy of Political and Social Science* 262 (March 1949) 118-29.

26. Chinese prefer to distinguish by a common "middle name" all persons born in the same generational cohort of a single lineage, but they do not continue a genealogical measurement of geo-generational distance from China. See Maurice Freedman, *Chinese Lineage and Society: Fukien and Kwangtung* (New York: Humanities Press, 1966), pp. 44-45, 179-180.

27. Norbeck, *op. cit.*, p. 94.

28. See Kathleen Tamagawa, *Holy Prayers in a Horse's Ear* (New York: Ray Long and Richard R. Smith, 1932).

29. See Daisuke Kitagawa, *Issei and Nisei: The Internment Years* (New York: Seabury Press, 1967), pp. 26-31.

30. The phenomena discussed here are analogous to the issues involved in romantic love and incest (withdrawal) on the one hand and group dissolution through loss of function on the other. For perceptive theoretical insights see Philip Slater, "Social Limitations on Libidinal Withdrawal," *American Journal of Sociology* LXVII (November 1961) 296-311 and Talcott Parsons, "The Incest Taboo in Relation to Social Structure," *British Journal of Sociology* V (June 1954) 101-17; Parsons, "The Superego and the Theory of Social Systems," *Psychiatry* 15 (February 1952) 15-25.

31. Broom and Kitsuse, *op. cit.*

32. Discussions of this group breakdown through withdrawal or transcendence usually focus on juvenile delinquency although the issues clearly go beyond this element of behavior. See, e.g., Harry H. L. Kitano, "Japanese-American Crime and Delinquency," *Journal of Psychology* 66 (1967) 253-63.

33. See, e.g., Ruth Benedict, *The Chrysanthemum and the Sword: Patterns of Japanese Culture* (Boston: Houghton Mifflin, 1946); Nyozekan Hasegawa, *The Japanese Character: A Cultural Profile* (Tokyo: Kodansha International, 1966); Fosco Maraini, *Meeting with Japan* (New York: Viking Press, 1960), pp. 22-23, 217-218 (translated by Eric Mosbacher).

34. Joseph K. Yamagiwa, "Language as an Expression of Japanese Culture,"

in John W. Hall and Richard K. Beardsley, eds., *Twelve Doors to Japan* (New York: McGraw-Hill, 1965), pp. 186-223.

35. Hajime Nakamura, *Ways of Thinking of Eastern Peoples: India-China-Tibet-Japan* (Honolulu: East-West Center Press, 1964), pp. 409-10 (edited by Philip P. Wiener).

36. See Benedict, *op. cit.,* pp. 48-49.

37. Among Nisei I have observed a quick jerk of the head in genuflection before elders, Issei, and visitors from Japan, but this vestigial bow is far from the careful employment of body idiom required of traditional Japanese.

38. Among my Nisei associates it is widely professed that the Japanese language contains no obscenities, and many Nisei utter English scatalogical phrases softly and under their breath. In contrast, Chinese Americans of the same generation, especially those who speak *Sze Yap* dialect, employ a rich variety of epithets, curses, and obscenities.

39. Clifford Geertz, *The Religion of Java* (London: Collier-Macmillan, The Free Press of Glencoe, 1960), pp. 241-42.

40. As a general phenomenon of human behavior, this suspiciousness has been described by Erving Goffman. See *The Presentation of Self in Everyday Life* (Edinburgh: University of Edinburgh Social Science Research Centre, Monograph No. 2, 1958), pp. 1-46.

41. See Hiroshi Wagatsuma, "The Social Perception of Skin Color in Japan," *Daedalus* 96 (Spring 1967) 407-43.

42. A few Jews came to Japan in the ninth century, and another group in the sixteenth, but it was not until the nineteenth century that the Jewish religion had even a small establishment there. In the early twentieth century Kobe became a center for European Jewish merchants, and this colony was enlarged by refugees from Nazi Germany.

43. I am indebted to the Rev. Taro Goto and Mr. Nobusuke Fukuda for explaining these terms and their origins to me.

44. George de Vos, "A Quantitative Rorschach Assessment of Maladjustment and Rigidity in Acculturating Japanese Americans," *Genetic Psychology Monographs* 52 (1955) 66.

45. Edward T. Hall, *The Hidden Dimension* (Garden City: Doubleday, 1966), pp. 139-44.

46. Bernard Rudofsky, *The Kimono Mind* (Garden City: Doubleday, 1965), pp. 159-61.

47. Japanese, like English, is a language that betrays the speaker's social and regional origins. Japanese Americans, highly conscious of the poor quality of their spoken Japanese and wary lest it betray peasant origins, tend to rely on English whenever possible.

48. See Ezra Vogel, "The Go-Between in a Developing Society, the Case of the Japanese Marriage Arranger," *Human Organization* 20 (Fall 1961) 112-20. For the go-between among Japanese in America see Shotaro Frank Miyamoto, *Social Solidarity Among the Japanese in Seattle* (Seattle: University of Washington Publications in the Social Sciences, Vol. II, December, 1939), pp. 87-88; Robert H. Ross and Emory S. Bogardus, "Four Types of *Nisei* Marriage Patterns," *Sociology*

and Social Research 25 (September 1940) 63-66; John F. Embree, "Acculturation Among the Japanese of Kona, Hawaii," Memoir of the American Anthropological Association. Supplement to *American Anthropologist* 43 (1941) 74-77; Toshio Yatsushiro, "The Japanese Americans," in Milton Barron, ed., *American Minorities* (New York: Alfred A. Knopf, 1962), p. 324.

49. Rudofsky, *op. cit.,* pp. 161-163.

50. For a discussion of information games see Stanford M. Lyman and Marvin B. Scott, "Game Frameworks," in *Sociology of the Absurd* (New York: Appleton-Century-Crofts, forthcoming).

51. For the most perceptive theoretical analysis of social occasions, and one that is applicable to the Japanese American scene, see Georg Simmel, "The Sociology of Sociability," *American Journal of Sociology* LV (November 1949) 254-61 (translated by Everett C. Hughes).

52. Cf. David Riesman, et al., "The Vanishing Host," *Human Organization* XIX (Spring 1960) 17-27.

53. John Embree, *The Japanese,* Smithsonian Institution War Background Studies Number Seven (Washington, D.C.: Smithsonian Institution, 1943), p. 25.

54. John Embree, *A Japanese Village: Suye Mura* (London: Kegan Paul, Trench, Trubner, 1946), pp. 155-56.

55. See Lyman and Scott, "Stage Fright and the Problem of Identity," in *Sociology of the Absurd, op. cit.*

56. See Marvin B. Scott and Stanford M. Lyman, "Accounts," *American Sociological Review* 33 (February 1968) 46-62.

57. Cf. Edward Gross and Gregory P. Stone, "Embarrassment and the Analysis of Role Requirements," *American Journal of Sociology* LXX (July 1964) 6-10; Erving Goffman, "Embarrassment and Social Organization," *American Journal of Sociology* LXII (November 1956) 264-71; Stanford M. Lyman and Marvin B. Scott, "Coolness in Everyday Life," in Marcello Truzzi, ed., *Sociology and Everyday Life* (Englewood Cliffs, N.J.: Prentice-Hall, 1968), pp. 92-101.

58. Cf. Georg Simmel, "The Metropolis and Mental Life," in *The Sociology of Georg Simmel* (Glencoe: The Free Press, 1950), pp. 409-26 (edited and translated by Kurt Wolff).

59. Georg Simmel, "The Aesthetic Significance of the Face," in *Georg Simmel, 1858–1918* (Columbus: Ohio State University Press, 1959), pp. 276-81 (edited by Kurt Wolff).

60. Georg Simmel, "Sociology of the Senses: Visual Interaction," in Robert E. Park and Ernest W. Burgess, *Introduction to the Science of Sociology* (Chicago: University of Chicago Press, 1921), pp. 356-61.

61. Cf. Erving Goffman, *Behavior in Public Places: Notes on the Social Organization of Gatherings* (London: Collier-Macmillan, the Free Press of Glencoe, 1963), pp. 38-42.

62. Cf. Mariani, *op. cit.,* p. 23.

63. Geertz, *Religion of Java, op. cit.,* pp. 245-47.

64. See Jerry Enomoto, "Perspectives: Enryo-Syndrome?" *Pacific Citizen* 64 (June 16, 1967) 1; "Perspectives: Enryo," *Ibid.* 65 (July 7, 1967) 1.

In 1953 John H. Burma wrote:

> There is evidence that Nisei leaders are not so aggressive and consistent in their leadership roles as are Caucasian leaders. . . . The problem involved here is that Nisei are likely to be much concerned with "doing the proper thing," meeting requirements placed upon them, and being careful not to do anything which would too much disturb the Japanese community or disrupt the *status quo*. This tends to penalize initiative and aggressiveness and to slow down the dynamics of leadership as the Caucasian knows it.

"Current Leadership Problems Among Japanese Americans," *Sociology and Social Research* 37 (January 1953) 162.

65. See three essays by L. Takeo Doi, "Japanese Language as an Expression of Japanese Psychology," *Western Speech* 20 (Spring 1956) 90-96; "'Amae': A Key Concept for Understanding Japanese Personality Structure," in Robert J. Smith and Richard K. Beardsley, eds., *Japanese Culture: Its Development and Characteristics* (Chicago: Aldine, 1962), pp. 132-39; "Giri-Ninjo: An Interpretation," in R. P. Dore, ed., *Aspects of Social Change in Modern Japan* (Princeton: Princeton University Press, 1967), pp. 327-36.

66. Doi, "'Amae'," *op. cit.,* p. 133.

67. See Charlotte E. Babcock and William Caudill, "Personal and Cultural Factors in Treating a Nisei Man," in Georgene Seward, ed., *Clinical Studies in Culture Conflict* (New York: Ronald Press, 1958), pp. 409-48; Charlotte E. Babcock, "Reflections on Dependency Phenomena as Seen in Nisei in the United States," in Smith and Beardsley, *op. cit.,* pp. 172-188.

68. For this last point I am indebted to Hideo Bernard Hata.

69. See Joseph L. Anderson and Donald Richie, *The Japanese Film* (New York: Grove Press, 1960), pp. 63-71, 223-228, 315-331.

70. Cf. Robert Frager, "The Psychology of the Samurai," *Psychology Today* 2 (January 1969) 48-53.

71. Douglas G. Haring, "Japanese National Character: Cultural Anthropology, Psychoanalysis, and History," in *Personal Character and Cultural Milieu* (Syracuse: Syracuse University Press, 1956), 3rd ed., compiled and edited by Douglas G. Haring, pp. 424-437; George A. De Vos, "Achievement Orientation, Social Self-Identity, and Japanese Economic Growth," *Asian Survey* 5 (December 1965) 575-89.

72. Reinhard Bendix, "A Case Study in Cultural and Educational Mobility: Japan and the Protestant Ethic," in Neil J. Smelser and Seymour Martin Lipset, eds., *Social Structure and Mobility in Economic Development* (Chicago: Aldine, 1966), pp. 266-67.

73. Although early student migrants were of samurai rank, the settler and sojourner immigrants who came after 1880 were largely of peasant, handicraft, and merchant origin. Some of these undoubtedly descended from noble lineage or *ronin* (masterless warrior) backgrounds. See Hirokichi Mutsu, "A Japanese View of Certain Japanese American Relations," *Overland Monthly* 32 (November 1898) 406-14; Yosaburo Yoshida, "Sources and Causes of Japanese Emigration," *Annals of the American Academy of Political and Social Science* XXIV

(September 1909) 157-67. The Japanese American History Project now carrying on research at UCLA may produce more data on the social origins of Issei.

74. George Sansom, *A History of Japan, 1334–1615* (Stanford: Stanford University Press, 1961), pp. 333, 398; *A History of Japan, 1615–1867* (Stanford: Stanford University Press, 1963), pp. 32-34, 54-58, 79, 92-93, 133-138; *Japan: A Short Cultural History* (New York: Appleton-Century-Crofts, 1943) rev. ed., pp. 356, 496-98.

75. Herbert Passin, *Society and Education in Japan* (New York; Bureau of Publications, Teacher's College, East Asian Institute, Columbia University, 1965), pp. 117-121, 177-179, 190-191, 226-228; R. P. Dore, *Education in Tokugawa Japan* (London: Routledge and Kegan Paul, 1965), pp. 124-251.

76. Passin, *op. cit.,* pp. 149-60; Dore, *op. cit.,* pp. 124-251.

77. George B. Sansom, *Japan: A Short Cultural History, op. cit.,* pp. 520-521.

78. Paul T. Takagi, "The Japanese Family in the United States: A Hypothesis on the Social Mobility of the Nisei," revised version of a paper presented at the annual meeting of the Kroeber Anthropological Society, Berkeley, April 30, 1966.

79. Tadashi Fukutake, *Japanese Rural Society* (London: Oxford University Press, 1967), pp. 39-59, 212-217 (translated by R. P. Dore).

80. Chie Nakane, *Kinship and Economic Organization in Rural Japan* (New York: Humanities Press, 1967), shows a distinct difference between Japanese rural social structure and that of China described in Maurice Freedman, *Lineage Organization in Southeastern China* (London: Athlone Press, 1958) and *Chinese Lineage and Society: Fukien and Kwangtung, op. cit.*

81. Fukutake, *op. cit.,* p. 40.

82. *Ibid.,* p. 212. See also Robert J. Smith, "The Japanese Rural Community: Norms, Sanctions, and Ostracism," *American Anthropologist* 63 (June 1961). Reprinted in Jack M. Potter, et al., eds., *Peasant Society: A Reader* (Boston: Little, Brown, 1967), pp. 246-255.

83. Sidney L. Gulick, *The American Japanese Problem* (New York: Charles Scribner's Sons, 1914), pp. 90-96; T. Iyenaga and Kenoske Sato, *Japan and the California Problem* (New York: G. P. Putnam's Sons, 1921), pp. 109-19.

84. See William Caudill, "Japanese American Personality and Acculturation," *Genetic Psychology Monographs* 45 (1952) 32. In rural areas and in some of the ghetto residences of urban *Nihonmachi,* the hot bath was transplanted from Japan.

85. Benedict, *op. cit.,* pp. 266-267. Personal interviews with Nisei indicate that *moxa* was used or threatened against naughty, overly excited, tantrum-throwing children. See also Monica Sone, *Nisei Daughter* (Boston: Little, Brown & Company, 1953), p. 28.

86. Douglas G. Haring, "Aspects of Personal Character in Japan," *Personal Character and Cultural Milieu, op. cit.,* pp. 417-19; Betty B. Lanham, "Aspects of Child Care in Japan: Preliminary Report," *ibid.,* pp. 565-583; Edward and Margaret Norbeck, "Child Training in a Japanese Fishing Community," *ibid.,* pp. 651-673; Benedict, *op. cit.,* pp. 261-264.

87. See, e.g., *The Autobiography of Yukichi Fukuzawa* (New York: Columbia University Press, 1966), pp. 113-14. (rev. transl. by Eiichi Kiyooka).

88. Caudill, *op. cit.*, p. 30.

89. Takagi, *op. cit.*

90. For the *Eta* in Florin see Winifred Raushenbush, "Their Place in the Sun," *Survey Graphic* LVI (May 1, 1926) 154-58; Hiroshi Ito (Pseud.), "Japan's Outcastes in the United States," in George de Vos and Hiroshi Wagatsuma, eds., *Japan's Invisible Race: Caste in Culture and Personality* (Berkeley: University of California Press, 1966), pp. 200-221.

91. Takagi, *op. cit.*

92. Cf. Edward Norbeck, "Age-Grading in Japan," *American Anthropologist* 55 (June 1953) 373-84.

93. Caudill, *op. cit.*, p. 30.

94. George A. DeVos and Keiichi Mizushima, "Organization and Social Function of Japanese Gangs: Historical Development and Modern Parallels," in R. P. Dore, ed., *Aspects of Social Change in Modern Japan, op. cit.*, pp. 289-326.

95. Takagi, *op. cit.;* Stanford M. Lyman, "The Nisei Personality," *Pacific Citizen* 62 (January 7, 1966) 3.

96. Geertz, *The Religion of Java, op. cit.*, p. 241.

97. Lyman and Scott, "Coolness in Everyday Life," *op. cit.*

98. *Ibid.*, p. 93.

99. Caudill, *op. cit.*, pp. 66-68.

100. For an excellent discussion of these phenomena in general see Erving Goffman, *Interaction Ritual: Essays on Face-To-Face Behavior* (Chicago: Aldine, 1967), pp. 218-226.

101. William Petersen, "Success Story, Japanese-American Style," *The New York Times Magazine,* January 9, 1966, p. 40.

102. Professor Harry H. L. Kitano has suggested that most Japanese Americans did not resist incarceration in detention camps during World War II because of their ingrained sense of fateful resignation: Joe Grant Masaoka, "Japanese tailor-made for Army order, says Kitano," *Pacific Citizen* 64 (June 9, 1967) 1-2.

103. There is cultural support for this phenomenon, summed up in the Buddhist ideal of *muga,* carrying on activities effortlessly, that is, having eliminated the observing self in one's acts. See Benedict, *op. cit.*, pp. 247-251.

104. Cf. the remark by Sapir: "We do not really know what a man's speech is until we have evaluated his social background. If a Japanese talks in a monotonous voice, we have not the right to assume that he is illustrating the same type of personality that one of us would be if we talked with his sentence melody." "Speech as a Personality Trait," *Selected Writings,* p. 539.

105. Caudill and de Vos, *op. cit.*, p. 1117.

106. Geertz, *Person, Time, and Conduct in Bali, op. cit.*, pp. 53-61; Goffman, *Interaction Ritual, op. cit.*, pp. 226-33; Lyman and Scott, "Stage Fright and Social Identity," *Sociology of the Absurd, op. cit.*

107. The Japanese term *jicho* sums up this sense. Literally "a self that is

weighty," it refers to circumspection in social relations. A person loses *jicho* when he commits an impropriety. See Benedict, *op. cit.,* pp. 219-222.

108. George de Vos and Hiroshi Wagatsuma, "Psycho-Cultural Significance of Concern over Death and Illness Among Rural Japanese," *International Journal of Social Psychiatry* V (Summer 1959) 5-19; George de Vos, "Social Values and Personal Attitudes in Primary Human Relations in Niike," *Occasional Papers,* Center for Japanese Studies, University of Michigan, 1965; Babcock and Caudill, *op. cit.,* pp. 436-437; Marvin K. Opler, "Cultural Dilemma of a Kibei Youth," *Culture and Social Psychiatry* (New York: Atherton Press, 1967), pp. 360-80.

109. Weston La Barre, "Some Observations on Character Structure In the Orient: The Japanese," in Bernard S. Silberman, ed., *Japanese Character and Culture* (Tucson: The University of Arizona Press, 1962), pp. 325-59, esp. pp. 349-51.

110. See Thomas S. Szasz, *The Myth of Mental Illness: Foundations of a Theory of Personal Conduct* (New York: Dell-Delta, 1967), pp. 100, 110, 129-130, 139-143, 248-258.

111. Ezra Vogel, "The Go-Between," *op. cit.*

112. Georg Simmel, "The Stranger," in *The Sociology of Georg Simmel, op. cit.,* pp. 402-408.

113. See Franz Alexander, "The Psychosomatic Approach in Medical Therapy," *The Scope of Psychoanalysis: Selected Papers of Franz Alexander, 1921-1961* (New York: Basic Books, 1961), pp. 345-58.

114. George de Vos, "A Comparison of the Personality Differences in Two Generations of Japanese Americans By Means of the Rorschach Test," *The Nagoya Journal of Medical Science* 17 (August 1954) 153-261.

115. See five articles by Emory S. Bogardus: "Current Problems of Japanese Americans," *Sociology and Social Research* 25 (July 1941) 562-71; "Culture Conflicts in Relocation Centers," *ibid.* 27 (May 1943) 381-90; "Relocation Centers as Planned Communities," *ibid.* 28 (January 1944) 218-34; "Resettlement Problems of Japanese Americans," *ibid.* 29 (June 1945) 218-226; "The Japanese Return to the West Coast," *ibid.* 31 (January 1947) 226-33.

116. For this concept see Alfred Schutz, "Some Structures of the Life-World," *Collected Papers III: Studies in Phenomenological Philosophy* (The Hague: Marinus Nijhoff, 1966), pp. 116-32. (ed. by I. Schutz).

117. See Dennie L. Briggs, "Social Adaptations Among Japanese American Youth: A Comparative Study," *Sociology and Social Research* 38 (May-June 1954) 293-300; Melvin S. Brooks and Ken Kunihiro, "Education in Assimilation of Japanese: A Study in the Houston Area of Texas," *Sociology and Social Research* 37 (September 1952) 16-22.

118. See T. Scott Miyakawa, "The Los Angeles Sansei," *Kashu Mainichi,* December 20, 1962, Part 2, pp. 1, 4.

119. For the "Hansen effect" see Marcus Lee Hansen, "The Third Generation in America," *Commentary* 14 (November 1952) 492-500; Eugene I. Bender and George Kagiwada, "Hansen's Law of 'Third-Generation Return' and the Study of American Religio-Ethnic Groups," paper presented at the annual meeting of

the Pacific Sociological Association, Vancouver, B.C., Canada, April, 1966. For its application to Japanese Americans, see George Kagiwada, "The Third Generation Hypothesis: Structural Assimilation Among Japanese-Americans," paper presented at the annual meeting of the Pacific Sociological Association, San Francisco, March, 1968.

120. See Harry H. L. Kitano, "Is There Sansei Delinquency?" *Kashu Mainichi, op. cit.*, p. 1.

121. See "A Sansei's Opinion," *Kashu Mainichi, op. cit.*, p. 2; Ken Yoshida, "Contra Costa Youth Trade Views with Nisei Parents," *Pacific Citizen* 64 (March 3, 1967) 4; Donald Kazama, "On Focus: The Sansei and Nisei," *Pacific Citizen* 64 (May 26, 1967) 4.

122. Recently World War II *Nisei* air ace Ben Kuroki observed that "We're losing our Japanese heritage through intermarriage." His public "blast" at intermarriage [*Pacific Citizen* 64 (February 17, 1967), p. 1] was criticized in letters to the editor [Ibid., 64 (April 14, 1967) 6] and by a young columnist: Ken Kuroiwa, "Mampitsu: Interracial Dating," *Ibid.*, 64 (March 24, 1967) 5.

123. "Sansei in California divided on Integration, FEPC Told," *Pacific Citizen* 64 (May 19, 1967) 1; Jeffrey Matsui, "Sounding Board: Anonymously Integrated," *Ibid.*, p. 4; Bill Strobel, "Japanese Heritage in the United States," *Oakland Tribune*, March, 1966. Reprinted in *Pacific Citizen* 62 (April 1, 1966) 1, 3, 4. See also Daisuke Kitagawa, "Assimilation or Pluralism?" in Arnold M. Rose and Caroline B. Rose, eds., *Minority Problems* (New York: Harper & Row, 1965), pp. 285-287.

124. Isao Horinouchi, *Educational Values and Preadaptation in the Acculturation of Japanese Americans*, Sacramento Anthropological Society Paper Number 7, Fall 1967.

125. Jitsuichi Masuoka, "Race Relations and Nisei Problems," *Sociology and Social Research* 30 (July 1946) 459.

Index

Acculturation 248–49, 251, 258, 260,
261, 264
    typology of 249
    of children 248–49, 256, 258
    of mothers 248–49
Aggression, prohibition of, *see* child
rearing, variables of
Aggressiveness, *see* child behavior,
patterns of
Agnes Irwin School for Girls 41
Agriculture, Japanese in California
86
Alien Land Acts (1913 and 1920) 76,
221, 236, 238
Amae-kodawari-sumanai complex 292
American Friends Service Committee
127, 131, 135, 136, 138
Ando, Taro 50
Anti-Alien Land Law, *see* Alien
Land Acts
Arai, Ryoichiro 157, 159, 160–61,
163, 168, 169–71
Asian Americans, socioeconomic
status of 217
Asiatic Exclusion League 93, 94, 95,
102, 107
Assimilation 187, 217, 274–75, 277
    behavioral 269
    structural 269, 271, 272–73,
276–77
Athletic ability, *see* child behavior,
patterns of
Authoritarianism, *see* child rearing,
variables of
Ayusawa, Iwao 204
Bache, Sophia Arabella (Irwin) 41
Banking 167–168, 175–176
Barnhart, Edward N. 74, 146
Baum, D. A. 20, 23
Bellingham (Wash.) Hindu Affair
103, 104–105
Bendix, Reinhard 293

Bethune (Mayor of Vancouver) 99,
102, 105, 107
Board of Immigration (Hawaii) 6,
14, 22–23, 24, 25, 46, 48
Bonin Islands 56–57
Bosworth, Allan R. 147, 148
Bowles, Gilbert 200
Bowser, William J. 111, 112, 117–18
British-Japanese relations 95,
102–103, 104, 113
Broom, Leonard 143, 280
Brown, Godfrey 49, 51
Bushido 187, 188, 190–192, 200, 201,
203, 304
Canadian Nippon Supply Co.
110–112, 116, 118
Caudill, William 281, 282
Character, of Japanese Americans,
    see Japanese Americans, character
of
Charmer 100
Child behavior, patterns of
    aggression, covert 257–58,
263–64
    aggressiveness 248, 256–57,
258, 263, 264
    athletic ability 255, 259–60
    disobedience 257, 263–64
    gregariousness 251, 254, 258,
259
    independence 251, 260
    passivity 244–45
    venturesomeness 254–55,
259–60
Child rearing, Japanese American, *see*
Japanese Americans, child-rearing
practices of
Child rearing, variables of
    authoritarianism 256, 261,
262–64
        punishment pattern as
index of 262

permissiveness 250, 252–54,
259, 260
prohibition of aggression 251,
256, 261, 263, 264
Children
accident rates of 246, 249–50,
252–53, 254, 255, 257, 258,
259, 260, 261, 264, 265
accident proneness of 255–56,
257
Chinda, Sutemi 80–81, 83
Chinese immigrants
discrimination against 73, 81,
83, 84–85, 96, 98, 117, 170
in California 83–85, 128
in Canada 96, 100, 106,
109–110, 117
to Hawaii 6
Chinese Exclusion Act 84
Cho, Kiyoko Takeda 188
Christianity 187, 188, 191, 192, 202
Chugai Bukka Shimpo 47
City of Tokyo 47
Consociates, *see* temporal categories
Constitution, Hawaiian
of 1887 50
of 1894 53
Contemporaries, *see* temporal
categories
Coping variables 250, 252, 255,
257–58, 260–61, 263
Cotterill, Frank 105
Date, Chushichi 157
De Long, Charles E. 33, 34, 43
de Vos, George 281
De Witt, John L. 77, 147, 239
Discrimination, *see* Chinese
immigrants, discrimination
against; Japanese Americans,
discrimination against; Japanese
Canadians, discrimination
against
Disobedience, *see* child behavior,
patterns of
Dole, Sanford 51, 53
Doshin Co. 175, 176, 177

Eaton, Allen H. 143
Elkinton, Joseph 193–94
Elkinton, Mary P., *see* Nitobe, Mary
P. E.
Enomoto, Takeaki (Buyō) 59
Etiquette, importance of
in Japanese culture 285–86,
301
in language 286–88
Evacuation, *see* Japanese Americans,
relocation of
Exposure variable (in accidents) 250,
251, 252–55, 258, 260–61
Family, behavior patterns of
detached family relations 251,
256, 257, 261, 262, 263
parent-child relations 256–57,
261, 262
traditional Oriental 244, 256,
262, 294
Federal Bureau of Investigation 128
Form, emphasis on in Nisei 289–90
Formosa (Taiwan) 189, 193
Fowke, Edith 144
Fowler, Arthur E. 94, 98, 103, 105
Frustration-aggression theory 256,
257, 262, 263
Fujita, Yoshiro 80–81
Fukuzawa, Yukichi 160, 161, 162,
163, 166, 167, 168, 180
Gan-nen-mono (First Year Men) 5,
34–35
embassy to settle complaints
of 28–32
Geertz, Clifford 282, 286, 297
Generation
concept of 270, 276
definition of 270, 271–72
Gentlemen's Agreement
(Canada-Japan) 114–115
Gentlemen's Agreement (U.S.-Japan)
76, 85, 120, 220
Gibson, Walter Murray 35, 45, 48,
49, 50
Gilbert, Dorothy 188
Girdner, Audrey 147

Giri 190, 191, 241
Gordon, Milton M. 217, 269
Gosei 283, 302; *see also* Japanese
    Americans, generations of
Gotoh, Saori 110–12, 116, 118
Green, William 50
Gregariousness, *see* child behavior,
    patterns of
Hamada, Hikozo (Heco, Joseph) 6–7
Hansen, Marcus L. 215, 268–69; *see*
    also third generation hypothesis
Harris, Charles C. 29, 30, 31, 33, 34
Harris, Townsend 7, 12
Hawaiian Gazette 8, 23, 24
Hawaiian Immigrants' Fund 48–50
Hawaiian immigration 3–4, 5–36,
    40–53
    inspectors and doctors for
        47–50
    sources of 46, 47
Hayami, Kenzo 176
Hayashi, Tadamichi 44, 57
Hayashi, Tadasu 108, 115
Heco, Joseph, *see* Hamada, Hikozo
Higashikuze, Michitomi 17, 18, 19
Hillebrand, William 6
Hinode Company 158–59, 163, 166,
    167, 170
Hooper, Isaac H. 29, 31
Hosokawa, Bill 142, 148
Hoshino, Chotaro 161, 164, 173
Iaukea, Curtis P. 45
Ichihashi, Yamato 146
Ichiya Shokai 58, 59, 67
Ie system 293–94
Iglehart, Charles 149
Immigrants, Japanese, *see also*
    Japanese Americans; Japanese
    emigration
    policy of Japanese government
        toward 28–32, 48–50,
        80–82, 106–108, 113–15
Immigration Act of 1907 (British
    Columbia) 95–96, 118
Immigration Convention,
    Japan-Hawaii 48–49

Immigration, European
    compared with Japanese 3, 40,
        73, 79, 213, 214
Immigration laws (U.S.), *see also*
    Japanese Exclusion Act of 1924
    of 1882 84
    of 1924 76, 84, 128, 196,
        220–21
Independence, *see* child behavior,
    patterns of; mother, role of
Inoue, Kaoru 42–43, 44, 45, 48, 49
Inouye, Daniel K. 149
Institute of Pacific Relations 189,
    196, 200, 201
Irwin, Agnes 41–42
Irwin, John 41, 51
Irwin, Iki (Takechi) 44
Irwin, Richard 41, 42, 43–44
Irwin, Robert Walker 3, 4, 36,
    40–53
Irwin, Sophy 41–42
Ishii, Kikujiro 99, 106
Ishitsuka, Eizō 65, 66, 67
Issei 78–79, 81–83, 86–87, 153–54,
    156–80, 221, 230, 236, 240, 268,
    283, 284, 285, 293–94, 302; *see*
    also Japanese Americans,
    generations of
Japan
    prefectures of, *see also ken*
        Hiroshima 46, 47, 231
        Yamaguchi 46, 47, 231
    Western traders in 158, 161,
        169, 172, 176
Japanese American Citizens League
    89, 139, 237, 240
Japanese American immigrant
    community 217–42
    churches of 232–34, 240
        Buddhist 232, 234
        Christian 232–34
    economy of 221–25
        business and professions
            in 233, 239
        business associations in
            224–25

credit system (*tanomoshi*)
  in 224
entrepreneurship in
  222–23
first employment of
  immigrants and 222
occupations in 223
family in 226–229, 241
  conflicts in 230
  economic role of 224
  etiquette in 229
  festivals observed in
    230
  linguistic barriers in
    228–29
  main and branch form
    of (*honke-bunke*)
    227–28, 294
  male primogeniture in
    228
  socialization of children
    in 228–29
  status obligations of 229
  values emphasized in
    230–31
  wife's role in 228
marriage in 226–27, 294
  arranged marriages 226
  baishakunin
    (go-between) for 226,
    288, 289
  "picture-bride" 226,
    294
newspapers in 237
norms in 228, 230
organization of 218, 241–42
  stages of 220–21
recreation of 237–38
schools in 234–36
  functions of 235–36
  Japanese Language
    School 235–36
Japanese American Research Project
  88, 180
Japanese Americans
  born in Hawaii 272

character of 281
  Nisei 284, 285, 292–93,
    297, 298–99, 303; *see
    also* Nisei, character
    of
child-rearing practices of 292,
  293–95
  Issei 294–95
  Nisei 303–304
delinquency rates of 87, 213,
  220, 304
discrimination against 73,
  76–77, 81, 82, 84–85, 139,
  146, 149, 170, 220–21, 236,
  238–39, 274–75, 279, 303
generations of 221, 268,
  271–72, 281, 283, 302; *see
  also* Gosei; Issei; Kibei;
  Nisei; Sansei; Yonsei
occupations of 127–128, 213
population of
  in California 73, 78–79,
    86–87
  in United States 73, 78,
    127
  on East Coast 153
relocation of 129–39, 140–50,
  238–39, 302
  centers of 74–75, 77,
    132–33, 134, 137
  factors causing 238–39
  post-war effects of
    239–40, 302
  protests against 134, 138
repatriation of 137–38, 140
Japanese and American Agency 163
Japanese Association of America 81
  of Seattle 236–37
Japanese Canadians
  discrimination against 92–120,
    144–46, 149
  relocation of 144–46, 149
  riots against 92–120
Japanese emigration
  to Canada 73–74, 109–116
  to Guam 14, 15

to Hawaii 3–4, 5–36, 40–53
to United States 73–74, 76–87, 220–21
Japanese Exclusion Act of 1924 196, 203; *see also* immigration laws, U.S.
Kaanapu, James 35–36
Kai, Oriye 175
Kaigaikogyo Kaisha 66, 67
Kaiser Foundation Health Plan 245–46, 250
Kalakaua, King 45, 50
Kamehameha IV 5, 6
Kamehameha V 6
Kaneko, Naokichi 65–66
Ken (prefectures) 224, 231–32, 241
control functions of 241
economic functions of 224
Kenjinkai (prefectural associations) of 231–32
social functions of 231–32
Kennan, George F. 82
Kibei 128, 138, 221, 283, 285, 302; *see also* Japanese Americans, generations of
King, W. L. Mackenzie 108–109, 116, 119
Kitagawa, Daisuke 141–42
Kitsuse, John K. 143, 280
Kluckholn, Florence 282
Komida, Kigi 58, 59
Komuchi, Tomotsune 158, 164
Konvitz, Milton F. 147
Koshinsha 59
Kuwano, Noburo 162
Labor
attitude toward Chinese and Japanese 84–85, 95, 103, 170
Laurier, Sir Wilfred 107, 116, 119
LaViolette, Forrest 144, 149
League of Nations 189, 196, 197 198, 200, 201
Lee, David J. 17, 20, 22, 23, 24
Lee, Rose Hum 280
Leighton, Alexander 143

Lemieux, Rodolphe 113–15
Lillibridge, Harlan P. 44–45
Lippmann, Walter 77
Listman, A. P. 105
Loftis, Anne 147
McBride, Richard 96
McCook, Edward M. 12–13
McWilliams, Carey 142, 147, 149
Maeda, Tamon 204
Makino, Tomisaburo (Saburo) 20, 22, 23–24, 25, 26, 28, 31, 32, 33, 48
Manchuria 196–98, 203
Mannheim, Karl 215, 270, 272, 276
Marriage, *see* Japanese American immigrant community, marriage in
Martin, Ralph G. 148
Masuda, Rinzo 157
Masuda, Takachi 42–43, 44, 46
Matson, Floyd W. 146
Matsue, Harutsugu 65–66
Matsunaga, Ichitarō 57, 58
Masuoka, Jitsuichi 305
Meiji era and government 3, 5, 7, 17, 34, 153, 156, 157–58, 160, 178, 188, 189, 193, 201, 202, 213, 218–19
Micronesia
German influence in 56, 59–60, 66
Japanese influence in 56–67
Japanese immigration to 61, 62
Mitsui Bussan Kaisha 43, 44, 46, 47, 49
Miwa, Hoichi 28–29
Morikawa, Hideshiro 99, 106
Morimura Arai Company 177
Morimura Brothers and Company 167
Morimura, Ichizaemon 161–62, 163, 167–69, 177, 180
Morimura, Toyo 157, 158, 161, 162, 163–64, 167–69, 170, 180

Mothers
    medical predisposition of
        249–50, 264–65
    roles of
        "egalitarian" 250,
            252–54, 258, 259, 260,
            261
        independent 252–54,
            258–59, 260
        "maternal" 253
        permissive 250, 252–54,
            259, 260
Murai, Yasukata 154, 168
Murayama, Sukichi 59, 60
Murphy, Thomas D. 148
Mutsu, Munemitsu 58, 83
Myer, Dillon 141
Nakamura, Jiro 48
Nakayama, Joji (George Nacayama)
    47–48, 51
Nantō Shōkai 57, 58, 59, 66, 67
Nanyō Bōeki Hioki Gōshi Kaisha 59,
    60, 67
Nanyō Bōeki Kaisha 59, 60–61, 63, 67
Nanyō Bōeki Murayama Gōmei Kaisha
    59
Nanyō Kōhatsu Kaisha 66, 67
Nanyo Shokusan Kaisha 64, 65, 66
Neumann, Paul 50, 52
Nihon Shokai 165
Nippu Shokai (Japanese-Hawaii
    Trading Company) 49
Nisei 86, 216, 221, 230, 237, 240,
    268, 269, 271–76, 280, 281, 282,
    283, 284–305; *see also* Japanese
    Americans, generations of
    as volunteers in U.S. armed
        forces 137, 138, 148
    character of 284, 285, 292–93,
        297, 298–99, 303
    psychosomatic diseases among
        301–302
    voting by 139
Nishimura, Ichimatsu 63–64
Nishimura Shokusan Kaisha 64, 65,
    66

Nishimura Sōshirō 62–63, 64
Nitobe, Inazo 187–205
Nitobe, Mary P. E. 188, 189, 194
Niwa, Yukuro 164, 165
Nobbe, Charles E. 280
Norman, W. H. Howard 145
Oakie, John H. 148
Oceanic group 157, 163, 169, 179
Okada, Heizo 42, 43
O'Keefe, D. D. 58
Okubo, Mine 141
Okuma, Shigenobu 50
Ozawa family (Kintaro, Tomi,
    Yotaro, Itoko, Arthur) 36
Park, Robert E. 268, 279–80
Parkes, Sir Harry 20, 21
Passivity, *see* child behavior,
    patterns of
Peirce, Henry A. 28, 29, 30, 32
Permissiveness, *see* child rearing,
    variables of; mothers, roles of
Petersen, William 213
Phelan, James D. 82, 86, 88
Phillips, Stephen H. 13, 26, 27, 28
Pluralism 269, 274, 277
Predecessors, *see* temporal categories
Punishment, *see* child rearing,
    variables of
Quakerism 187, 188, 190, 192–93,
    195, 198, 200, 201, 202
Raushenbush, Winifred 280
Recife 16, 17
Reischauer, Edwin O. 153, 213–14
Relocation, *see* Japanese Americans,
    relocation of
Repatriation, *see* Japanese
    Americans, repatriation of
Revolution, Hawaiian (1893) 51
Richardson, B. and Son 173–74
Ridicule, use of by Nisei 294–96,
    299
Riemer, Ruth 143
Ringle, Kenneth D. 149
Roosevelt, Theodore 76
Rostow, Eugene V. 147
Rowell, Chester 280

Russo-Japanese War 192, 193–95, 196, 198, 202

Saburo, *see* Makino, Tomisaburo

Sakuma, Yonekichi 21, 36

Samoto, Tsunekichi 59, 60

Samurai ethic 162, 190–93, 203, 219, 292–93

Sandai Shoten 165

Sandwell, Bernard K. 145–46

San Francisco School Board Affair 76

Sansei 221, 268, 269, 272–76, 283, 284, 285, 288, 302–305; *see also* Japanese Americans, generations of

Sapporo Agricultural College 188, 193

Sato and Company 164–65

Sato Arai Company 164, 165, 175, 176

Sato, Momotaro 157, 158–60, 161, 163–67, 170, 175–76, 177

Sato, Shochu 159

Sato, Susumu 159, 164

Sato, Taizen 159

Scarr, Henry A. 282

Schmid, Calvin 213, 217, 241, 280

Schutz, Alfred 282

Schwantes, Robert S. 199

Scioto 5, 16–17, 18–22, 23, 29, 30

Sekine, Sentarō 58, 59–60

Self-control, importance of to Nisei 286, 290–91, 295, 297

Senshu Kaisha 42–43

Shima, George 86

Shiroyama, Seiichi 26–27

Silk, trade in 158–59, 160, 161, 168, 169, 171–78

Sino-Japanese War 192, 193, 195, 198, 202

Smith, Bradford K. 146

Sone, Monica 141–42

Stereotypes, racial 279–81

Successors, *see* temporal categories

Sugar, cultivation of in Micronesia 63–67

Suzuki Brothers Trading Company 65

Suzuki, Toichi 157

Taguchi, Ukichi 57–58, 66, 67

Takagi, Saburo 160, 176

Takahashi, Koreikiyo 160

Takatsuhisa, Ueimon 65

Takazaki, Goroku 57

Teasing, use of by Nisei 294–97, 299

Temporal categories
    consociates 282, 283, 285, 300, 301
    contemporaries 282, 283, 284, 285
    defined, 282
    predecessors 282, 283
    successors, 282, 283, 305

tenBroek, Jacobus 146, 147

Terashima, Tozo 17–18, 19, 20, 34

Third generation hypothesis (Hansen) 215, 269, 271, 274–77, 304; *see also* Hansen, Marcus L.

Thomas, Dorothy Swaine 142

Tokio Emigration Company 112

Tokugawa Shogunate 3, 7, 17, 18, 161, 162, 178, 218

Tokyo Imperial University 188

Tomita, Tetsunosuke 160, 164, 169

Tōyō Seitō Kaisha (Orient Sugar Company) 65

Tōyō Takushoku Kaisha 65, 67

Treaty negotiations, Japan-Hawaii 7–13

Treaty of Tordesillas 56

Triple Intervention 60, 193, 195, 202

Tule Lake Relocation Center 132, 137

Uchimura, Kanzo 194

Ueno, Eijiro 165

Ueno, Keisuke 28–33

United States-Japan trade 153, 156, 158, 179

Vancouver Riots of 1907 92–120
    commission of inquiry into 108–109
    press reaction to 101–106

United States role in 93, 95, 103, 105

Van Reed, Eugene 3–4, 5, 6, 7–20, 21, 22, 23, 25, 26, 27, 28, 30, 31, 32, 33–35, 45

Van Valkenburgh, Robert B. 9, 12–13, 20–21, 28, 33

Varigny, Charles de 8–10, 13–18, 20, 22, 23, 25

Venturesomeness, *see* child behavior, patterns of

von Briesen, Richard 163, 164, 166

Wakefield, Harold 199

Walsh, Hall and Company 42, 43

War Relocation Authority 135, 136, 140–41

Waterman, D. C. 10, 11, 12, 13

Weber, Max 171, 180

Wodehouse, James H. 28, 29, 32

Worden, William L. 149

Wyllie, Robert C. 5, 6, 7–8

Yanaihara, Tadao 204

Yasaka, Takagi 204

Yokohama Kiito Kabushiki Kaisha 177

Yonsei 268, 284, 302; *see also* Japanese Americans, generations of

Yoshy, Frederick 110–12, 116

Young, W. A. 95, 103

backs in old areas of influence. There have been mutinies in Congo and Guinea and problems in the Central African Republic. France dispatched troops to the CAR in April 1996 when the elected government . . . was threatened by an Army mutiny, triggered . . . by the complaint that its soldiers had not been paid.

The French operation has now become overwhelmed. To help quell the revolt and keep French soldiers out of danger, the French military budget is now funding salaries for the CAR military. But the determination to act quickly, and clearly, to support a political leadership seems to have eroded, and with it France's earlier capacity to dictate domestic affairs in many African countries.

The arc of indiscriminate warfare, often fought through local tribal surrogates in Africa, began with the collapse into genocide of France's client Rwanda in 1994. The last French troops withdrew in August that year. Within four years, the emerging victors were the US government and American companies. In December 1997, even as France was announcing a reduction in its military bases in Africa from 8,000 to 5,000 men (spread about the continent in tiny groups), US Secretary of State Madeleine Albright visited six African states once subject to French influence. Paris was paying the price of backing the old – and defeated – regimes.

As the International Institute of Strategic Studies noted, France's support for Rwanda in 1994 and its subsequent advocacy of military intervention in Zaïre (the Democratic Republic of Congo, or DROC) two years later 'put it at odds with the new administrations'. The beneficiaries included American Mineral Fields, which acquired a $1 billion concession to exploit copper and cobalt in Lubumbashi.

The pressure on French resources, in an increasingly turbulent world, could be measured in other ways. In 1997, a French general, Jean-Philipe Douin, observed that France had intervened in trouble spots around the world twelve times between 1950 and 1980; twenty times between 1980 and 1990 and more than thirty times between 1990 and 1997: a total of at least sixty-two such operations. Most of these operations did not involve the Legion. Other elements of the professional French army – the *armée de métier* – were now being employed to project French power in a way which pointed to the shape of things to come: a drastic reduction in the Legion's role and manpower in an exclusively professional army and an increasing reliance on joint operations with allies such as the UK.

One of the few legionnaires left on the Continent to salute the sunset of France's African empire was a young Scot, Corporal William Donaldson, from Dundee. Like many before him, Donaldson was seeking a new life and a new identity as 'Legionnaire Alan Dunn' after one fight, and one conviction, too many back home. He became a good, disciplined soldier.

On 19 February 1997, Donaldson was one of a few hundred men of the 2nd Legion Parachute Regiment ('Deuxième Rep') around Bangui, capital of the Central African Republic. As night fell, a local military mutiny was still smouldering after much wild shooting earlier in the day. Donaldson recalled:

My section was in a ditch alongside the road near St Jacques's Church. It was pitch dark. We were supposed to stop all cars. A taxi came along. Someone inside it started shooting at my buddies further up the road. The taxi was coming towards me. I aimed my Minimi machine-gun but I knew my arc of fire was limited to just a degree or so: other legionnaires were almost opposite me and others were just off to my right a wee bit . . . I got the taxi in my sights and gave it one good rattle. One guy – the driver – was killed. Another was wounded. Local police found his body later. Somehow he'd walked away from the wreck to die alone.

A citation commended Donaldson's sang-froid and quick

reactions. It was one small fragment of the disorder that some academic experts have come to call 'Africa's first world war'; one fought, almost exclusively, by Africans. There were no glorious victories – or defeats – here: just, as one anonymous IISS expert noted, 'the vacuum that opened when many of France's African allies – some of them notoriously corrupt – were deposed'.

A year later, Donaldson decided to take his chance as a civilian. This was a mistake. He had hoped that five years of dedicated soldiering for France in Guiana, Chad and elsewhere would win respect back home in Scotland. Instead, as he admitted: 'They think if you served with the Foreign Legion you must be a hardened criminal.' He was now aged thirty-two. His dreams of working as a bodyguard in the world's expanding protection industry shrank in Dundee to occasional work as a nightclub bouncer.

He was a depressed, anxious man – though still physically strong – when the author interviewed him for this history in the autumn of 1998. On 11 December that year he drove his car off the road two minutes from home. He hit a wall and died. No other vehicle was involved. He was an expert driver: it was one of his military specialities. But five years earlier, as he passed his first four-month selection course, his commanding officer had warned him:

The major problem in the future will be boredom . . . or becoming discouraged . . . So keep in mind what I tell you today. Every one of you is capable of overcoming the obstacles ahead, otherwise you would not be here. Also keep in mind you are not left to yourself. You may always count on the Legionnaire's solidarity. You have comrades and superiors who will help you. Do not hesitate to call on them whenever you encounter problems that are too big for you.

Isolated from that support, Donaldson could no longer summon up help with the battle-cry *A moi, la Légion!* when he met his early death. In a changing world, where warfare was no longer a matter of noble self-sacrifice (however illusory the cause), the values he had sweated to acquire were no longer marketable in Britain.

The Legion's most senior commander, Général de Corps d'Armée Christian Piquemal, noted the decline in France also. His message commemorating the annual Camerone festival in 1999 flagged the latest cut: the upcoming dissolution of the Legion's 5th Regiment, founded in 1930. As he put it: 'Camerone 99 marks the delicate transformation of the Legion imposed by the reorganization of the army.'

It was not only in Africa that the world as the Legion had known it was changing. In February 1996, President Chirac unveiled dramatic cuts in the entire French armed forces. Not only was the sacred cow of conscription to be put peacefully to sleep by 2002, but the remaining, professional force would be slimmed down from 400,000 men to 250,000. The land-based element of the nuclear deterrent was being dismantled. A new, professional army modelled on Britain's would include a 50,000-strong rapid reaction force to react to crises overseas, in conjunction with the British, thanks to the St Malo agreement of December 1998, which asserted: 'The European Union must have the capacity for autonomous action, backed by credible military force.' This did not please the US, or NATO.

The Legion was effectively dismembered by this process. Not only was the total 8,600 force to be cut by 10 per cent, but, by committing other professionals to wider service overseas, Paris now required the Legion to give up its former domination of its traditional bases in Guiana, Polynesia, Mayotte and Djibouti. Other regiments would occupy such garrisons, which had been 50 per cent of the Legion's far horizons. Only specialist engineers and others could still count upon such exotic postings. A further decision imposed 300 new NCOs on the reduced Legion, prompting fears of *banalisation*, or standardization in an army aiming at central control and, perhaps, dilution of an NCO corps which had enjoyed godlike powers hitherto.

In May 1999, as if sensing that it was time to record the final years of the Old Legion, the one that had been the true *armée de métier* when all else failed, the journal *Képi Blanc* listed the Legion's operations beyond the French mainland from 1990 onwards. The Gulf War, 1990–91, was mentioned of course. Other operations, unsung even in France, included the re-insertion of French troops into Chad and an intervention in Gabon from March to June 1990, Operation Requin. 'The country was prey to serious troubles, accompanied by violence and pillage. At Port-Gentil and Libreville, legionnaires assisted the evacuation of 2,000 French residents and foreigners.'

From October, the focus for such interventions had shifted to the volcanic centre of the emerging African war, Rwanda, soon to be the bloody theatre of a million dead, most of them civilians. Operation Noroit protected Europeans in Kigali: 'The 4th company of 2e REP, through its solid presence, restored calm and reassured a worried populace.' On 22 June 1994, the UN had approved a new French intervention, in a situation that had now slipped beyond control. The Legion ran a 'safe haven' in southern Rwanda, known as Operation Turquoise. The elements involved in this humanitarian mission were the 1st Company, Second Legion Infantry Regiment (2 REI); 3rd Company, 13 Demi Brigade (13 DBLE) and the CRAP. The intention was to halt the massacre of the ruling Hutus by the Tutsi majority 'to neutralize armed bands and halt convoys of arms and ammunition'.

The Legion's journal, *Képi Blanc*, described how the intervention halted looting, racketeering and murder and restored civil police structures. The intervention ended in August. A year later, Paris granted a campaign clasp, to be attached to the Foreign Service Medal, for the Rwanda contingent. Not everyone was so impressed by the outcome. As the investigative journalist and author Linda Melvern put it in September 2000:

> France's role in Rwanda had been crucial. Without French support the Hutu regime would never have lasted as long as it did. France had helped arm Hutu Power, and French soldiers had been closely involved with the Rwandan military.
>
> In French government, military and intelligence circles there were fears that the Tutsi Rwandan Patriotic Front, whose soldiers had grown up in refugee camps in English-speaking Uganda, would overrun French-speaking Rwanda. In Paris, the RPF invasion in 1990 [from Uganda] was seen as a Ugandan plot, part of an anglophone conspiracy to expand influence in Africa.

Two prominent human rights watchdogs (the International Federation of Human Rights Leagues in Paris and Human Rights Watch in New York) published their findings in April 1999. They concluded that, early in 1994, a Canadian officer commanding the United Nations Assistance Mission in Rwanda, Lieutenant-General Romeo Dallaire, had issued a warning of Hutu plans to massacre Tutsis. UN officials consistently refused to send reinforcements or allow peacekeepers to intervene. On 7 April, the first day of the genocide, ten Belgian peacekeepers were killed, prompting Belgium to withdraw its troops. Belgium now supported the US and British opposition to any enlargement of the peacekeepers' mandate as the massacres continued.

As a British general, Sir Michael Rose, wrote later:

> The peacekeeping mission in the Balkans was the largest the world has ever seen. 36,000 peacekeepers were deployed in an operation which cost billions of dollars. Yet when General Dallaire asked for 3,000 soldiers to go to Rwanda to stop what was a genuine genocide in which at least a million people died, the world failed

to respond. What is the moral basis for such inequality?

France was accused of the wrong sort of intervention: sending arms to the Rwandan Hutu government before and during the genocide. Alison Des Forges, a Rwanda scholar and author of the report, asserts: 'The Americans were interested in saving money, the Belgians in saving face and the French in saving their ally, the genocidal government.' That ally – a European-educated elite which sought to perpetuate its grip on power – had planned the killings as a deliberate policy, the report concluded. If so, this was not a spontaneous explosion of ethnic rivalries, an African madness. As one summary of Des Forges puts it:

> Detailed official memos reproduced in the study show that soldiers, veterans, police and local administrators encouraged the killings by spreading fear about the Tutsis. Hutu authorities gave food, drinks, drugs, uniforms and small sums of cash to Rwanda's jobless Hutu young people to encourage them to kill. Hutus reluctant to join in the slaughter were swiftly killed.

The murders went on hold only when the Tutsi rebel movement, the Rwandan Patriotic Front, toppled the Hutu-led government and army. In their turn, 'the Tutsi rebels also committed atrocities, killing tens of thousands of unarmed civilians after their victory'. An official UN report in December 1994 blamed the Hutu government for creating a body count of 500,000 and 40,000 orphans during the first phase of the drive to eliminate all Tutsis. By that time, 1.7 million Hutu refugees were quartered in Zaïre alone. In Rwanda, 65,000 Hutu suspects were crowded into human hen-batteries as they awaited the operation of a slow, idiosyncratic judicial process.

By 1998 most of sub-Saharan Africa was at war. Of forty-five countries in the region, twenty were involved in armed conflict, one way or another. The epicentre was Zaïre (now

the Democratic Republic of Congo, or DROC), where
France's former clients, the Hutu, guilty of the 1994
massacres, supported the successful seizure of the country
by Laurent Kabila. In December 1998, Kabila visited Paris
to drum up support for his next campaign. This time
around, France was not interested in yet further engagement
in Africa. Its eyes and its strategy had turned to Europe and
the alliance with Britain. Future military adventures beyond
Europe would be as part of that alliance, using rapid
reaction forces for short, sharp interventions supported
by air power in an effort to create a new world order
that acknowledged US supremacy without becoming its
prisoner.

This was a new form of warfare, more concerned with
economic intelligence than occupying and holding disputed
territory. It was a style of conflict for which the Legion was
not well suited in a rapidly changing world; a world of political correctness which left the Legion marooned on an island
of admirable but anachronistic values. By 1999 France had
more women in uniform than any other Nato army; around
8,500 (compared with 7,867 Legion soldiers of all ranks),
and representing 8 per cent of the French army. Only one
unit still retained its all-male status. This was the Foreign
Legion. With the absorption of the Legion into a reformed,
professional army, 'harmonization' pointed towards the
creation of female legionnaires. In its 168 years, the Legion
had accepted only one woman – the English Susan Travers
('La Miss') – into its ranks and on paper her gender was
male. But she – as she revealed in a newspaper interview at
the age of ninety-two, in December 2000 – was the mistress
of the Legion hero General Pierre Koenig as well as his
chauffeur during the epic battle of Bir Hakeim (see Chapter
11).

Gender equality in the French forces was the uneasy bed-
fellow of the old military realities of blood and sacrifice,
though not the new, casualty-free, air assault from high alti-
tude as practised by Nato in Kosovo, 1999. Women were

barred under French law from 'direct and prolonged combat with hostile forces'. Yet according to a Defence Ministry report, women had 'conquered' all the traditional male bastions of the armed forces, serving as commandos, mechanics and, in the case of Lieutenant Caroline Aigle, as a fighter pilot. The Legion resisted the suggestion that military harmonization, under the New Order, should go this far. General Piquemal told the magazine *l'Express*: 'The presence of women is incompatible with the very nature of the Legion. One essential principle is cohesion and camaraderie among men. The presence of women would mean the disappearance of the Legion. Women have their place in the Army but not with us.

As *The Times* of London observed in 1999:

Commanding officers have always argued that, as the only fully professional unit in France, the Legion has a special status. They live and fight together. However, President Chirac's decision to phase out conscription has 'cast doubts over our specificity' according to General Piquemal. 'The changes bring risks. The biggest is that we could have to fall into line with the rest of the armed forces.'

The Times, noting that the Legion would lose its unique professional status by 2002, reported: 'Although generals in other regiments are careful not to make public statements on the issue, they have privately made it plain that this is precisely what they would like.'

The rearguard action against women was the battle the Legion lost, and one which symbolized the death of the old order. In October 2000, the French Defence Ministry imposed the change by decree. As the Ministry's spokeswoman Christine Triche put it: 'It is true that there is reluctance to accept this move. This is not a natural evolution for them.' This was an understatement of which a Whitehall civil servant would have been proud.

Meanwhile, as the French military establishment ticked off the calendar days bringing closer the end of the Legion as it had existed hitherto, the country's foreign volunteers were still handed the jobs others preferred to avoid. As *The Times* put it: 'Legionnaires . . . have little contact with the rest of France's forces. Also, they are often sent on the most dangerous missions, such as mine-clearance in Kosovo.' The British army, *The Times* might have observed, used its own foreign mercenaries, the Gurkhas – two of whom were killed in Kosovo – for the same purpose. One of those casualties was a British officer.

The Balkans had other lessons for the French military establishment, which it had to learn the hard way, as the bloodless victories the public had come to expect proved to be a process of military self-deception. Its born-again army discovered the sort of ethnic warfare – sometimes comfortingly described as 'peace-keeping' – familiar to British soldiers from Cyprus to Ulster. In 1994, as Lieutenant-General Sir Michael Rose recalled, 'a handful of women held a French convoy hostage for five weeks only a few miles from Sarajevo'. This occurred on a main supply route crossing two mountain passes, through narrow defiles, over forty-four bridges. It was a place where 'a few determined men can deny the route . . . by direct or indirect fire, mining, destroying bridges or even getting the civilian population to block the road'.

The Legion, many of whose volunteers are Serbs, took such annoyances in their stride. Things got no better for the peacetime soldiers of the regular French army. Following Nato's first offensive operation in its fifty-year history – the aerial bombardment to expel the Yugoslav (Serb) army from Kosovo province in 1999, France was allocated control of the turbulent northern sector, including the hell's brew of Mitrovica, a city divided by a river and ancient racial hatreds wearily described by Prime Minister Disraeli in 1878: 'Political intrigues, constant rivalries, a total absence of all public spirit . . . hatred of all races, animosities of rival religions and absence of any controlling power'. The French contingent of 4,000 – the largest among a force totalling 7,200 in this sector – suffered forty-two wounded during the first three months of 2000. A newspaper cartoon told the story: a graffiti-laden wall (*'Mort aux Serbs!' 'Mort aux Albanians!' 'Mort aux Francais!'*) and a wry comment from a sandbagged Allied, K-For position: 'Liberté. Egalité. Fraternité.'

Corporal Willi Othelot, a soldier serving with one of France's orthodox units, like most of his battalion, 'joined the army very recently' at the age of twenty-seven and found himself a new role in life: as a walking target for snipers and shocked by the spectacle of a comrade lying, bleeding. Another disturbed by the Kosovo experience was Sergeant-Major (Adjutant) Lebreton, seventeen years a soldier but without combat experience until he arrived in Mitrovica on 3 February 2000. 'Next day a grenade exploded in an Albanian apartment in the [Serb-dominant] north of the city. A pregnant woman and a kid were killed. I was there. A crowd of Serbs spat on the surviving children as they came out, eyes full of hatred. How do you forget that?'

Well, at least, a sympathetic reporter suggested, he could go home soon to his daughters, to start to forget. Not quite. His wife, also a serving soldier, would be sent to Mitrovica to replace him.

If the Legion's separateness from the rest of the French army was eroded by the Chirac reforms, there was also at last a grudging recognition of the Legion's wounded as French nationals by right, regardless of their length of service. Until 1999 a legionnaire could claim French citizenship after three years' service unless he was injured within that time. His reward, in that case: discharge without right of French citizenship. In September 1999, debating a new Nationality Act, the Justice Minister Elisabeth Guigou ruled that the government would make 'no exceptions' to the three-year rule. In doing so she overlooked the continuing mystique and political power of the Legion even at this cynical *fin de siècle*. Recalling Pascal Bonnetti's famous verse, 'The Foreign Volunteer, 1914',

> *Qui sait si l'inconnu qui dort sous l'arche immense . . .*
> *N'est pas cet étranger devenu fils de France*
> *Non par le sang reçu mais par le sang versé?*

> *[Who knows this unknown man sleeping under the arched*
>   *sky . . .*
> *Has he not become a son of France*
> *Not through the blood inherited, but the blood he shed?]*

the tribal elders raised a storm in Paris. *Le sang versé* – blood sacrifice – became the mantra of a potent political and media campaign. The old lion Pierre Messmer, a former Prime Minister and a Legion hero of Bir Hakeim fifty years earlier, denounced Guigou's ruling.

The number of Legion casualties – and therefore the cost to France of reform – was now minimal: just eight dead and sixteen wounded since 1995 in the Balkans, the Central African Republic and the Congo. But historically, France owed rather more than that to the citizens it accepted through the blood they shed. Approximately 35,000 legionnaires have died for France since 1831. Of those, 10,000 lost their lives in Vietnam, 1945–54, and almost 2,000 in Algeria, 1954–62. The number of wounded, many crippled for life, runs to hundreds of thousands. One of these was Corporal Mariuz Novakowski, from Poland. As a result of wounds he suffered while peacekeeping in Sarajevo in 1993 he had a leg amputated in Les Invalides military hospital in Paris. The Defence Minister, François Leotard, during a visit to the hospital, asked the young legionnaire how France could reward his service. Novakowski said he wanted 'neither a medal nor money, sir, but to be French'.

Initially, this cut no ice with that personification of French bureaucracy, Le Pouvoir. As Madame Guigou's aide,

Francis Cavarrac, put it, the government did not want to disappoint the Legion but it would not extend the citizenship rights the soldiers already enjoyed. He added: 'In particular, we want to be able to assess the degree of these people's attachment to France. Do they really want to be French, or just not to be who they actually are?' At that time, the Legion's 7,867 men, representing 138 nations, were bonded together by a unique brotherhood, in which only one out of every twenty applicants now passed initial selection. Of these, 46 per cent were Slavs; 28 per cent French.

The Legion pressed its case in the National Assembly, where MPs voted unanimously to overturn the three-year rule. The debate raised an interesting, if unanswerable, philosophical issue. What does 'French' mean? What 'France' does the foreign volunteer now risk his life for? As nation states decline under the pressure of multinational forces, in a world dominated by a single superpower, the old verities no longer hold good for any nation – including Britain – that lays claim to a military tradition of obedience and self-sacrifice.

It is possible that Monsieur Cavarrac, unintentionally, identified the secret of maintaining the sacrificial tradition in a culture of bloodless victory and hedonistic risk-avoidance. The Legion proclaims that 'The Legion is Our Country', not France. It is that dimension which still worries political France, hedging its bets, with one eye on the inconvenient loyalty and commitment of the Legion 'rebels' in Algeria.

Yet it is just such tribalism, uniquely expressed as a *multinational* value by the Legion, that is the way ahead for armies of the future. The strategic failures of Allied campaigns in Iraq and Kosovo have demonstrated that the New World Order alternative – high-tech, remote warfare; computerized games magnified by slick media-management as a perception of war, but without *le sang versé* – will not work. War is part of the human condition. Regrettably, warfare requires sacrifice. Sensible people prefer that the sacrifice be made by others. The soldier's agenda pays little heed to politics; less to expediency. The legionnaire has a rendezvous with himself and kindred spirits, as well as, in due time, a rendezvous with death.

Appendix I

Foreign Legion Campaign Chronology

1831	Foundation and start of Algerian Conquest
1835–39	Spanish Civil War (First Foreign Legion assigned to Spain)
1835	New Foreign Legion founded: joins Armée d'Afrique in Algeria
1839	Survivors of Spanish campaign join the new Legion
1854–55	Crimea
1859	Northern Italy
1863–67	Mexico
1870–71	Orléans, Alpine France, Paris
1882–1908	Saharan Morocco ('South Oranais')
1883	Tonkin, Indo-China
1885	Formosa
1892	Dahomey
1893	Sudan
1895	Madagascar
1907–14	Morocco
1914–18	Western Front (France) Eastern Front (Dardanelles; Serbia)
1918–20	Northern Russia
1918–33	Morocco
1917–27	Syria
1940	Battle of France prior to surrender of May 1940
1940	Norway, 13 Demi-Brigade (13 DBLE)
1940–45	Free French legionnaires of 13 DBLE supporting de Gaulle after French surrender of May 1940 Dakar Eritrea Lebanon Syria Opposing Vichy French forces including 6 Foreign Legion Infantry Regiment.

1940–45		Bir Hakeim, Western Desert
		El Himeimat (Alamein flank)
		Tunisia
		Italy
		Southern France
		Alsace
		Western France (Gironde)
		Strasbourg
		Colmar
		French Alps
1940–42	Legionnaires loyal to Vichy France	North Africa
		Indo-China
		French West Africa
	Syria	Opposing Allied forces
	Lebanon	including 13 DBLE
(1942	Vichy overrun by Germany following Vichy's surrender to Allied landing in North Africa. France changes sides.)	
1942–45	Legion other than Free French and Indo-Chinese garrison	Tunisia (Opposing Axis forces)
		Southern France
		Vosges, Eastern France
		Colmar
		Karlsruhe, Germany
		Stuttgart
		Arlberg, Austria
1940–45	5 Foreign Legion Infantry Regiment	Indo-China: Neutral during Japanese occupation of French Indo-China
March 1945	Japanese attack Legion bases	Legion survivors of Japanese massacres march into China; return after Japanese surrender. 5 Foreign Legion Infantry Regiment then disbanded

August 1945	Japan surrenders to Ho Chi Minh's Viet Minh resistance movement
Sep. 1945	Ho Chi Minh's Vietnamese Republic declared. Hostilities between French and Vietnamese
1945–54	Indo-China
1954–62	Algeria, War of Independence
1961–	Irregular criminal activity by some legionnaires supporting Secret Army Organization opposed to Algerian independence and de Gaulle's U-turn on this issue.
1969–71	Chad
1976	Djibouti (hostage rescue)
1978	Kolwezi, Zaïre
1978–80	Chad
1982–83	Beirut (with multinational peacekeeping force)
1983–84	Chad (confrontation with Libya)
1990	Gabon
	Rwanda
1990–91	The Gulf War (as part of US-led alliance against Iraq)
1991–92	Djibouti (guerrilla activity)
1993	Sarajevo
1994	Rwanda
1996–97	Central African Republic
1996–98	Bosnia (Stabfor)
1999 onward	Kosovo
2002	Modernization plan complete: Legion strength cut to 7,867 and diluted

Legion's garrison deployments: Mainland France
Corsica
Djibouti, Gulf of Aden
Mayotte, Indian Ocean
French Guiana

Appendix II

Sous Lieutenant Jean Nicolas Napoleon Vilain

In 1849 an award for bravery was created by the British for non-commissioned officers. (At that time the Victoria Cross had not yet been initiated.) This award had been instituted for the purpose of rewarding British NCOs for outstanding acts of bravery on the field of combat. It was very rarely granted to foreign troops, except where particular acts of gallantry by the individual had resulted in saving British lives. This medal had been given the designation of 'Meritorious Service Medal'. A record of all the recipients of this decoration can be found in the Public Office at Kew.

Up to 1987 and the 124th anniversary of the Battle of Camerone, no Foreign Legion historian, either British or French, has uncovered the fact that Lieutenant Jean Nicolas Napoleon Vilain, at the time of his death on 30 April 1863, wore on his breast *three* decorations for bravery: Chevalier de l'Ordre Imperial de la Legion d'Honneur, gained at Solferino on 17 June 1859; the Medaille d'Or won during the battle of Magenta, 1859 and the British Meritorious Service Medal, granted by Queen Victoria for his services rendered to the British during the Assault of Malakoff, Sebastopol on 18 June 1855.

All of these awards had been won by Vilain either in the grade of Sergeant or Sergeant Major. This was the anniversary of the Battle of Waterloo, a day at Sebastopol during which the combined British and French forces had suffered 6,000 deaths in 24 hours.

Bibliography

Titles in English

DMS Market Intelligence, *Rapid Deployment Force*. DMS Inc., 1980.

International Institute for Strategic Studies, *The Military Balance, 1985–1986*.

International Institute for Strategic Studies, *Strategic Survey 1990–1991*; *Strategic Survey 1994–1995*; *Strategic Survey 1995–1996*; *Strategic Survey 1996–1997*; *Strategic Survey 1998–1999*.

Pentagon Task Force, *The Pentagon Papers, The Defense Department History of United States Decisionmaking on Vietnam, Volume One*. Boston: Beacon Press, 1971.

Behr, Edward, *The Algerian Problem*. London: Hodder and Stoughton, 1961.

Billière, Peter de la, *Storm Command: A Personal Account of the Gulf War*. London: HarperCollins, 1992.

Chipman, John, *French Military Policy and African Security*. London: International Institute for Strategic Studies, 1985.

Cobban, Alfred, *A History of Modern France, Vol. 2: 1799–1871*. Harmondsworth: Penguin Books, 1965.

de Quetteville, Harry, 'Women to Join Foreign Legion'. London: *Daily Telegraph*, 13 October 2000.

Des Forges, Alison, *Leave None to Tell the Story*. New York: Human Rights Watch, and Paris: International Federation of Human Rights Leagues.

Garrett, Richard, *General Gordon*. London: Arthur Barker, 1974.

George, Sir Arthur, *Life of Lord Kitchener*. London: Macmillan, 1920.

Goebbels, Dr J., *The Goebbels Diaries, 1939–41*. London: Hamish Hamilton, 1982.

Gooch, G. P., *History of Modern Europe 1871–1919*. London: Cassell, 1923.

Gourevitch, Philip, *We Wish to Inform You that Tomorrow We Will be Killed with Our Families*. London: Picador, 2000.

Grant, A. J. C. and H. Temperley, *Europe in the Nineteenth and Twentieth Centuries (1789–1939)*. London: Longmans, Green & Co., 1940.

Grauwin, Paul, *Doctor at Dien Bien Phu*. London: Hutchinson, 1955.

Guedella, Philip, *The Two Marshals*. London: Hodder and Stoughton, 1943.

Halliday, E. M., *The Ignorant Armies – The Anglo-American Archangel Expedition 1918–19*. London: Weidenfeld and Nicolson, 1960.

Hamilton, Iain, *Koestler, a Biography*. London: Secker and Warburg, 1982.

Henley, Jon, 'I think actually they thought I was a man' (Interview with Susan Travers). London: *Guardian*, 7 December 2000.

Herbert, Susannah, '37 years on, France says it did fight Algerians'. London: *Daily Telegraph*, 11 June 1999.

Heuser, Dr Beatrice, 'The Transformation of France's Armed Forces'. London: *RUSI Journal*, February 1997.

Hirst, David, *The Gun and the Olive Branch – The Roots of Violence in the Middle East*. London: Faber and Faber, 1977.

Horne, Alistair, *The French Army and Politics*. London: Macmillan, 1984.

Ironside, Lord, *Archangel 1918–19*. London: Constable, 1953.

Jacobson, Philip, 'France Hints at Readiness to Break Ranks over Kuwait'. London: *The Times*, 5 December 1990.

John, Colin, *Nothing to Lose*. London: Cassell, 1955.

Johnson, Paul, *A History of the Modern World (from 1917 to the 1980s)*. London: Weidenfeld and Nicolson, 1983.

Kingsford, C. L., *The Story of the Royal Warwickshire Regiment*. London: George Newnes, 1921.

La Guardia, Anton, 'Slaughter of Tutsis blamed on the West'. London: *Daily Telegraph*, 1 April 1999.

McLeave, Hugh, *The Damned Die Hard*. Farnborough: Saxon House, D. C. Heath, 1974.

Maurice, J. F., et al., *The Franco-German War 1870–71 by Generals and Other Officers who took part in the Campaign*. London: A. Sonnenschein & Co., 1900.

Mockler, Anthony, *Our Enemies the French*. London: Leo Cooper, 1976.

Moorehead, Alan, *African Trilogy*. London: Lansborough, 1959.

Munro, Sir Alan, 'Politics & Diplomacy Behind the Gulf War: "An Arabian Affair"'. London: *RUSI Journal*, April 1996.

Murray, Simon, *Legionnaire – An Englishman in the French Foreign Legion*. London: Sidgwick and Jackson, 1978.

Osburn, Arthur, *Unwilling Passenger*. London: Faber and Faber, 1932.

Parker, John, *Inside the Foreign Legion*. London: Piatkus, 1998.

Paxton, Robert O., *Parades and Politics at Vichy*. Princeton: Yale University Press, 1966.

Pitt, Barrie, *The Crucible of War – Year of Alamein, 1942*. London: Jonathan Cape, 1982.

Porch, Douglas, *The Conquest of the Sahara*. London: Jonathan Cape, 1985.

Rose, Sir Michael, 'A Year in Bosnia . . .'. London: *RUSI Journal*, June 1995.

—— 'Are We Creating a Universal Culture of Violence? The Global Challenges of Peacekeeping'. London: *RUSI Journal*, April/May 1999.

Sage, Adam, 'Legion Fights March of Sex Equality'. London: *The Times*, 19 July 1999.

Shaplen, Robert, *The Lost Revolution – Vietnam 1945–65*. London: André Deutsch, 1966.

Shearer, David, 'Africa's Great War'. *Survival: The IISS Quarterly*, summer 1999.

Terrill, Andrew, 'Chemical Warfare and "Desert Storm": The Disaster That Never Came'. Ilford: *Small Wars & Insurgencies*, autumn 1993.

Tombs, Robert, *The War Against Paris 1871*. Cambridge: Cambridge University Press, 1981.

Whitehouse, Arch, *Legion of the Lafayette*. New York: Modern Literary Editions Publishing Company and Doubleday & Co., 1962.

Windrow, Martin, *Uniforms of the French Foreign Legion 1831–1981*. Poole: Blandford Press, 1982.

Wood, H. F., *Adventure in North Russia: Allied operations against the Bolsheviks, 1919. Canadian Army Journal*, Vol. 11, No. 4.

Yost, David S., *France's Deterrent Posture and Security in Europe*. London: International Institute for Strategic Studies, 1985.

Young, John Robert, et al., *The French Foreign Legion*. London: Thames and Hudson, 1984.

Young, Brig. Peter, *A Dictionary of Battles (1816–1976)*. London: New English Library, 1977.

Zeldin, Theodore, *The French*. London: Collins, 1983.

Titles in French

'Mémorial de Nos Compagnons – Lieutenant Jean Deve, dit "Dewey"', *Journal de la Treizième Demi-Brigade*, 1984.

Képi Blanc editorial team, *La Légion Étrangère à 150 Ans*. Aubagne: Service Information et Historique de la Légion Étrangère, 1981.

Képi Blanc. Aubagne, March 1991, July 1991, May 1999.

Documents Diplomatiques Français, 1871–1914, Tome XI. Serie 2. Imp. Nationale.

'Kosovo: les Français dans le piège' Paris: *Aujourd'hui*, 24 March 2000.

Andoque, Nicolas d', *1955–1962 Guerre et Paix en Algérie – L'épopée silencieuse des SAS*. Paris: Société de Production Litteraire, 1977.

Bonnencarré, Paul, *La Guerre Cruelle – La Légion Étrangère en Algérie*. Paris: Fayard, 1972.

Chastenet, Jacques, *Jours Inquiets et Jours Sanglants – Histoire de la Troisième Republique*. Paris: Hachette, 1955.

Courrière, Yves, *La Guerre d'Algérie*. Vol. 1: *Les Fils de la Toussaint*; Vol. 2: *Le Temps des Léopards*; Vol. 3: *L'heure des Colonels*; Vol. 4: *Lex Feux du Désespoir*. Paris: Fayard, 1968.

Decoux, Adml., *A la Barre de l'Indo-Chine*. Paris: Plon, 1949.

La Délégation Française auprès de la Commission Allemande de l'Armistice, Tomes II and III. Paris: Imp. Nationale, 1950, 1952.

Devillers, Philippe, *Histoire du Viet-Nam de 1940 à 1952*. Paris: Editions du Seuil, 1952.

De Vivie, François-Xavier et al., *La Légion Étrangère 150e anniversaire*. *Historia Special*, No. 414 bis. Paris: Librairie Jules Tallandier, 1981; *Les Paras*. *Historia Special*, No. 391 bis, 1979.

El-Kader, Abd, *Lettre aux Français* (translated from the Arabic by Réné R. Khawam). Paris: Editions Phebus, 1977.

Fleury, Georges, *Mourir à Lang Son*. Paris: Editions Grasset et Fasquelle, 1985.

Gandy, Alain, *Royale Étrangère – Légionnaires Cavaliers au Combat 1921–1984*. Paris: Presses de la Cité, 1985.

Gauchon, Pascal and Patrick Buisson, *OAS – Jean Pied Noir*. Bievres, France, 1984.

Huré, Gen. R., et al., *L'Armée d'Afrique, 1830–1962*. Paris-Limoges: Charles-Lavauzelle, 1977.

Jauffret, J.-Ch., *Armée et pouvoir politique. La question des troupes spéciales chargées du maintien de l'order en France de 1871 à 1914*. Paris: Revue Historique, Presses Universitaires de France, 1983.

Koenig, Gen. Pierre, *Ce Jour-là: Bir Hakeim*. Paris: Editions Robert Laffont, 1971.

Lasserre, Jean, et al., *Bir Hakeim*. Orly: Icare, 1971.

Le Mire, Col. Henri, *Histoire Militaire de la Guerre d'Algérie*. Paris: Albin Michel, 1982.

Massu, Gen. Jacques, *La Vraie Bataille d'Alger*. Paris: Plon, 1971.

Mordal, Jacques, *Bir Hakeim*. Paris: Presses de la Cité, 1970.

Sabattier, G., *Le Destin de l'Indochine*. Paris: Plon, 1952.

Saint-Hillier, Gen. de CA, *Bir Hakeim 26 mai – 11 juin 1942*. Paris: Almanach du Combattant, 1982.

Sergent, Pierre, *Paras-Legion – le 2ème BEP en Indochine*. Paris: Presses de la Cité, 1982.

—— *Je Ne Regrette Rien – La poignante histoire des légionnaires parachutistes du 1er REP*. Paris: Librairie Arthème Fayard, 1972.

—— *Ma Peau au Bout de mes Idées*. Paris: La Table Ronde, 1967.

—— *La Légion*. Paris: Graphiques Lafayette, 1985.

Spartacus, Col., *Operation Manta – Tchad 1983–1984*. Paris: Plon, 1985.

Villaume, Col., et al., *Légion Étrangère 1831–1981: Revue Historique des Armées, No. Special 1981*. Vincennes: Service Historiques des Armées, 1980.

Yacono, Xavier, *Que Sais-je: Histoire de la colonisation française*. Paris: Presses Universitaires de France, 1984.

Ysquierdo, Antoine, *Une Guerre Pour Rien – Le 1er REP cinq ans après*. Paris: La Table Ronde, 1966.

Postscript

The Legion Reformed

In 2001 the Legion published a glossy brochure – *Agenda 2001* – inviting new volunteers to make contact at any one of seventeen recruitment centres in France. As if to emphasize its undiminished spirit the Legion's commandant, General Bernard Grail, opened the publication with the words: 'The Legion occupies a place apart in the French Army.'

This brave sentiment was not sustained by the new Order of Battle, itemizing the Legion's new structure. According to *Agenda 2001* the Legion's ten regiments, comprising 5,768 legionnaires, 1,705 NCOs and 394 officers, would be dispersed as follows:

Non-combat units:
    1 RE – Administration, support (Aubagne, France)
    4 RE – Basic training (Castelnaudry, France)

Combat units:
Under command of 11 Para Brigade of regular French Army:
    2 REP (paras) based at Calvi, Corsica
Under command of 6 Light Armoured Brigade of regular French Army:
    1 REC (cavalry) based at Orange, France
    1 REG (engineers) based at Laudun, France
    2 REI (infantry) based at Nîmes, France
Under command of 27 Mountain Infantry Brigade of regular French Army:
    2 REG (engineers) based at St Christol, France

Under local command overseas:
   3 REI (Infantry) based at Kourou, French Guiana
   13 DBLE (mixed) based at Djibouti
   Legion detachment, Mayotte.

No Legion bases now existed in sub-Saharan Africa, the Maghrib or the Pacific. Many legionnaires serving in Guiana, Djibouti and Mayotte would be there for short four-month tours. Others would serve alongside their French comrades on intervention operations – peacekeeping; aided evacuation tasks, etc. – wherever necessary.

   Agenda 2001 did not discuss the possibility of women, including foreign women, serving with the Legion though it did note the rising percentage of men from Russia, Ukraine, Poland, Hungary, Rumania and Slovakia now serving: in all, 46 per cent of the strength was categorized as 'Slav'.

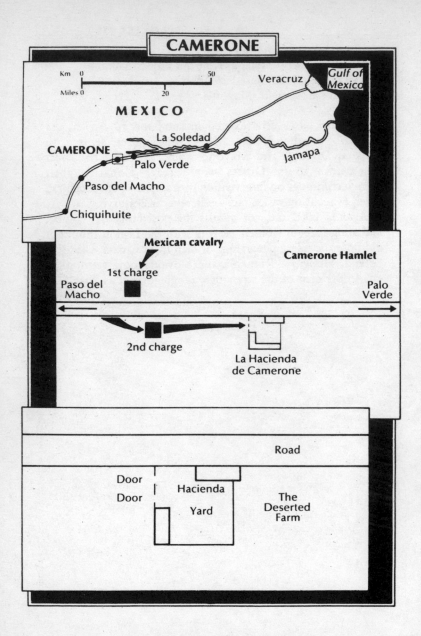

CAMERONE

Km 0   50

Miles 0   20

Veracruz

Gulf of Mexico

MEXICO

La Soledad

CAMERONE

Palo Verde

Jamapa

Paso del Macho

Chiquihuite

Mexican cavalry

Camerone Hamlet

1st charge

Paso del Macho

Palo Verde

2nd charge

La Hacienda de Camerone

Road

Door

Hacienda

Door

Yard

The Deserted Farm

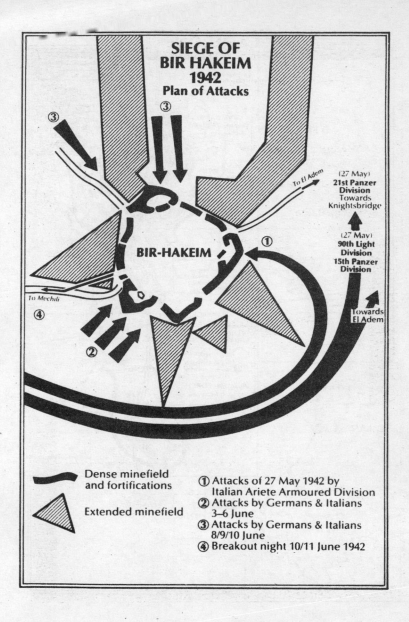

SIEGE OF BIR HAKEIM 1942
Plan of Attacks

BIR-HAKEIM

To El Adem

(27 May)
21st Panzer Division
Towards
Knightsbridge

(27 May)
**90th Light Division
15th Panzer Division**

Towards
El Adem

To Mechili

Dense minefield
and fortifications

Extended minefield

① Attacks of 27 May 1942 by
Italian Ariete Armoured Division
② Attacks by Germans & Italians
3–6 June
③ Attacks by Germans & Italians
8/9/10 June
④ Breakout night 10/11 June 1942

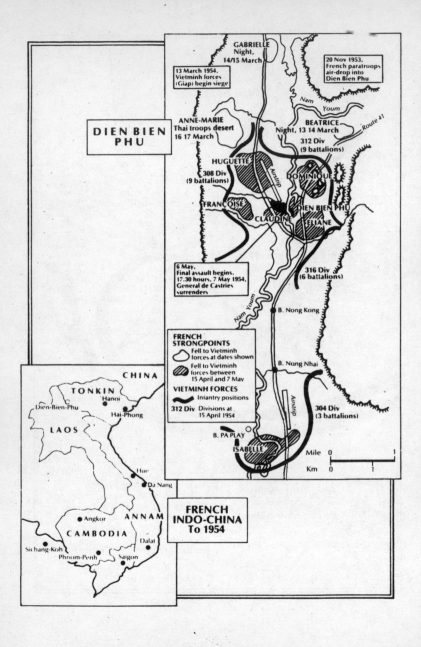

DIEN BIEN PHU

GABRIELLE
Night,
14/15 March

20 Nov 1953,
French paratroops
air-drop into
Dien Bien Phu

13 March 1954,
Vietminh forces
(Giap) begin siege

ANNE-MARIE
Thai troops desert
16 17 March

BEATRICE
Night, 13 14 March
312 Div
(9 battalions)

Nam Youm

Route 41

HUGUETTE
308 Div
(9 battalions)

DOMINIQUE

Airstrip

FRANCOISE

DIEN BIEN PHU

CLAUDINE

ELIANE

6 May,
Final assault begins.
17.30 hours, 7 May 1954,
General de Castries
surrenders

316 Div
(6 battalions)

Nam Youm

B. Nong Kong

FRENCH
STRONGPOINTS
Fell to Vietminh
forces at dates shown
Fell to Vietminh
forces between
15 April and 7 May
VIETMINH FORCES
Infantry positions
312 Div Divisions at
15 April 1954

B. Nong Nhai

Airstrip

304 Div
(3 battalions)

CHINA

TONKIN

Hanoi

Dien-Bien-Phu

Hai-Phong

LAOS

B. PA PLAY

ISABELLE

Mile 0   1

Km   0   1

Hue

Da Nang

ANNAM

FRENCH
INDO-CHINA
To 1954

Angkor

CAMBODIA

Dalat

Si chang-Koh

Phnom-Penh

Saigon

Index

Aage, Prince, of Denmark 186, 191
Abd-el-Aziz, Sultan of Morocco 154
Aberdeen, Lord 70
Africa: scramble for 127, 132–4, 135
African Light Infantry (Bats d'Af) 45, 70
Agadir Incident, 1911 155–6
Agence France-Presse 311
Ahmad, *dey* of Constantine 57
Aigle, Lt Caroline 411
Alcheik, Jim 353
Alexander, King of Serbia 167
Algeciras Conference, 1906 148
Algeria
  Armé de Libération Nationale
    (ALN) 300–301, 303–15 passim,
    323, 327, 329, 331, 333, 336,
    337, 339, 355, 356–7
  Barbouzes, Les 352
  'C' Force 354
  Delta Force 348–9, 350, 355, 356,
    357
  FLN 313
  French settlers ('*Pieds Noirs*') 300,
    327, 328, 329, 336, 341–2, 344,
    347, 349, 356
  history of French in: first French
    incursion 38, 40–1, 44–9; progress
    of French conquest, 1835–47
    56–63; colonisation 63; subduing
    the Kabylie 72–3; French punitive
    expedition, 1903 143; unrest on
    VE-Day, 1945 302–3; War of
    Liberation, 1954–8 302–25; use of
    torture 310–15 *passim*; settlers'
    revolt, 1958 328–9; French
    acceptance of war 401; *See also* De
    Gaulle, Gen. Charles
  Movement for Co-operation (MPC)
    352
  Organisation de l'Armée Secrète
    (OAS) 345, 348, 349, 352, 354,
    355, 364
Algerian Tirailleurs (Turcos) 45, 70,

74, 78, 79, 99, 100, 158, 201, 301,
  365
Algiers
  history of French in: reconnoitring
    38, 39; landing, 1830 38, 41;
    reasons for French assault 39–40;
    Battle of, 1957 312, 315, 330
  Kasbah 308
  slave market 39–40
Algiers Echo 346
Allenby, Gen. 197
Alonzo, Leg. 232
Amelot, Sec. Lt 130
Amilakvari, Lt-Col. Dimitri 28, 223,
  226, 248, 251, 260–5 *passim*
André, Gen. 140
Arago, Major 101
Archinard, Col. Louis 133
Armée d'Afrique 38, 44, 45, 47, 49,
  57, 58, 63, 65, 78, 91, 92, 102, 105,
  113, 115, 135, 188, 196, 201, 204,
  210, 228, 365
  in Crimean War 70
  in Franco-Prussian War 99, 103
  in World War I 158, 177
Armée d'Orient, 1915 166
  Régiment de Marche d'Afrique 166
Ascherson, Neal 19
As-Salman (Iraq) 396–7, 399
Aubagne: Legion depot at 34, 132,
  369
Aumale, Duke of 62
Austria
  defeated by Prussia, 1866 93, 94, 96
  defeated in Italy, 1858–9 74–9

Bablon, Major 227
Babonneau, Major 248, 250, 251, 252,
  266
Bach, Jimmy, Leg. 179–80
Baer, Leg. Rif 169
Balfour, A. J. (Lord) 197
Balkans, the, 402, 412

Bangerter, Leg. 173
Bao Dai, Emperor of Vietnam 272, 275, 281, 284, 285
Barbary Coast pirates 37, 40
Barbateau, Capt. 181, 182
Barre, Major 135
Bay Vien, Le Van 284
Bazaine, Lt Achille (later Marshal) 25, 44, 55, 59, 66, 67, 71, 91, 93, 108, 109, 110
    marital problems 91–2
    military career: campaigns in Mexico, 1860s 91, 92; evacuates French from Mexico 94; made scapegoat for Mexican fiasco 94; surrenders Metz in Franco-Prussian War 108–9; court-martialled 109–10; imprisoned 110; escape into exile and death 110
Bazaine, the Mesdames 67–8, 71, 92
Behanzin, King of Dahomey 127–131 passim
Beasting 14
Behr, Edward: The Algerian Problem 61, 299, 300, 311, 313
Belackem, Krim 312
Bellec, Lt 260
Ben Bella 301
Benedetti, Ambassador 98
Berg, Corp. 90
Bergot, Erwan 42
Bernelle, Col. Joseph 50–3 passim
Bernelle, Mme Tharsile 50, 51, 53
Berset, Sgt Samuel-Benoit 52
Bertrand, Col. 142
Bethouart, Gen. 218, 220
Beulin, Corp. 120
Biallas, Rudolfo 205, 235
Bichemin, Major 142, 144
Bidault, Georges 296
Billod, Leg. 90
Billotte, Gen. Pierre 311
Bir Hakeim 23, 68, 211, 221
    French defence, 1942 237 et seq.
    French evacuation 259–68
    strategic importance 23
Bismarck, Prince Otto von 97, 98, 106, 111, 113, 141
Blanc, Col. Marcel 217
Blum, Léon 280
Bobillot, Sgt 119, 120, 126
Bokassa, Pres., of Central African Republic 389

Boldini, Lt 48
Bonetti, Pascal 30
Bonnelet, Capt. 146
Bonnier, Lt-Col. Eugène 133
Borelli, Capt. de 111, 119, 122, 124, 125, 365
Bosnia, 402
Bou-Amama 114, 115
Boufflack, Sgt 260
Bougenot, André 294
Bourbaki, Gen. 85
Bourges-Manoury, Maurice 314
Boutin, Major 38
Bridges, Major Tom 165
Brothier, Col. 27
'Brückler', Sgt 212
Brundsaux, Capt. Paul 129, 131, 137, 140
    statue at Aubagne 132
Brunswick, Leg. (later Sgt) 90, 103
Bucereau, Colour-Sgt 230
Bugeaud, Gen. Thomas-Robert 59–62 passim
Bullard, Eugene 180
Byricnter, Corp. 231

Cambas, Col. 83, 88
Camerone, Mexico: Legion defence of, 1963 31, 32, 82, 83–91
Canrobert, Gen. François 66, 67
Cao Bang, Indo-China: French disaster at, 1950 285–6
Carbillet, Capt. 198
Carles, Lt-Col. Pierre 34, 96
Carlist Legion 54, 55
Carlos, Don, of Spain 42, 49, 54
Carlotta, Empress 94
Carpentier, Gen. 285
Castaing, Lt 200
Casteinau, Gen. 94
Catteau, Leg. Victor 88
Cattelin, Capt. 119, 122
Cavarrac, Francis 415
Cavour, Count 74
Cecconi, Sgt Marius 93
Cédile, Col. Jean 277, 278
Cendrars, Blaise 158
Central African Republic 402–3, 404–5
Chad 372–3, 384–5, 387–9
Challe, Gen. 332, 341, 342, 343, 345, 346, 347
Chancy, Marshal 96, 107

Changarnier, Gen. 60
Charles X, King of France 21, 39, 40
Charton, Col. 287
Chasseurs d'Afrique 45, 78, 99, 222, 365
Chavigny, Dr Paul 28
Chenel, Sec. Lt 214, 215
Chevenement, Jean-Pierre 394–5
Cheysson, Monsieur 389
Chipman, John 389
Chirac, Jacques 406, 411
Christ, Sgt 231
Christian, Leg. 155
Churchill, Winston 141, 148, 220, 236, 294, 295
Clauzel, Count Bertrand 41, 44, 57
Clemenceau, Georges 118, 189
Clermont-Tonnerre, Count 37, 40
Clinchant, Gen. 105
Cobban, Alfred: A History of Modern France 56, 59, 98
Coevoet, Capt. 382
Collot, Capt. 224
Combe, Col. Michel 28, 58
Combes, Emile 140
Conrad, Col. 28, 50–5
Conrad, Leg. 90
Conscription 401, 406
Constantine, Algeria: French capture, 1837 57–8
Constantine, Leg. Laurent 88
Corta, Capt. 186
Cot, Col. 166
Coty, Pres., of France 331
Crimean War 65–71
  battle of the Alma 66–7
  Charge of the Light Brigade 65
  fall of Sebastopol 70–1
Cros, Col. 163

Dahomey: Dodds' campaign, 1892 127–32
Daily Telegraph 151
Dallaire, Lt-Gen. Romeo, 408
D'Amade, Gen. 153, 156
Damascus: Omayyad Mosque 63
Damrémont, Gen. 58
Danjou, Capt. Jean 84, 85, 86, 89, 90
  wooden hand 89–90
D'Argenlieu, Adm. 279, 281
Darlan, Adm. Jean 228
Daumont, Col. 201
De Bourmont, Count Louis 38, 40, 41

De Brian, Major 92
De Castries, Capt. 114
De Chabrières, Col. Granet Lacroix 28, 75
De Chastenet, Major 373
De Foucauld, Charles 112, 143, 144
De Gaulle, Gen. Charles 32–3, 35, 216, 220, 221, 236, 312, 326, 327, 331, 367, 373
  career from 1940: looks for support in French colonies 220; becomes president, 1958 331–2; deals with Algerian problem 332, 334, 335–8, 342, 343, 345–9 passim, 355, 356, 359, 363, 364; makes cuts in African forces, 1959–64 365; makes cuts in French army 366 reshapes French outlook 366–7
De Grandmaison, Col. 157
De la Barre de Nanteuil, Gen. H. 287
De la Bigne, Lt Michel 339
De la Billière, Gen. Sir Peter 394, 400
De Lamaze, Col. Jean de Pradel 177
De la Moricière, Col. 58, 62
De la Tour, Col. 28
De Lannurien, Capt. 172
De Larminat, Col. (later Gen.) 221, 265, 359
De Lasalle, Comte 27
De l'Isle, Gen. Brière 124, 125
De Nedde, Lt 229–30
De Negrier, Col. François 19, 113, 114, 115, 117, 118
De Sairigné, Capt. (later Col.) Gabriel 28, 227, 248, 249, 253, 262, 283
De Seguins-Passiz, Gen. Hubert 282
De Soria, Lt 150
De Susbielle, Capt. 144, 145
De Tassigny, Gen. Jean de Lattre 228, 288
De Tocqueville, Alexis 19
De Tscharner, Capt. 169
De Verdilhac, Gen. 223
Degueldre, Lt Roger 330, 336–40 passim
  part in Algerian mutiny, 1960–2 348, 349, 356, 357–64
  trial and execution 358–62
Delarue, Father 35, 312, 338
Delcaretto, Corp. Adolfi 87
Dennikin, Gen. 190
Dentz, Gen. 220

Depoorter, Col. 381
Des Forges, Alison 409
D'Eu, Lt-Col. Clement 142
Deve (or Dewey), Lt Jean 256, 261
D'Hilliers, Marshal Baraguey 77
Dia, Capt. 120, 125
Diaz, Antonio 83
Dicken, Leg. Peter 87
Dien Bien Phu 31, 68, 126, 289–94, 305
Dodds, Col. Alfred-Amédée 128, 129, 130, 132
Dominé, Major 119–23 passim, 125
Donaldson, Corporal Willliam 404–5
Dorian, Jean-Pierre 185
Doumergue, Pres. Gaston 195
Dovecar, Sgt 'Boby' 322, 330, 337, 345, 350–1
   executed by firing squad 358
Doze, SM 58
Dreyfus, Capt. Alfred 139
Drude, Capt. Antoine 129
Dubois, Leg. 87
Duchesne, Gen. Charles 135, 137
Dufour, Col. Henri 334, 338
Dulles, John Foster 294
Dumoustier, Sec. Lt 51
Dunant, Henri 77
Dupetit, Lt 199, 201
Duriez, Lt-Col. 28, 171, 177, 178
Dutailly, Lt-Col. Henry 35
Duval, Gen. 302
Duval, Pierre 39
Duvivier, Col. 44

Eckstein, Colour-Sgt 260, 267
Economist, The 265, 388
Edward VII, King 151, 152
El-Kader, Abd- 46–7, 48, 56, 59, 60
   defeated by French in Algeria 62–3
   exiled to Damascus 63–4
Elkington, Leg. John Ford 164–6
El-Krim, Abd 189, 192–4, 196
Ely, Gen. Paul 328
Emerson, Ralph Waldo 96
Entente Cordiale, 1904 147, 148
Erulin, Col. 377, 379, 380, 381
Espinasse, Capt. (later Gen.) Louis 44, 62, 76
Estoup, Capt. 307, 345
Etienne, Eugène 110, 118
Eugénie, Empress 97, 98

Fairfax, Col. 168
Fashoda Incident, 1898 134
Faulques, Lt Roger 287
Faurax, Major 129
Feisal, King of Iraq 197
Ferrary, Capt. 51
Ferry, Jules 112, 116, 118
Finala, Sgt 93
Fiore, Lt 188
Fisk, Robert, 395
Flatters, Col. Paul 118
Flavinius, Marcus 34
Flores, Leg. 309
Foch, Marshal Ferdinand 185, 189
Foreign Legion
   attitude of French army to 32–3
   brotherhood of 27
   casualty figures 414
   devotion of men to officers 28
   different types of commission 33
   divided loyalty in World War II 23, 32–3
   expendability 19
   and French citizenship 413–15
   history: foundation, 1831 21–2, 42–3; sent to Algiers, 1831 42, 45; ceded to Spanish government, 1835 42; role in Algerian war, 1832–5 46–8; role in Carlist War in Spain, 1835–8 48–56; regiment returns to France, 1839 55; role in conquest of Algeria, 1835–47 56–62 passim; role in Crimean War 66; actions against Algerian Kabylie, 1857–8 72–3; part in Italian campaign, 1858–9 72–9; exploits in Mexico, 1862–7 81–94; desertions to US from Mexico 92–3; question of German legionnaires and Franco-Prussian War 96, 98, 106, 107; role in Franco-Prussian War, 1870–1 99–106 passim; position in 1870s 113; mounted infantry formed, 1881 113–14; role in Indo-China, 1883–5 115–26; campaign in Dahomey, 1892 127–32; African expeditions, 1890s 132–4; campaign in Madagascar, 1894 135–8; fighting in Algeria, 1901 143–6; moves into Morocco, early twentieth c. 148–9, 154–5; desertions, early twentieth c.

153–4; 'duration only' *régiments de marche*, World War I 158–61 *passim*; actions on Western Front, 1914–18 159–67, 167–79; actions against Turks, 1915–16 166; actions in N. Russia, 1918–20 180–3; decorations and casualties in World War I 177; composition after World War I 184–8; desertions in 1920s 187; return to N. Africa 187–8; Moroccan campaigns, 1920s 191, 192–6; beginning of motorization, 1930 194; Syrian campaigns 197–204; German demand for repatriation of German legionnaires after fall of France, 1940 205, 208–9, 210; Nazi-wanted legionnaires sent to Indo-China, 1940 214; German use of, World War II 213, 215, 222–3, 223–4; Allied use of, World War II 216–18, 220, 225–34, 237 *et seq.*; recruits Germans, 1945 235–6; march of 5 REI from Indo-China to China, 1945 273–4; service in Indo-China, 1946–54 280, 282–4, 285–98 *passim*; service in Algerian War, 1955–9 305–25, 330, 331, 333–9 *passim*; mutiny of 1961, Algeria 338, 340, 341–7; dissolution of 1 REP 347; punishments for mutineers 358–63; strength cut by de Gaulle, 1960s 365; dispersion after leaving Africa 369; intervention in Chad, 1969 372–3; intervention in Djibouti, 1978 374; intervention in Zaire, 1978 375–82; intervention in Chad, 1978 383–5; joins peacekeeping force in Beirut, 1982 385–6; third intervention in Chad 388–9; garrison roles today 389; in Gulf War 393–400; in Africa 403–10
importance of ritual 30–1
Képi Blanc, Le, journal 34, 397, 407
legionnaire's right to *nom-de-guerre* 26
main role outside France 21–2, 25, 26
motto 43
nationalities comprising 158, 159, 367–8

officered by French 27–30 *passim*, 33–4
periods of recruitment due to economic hardship 26
present-day 34, 35, 369, 402
reasons for Algerian mutiny, 1961 35, 299–300, 331–2, 334
reforms to 13–14, 406
romance of 26–7, 390–91, 397
sanctuary for outcasts 25–6, 42
scapegoat role 21
suicide explanation of legionnaire's motivation 29
women in 13–14, 410–11
Foreign Legion units
1st Battalion 60, 115
3rd Ballation 116
4th Battalion 116
Bataillons Étrangers de Parachutistes
1 BEP 283, 286, 287
2 BEP 291, 292, 293, 294
Brigades and Demi-Brigades
1st Brigade 161
13th Demi-Brigade 216, 217, 219, 220, 221, 226–7, 232–3, 240, 269, 279, 283, 288, 290, 357, 369, 374
2/13 DBLE 283
3/13 DBLE 290, 407
Régiments Étrangers
1 RE 70, 72, 76, 110, 119, 142, 146, 155, 158, 159, 185, 366
2 RE 62, 73, 75, 142, 143, 144, 158
5 RE 99, 100, 102
Régiments Étrangers de Cavalerie
1 REC 190, 191, 198, 229, 283, 369, 374, 383, 386, 396, 399
2 REC 393
Régiment Étranger de Genie
6REG 398
Régiments Étrangers d'Infanterie
1 REI 228, 229, 231–2
1/1 REI 228
1/3 REI 230
2 REI 192, 194, 229, 279, 383, 385, 386, 393, 394, 397–8, 399, 407
2/1 REI 229
3 REI 189, 229, 231, 279, 283, 290, 297, 335, 350, 357, 369, 389
3/3 REI 293
4 REI 197, 198, 199, 369
5 REI 214, 215, 273, 274, 290, 335, 369, 390

Cont. Foreign Legion units
6 REI 205, 215, 221, 222, 228, 231, 269, 317
11 REI 219
12 REI 219
Régiments Étrangers d'Infanterie de Marche
1 REI(M) 229
3 REI(M) 229
Régiment de Marche de la Légion Étrangère (Marching Regiment) 166, 168, 169, 171, 172, 174–8 *passim*, 399
Régiments de Marche de Volontiers Étrangers
21st RMVE 219
22 RMVE 219
23 RMVE 219
Régiments Étrangers de Parachutistes
1 REP 34, 35, 306, 307, 308, 312, 315, 316, 317, 319, 320, 324, 326, 329, 330, 331, 332, 333, 334, 336–45 *passim*, 347, 348, 357, 358, 362, 366
2 REP 333, 349, 362, 366, 370, 371–7 *passim*, 382, 385–6, 396–7, 407
Forey, Gen. Elie Frédéric 80, 83, 91, 390
France
fears at start of World War II 208
fluctuating attitudes to army 24
French Division of SS 211
history: revolution of 1830 21; political instability, nineteenth c. 24; imperialism, 1881–1907 111–12; African colonial policy decided by soldiers 133; discontent with army, early twentieth c. 138–140; Dreyfus case 139; problem of desertion from army, early twentieth c. 153; belief in the offensive, 1914–15 160, 166; surrender to Germany, 1940 205, 219–20; Unoccupied France seized by Germans, 1942 227; World War II collaboration with enemy 270–1; reshaped by de Gaulle, 1960s, 366–7; interventionist strategy and forces today 370, 371–3, 389
loss of empire 1533–1815 22
Maginot Line 219

and Nato 392
relation with Foreign Legion 36, 392–3, 396
reorganization of Army 13, 400–1, 406
successful period of imperialism 1830–1940 23
use of mercenaries 19
Vichy government 206, 215, 216
Franco-Prussian War, 1870 22, 25, 96–106
causes 97–8
Ems telegram 98
Foreign Legion losses 32
indifference to sick legionnaires 35–6, 102
progress: surrender of Napoleon III at Sedan 100; battle for Orléans 102–3; surrender of Metz 103, 108–9; siege of Paris 100, 103, 105
Franz Josef, Emperor 77, 81
French Guiana: Ariane base 389
Frey, Roger 354

Gabin, Jean 205
Gabon 407
Gaddafi, Col. 374, 384, 385, 387, 388, 389
Gaertner, Leg. 90
Gaillard, Prime Minister 326
Galliéni, Gen. Joseph 19, 127
Gallipoli, 1915–16 166
Gambert, Major 163
Gambetta, Léon 100, 102, 108
Gambiez, Lt (later Gen.) 194, 342, 345
Gamelin, Gen. 208
Gardy, Lt (later Gen.) 201–2, 203, 350
Gardy, Nicole 350
Garibaldi, Capt. Bruno 161
Garibaldi, Lt-Col. Giuseppe 161
Garibaldi, the Patriot 104
Gaucher, Col. 28
Gavoury, Police Commissioner 350
Gazeaux, Squadron SM 200, 203
Gemayel, Pres., of Lebanon 386
Gendarmerie d'Afrique 45
Genocide 392, 403
George V, King 166
George, Sir Arthur 99
Germann, Capt. 172
Germany
encourages legionnaires to desert 149–54 *passim*

question of German legionnaires fighting against 96, 99, 107, 205, 208–10, 211
reaction to French designs on Morocco 148
See also Franco-Prussian War, Prussia, and World Wars I and II
Germays, Sgt Jean 87
Giap, Gen. V. Nguyen 286, 288, 290
Gilson, Leg. 231
Giovaninelli, Col. 123, 12AH5
Girardet, Raoul 227
Giscard d'Estaing, Pres. Valéry 364
Glaspie, April, 393
Godard, Col. Yves 349
Godot, Lt 337, 344–5
Goebbels, Dr Joseph 205, 211, 215, 220
Gohier, Urbain 127, 138
The Army Against the Nation 138
Gombeaud, Major 231
Gordon, Lt (later Gen.) Charles 69
Gorzki, Leg. 90
Goudeau, Jean-Claude 299, 310
Goukouni Ouedeye, Gen. 383, 384, 387
Goums 45, 163
Grancher, Capt. 202
Grant, A. J. C. and Temperley, H.: *Europe in the Nineteenth and Twentieth Centuries* 81–2, 98, 147
Gras, Col. (later Gen.) 376, 377–8, 381–2
Grauwin, Dr Paul 292–3
Doctor at Dien Bien Phu 292
Greenpeace 402
Grimby, Lt 224
Guedalla, Philip: *the Two Marshals* 60, 71, 108
Guéninchault, Col. 28
Guigou, Elisabeth 413–4
Guilhem, Col. 28
Guiraud, Col. Maurice 341
Gulf War (1990–1) 393–400

Habré, Hissen 383, 387
Hacq, Michel 354
Haig, FM Sir Douglas 175
Haller, Leg. 90
Halliday, E. M.: *The Ignorant Armies* 181
Hamilton, Iain 207
Hardinge, Sir Charles (later Lord) 151

Harkis 45
Hascoet, Sgt 257
Hastings, Max 36
Heinz, Corp. 292
Herbinger, Lt-Col 117
Hernu, Charles 388, 390
Heuser, Dr Beatrice 401
Himmler, Heinrich 234
Hinderschmitt, Leg. 122
Ho Chi Minh 272–5 *passim*, 278, 280, 281
Horain, Major 48
Horne, Alistair
French Army and Politics, The 24, 139–40, 154, 366
on use of torture in Algeria 311
Housman, A. E.: 'Epitaph On An Army of Mercenaries' 390
Hugo, Victor 59
Hunter-Choat, Brig. A, OBE 89, 90, 363
Huré, Gen. R. et al.: *L'Armee d'Afrique* 42, 47, 58, 78, 177, 211, 287
Husband, Sec. Lt Edward 122
Husein, Khodja 39
Hussein, Saddam 393, 395, 399

Indo-China
'Black Flag' brigands 115, 284
French connection: French take over, 1880s 115–25; collaboration with Japanese, 1940–1 271; French return after World War II 276–81; Franco-Viet Minh War, 1946–54 280–98; thoughts of nuclear strike, 1954 294–6
numbers of French troops, 1953 282
Viet Minh 272, 275, 276, 277, 284, 285, 286, 289, 290, 291, 293
International Red Cross: founded 77
Ironside, Gen. (later Lord) 181, 182
Archangel, 1917–19 182
Isabella II, Queen of Spain 42, 49, 97
Itzkowitz, Leg. Eliahu 296–7, 298

Jacobson, Philip 395
Japanese
absorb Indo-China, 1940–1 271
murder of legionnaires, 1945 273
troops used to keep order by French and English 277
Jeannin, Leg. 90

Jeanningros, Col. Pierre 83, 89
Jeanpierre, Capt. (later Col) Pierre 28, 287, 309, 315, 316, 317–18, 322, 323, 324, 325
Joffre, Marshal Joseph 160, 167, 170
Johnson, Paul 91
    A History of the Modern World 92, 208, 217, 366–7
Joinville, Prince de 63
Jonnart, Célestin 143, 146
Josevitch, Lt 48
Jouhaud, Gen. Edmond 338, 346
Joxe, Pierre 394, 395
Joyeux 58, 60, 69, 99, 105, 117, 141, 144, 156, 158, 187
Juárez, Pres. Benito Pablo, of Mexico 80–1, 82, 92, 93
Juin, Gen. Alphonse 227, 232
Jünger, Ernst 158
Just, Herr 150

Kapf, Leg. 203
Karageorgevic, Sgt 99
    becomes King Peter I of Serbia, 1903 99
Kesselring, Gen. 232, 253
Kitchener, Lord, of Khartoum 99, 134
Klems, Sgt Joseph 191, 192, 196
Koenig, Gen. Pierre 237, 241, 242, 243, 245–60 passim, 261–8 passim
Koestler, Arthur 205–7, 208
Kosovo 402, 410, 412–3
Kunassec, Leg. 90, 192

La Pointe, Ali 308, 309
Labruyère, Sec. Lt 231
Lacoste, Capt. 354–8 passim
Lacoste, Robert 307, 311, 314, 330
Lafayette Squadron 178–80
Lai, Drummer 84, 89, 90
Laine, Lt Ramon 86
Lalande, Capt. (later Col.) 267
Lambert, Col. 232
Landriau, Capt, 198–201, 202
Laniel, Premier 294
Lansdale, Col. 284
Lapeyre, Lt Pol 193
Lappara, Major 230, 231
Laroche, Corp. 380
Lassen, Anders 320
Lawrence, T. E. 197
Le Mire, Col. Henri: Histoire Militaire de la Guerre d'Algérie 336

Le Pen, Jean Marie 310, 313, 364
Le Petit, Major 168
Lebanon
    Franco-British War, 1941 225
    PLO evacuated from Beirut, 1982 386
Lebeau, Col. 53
Lebreton, Sgt-Maj. (Adj) 413
Leclerc, Gen. Jacques 279, 281, 282
Lejeune, Max 314
Lemonnier, Gen. 273
Léonhard (Léonard), Leg. 90
Leopold, Prince of Hohenzollern-Sigmaringen 97
Leotard, François 414
Letulle, Major 142
Libération, Paris 309, 310, 313, 314
Lihaut, Corp. 71
Liskutin, Miroslav 207
    Stormy Skies – Reminiscences of an Aviator 207
Liu-Xan-Phuc 119
Louis-Philippe, King of France 21, 22, 41, 42, 43, 49, 54, 55, 56, 59, 62, 97
    sends rabble to fight in Algeria 42
    toppled by 1848 Revolution 64–5
Lyautey, Gen. Hubert 146, 155, 156, 163, 187, 190, 191, 193, 194

MacArthur, Douglas II 294
Maclean, Sir H. 149
McLeave, Hugh: The Damned Die Hard 21, 28, 76, 88, 177
MacMahon, Lt-Col. (later Marshal) 62, 64, 71, 73, 74, 75, 76, 110
Madagascar: French expedition of 1894 135–8
Mader, SM Max-Emmanuel 173–4, 176
Magenta, battle of 1859 75–6
Magrin-Vernerey, Lt-Col. ('Monclar') 217, 220, 223
Maigret, Monsieur 150
Maine, Corp. 88, 90
Maire, Capt. (later Col.) Fernand 126, 172, 176, 184, 185–7, 219
Maire, SM Victor 75
Malloum, Gen. Félix 383
Malraux, André 335
Mangin, Corp. 90
Mangin, Major Paul 73
Marchand, Capt. Jean Baptist 134

María Cristina, Queen, of Spain 42, 49, 55, 97
Martin, Lt 137
Martinez, Col. 83
Martinez, Col. Jose 75
Marty, Leg. 230
Masson, Col. 241
Massone, Lt 114
Massu, Gen. Jacques 305, 317, 311, 313, 318, 329, 336, 348, 364
Mata Hari 25
Maudet, Sec. Lt 84, 88, 90
Maurice, J. F. et al: *The Franco-German War* 101, 108, 109
Maximilian, Emperor of Mexico 81, 91, 93
Mellec, Abbé 243
Melvern, Linda 408
Ménestral, Col. 142
Menshikov, Prince 67
Merlet, Leg. 90
Messmer, Capt. Pierre 32, 245, 254, 267, 347, 414
Mexico
    French invasion, 1862 81–2
    French movements 90–1, 92–5
    Legion's defence of Cameone 85–8
    withdrawal of French, 1867 93–5
M'Hidi, Larbi Ben 308
Milan, Col. Francisco 80, 86–9 *passim*
Mine clearance 398, 412
Minnaert, Leg. (later Sgt) 116, 133
Minute 299, 310
Miramon, Pres. Miguel, of Mexico 80
Mitterand, François (later President) 306, 310, 314, 388
Mockler, Tony: *Our Enemies the French* 223, 225
Molé, Count 113
Mollet, Guy 314
Monnerot, Guy and Mme 302–4, 333
Moorehead, Alan: *African Trilogy* 211
Mori, Sgt 73
Morin, Capt. 283
Morin, Corp. 380
Morny, Duke de 80
Morocco 141
    French invasion, 1844 62–3
    French invasion, early twentieth c. 146–7, 148–9, 154–5
    French overrun, 1920s 192–6
Morzycki, Sgt 85, 87, 88
Mouley-Hafid, Sultan of Morocco 154

Moulin (or Porshmann), SM 234
Moullinay, Capt. 119, 120, 121, 125
Muller, Sgt 273
Mullet, Major 163
Munro, Sir Alan 394
Murati, Corp. Horst 284
Murray, Simon 33, 333, 362

Napoleon 19, 24, 36, 37, 38
Napoleon III 64, 70, 82, 91, 94
    comes to power 65
    plan to conquer Mexico, 1862 80–2, 93
    support for Italian unification 73–9 *passim*, 94
    surrenders to Prussians, 1870 100
Nationality 413–15
Navarre, Gen. Henri 288, 296
Nemours, Duke of 58
N'Guyen, van Suong, 400
Nicolas, Sgt 256–7
Nishiara, Gen. 271
Nivelle, Gen. Robert 170, 171, 174
Nogues, Gen. Auguste 215, 227
Noire, Major 163
Novakowski, Corporal Mariux 414

Oberhoffer, Lt-Gen. Franz 104
Observer 19
Ochsenbein, Gen. 76
Odintzoff, Leg. 199
Ollivier, Emile 98
Operation Punch (Gulf War) 396
Orléans, Duke of 59
Osburn, Arthur: *Unwilling Passenger* 165
Othelot, Corporal Willi 413

Palin, Corp. Ray 309
Palmaert, Leg. 90
Paris Commune, 1870 22, 106, 107
Parker, John 395
Paxton, Robert O.: *Parades and Politics at Vichy* 213–14, 216
Pein. Col. Theodor 28, 163, 164, 174
Pélissier, Col. (later Marshal) 61, 68, 71
Perrin, Monsieur 351
Pershing, Gen. 175
Pétain, Marshal Philippe 167, 170, 171, 174, 175, 206, 216
    defeats Abd el-Krim, 1926 194
Pflimlin, Pierre 331

Piaf, Edith 13, 26, 347
Picot, Georges 197
Piquemal, General Christian 13, 406, 411
Pirizinger, André Sgt 90
Piroth, Col. Charles 290
Pitt, Barrie: *The Crucible of War: Year of Alamein, 1942* 212
Poincaré, Raymond 160
Pointurier, Lt 144
Popoff, Sgt 203
Porch, Douglas 163
  The Conquest of the Sahara 43, 133, 134
Porter, Cole 158
Poulet, Capt. 380
Prestissimo, Col. 243, 244
Protegma, Leg. 309
Proye, SM 123
Prussia 96, 97, 98
  defeats Austria, 1866 93, 94
  See also Franco-Prussian War
Puchois, Major 266

Rachef, Leg. Alberto 267
Raffalli, Col. 28
Raglan, Lord 66, 67, 68
Rambouillet: Legion 'nursery' 159
Ranavalona III, Queen of Madagascar 137
Randon, Marshal Jacques de 72, 73, 93
Reuss, Leg. Johan 87
Reynaud, Paul 207
Ridgway, Gen. Matthew 295
Riet, Major 189
Robaglia, Jean 28
Robert, Lt 200
Robitaille, Col. 224
Rollet, Col. Paul 174–8 *passim*, 184, 186, 187, 189
Rommel, Gen. Erwin 239, 245, 246, 249, 250, 252, 253, 254, 255
Roosevelt, Pres. Franklin D. 270, 271, 276, 327
Rose, Sir Michael 408, 412
Roulet, Capt. 136
Russia
  Allied forces in, 1918–20 181–3
  Revolution, 1917 180
  signs peace treaty with Germany, 1917 175, 181

Rwanda 403, 407–9
Ryder, Gen. Charles 227

Sa'adi, Yacef 308, 313
Sacrifice, 415–16
Sadok, *Caid* Hadj 303–4
Sahara: French expeditions into, 1900 141–3
Saïda, N. Africa 158
St Arnaud, Col. (later Marshal) Leroy de 37, 44, 58–9, 61, 66, 68, 131
Saint-Hillier, Gen. Bernard 340, 342
Saint-Marc, Major Élie Denoix de 330, 336, 340, 341, 342, 347
  given ten years' imprisonment 363
Salan, Gen. Raoul 328, 332, 346, 355
  receives life sentence 358
Samarine, Leg. 181, 182, 184
Sarrail, Gen. 167, 198, 199
Sartre, Jean-Paul 24
Saussier, Capt. 84
Savary, Gen. 45, 46
Schaffner, Leg. 90
Schelmann, Leg. 120
Schelmann, Maréchal de Logis 200
Schiffer, Leg. 90
Schlegelmilch, Nicolas 269
Schlesser, Gen. 234
Schreiblich, Leg. 90
Seeger, Leg. Alan 31, 35, 157, 158, 169
Seffrin, Leg. 90
Segers, Leg. 90
Segrétain, Col. Pierre 28
Selchauhansen, Lt Christian 145
Senghor, Pres., of Mali 389
Sergent, Capt. Pierre 52, 183, 323, 329–30, 332, 339, 344, 346, 355, 364
  La Légion 53
Serval, SM 200
Sidi-bel-Abbès Legion HQ 64, 72, 82, 126, 129, 134, 158, 187, 189, 335, 337, 365, 369
Simon, Capt. (later Gen.) Jean 267
Simonot, Lt 309, 324
Si-Slimane 114
Solferino, battle of, 1859 77–8
Souetre, Capt. Jean-René 339
Soult, Marshal Joseph 22, 42
Spahis 45, 70, 79, 104, 143, 144, 156, 158, 201, 202, 365

Spain
  Carlist War of 1835–8 49–55
  defeated by Abd el-Krim, 1921
    189–90
Special Air Service 24
Stanescu, Corp. 297, 298
Stoffel, Col. 45
Streibler, Leg. Thiebald 124, 125
Sudre, Admiral Chef Gerard 399–400
Suetonius 34
Suzzoni, Col. 100
Sykes, Sir Mark 197
Syria 23
  French collaboration with enemy
    271
  under French rule: comes under
    French mandate, 1921 197–8;
    French campaigns, 1920s 198–204;
    Free French v Vichy French, 1941
    211; Franco-British War, 1941
    221–7
Szuts, SM Istvan 335

Tahon, Lt 137
Tardieu: Le Mystère d'Agadir 152
Tasnady, SM Laslo 305, 309, 319–21,
  334–5
Templer, Sir Gerald 288
Tenne, Leg. Claude 351
Thevenet, Sgt 122
Thiers, Adolphe 57
Tillon, Germaine 313
Timmermans, Leg. Jean 87
Tisserand, Corp. 145, 146
Tissier, SM 145
Tombalbaye, Pres. N'Garta, of Chad
  372–3, 374, 383
Tomkins, Capt. 250
Tonel, CSM Henri 87
Travers, Susan 13, 268–9, 410
  during siege of Big Hakeim 237–8,
    241, 245–8, 249, 251–2
  escape from Big Hakeim 259–66
    passim
  Legion service in Vietnam 268–9
  marriage and retirement 269
Trézel, Gen. Camille 47
Triche, Christine 411
Trotsky, Leon 183
Tsakiropolous, Leg. 273
Turnbull, Lt-Col. Patrick 367, 368, 369
Tuyen Quang, Indo-China 118–26,
  274, 365

United States of America
  and Africa, 403
  history: attacks Barbary pirates,
    1801 40; Civil War, 1861–5 80,
    93; encourages French to leave
    Mexico 93; enters World War I
    174; concern over French position
    in Indo-China, 1954 294–6
  Officer of Strategic Services (OSS)
    272
  Pentagon Papers, The 271, 275, 281

Valée, Marshal Sylvain 60
Valko, SM Janos 335
Valliez, Sgt 71
Van de Bulcke, Leg. 90
Vauchez, Capt. 145
Vaury, Leg. 120
Verius, Leg. 90
Vezinet, Gen. 344, 345
Victor Emmanuel, King of Italy 76
Vienot, Col. 28, 70
Vignol, Col. 209
Villain, Sec. Lt Napoleon 84, 86
Villaume, Col. et al.: Revue Historique
  des Armées 34, 217, 230
Von Arnim, Gen. 232
Von Bolt, Prince Ernst von Milson
  103, 132
Von Bülow, Chancellor 150, 152
Von der Goltz-Pasha, Baron 108
Von der Tann, Gen. 102, 103
Von Etzdorf, Baron Rudiget 207
Von Falkenhayn, Gen. 167
Von Heinleth, Gen. Adolf 32, 96,
  100
Von Moltke, Gen. Adolf 103
Von Rundstedt, Gen. 218
Von Stulpnagel, Gen. 209
Voyron, Gen. 136

Waddell, Major James 169, 175
Wagner, Capt. 255, 256
Waterloo, Battle of 21, 24, 28, 39
Welles, Sumner 271
Wenzel, Leg. Geoffrey 88
Weygand, Gen. 215
Wilhelm I, Kaiser 96, 97, 98
Wilhelm II, Kaiser 148, 150–2, 153
Women in the Legion 13–14, 410–11
Worden, James 240
Worden, Jim: The Wayward
  Legionnaire 15, 212–13

World War I
  progress: early German success 160;
    battle for Verdun 167; battle of the
    Somme, 1916 167–70; French
    failure under Nivelle 170–1;
    French mutinies of 1917 170, 171;
    battles of 1918 175–7
  volunteers 157–8, 159
World War II: fall of France, 1940
  205, 219–20; Norway campaign,
  1940 217–18; Italy's entrance, 1940
  218; Near East actions, 1941 221–6;
  Allied N. African invasion, 1942
  227; N. African campaign, 1942–3
  226–32, 237 et seq.; Italian
  campaign, 1943 232–3; campaign in
  Europe, 1944–5 233–4

Wrangel, Gen. 190

Yacono, Prof. Xavier: Histoire de la
  colonisation française 19
Young, John Robert et al.: The French
  Foreign Legion 42
Ysquierdo, Lt Antoine 305, 306, 320,
  324, 332, 335
Yudenitch, Gen. 183

Zaïre 403, 410
  Legion intervention, 1978 374–83
Zeller, Gen. André 346
Zey, Leg. 90
Zola, Emile: J'Accuse 139
Zouaves 44, 58, 67–72 passim, 74, 99,
  100, 103, 156, 158, 161, 163, 365